SAP BW Data Modeling

SAP PRESS

SAP PRESS is issued by
Bernhard Hochlehnert, SAP AG

SAP PRESS is a joint initiative of SAP and Galileo Press. The know-how offered by SAP specialists combined with the expertise of the publishing house Galileo Press offers the reader expert books in the field. SAP PRESS features first-hand information and expert advice, and provides useful skills for professional decision-making.

SAP PRESS offers a variety of books on technical and business related topics for the SAP user. For further information, please visit our website:
www.sap-press.com.

Steffen Karch, Loren Heilig
SAP NetWeaver Roadmap
2005, 312 pp., ISBN 1-59229-041-8

Norber Egger
SAP BW Professional
Tips and tricks for dealing with the SAP Business Information Warehouse
2004, 450 pp., ISBN 1-59229-017-5

Arnd Goebel, Dirk Ritthaler
SAP Enterprise Portal
Technology and programming
2005, 310 pp., ISBN 1-59229-018-3

Roland Fischer
Business Planning with SAP SEM
2004, 403 pp., ISBN 1-59229-033-7

Norbert Egger, Jean-Marie R. Fiechter, Jens Rohlf

SAP BW Data Modeling

SAP PRESS

SAP PRESS is an imprint of Galileo Press,
Fort Lee (NJ), USA
Bonn, Germany

German Edition first published 2004 by
Galileo Press.

Translation Lemoine International, Inc., Salt Lake City, UT
Copy Editor Nancy Etscovitz, UCG, Inc., Boston, MA
Cover Design Silke Braun, Galileo Press, Germany
Printed in Germany

ISBN 1-59229-043-4

Contents

Preface 13

Foreword 15

Introduction and Overview 17

Introduction ... 17
Structure of the Book ... 18
Working with This Book ... 19
After You've Read the Book 20
Acknowledgements ... 20

1 Data Warehousing Concepts 23

1.1 Introduction ... 23
1.2 OLTP and DWH: Different Requirements ... 24
1.3 Historical Observations ... 26
1.4 Typical Characteristics of Data Warehouses ... 29
1.4.1 Subject-oriented ... 30
1.4.2 Integrated ... 31
1.4.3 Time Variance ... 32
1.4.4 Non-volatility ... 33
1.5 Data Warehouse Architecture ... 34
1.5.1 Layers of the Logical Architecture ... 37
1.5.2 Data Acquisition (ETL) ... 38
1.5.3 Data Storage and Query Optimization ... 41
1.5.4 Data Provision ... 47
1.5.5 Administration ... 50
1.6 OLAP Designs ... 51
1.6.1 Multidimensional OLAP (MOLAP) ... 51
1.6.2 Relational OLAP (ROLAP) ... 52
1.6.3 Hybrid OLAP (HOLAP) ... 53
1.7 The Multidimensional Data Model ... 54
1.7.1 Key Figures and Fact Tables ... 55
1.7.2 Characteristics and Dimensions ... 55
1.7.3 Special Dimensions ... 57

1.8 **Navigation in Multidimensional Data Sets** 58
1.8.1 Slicing, Dicing, Ranging, and Rotation 58
1.8.2 Drilldown and Rollup 60
1.8.3 Drill Across 60
1.8.4 Drill Through 60
1.9 **The Classic Star Schema** 61
1.10 **The Classic Snowflake Schema** 62
1.11 **The Enhanced Star Schema of SAP BW** 62

2 SAP Business Information Warehouse—Overview of Components 67

2.1 **The Architecture of SAP BW** 67
2.2 **Data Storage in SAP BW** 69
2.2.1 InfoObjects as the Basis 69
2.2.2 InfoProviders 70
2.3 **Data Acquisition** 75
2.3.1 Components of the Data Acquisition Process: Sources of Data and Their DataSources 75
2.3.2 Components of the Data Acquisition Process: InfoSources 77
2.3.3 Components of the Data Acquisition Process: Update Rules 78
2.3.4 Components of the Data Acquisition Process: Requesting the Data Transfer and Monitoring 79
2.3.5 Components of the Data Acquisition Process: Persistent Staging Area (PSA) 80
2.3.6 The ETL Process 80
2.4 **Reporting and Analysis Tools** 81
2.4.1 SAP BW Components and Third-Party Tools 81
2.4.2 SAP Business Explorer Query Designer 83
2.4.3 Web Application Designer 85
2.4.4 The Runtime Environment of Web Applications 88
2.4.5 SAP Business Explorer Analyzer 88
2.4.6 SAP Business Explorer Information Broadcasting 90
2.4.7 Additional SAP BW Reporting Functions 91
2.4.8 The Reporting Agent 92
2.4.9 Reporting Functionality and Frontends for SAP BW 94
2.5 **Open Hub Service** 96
2.6 **Additional Functions and Components** 96
2.7 **SAP Business Content** 97
2.8 **The Position of SAP Business Information Warehouse** 99

3 Introduction to Data Modeling 101

3.1 Introduction ... 101
3.2 Some Theory ... 103
3.3 Conceptual Approaches to Modeling: Excursus ... 105
3.3.1 Designs Based on the Entity Relationship Model ... 105
3.3.2 Designs Based on the Object-Oriented Model ... 109
3.3.3 Designs Without Reference to a Conventional Model ... 112
3.4 Back to Practice: Procedures for DWH Projects ... 113
3.5 Modeling (Conceptual and Physical Schema) ... 116
3.5.1 Determining All the Required Objects (Characteristics, Attributes, and Key Figures) ... 116
3.5.2 Displaying the Relations Between Individual Objects ... 117
3.5.3 Dimensioning of Key Figures ... 117
3.5.4 A Step Toward a Physical Data Model: Determining the Objects Relevant to Reporting ... 119
3.5.5 The Golden Rules of Dimensional Modeling ... 120

4 Sample Scenario 121

4.1 The Model Company: CubeServ Engines ... 121
4.1.1 Company Structure ... 121
4.1.2 Infrastructure ... 122
4.2 Requirements of the Case Study ... 124
4.2.1 Requirements of the Analytical Applications ... 124
4.2.2 Planning Requirements ... 126
4.3 Procedure and the SAP Components Involved ... 127
4.4 Details on Data Modeling ... 128
4.4.1 InfoProviders ... 128
4.4.2 InfoObjects ... 129
4.5 A Look Ahead: Additional Steps in the Implementation ... 131

5 InfoObjects of SAP BW 133

5.1 InfoAreas and InfoObjectCatalogs ... 133
5.1.1 Creating Structures and Hierarchies ... 133
5.1.2 Setting Up InfoAreas ... 135
5.1.3 Setting Up InfoObjectCatalogs ... 139
5.2 InfoObjects of SAP Business Content ... 142
5.2.1 Activating an Individual InfoObject of SAP Business Content ... 143
5.2.2 Transferring an SAP Business Content InfoObject into an InfoObjectCatalog ... 148

5.2.3 Transferring an SAP Business Content InfoObject In Data Flow Before ... 150
5.2.4 Transferring SAP Business Content InfoObjects by Selecting InfoCubes In Data Flow Flow Before ... 151
5.2.5 Simultaneous Transfer of Several SAP Business Content InfoObjects into an InfoObjectCatalog ... 153

5.3 Configuration of Your Own InfoObjects Based on SAP Business Content InfoObjects ... 157

5.3.1 The Need for Configuration of Your Own InfoObjects: Example ... 157
5.3.2 Creating Your Own InfoObject with Reference to an InfoObject of SAP Business Content ... 159
5.3.3 Creating Your Own InfoObject Based on InfoObjects of SAP Business Content with a Template ... 161

5.4 Modifying SAP Business Content InfoObjects ... 162

5.4.1 Inserting Attributes into SAP Business Content InfoObjects ... 162
5.4.2 Modifying the Properties of SAP Business Content InfoObjects ... 165
5.4.3 Source System Compounding ... 169

5.5 Creating Your Own InfoObjects ... 172

5.5.1 Introduction ... 172
5.5.2 Creation of an InfoObject—"Characteristic" Type: The Harmonized Version ... 173
5.5.3 Creation of an InfoObject—"Key Figure" Type: Sales Order Stock in Document and Group Currency ... 182

6 InfoProviders of SAP BW 189

6.1 Selective Approach ... 189

6.2 Characteristics as a Basis for Master Data Reporting ... 189

6.3 Financial Reporting ... 192

6.3.1 Introduction ... 192
6.3.2 The Components of an ODS Object ... 193
6.3.3 Configuring an ODS Object to Consolidate the Actual Data on the Basis of an SAP Business Content ODS Object ... 195
6.3.4 Creating an InfoCube to Store the Actual Data on the Basis of an SAP Business Content BasicCubes ... 199
6.3.5 Creating an InfoCube to Store Plan Data with a Template ... 210
6.3.6 Creating a MultiProvider as a Basis for Plan-Actual Comparisons ... 216

6.4 Profitability Analysis ... 223

6.4.1 Data Model and Data Flow: Overview ... 223
6.4.2 ODS: Profitability Analysis—Actual Data ... 224
6.4.3 Creating an InfoSet for Document Reporting in the Profitability Analysis ... 233
6.4.4 Creating an InfoCube for Actual Data of the Profitability Analysis ... 235

6.4.5 Creating an InfoCube for Plan Data of the Profitability Analysis ... 241
6.4.6 Creating a MultiProvider as a Basis for Plan-Actual Comparisons ... 246

6.5 Sales & Distribution ... **252**

6.5.1 Requirements to Incoming-Order and Sales-Order-Stock Reporting ... 252
6.5.2 ODS Objects for Incoming-Order Reporting: Usability of SAP Business Content and the Need for Enhancements ... 253
6.5.3 Creating ODS Objects for Incoming-Order Reporting ... 254
6.5.4 Creating an InfoSet for Reporting with the Allocations of Sales Document Items ... 260
6.5.5 Creating InfoCubes for Incoming-Order Reporting ... 265
6.5.6 Creating a MultiProvider for Incoming-Order Reporting ... 271
6.5.7 Creating the InfoCube for Analysis of Sales Order Stocks ... 274

7 SAP Business Content 285

7.1 Elements of SAP Business Content ... **286**

7.2 Fundamental Problems of SAP Business Content ... **286**

7.2.1 Technical Problems ... 287
7.2.2 Data Model ... 287

7.3 Using SAP Business Content Versus Proprietary Objects ... **292**

7.4 SAP Business Content in Selected Application Areas ... **293**

7.4.1 Business Content for Financials ... 293
7.4.2 Business Content for Supply Chain Performance Management .. 295
7.4.3 Business Content for Human Resources ... 300

7.5 Conclusion ... **303**

A Abbreviations 305

B InfoObjectCatalogs 307

B.1 InfoObjectCatalog ZECOPA01CHA01 ... **307**
B.2 InfoObjectCatalog ZECOPA01KYF01 ... **308**
B.3 InfoObjectCatalog ZEFIGL01CHA01 ... **309**
B.4 InfoObjectCatalog ZEFIGL01KYF01 ... **309**
B.5 InfoObjectCatalog ZESALES01VAHDRCHA01 ... **309**
B.6 InfoObjectCatalog ZESALES01VAHDRKYF01 ... **310**
B.7 InfoObjectCatalog ZESALES01VAITMCHA01 ... **311**
B.8 InfoObjectCatalog ZESALES01VAITMKYF01 ... **312**
B.9 InfoObjectCatalog ZESALES01VASCLCHA01 ... **312**
B.10 InfoObjectCatalog ZESALES01VASCLKYF01 ... **313**

C ODS Objects 315

C.1 ODS Object ZECOPAO1 ... 315
C.1.1 Key Fields ... 315
C.1.2 Characteristics ... 316
C.1.3 Key Figures ... 317
C.2 ODS Object ZEFIGLO1 ... 318
C.2.1 Key Fields ... 319
C.2.2 Characteristics ... 319
C.2.3 Key Figures ... 319
C.3 ODS Object ZEVAHDO1 ... 320
C.3.1 Key Fields ... 320
C.3.2 Characteristics ... 320
C.3.3 Key Figures ... 321
C.3.4 Navigation Attributes ... 322
C.4 ODS Object ZEVAHDO2 ... 323
C.4.1 Key Fields ... 323
C.4.2 Characteristics ... 323
C.4.3 Key Figures ... 325
C.4.4 Navigation Attributes ... 325
C.5 ODS Object ZEVAHDO3 ... 326
C.5.1 Key Fields ... 326
C.5.2 Characteristics ... 327
C.5.3 Key Figures ... 328
C.5.4 Navigation Attributes ... 328
C.6 ODS Object ZEVAHDO4 ... 328
C.6.1 Key Fields ... 329
C.6.2 Characteristics ... 329
C.6.3 Key Figures ... 329

D InfoCube »Actual Data: Profit and Loss Statement« 331

D.1 InfoAreas with InfoCubes ... 331
D.1.1 InfoArea ZECOPA01 Profit and Loss Statement ... 331
D.1.2 InfoArea ZEFIGL01 Financials—General Ledger ... 331
D.1.3 InfoArea ZESALES01 Sales ... 331
D.2 InfoCube ZECOPAC1 ... 332
D.3 InfoCube ZECOPAC2 ... 335
D.4 InfoCube ZEFIGLC1 ... 337
D.5 InfoCube ZEFIGLC2 ... 339
D.6 InfoCube ZEKDABC1 ... 340
D.7 InfoCube ZEVAHDC1 ... 342
D.8 Dimension ZEKDABC13 Distribution Channel ... 343

D.9 InfoCube ZEVAHDC2 345
D.10 Dimension ZEVAHDC23 Data Type 346
D.11 InfoCube ZEVAHDC3 348
D.12 Dimension ZEVAHDC33 Data Type 348

E MultiProviders 351

E.1 MultiProvider ZECOPAM1 351
E.2 MultiProvider ZEFIGLM1 354
E.3 MultiProvider ZEVAHDM1 355

F InfoSets 359

F.1 InfoSet ZECOPAI1 359
F.1.1 ODS ZECOPAO1 Profit and Loss Statement 359
F.2 InfoSet ZEVAHDI1 362
F.2.1 ODS ZEVAHDO4 Sales Document Schedule Lines (Order) 362
F.2.2 ODS ZEVAHDO2 Sales Document Item Data (Order) 362
F.2.3 Link 364

G Transaction Codes 365

G.1 Transactions in SAP BW 365
G.2 SAP R/3 Transactions Relevant to SAP BW 368

H Metadata Tables 369

H.1 InfoObject 369
H.2 InfoCube 369
H.3 Aggregate 370
H.4 ODS Object 370
H.5 PSA 370
H.6 DataSource (= OLTP Source) 370
H.7 InfoSource 370
H.8 Communications Structure 371
H.9 Transfer Structure 371
H.10 Mapping 371
H.11 SAP BW Statistics 371

I Glossary 373

J Literature 423

J.1 The SAP BW Library 424

Authors 427

Index 429

Preface

It is with pleasure that I have accepted a request from Norbert Egger to write a preface for this book, *SAP BW Data Modeling*. This book will substantially contribute to the success of SAP BW projects in many companies.

Many customers already use SAP BW as a strategic tool for companywide control of important processes. The implementation teams at customer sites fulfill the requirements of countless projects and thus serve numerous users. During the past few years, more and more "casual users"—those who generally query prepared information—have joined the analysts and power users previously served by the teams.

All these users must access a swiftly increasing volume of data. Just a few years ago, SAP BW systems larger than one terabyte were usually considered an exception. In many companies, such systems are now the rule or will be in the near future.

Projects based on such systems require accurate data modeling. By "accurate," we mean more than just the ability to handle existing volumes. Accuracy is urgently needed in preparing the systems for future requirements and in keeping them flexible enough to meet the changing requirements of business intelligence systems, which ultimately reflect business changes in general.

Norbert Egger and his co-authors combine their rich experience from many successful implementations of SAP BW with their profound knowledge of SAP BW 3.5, particularly its new features. This marriage of experience and knowledge yields tips and suggestions that this book provides in an easily readable form.

I hope that all readers learn from this book and enjoy reading it. And I'm sure that, as readers, you'll be able to implement many suggestions from the book in your projects.

Walldorf, June 2005
Heinz Häfner
Vice President Business Intelligence: SAP AG

Foreword

Background

When Wiebke Hübner, then an editor at SAP PRESS, asked me in December 2002 if I wanted to write a book on SAP BW, I waved her off. Such a book would have to consist of too many pages to offer an adequate presentation, I thought. I also believed that a viable market for such a book would not exist, so the effort would be of no value. Luckily, she remained insistent, which resulted in our first book on SAP Business Information Warehouse, *SAP BW Professional*. I paid particular attention to the rapid development of the reporting functionality in SAP BW 3.x and other topics in that book.

Thanks to readers

Besides the fact that writing the book proved enjoyable to me, the general interest that this work generated afterwards surprised me a great deal. That's why I'm so pleased to thank you, the readers, at the very beginning of this book for your great interest and the wonderful feedback that you've provided. You should note that a second edition of the first book has already been published in several languages.

My vision

I hope to contribute to companies being able to meet the challenges of adequately mining and using information. That includes the successful use of business intelligence tools. In SAP BW, SAP has offered a very powerful tool for several years now. However, implementations often fail to reach an appropriate standard, so that the question often arises regarding the ability of such a product to function in real life. Therefore, my hope is to increase knowledge about the options and functionality of business intelligence tools so that future implementations and the operation of these solutions are more successful and useful.

The idea of a compendium

Based on the great interest shown in the first book, the rapid development of SAP Business Intelligence components, and the welcome growth of our company, the management of the CubeServ Group decided to approach the topic even more consistently in collaboration with SAP PRESS. Gradually, we happened upon the idea of offering a comprehensive compendium—a compendium that would describe the functionality of SAP BW in even greater detail.

The SAP BW Library

It became readily apparent that one book and one individual involved in the life of a project could not complete such a monumental task: The functionality (luckily) is too vast and such a book would be too comprehensive. We therefore needed to create a multivolume work that would focus on specific aspects, such as data modeling, extraction, transformation, and loading (ETL) processes, reporting, or planning. The notion of a new series, the *SAP BW Library*, began to take shape.

Because our wonderful CubeServ team consists of many highly motivated co-workers, we were quickly able to create a team of authors that was willing to split up the work and produce a book on each topic.

I'm very pleased to be able to present our readers with the first volume of the *SAP BW Library*. Because several authors are already working on the forthcoming volumes, I'm confident that, step by step, this series will offer you a comprehensive description of the functionality of SAP BW. If interest continues to remain high, additional books will appear after the first group of four volumes and address SAP Business Intelligence tools in even more detail.

Jona, Switzerland—June 2005 **Norbert Egger**

Introduction and Overview

The ability to mine and use information adequately is increasingly becoming a global key competency of companies. In addition to good management methods and an appropriate organization, successful implementation of data-warehouse processes is the fundamental precondition for companies to react to new opportunities and risks in a timely and appropriate manner.

Introduction

Volume 1 of the SAP BW Library

This book is the first volume of a new series, the *SAP BW Library*; all its authors are considered experts in business intelligence and work at the CubeServ Group.[1] This volume addresses the fundamentals of *data modeling*; the forthcoming volumes of the SAP BW Library deal with other topics—first the basics are introduced and then the topic itself is addressed in more detail. The topics include *data retrieval*, *reporting*, *analysis*, *planning*, and *simulation*.

Comprehensive case study

To enable easy access to the complex subject matter of SAP Business Information Warehouse (SAP BW), we've decided to work as close to the actual implementation and with as many examples as possible in all volumes of the *SAP BW Library*. Therefore, the foundation for our books is a uniform case study developed by the authors: a virtual company (CubeServ Engines). The case study will be used to present and communicate all the important requirements of business intelligence applications in a manner that reflects real life experiences.

Goal of this book

The first goal of this book is to introduce the basic concepts (data warehouse and so on) of SAP BW. A second goal is to present the steps involved in implementing a data model in SAP BW systematically and step by step. Our case study should serve as an unbroken thread as you go through the material.

The detailed description of the components and implementation steps will enable the various groups within a company that deal with SAP BW to comprehend the material even if they have no deeper understanding of IT. We hope to use this procedure to make SAP BW projects more successful so that employees of user and IT departments, application

1 See Appendix L for an overview of the forthcoming volumes of the *SAP BW Library*.

experts, and consultants can gain a profound understanding and find a common basis of knowledge and language.

Structure of the Book

Four topic areas

This book can be divided into four essential areas:

1. Background and theoretical basics of SAP BW data modeling (Chapters 1–3)
2. Presentation of the case study (Chapter 4)
3. Detailed presentation of three major topic areas: InfoObjects, InfoProviders, and SAP Business Content (Chapters 5–7)
4. Additional supporting information (Appendices)

Chapter 1 Data warehousing concepts

Chapter 1 gives you an overview of the basic concepts and architecture of data warehouse systems. The chapter examines the theoretical and historical background and the basic modeling schema.

Chapter 2 Overview of components

Chapter 2 provides a general overview of the architecture and functionality of SAP BW. This chapter presents all the important innovations, enhancements, and improvements of SAP BW 3.5

Chapter 3 Data modeling

Chapter 3 provides an overview of the basic concepts of data modeling. The quality of data modeling and the power of the underlying systems determine the performance and successful use of a data warehouse.

Chapter 4 Sample scenario

Chapter 4 offers you an overview of the basic elements of the case study used in all volumes of the SAP BW Library. In light of the topic of this book, the chapter then looks at specific aspects of *data modeling* in detail.

Chapter 5 InfoObjects

As InfoObjects, characteristics and key figures form the foundation of the data model in SAP BW. Chapter 5 shows you how to use and configure the InfoObjects of SAP Business Content and how to define your own InfoObjects.

Chapter 6 InfoProviders

Chapter 6 sets up the InfoProviders of our case study step by step. It also examines the individual types of InfoProviders in detail. The chapter uses examples to show you how to create InfoProviders and explains the distinctive features that you must consider.

Chapter 7 SAP Business Content

Chapter 7 describes the preconfigured solution, SAP Business Content, which SAP delivers with SAP BW. In particular, it addresses the solution's strengths and weaknesses and recommends how you can best use SAP Business Content for your own purposes.

Appendices: Overviews and glossary

The appendices provide additional assistance for your daily work: overviews, documentation on various data models, and, in particular, a comprehensive glossary.

Working with This Book

As noted, the goal of this book is to offer users of SAP BW from various areas and differing levels of knowledge a strong foundation for modeling data with SAP BW.

What do you want to know?

Readers with various levels of knowledge and individual needs for information can easily use this book.

- Readers who wish to study SAP Business Information Warehouse starting from its conceptual design should begin by reading the theoretical approach in Chapter 1, *Data Warehousing Concepts*.
- Readers primarily interested in a quick overview of SAP BW and the enhancements in SAP BW 3.5 should begin with Chapter 2, *SAP Business Information Warehouse—Overview of Components*, and then read the details in the following chapters if they wish.
- Chapter 1 (*Data Warehousing Concepts*), Chapter 2 (*SAP Business Information Warehouse—Overview of Components*), and Chapter 7 (*SAP Business Content*) are especially appropriate for readers who want an overview of the topic.
- Readers interested in individual aspects, such as integration of source systems, profitability key figures, use of Operational Data Source (ODS) objects, and so on, can and should use this book as reference material. They can find information on specific topics with the table of contents, the index, and the glossary.

Special symbols

To make it even easier for you to use this book, we have adopted special symbols to indicate information that might be particularly important to you.

- **Step by step**
  An important component of this book is to introduce complex work with SAP BW step by step and explain it to you exactly. This icon refers you to the beginning of a step-by-step explanation.
- **Note**
  Sections of text with this icon offer you helpful hints and detailed information to accelerate and simplify your work.

- **Recommendations**
  This book offers tips and recommendations that have been proven successful in our daily consulting work. This icon indicates our practical suggestions.
- **Caution**
  Particular attention is required when you see this icon. The accompanying text tells you why this is the case.

After You've Read the Book ...

Even after you've read the book, we'd like to continue to assist you with advice and help. We offer the following options.

- **SAP BW Forum**
  Under the motto of "Meet the Experts," you can use an Internet forum to send additional questions to the authors and share them with the business intelligence community. Stop by for a visit: *www.bw-forum.com*.
- **Email to CubeServ**
  If you have additional questions, you're invited to send them to the authors directly by email. See Appendix K, *Authors*, for their email addresses.
- **Information on the CubeServ Web site**
  You can also receive additional information from the CubeServ Group by email. You can register for this service by sending an email that contains your personal registration code for this book to *bw-books@cubeserv.com.*

Acknowledgements

Books are never produced without the support and collaboration of many. That's why we'd like to express our special thanks to the following people for their collaboration, help, and patience.

Norbert Egger
Because various co-workers on our CubeServ team are creating the SAP BW Library, I'd like to thank all the authors sincerely for their participation. Without them, work on this book would have been impossible because it requires comprehensive and specialized knowledge. I also wish to thank all the employees of the CubeServ Group. I'd like to thank SAP, especially Dr. Heinz Häfner, and the publisher for their cooperation and

patience with me. Above all, I thank my family, especially my beloved wife. Despite all my writing efforts, we were married last year. She supported me during this work by taking over all the tasks of managing the family and with a great deal of patience and care.

Jean-Marie R. Fiechter
I wish to thank Wiebke Hübner for all her help. But I'd especially like to thank my wife, Karin, and my two children, Patrick and Olivier, for the patience and understanding they showed me as I wrote my sections of this book. I wish to dedicate my work to all three of them.

Jens Rohlf
Without the support of and feedback from all employees at the CubeServ Group, the creation of this book would have been impossible—many thanks.

I'd especially like to thank my wife, Claudia, for the time and space she gave me as I worked on the book.

Jona, Switzerland and Flörsheim am Main, Germany—April 2005
Norbert Egger
Jean-Marie R. Fiechter
Jens Rohlf

1 Data Warehousing Concepts

Data warehouse systems enable efficient access to integrated information from heterogeneous sources of information. In the past few years, they have become one of the most important components of modern decision-support systems. According to studies by IDC and Meta Group, $15 billion was spent in 2000 for data warehouse projects, of which $5 billion covered software costs. Forecasts predict annual growth to exceed 25 % by 2005.[1] *This chapter provides an overview of the basic concepts and architecture of data warehouse systems.*

1.1 Introduction

Computers have promised us the source of wisdom, but have delivered only a flood of data.[2]

This quotation succinctly captures the problem of the *information society*. In most companies, data is collected, stored, evaluated, recombined, and saved yet again, so that the quantity of information doubles ever more quickly. And the problem also affects research and education. The information does not flow into one location, one pot, from which it can be easily extracted. Instead, it's stored in several different locations.

Main benefit

The main benefit of a data warehouse (DWH) system lies in its ability to derive information from data stored in operational systems in a form that is inappropriate for analysis. Such a system merges information from the most important systems across the whole value chain in a manner that enables quick and targeted decisions at all company levels. The data warehouse unifies information on vendors, products, production, warehouse stocks, partners, customers, and so on into a holistic view and does so independently of the data's source platform.

Data Warehouse and OLAP

For several years, two terms have become preeminent in the area of information retrieval:

1 Various reports and research papers, in particular: *Worldwide Business Intelligence Tools Forecast & Worldwide Data Warehousing Tools Forecast* by IDC.

2 Christoph Breitner, University of Karlsruhe.

- **Data Warehouse (DWH)**
  As a data pool to retrieve consolidated, historical, and consistent information
- **Online Analytical Processing (OLAP)**
  As the description for the multidimensional analysis concept

Later sections of this chapter address both topics in more detail.

1.2 OLTP and DWH: Different Requirements

OLTP systems

All operational information systems, for example, enterprise resource planning (ERP) software like SAP R/3, PeopleSoft, or Siebel, are *transaction-oriented*. They are also called *Online Transaction Processing (OLTP) systems*.

Users of OLTP systems run the "day-to-day" business of a company. They accept orders, create new customers, post payments, and so on. The tasks can be forecast and planned. They repeat often and almost always involve a single entity (order, customer, and so on). With a few exceptions, reporting options are limited to simple lists.

The task of OLTP systems therefore consists of processing many "atomic" procedures, such as orders. In general, each of these processes requires only a limited amount of data.

OLTP systems run on databases that are continuously updated: new records are inserted and old records are updated, corrected, or deleted. The organization of data mostly follows the relational model (normalized according to E.F. Codd)[3] to ensure limited redundancy and high performance of write and update procedures.

Data warehouse systems

The users of a data warehouse (DWH) observe, analyze, and make decisions based on the data in the data warehouse. For example, they compare orders across various periods, ask for financial data, and group customers according to their behavior. Their queries are usually different each time and pertain simultaneously to countless entities.

Unlike the environment in an OLTP system, only a few transactions occur in a data warehouse. However, the transactions involve very large sets of data, primarily regarding procedures that load data into the data warehouse. The data warehouse stores its data such that it offers the optimal performance for read operations. It can do so because data is not modi-

3 See Codd, 1983.

fied after its initial transformation, adaptation, and aggregation; rather every version of the data is stored redundantly.

The size of the database results from these facts. Although OLTP requires "only" a few gigabytes to store data, redundant storage in a DWH requires many gigabytes or even terabytes. The increase in size is also required because users link data from external information sources to internal company data in the data warehouse.

Both qualitative and quantitative differences exist between OLTP and DWH. Table 1.1 summarizes the qualitative differentiating characteristics outlined above.

Qualitative differences

Operational environment (OLTP) (also called operational systems)	Data warehouse environment (DWH) (also called informational or analytical systems)
Pertains to the day-to-day work	Consists of analytical applications and strategic decision-making
Application-oriented	Object or subject-oriented
Ongoing and volatile	Consistent and historical
Optimized for data entry (*write*, *delete*, and *update*)	Optimized for information output (*read*)
Many small transactions	Very complex queries
Static and stable applications	Dynamic applications
Normalized data	Denormalized and multidimensional data
Maintains transactional consistency	Time-based versioning

Table 1.1 Differences Between OLTP and DWH Solutions

Quantitative differences: System load

Let's look at the system load (see Figure 1.1): OLTP systems process a relatively small amount of data, such as that required for account movements. The required quantity of data is usually limited to a detailed specification of values. The simultaneous actions of many employees and the related applications access many transactions on the database in parallel. The operational system is set up to handle this system load and usually meets the required response time in sub-seconds range.

In DWH systems, however, each transaction accesses a very large quantity of data. Analytical results require an aggregation of the values along a hierarchy tree, especially when a high level of detail for individual values is involved. This procedure demands a great deal of effort and creates short-term peak loads. For analyses, users are satisfied with response times that range from a few seconds to a few minutes.

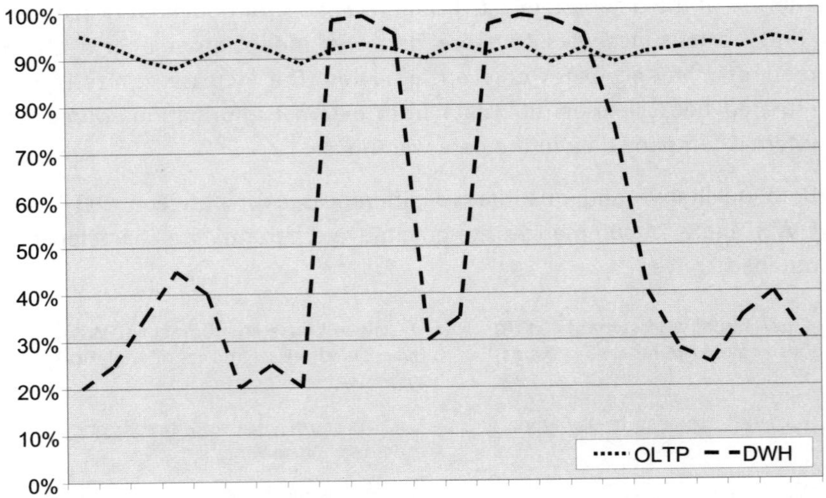

Figure 1.1 Comparison of System Load: OLTP and Data Warehouse

System stress

Despite some peaks, the stress on OLTP system hardware remains relatively constant over time. A DWH, however, has a very strong binary pattern. The system either works to its full capacity or is almost completely underutilized. Calculation of an average load to determine the system size is therefore as meaningless as calculating the average load in tunnels for the prediction of traffic jams.

Separation of OLTP and DWH

This fundamental difference is likely the most important reason for not combining OLTP and DWH systems. You can effectively optimize a system environment either for operational or analytical data processing: There is no such thing as a compromise solution.

1.3 Historical Observations

1960s MIS euphoria

In the early 1960s, many companies faced a changing market after many years of uninterrupted growth. Companies were increasingly confronted with heterogeneous customer desires in an international market. They had to master completely new situations for decision-making, but didn't have any of the basic information they needed to do so. Consequently, various companies developed their own Management Information Systems (MIS) to consolidate and format all the required data from individual areas in the company. The goal of this strategy was to develop an automatic decision generator. The expectation was to attain significant relief for company management.

However, the majority of these attempts failed for technical reasons inherent with their design. The storage and processing capacity of the hardware was insufficient and the programming languages used at the time were inappropriate. After a euphoric phase, a period of despair ensued. The term mis-information-systems was coined. But many thought that the cumbersome architecture of mainframe computers was the only reason for failure and hoped for rapid technological improvements.

1970s The era of controllers and DSS

In the 1970s, the start of globalization and the appearance of new companies on the market forced the increasing automation of processes and decisions. At the beginning of the 1980s, upper management and controllers thought that the time was ripe for a better solution. Their hopes were planted with the initial triumph of the PC (especially the initial experience with spreadsheet programs) and the development of controlling approaches paired with better-structured accounting. Today we know that accounting can measure only effects; it cannot tell us anything about causes.

A study by the Massachusetts Institute of Technology (MIT) showed that managers wanted query and analysis instruments based on flexible database systems that allowed them to perform what-if scenarios and ad-hoc analyses. *Decision-support systems (DSS)* were born. Three main reasons contributed to the failure of this DSS design:

1. The DSS offerings of the time used complex languages and rigid model structures; they required a great deal of effort to learn and had prohibitively high start-up costs.
2. To justify the enormous investments in the DSS infrastructure and the high cost of IT specialists, increasingly more lists and reports added to ever-higher mountains of paper. The sheer quantity and resulting unmanageability of the reports and lists made it impossible to make reasonable management decisions. The perfect vicious circle!
3. It soon became apparent that endless lists of numbers for the controller did not determine the success of an enterprise. Success depended on the consistent implementation of strategic goals, coupled with quick decisions.

1980s EIS This realization pushed the evolution of informational systems onto a completely new track. Companies no longer looked for an automatic decision generator and its magic or coincidental results or for a semiautomatic decision system supported by expensive specialists. They thought they were on the right track when they attempted to implement the "doable." And the doable looked like this:

1. Upper management was to be supported by Executive Information Systems (EIS).
2. If a decision-maker needed information, it was to be made available at the push of a button.
3. No one wanted to be limited to a company's own data, but instead wanted to be able to integrate external data.

As a result of this scenario, a new meaning was developed for EIS, "everybody's information system," although even then some critics spoke of NIS, "nobody's information system." But the EIS approach also failed technologically. It was too expensive and didn't offer an acceptable level of performance. The continuing weaknesses of EIS tools, especially regarding the integration of external data, and a lack of acceptance among upper management also contributed to the failure of this approach. Instead, divisional solutions came into being, such as marketing, sales, financial, and product information systems.

1990s Data warehousing Only the poor economic conditions at the beginning of the 1990s and an increasingly competitive enterprise environment sensitized decision-makers to the need to distill the correct data from the abundance of the data available. The term *data warehouse* was born to describe a central supplier of all information relevant for decisions.

Before we begin to discuss the concept of the data warehouse, let us use Figure 1.2 to clarify the evolution so far. The figure shows the support level of management by the individual approaches and the (r)evolution in the requirements of information systems that occurred between DSS and EIS.

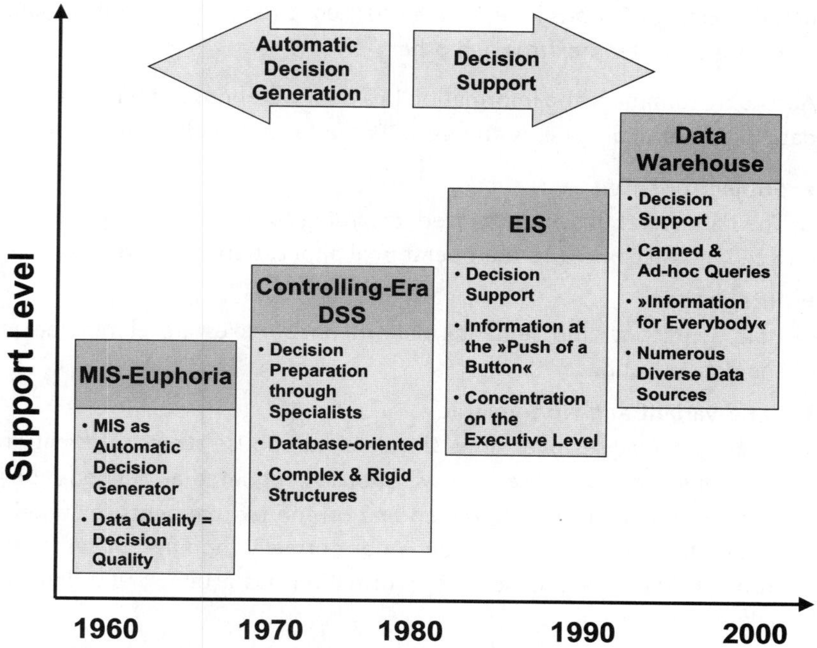

Figure 1.2 From Management Information Systems to Data Warehouse

1.4 Typical Characteristics of Data Warehouses

Data warehousing according to Inmon

The famous American consultant, William (Bill) Inmon, is considered to be the spiritual father of data warehousing and has molded the concept and its terminology as no one else could. He defines the data warehouse as a data pot in which decision-makers can find all necessary information and thus satisfy their need for information. His book, *Building the Data Warehouse*, has become the standard on the subject.[4]

The derivative of *warehouse* (i.e., "Warenhaus" or department store) is an apt analogy. A data warehouse can also be described as a self-service store for information. In fact, many characteristics of a data warehouse are identical to those of a traditional department store. The data warehouse is the central storage point for data (which primarily offers read access) and guarantees the formatting and availability of all required information. As is the case in a self-service store, end users (customers) independently take a product, in this case information, from the shelves and put it into their shopping baskets. The shelves are arranged by prod-

4 Inmon, 2002.

uct; the supply of goods is customer-oriented. Similar goods from various sources are located next to each other.

Typical characteristics

According to Inmon, the information in a data warehouse differs from the data in operational systems and exhibits the following characteristics.

- **Subject-oriented**
  The data warehouse is organized according to the subjects to be analyzed, not according to the operational application structure.
- **Integrated**
  Both syntactical and semantic data inconsistencies are eliminated in the data warehouse.
- **Time-variant and Non-volatile**
  To enable analyses over time, the data warehouse stores information over longer periods. The data warehouse is updated at defined intervals (hour, day, or month, depending on the requirements for timeliness). Once stored, information is not normally modified or removed from the data warehouse. The information has a temporally defined validity.

The following paragraphs explain these characteristics in more detail.

1.4.1 Subject-oriented

Subject-oriented

A data warehouse is structured according to the core subjects of an organization. This subject-oriented approach differs from that of an operational application, which is set up for efficient processing of day-to-day business and is therefore oriented toward objects like "order process for Miller." However, the data processed in an operational application is inappropriate for supporting decisions. Instead, applications are devoted to specific processes: orders, invoicing, production control, and so on.

The data warehouse concept, however, is focused on object and subject areas, like products and customers, even though the data comes from the corresponding operational applications (see Figure 1.3). Operational data necessary for running only operational processes and not involved in the process of supporting decision-making has no place in a data warehouse. To return to the metaphor of an actual department store, this means that a buyer preselects goods and places on the shelves only those goods for which demand likely exists. The buyer tries to avoid shelf-warmers.

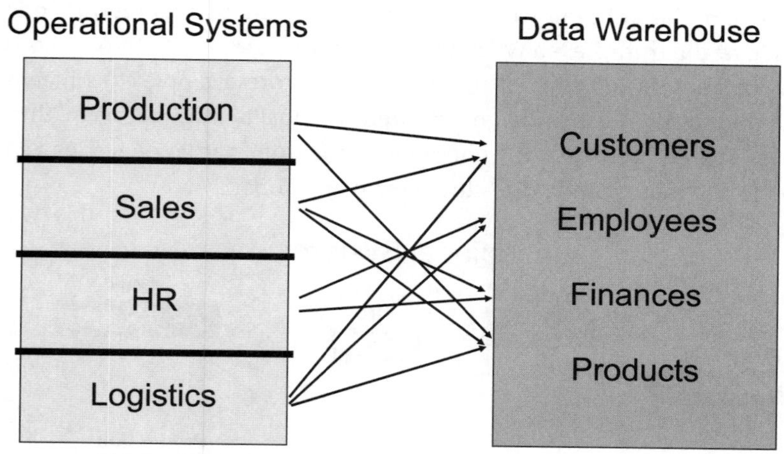

Figure 1.3 Application Focus (in OLTP Systems) Versus Subject Focus (in DWH Systems)

1.4.2 Integrated

Integrated

One of the central characteristics of a data warehouse is that when data is collected from the operational systems, it is brought to a consistent level in terms of both syntax and semantics. This uniformity comprises completely different aspects and usually refers to the formats, units, and coding (see Figure 1.4). In addition, designers must agree on the characteristics stored in the data warehouse, because the various operational systems often describe the same concept with different characteristics and various subject areas with the same characteristics.

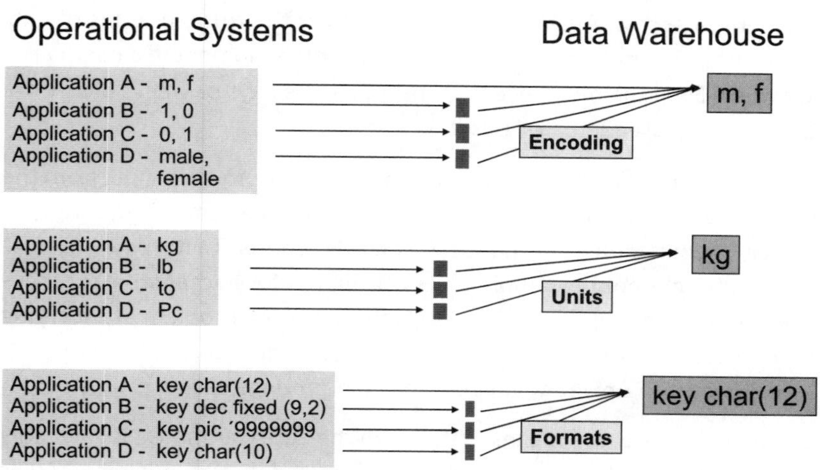

Figure 1.4 Integration (Coding, Units, and Formats)

The goal of this uniformity is a consistent set of data that represents "one source of the truth," even when the data sources are very heterogeneous (see Figure 1.5). In terms of the department store example, this means that the goods must undergo an intensive quality control when they arrive. The control sorts out unusable goods from partial deliveries and then formats and standardizes the remaining goods.

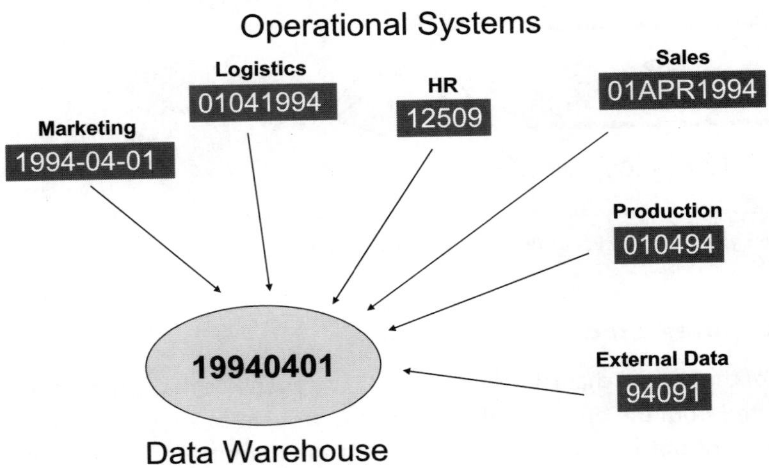

Figure 1.5 Data Integration (Uniformity)

1.4.3 Time Variance

Time variant The time variance of the data stored in the data warehouse is seen in various ways. Operational systems work with exact timeliness at the moment of access. A DWH, however, looks at the truth in terms of only a specific point in time. Every data load records a moment in a company's activities. Even the most recent snapshot can be days or weeks old by the time the end user actually uses it.

But this apparent deficit of the data warehouse approach results from the way it is used. Views of long- and mid-term periods (annual, monthly, or weekly examinations) are the focus of DWH reports. That's why information that might not be completely up-to-date is fully acceptable for these evaluations. This approach also avoids the annoying problem of executing two analyses consecutively, only to have each deliver a different result. Direct access to operational data can often produce such a problem.

Validity period The time variance also means that data in the data warehouse is valid only at a specific time for a specific period. This validity period is recorded as part of the key for all the relevant data in the data warehouse. Temporal analyses (historical views of the changes over a given period) are possible because the data already in the data warehouse is not modified, but updated data is added to it with a new validity period.

The goal of our "department store" is not to follow all fashion trends all the time, but to maintain an established supply of goods over the long term with periodic deliveries of goods. New models don't replace existing models; rather, they supplement existing models.

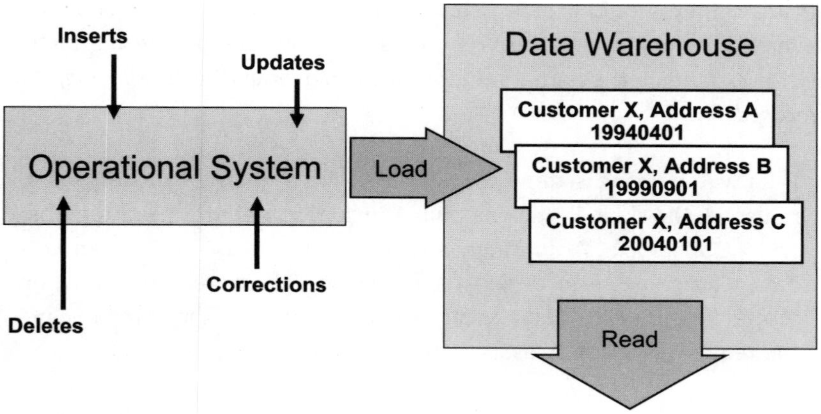

Figure 1.6 Time Variant and Non-Volatility of Data

1.4.4 Non-volatility

Non-volatile

The storage of data over long periods requires well-planned processes, tailored system landscapes, and optimized storage procedures to minimize the scope of the information to be stored and the runtime of individual analyses and reports. By contrast, data of operational applications ultimately remains in the system only until processing of a specific order is completed. Then, the data is archived or deleted to improve the performance of the system in order to avoid unacceptable response times.

The optimization of data access and the loading of data are important issues in modeling data warehouses. Updating data (modifying contents) is also avoided as much as possible because the data of a data warehouse has a documentary character (see Figure 1.6).

In our example, the requirement of non-volatility would mean that the department store has extensive storage capacity and guarantees the availability of goods over the long term.

1.5 Data Warehouse Architecture

Architecture is defined as a set of rules of structures that provide the framework for the overall design of a system or product.

Think big, start focused

According to Inmon, the devil is in the details of data warehouse architecture. He estimates that 80 % of the effort must be invested in setting up the model and in data acquisition: access, cleansing, and so on. He recommends that beginners don't start with an enterprise-wide superstore. Instead, they should proceed step by step to set up partial DWHs wherever the benefit is greatest. They must keep an eye on the big picture while expanding the partial solutions into an overall DWH: *Think big, start focused.*

> Data warehousing is an iterative process. No one can buy a data warehouse off the shelf. It must be built, much as something is put together with LEGO blocks. Accordingly, there's no simple, uniform design for a data warehouse. The design of a specific data warehouse varies in scope, functionality, and appearance, depending on the company and the requirements of its users.

The design and creation of a data warehouse demands professional support to avoid a protracted process that produces a flop.

The three layers of a data warehouse

Data warehouse architecture consists of three layers (see Figure 1.7):

- **The conceptual layer**
  This layer defines the vision, goals, and strategy of the data warehouse, which must be consistent with the vision, goals, and strategy of the company. The "guardrails" (rough requirements) and the need for integration with other systems are derived from these items. A company-wide, rough subject data model can also be created here.
- **The logical layer**
  This layer defines the scope of the system and solution (according to phases) and the required infrastructure. It also creates application models and a detailed, logical data model. It adheres to business processes and business rules.
- **The physical layer**
  This layer defines the technical implementation of the DWH infrastructure, the software, and data communication. It creates the physical data model and detailed process, application, and program definitions.

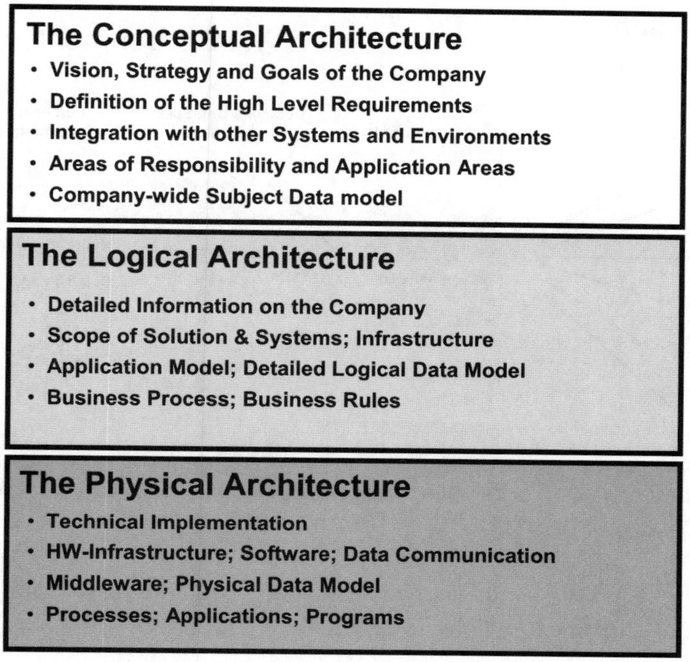

The Conceptual Architecture
• Vision, Strategy and Goals of the Company
• Definition of the High Level Requirements
• Integration with other Systems and Environments
• Areas of Responsibility and Application Areas
• Company-wide Subject Data model
The Logical Architecture
• Detailed Information on the Company
• Scope of Solution & Systems; Infrastructure
• Application Model; Detailed Logical Data Model
• Business Process; Business Rules
The Physical Architecture
• Technical Implementation
• HW-Infrastructure; Software; Data Communication
• Middleware; Physical Data Model
• Processes; Applications; Programs

Figure 1.7 The Three Layers of a Data Warehouse Architecture

Overall goal

The overall goal of a data warehouse architecture should be to describe an integrated environment that covers the needs of a company and that can be implemented iteratively (see Figure 1.8). This integrated environment covers all aspects of data warehousing processes: data acquisition, data storage with detailed data, lightly and heavily aggregated data, and the provision of analyses and reports—and does so by including a comprehensive and consistent metadata repository.

SAP Business Information Warehouse

SAP Business Information Warehouse (SAP BW) is a good example of an integrated DWH environment. Starting with data acquisition, data storage with detailed data, lightly and heavily aggregated data, and ending with the provision of analyses and reports, it covers all aspects of a modern data warehouse environment (see Figure 1.9). As required, SAP BW includes a comprehensive and consistent metadata repository.

The architecture is therefore a framework of rules or structures within which the system is constructed. The architecture for a data warehouse has specific characteristics that distinguish it from other systems: an iterative implementation instead of a big bang, for example.

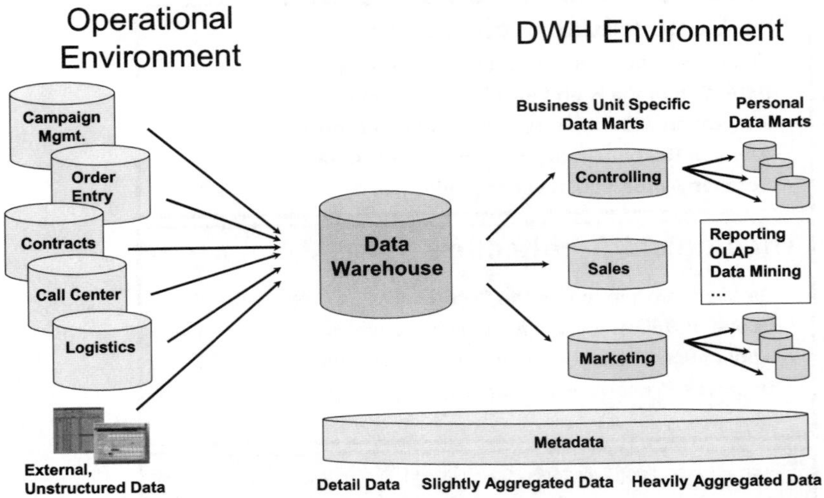

Figure 1.8 Integrated DWH Environment

The following sections examine individual elements required for a logical data warehouse architecture in more detail.

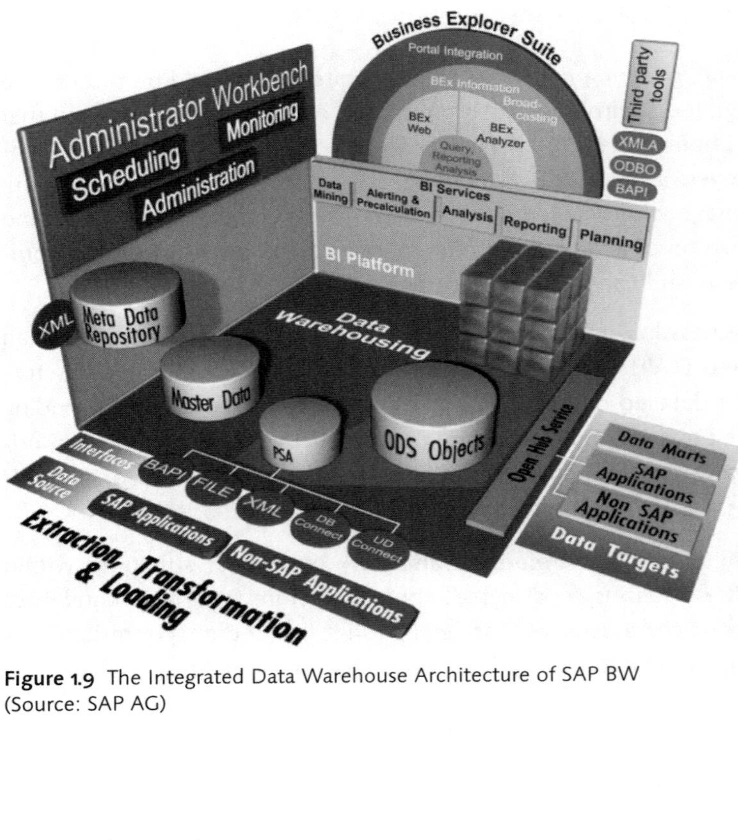

Figure 1.9 The Integrated Data Warehouse Architecture of SAP BW (Source: SAP AG)

1.5.1 Layers of the Logical Architecture

Figure 1.10 illustrates the logical architecture of a data warehouse system. The system can be subdivided into three layers:

- **Data acquisition layer with interfaces to operational systems**
  The data acquisition layer contains tools to extract data from operational sources, to format data, and to load data into the data warehouse.
- **Data storage layer with the actual data warehouse**
  The data storage layer uses special indexing procedures and explicitly uses redundancies and aggregations to minimize access times.
- **Data presentation layer with interfaces to end applications and presentation tools**
  The data presentation layer usually consists of one or more data marts that provide the required (multidimensional and tabular) structures for end-user applications and presentation tools.

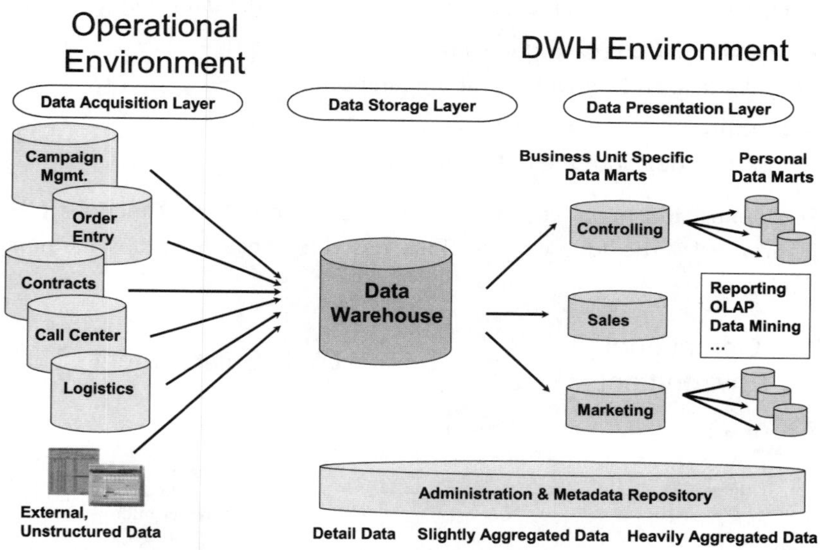

Figure 1.10 Characteristics of an Integrated Data Warehouse Environment

All layers provide administrative functions supported by a comprehensive and consistent metadata repository. The repository contains information on the data stored in the data warehouse.

1.5.2 Data Acquisition (ETL)

At the data acquisition layer, the data needed by users is collected from the heterogeneous operational data sources so that it then can be stored in the data warehouse. After the initial data import, the data warehouse must be reloaded with new data according to user-defined requirements for timeliness and consistency. Users have two methods for a reload:

- Reloading all data (reloading, full load)
- Incremental data acquisition (incremental load, delta load)

Instead of deleting and reloading the data in the data warehouse, incremental data acquisition loads only the changes in operational data into the data warehouse.

Data acquisition, also called *extraction*, *transformation*, and *loading (ETL)* is divided into three steps:

- **Extraction**
  Filtering of the required data from the operational data sources
- **Transformation (data cleansing)**
  Syntactical and semantic data preparation
- **Loading**
  Inserting data into the data warehouse

Scheduling and metadata management round out these functions (see Figure 1.11). The following sections describe these functions in more details.

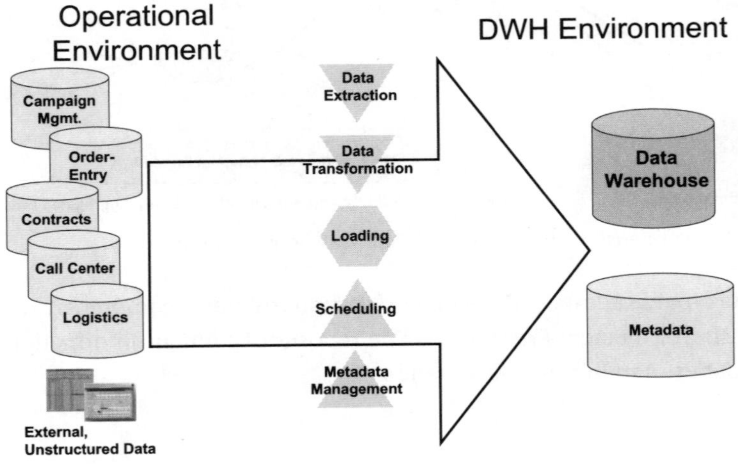

Figure 1.11 The ETL Process

Extraction from Source Systems

In terms of data acquisition, the initial load and a complete *reload* of the data pose no difficulties. Extraction

However, an incremental data import first requires extraction of the modifications relevant to the data warehouse from the operational systems. You have various options, depending on the operational application:

- **Triggers**
  If the operational database supports the use of SQL triggers, you can use them to retrieve the data. Triggers allow definition of database operations that are run automatically by specific events. Triggers used to extract data run every time the operational data set is modified and store the changes in an appropriate modification table. The data records in the modification table can then be transferred to the data warehouse at regular intervals.

- **Log files**
  You can often use the log files (*logs*) of the operational database systems for extraction. Most database systems support log files as a way of recreating a consistent state for the database (*recovery*) after a system failure. Special programs can evaluate log files and extract the data manipulation operations that they contain. The data is then transferred into the data warehouse.

- **Monitor programs**
  In some circumstances, neither triggers nor log files can be used to extract data, so the only remaining option is to access the operational data set. In this case, you can use special monitoring programs to extract the relevant modifications. Such programs periodically generate a snapshot of the data and then calculate the difference between the current snapshot and the previous one (*differential snapshot algorithm*).

- **Modification of the operational application systems**
  If the operational system storing the data doesn't support triggers or log files, and you cannot use a monitoring program, you must modify the operational system itself so that it logs every modification it executes in a separate database. You can then periodically transfer the relevant modifications into the data warehouse. Some manufacturers of operational application systems have adjusted their software to enable the automatic transfer of differential data to specific data warehouse systems. One example is the integration of the ERP solution, SAP R/3, with SAP Business Information Warehouse.

Note that sometimes in order to reduce the number of data records to be transferred, an update of the data warehouse requires filtering of the relevant modifications and executing queries and transformations on the operational data.

Data Cleansing

Transformation

A uniform data schema is set for the data warehouse during the development phase. The data from the various operational systems must then be transformed into the data warehouse format during loading. In addition, the heterogeneity of the data sources and the operational systems frequently leads to inconsistencies and even to erroneous data. For example, the following problems can occur: The use of different attribute values for the same attributes, missing values, different formatting of the data, and so on.

In order to create a clean and consistent data warehouse, these problems must be eliminated. The data-cleansing tools on the market can be subdivided into the following groups:

- **Data-migration tools**
  This category of data-cleansing tools permits the definition of simple transformation rules to transform the data from the source system into the target format. For example, transformation of attribute value "male" to "m" or "1."
- **Data-scrubbing and data-cleansing tools**
  Data-scrubbing tools use area-specific knowledge to cleanse the data from the operational sources. For example, they might use a table of all postal codes, localities, and street names to check and correct addresses. In terms of technology, these tools frequently use fuzzy logic and neural networks.
- **Data-auditing tools**
  You can use data-auditing tools to recognize rules and relationships between data. The tools then verify whether the rules have been violated. Because it is almost impossible to determine with absolute certainty whether an error is present, the tools simply notify you of possible errors, which you must then correct manually. Such tools can use statistical evaluations to determine that the discrepancies between specific values might indicate the presence of incorrect entries. This type of data analysis is usually based on data-mining techniques.

Inserting Data in the DWH

Loading

The actual insertion of the data into the data warehouse occurs after extraction of the required data from the source system and the follow-up data cleansing. Most systems also perform the following tasks along with the insertion:

- Checking the integrity constraints
- Calculating aggregations
- Generating indices

To reduce the load on the operational systems to a minimum, you can decouple the actual insertion of data into the data warehouse from the transmission of data from the operational systems. You would use *operational data stores (ODS)* to do so. An ODS stores data from the operational systems in an almost unmodified form until it can be inserted into the data warehouse. To reduce the length of the load process, you can execute data cleansing and aggregation operations within the ODS tables.

Data is loaded into the data warehouse based on user-defined timeliness and consistency requirements. To avoid inconsistent results from queries, you cannot access the data in the data warehouse during the update. However, a "query copy" of the data can be made available during the update. For this reason, most data warehouses are updated when few queries on the data occur—nights and weekends. In addition to updating the actual data warehouse, you also must update the data basis for the data mart system in use while loading the data. For relational data mart systems, this data basis is normally identical to the data warehouse. However, multidimensional data mart systems (OLAP systems) are based on multidimensional database systems that must also be brought up-to-date. Section 1.6 examines the various OLAP technologies in more detail.

1.5.3 Data Storage and Query Optimization

Views

In simple terms, the data storage layer of a data warehouse consists only of the data and its relationships. The relationships are derived from the corresponding relationship in the source system and stored permanently. In terms of the database technology, *materialized views* are used to depict these relationships. Operational systems, however, usually use virtual (also called "normal") *views* that store only the definition of a query, so that the result must be recalculated at each new access.

Materialized views

Materialized views mean that the results don't have to be recalculated for each query; they can be precalculated, which means a significant improvement in performance. However, the modified data from the affected relationships in the source systems must be loaded into the data warehouse at regular intervals.

Because a data warehouse rarely uses real-time data, materialized views don't have to be updated every time the data in the source system is modified. A deferred update at regular intervals is usually satisfactory.

Because a data warehouse should also ensure seamless access to integrated and historical data, it must sometimes deal with huge volumes of data (several gigabytes up to tens of terabytes). Such large volumes of data require special techniques for the efficient processing of queries.

The following section looks at the two most common options for query optimization: the use of aggregates and special indexing procedures. Thereafter we will explain in more detail the various organizational and distribution types of the data storage layer of a data warehouse.

Optimization

Aggregates

In addition to materialized views, *aggregates* (also called *aggregation tables* or *preaggregations*) are built in the data warehouse to optimize queries. Such aggregates are nothing more than materialized views that usually contain the data being used in a preaggregated form. These aggregates allow you to respond to user-defined queries directly from the preaggregated values instead of having to calculate them from the detailed data each time.

> The only drawbacks of these aggregates are the increased need for memory and the additional effort involved during the loading of the data warehouse.

Two challenges arise from the use of aggregates:

1. The correct choice of the aggregates to be built (considering the need for memory and the effort required in an update) and the expected use of these aggregates to process queries. The need for additional memory and the effort involved in the update make it impossible to calculate all combinations of aggregates. In addition, only a few of these combinations are actually used. Good data warehouse systems offer tools to determine the optimal combinations of aggregates.

2. The automatic (transparent to the end user) use of the available aggregates (if appropriate). This option is also a characteristic of a good DWH.

Figure 1.12 illustrates the inner structure of a data warehouse and the distinction between detail data and aggregated data.

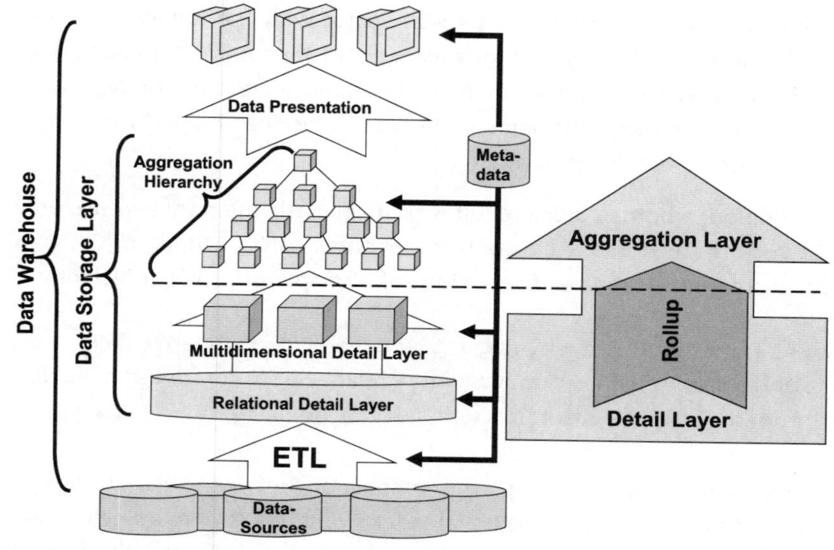

Figure 1.12 The Various Layers of a Data Warehouse

Relational, detailed data layer

The materialized views fed directly from the source system are assigned to the detailed layer of the data warehouse. These tables serve as a consistent foundation for the other layers in the data warehouse. To prepare for future modifications that might be desired and to contribute to greater flexibility of the data warehouse, the relational, detailed data is often stored at a greater level of detail than is currently required.

Aggregation layer

The multidimensional detail data layer forms the basic layer for processing queries; the aggregation layer contains aggregates for efficient processing of the queries.

Aggregation hierarchies

Aggregation hierarchies are created when aggregates are built on the basis of other aggregates. The terms *upflow* or *rollup* are often used to describe the flow of information within such aggregate hierarchies.

The division into a relational, detail data layer and various multidimensional, aggregation layers also allows you to meet simultaneous requirements for updating, and does so without affecting the consistency of the data.

Indexing schemes In addition to aggregates, indexing schemes are often used to accelerate the execution of queries. Studies of data warehouses over several years have shown that in addition to the usual indices, two specific indexing schemes are especially appropriate: the *bitmap index* and the *join index*.

Bitmap index Bitmap indices allow very efficient determination of the attribute properties of a data record. For example, a bitmap index for the four points of the compass would contain a two-bit vector with the following values: 00 for north, 01 for east, 10 for west, and 11 for south. The selection of all data records with the south attribute would therefore require a Boolean comparison with the value of 11. Such a task can be performed by a computer extremely efficiently.

In addition, a bitmap index requires relatively little memory because only bit vectors are stored. And Boolean operators (AND, OR, and XOR) can calculate intersections and set unions of bitmap indices very efficiently.

But something of a downside is also involved: Bitmap indices are appropriate only for attributes with a relatively small number of value properties (i.e., for attributes with a high cardinality).

Join index A join index, however, maps the connection between relationships in terms of a common key; traditional index structures refer to a single table. To implement a join index, the references to all records (and the foreign key of the second table) are stored for each primary key of the first table. This approach permits extremely efficient calculation of joins between two tables.

Star index The literature also uses the term *star index* for the enhancement of the join-index concept into a multidimensional model (star schema). A star index permits the storage of all relationships between a fact table and dimension tables that belong to it so that it can very efficiently determine the records that belong to one or more dimension table elements.

Organizational Forms

Implementation of the data storage layer of a data warehouse essentially involves the following four types of organization:[5]

- **Virtual data warehouse system**
  Unlike the other distribution types, a virtual data warehouse does not involve separate storage of the data. The required data is read, pro-

5 See also Inmon, 2002.

cessed, and presented by direct access to the underlying operational source system (see Figure 1.13).

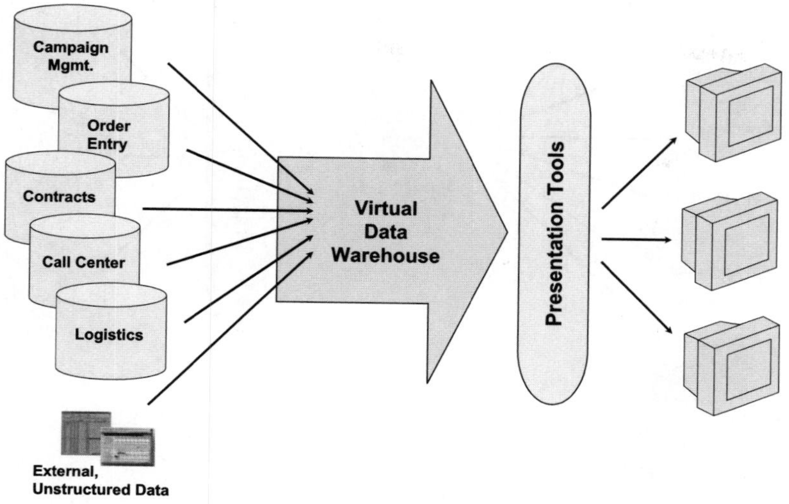

Figure 1.13 Virtual Data Warehouse

Because it does not require any complicated infrastructure, such a solution can be implemented quickly and (at first glance) economically. However, such a solution is extremely deleterious because it places a heavy load on the operational system and its options to consolidate and historicize data are very limited.

- **Central data warehouse system**
  The traditional design of a data warehouse: all data is managed in a central, logical data pool (see Figure 1.14). The additional work required to format and store this redundant data is well worth the effort, because it creates a single, company-wide base of data that has been historicized and consolidated. However, the high degree of complexity that such a project involves remains a challenge.

- **Distributed data warehouse system**
  A distributed data warehouse system is based on distributed database systems and uses their mechanisms to create sufficient synchronization among the individual, distributed subsystems (see Figure 1.15). The challenge here lies in the proper distribution of data across the subsystems of the data warehouse. The effort involved in preparing a single, company-wide set of data can be relatively large. Therefore, a distributed data warehouse system is best suited for highly decentralized organizations.

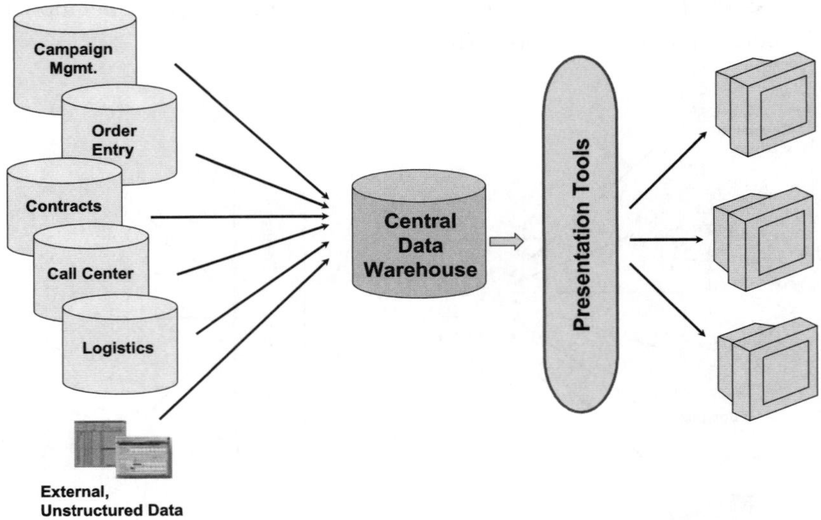

Figure 1.14 Central Data Warehouse

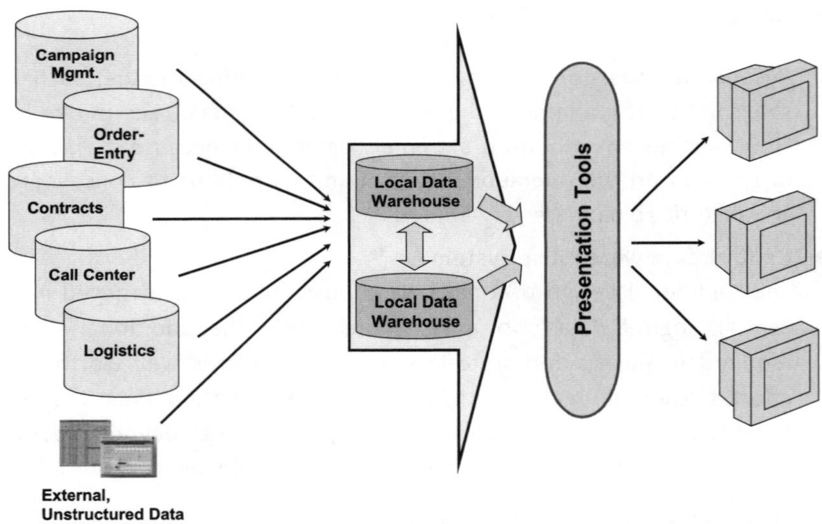

Figure 1.15 Distributed Data Warehouse

- **Data marts with a central data warehouse**

  Data marts are specific organizational or geographical subsets of a data warehouse. They enable the iterative implementation of data warehouse systems. Data marts built on a central data warehouse enable the extraction of subject-specific data (from the underlying data warehouse) for individual groups of decision-makers (see Figure 1.16).

According to Inmon, the proliferation of independent data marts without a central data warehouse results in chaos.

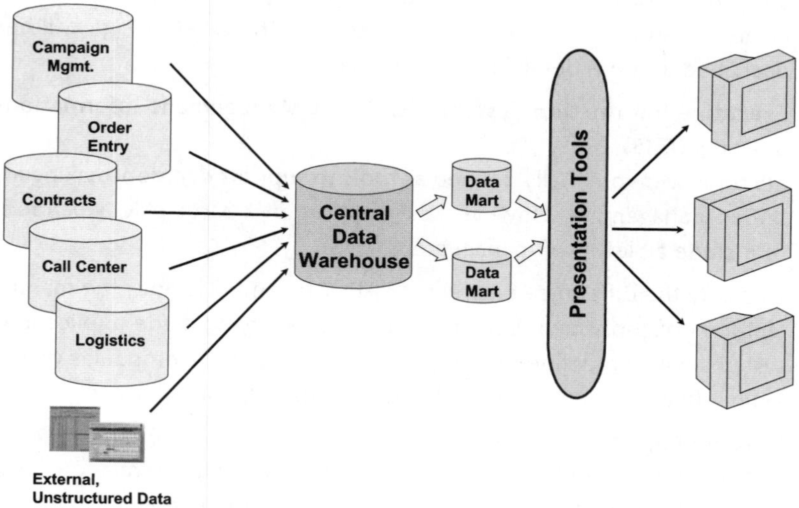

Figure 1.16 Data Marts with a Central Data Warehouse

1.5.4 Data Provision

To convert the data collected in a data warehouse into information that is relevant to the business demands, the data must be prepared before it can be presented properly to a target group. The preparation entails not only the automated creation of standard reports, but also comprehensive (and complex) analytical modeling and processing of the data.

Preparation

Subsets (organizational, geographical, temporal, and so on) of data from the data warehouse are usually sufficient to mine the desired information. To accelerate and simplify the work of analysis and presentation tools, the required data is often extracted from the detail layer of the data warehouse and stored in a specific and optimal format (the data marts) for the target tool. In rough terms, the following categories of tools can be differentiated:

- **Simple report and query tools**
  Programs that allows user-friendly definition of reports and queries.
- **Multidimensional analysis tools**
  To clarify the difference between data handling and a transaction-oriented system, one also speaks of *online analytical processing* (OLAP) in

this context. Special requirements exist for analytical tasks with OLAP support, particularly in terms of the speed of information delivery, the analysis options in the system, and the security and complexity of calculations, and the data sets to be processed. The OLAP design will be described in more detail later in this chapter.

- **Executive Information Systems (EIS) and Management Information Systems (MIS)**
  EIS tools were originally defined as tools to support decision-making in upper management. However, the application area quickly expanded to include all levels of management (MIS).

  To clarify the difference between OLAP, MIS, and EIS tools, the manufacturers of tools have begun to call simpler, ready-made application systems with predefined reports for specific areas of companies (marketing, finances, purchasing, HR, and so on) MIS and EIS tools.

- **Data-mining tools**
  Data mining is the process of finding previously unknown relationships and trends in large data sets. Data mining uses mathematical and statistical techniques from artificial intelligence (AI): neural networks, fuzzy logic, clustering, associations, regressions, chaos theory, machine learning, and so on.

  This book does not examine this group of tools. Given the rising popularity of data warehouse systems, we can assume that data mining techniques will increasingly be integrated as front-end tools.

- **Tools for application development**
  This group of front-end tools includes all application systems created individually for information mining. Development of these applications requires application development tools that support access to data warehouse systems. Today, application-development tools are already integrated into most data warehouse systems.

Presentation

The setup of a DWH and the preparation of data in a format specific to, and optimized for, the target tool serve one purpose: to present information relevant to decision-making and thus promote actions beneficial to the company.

The extremely varied needs of users, illustrated in Figure 1.17, are of paramount importance here. These differences demand that business-relevant information and facts oriented to decision-making be made available in various forms. The main categories include the following:

- **Standard reporting**
  Static or dynamic presentation of facts, often in a spreadsheet but increasingly in a multidimensional form—usually with comprehensive options for presentation and further distribution. Web server, publish, and subscribe processes, and portals (on the intranets, extranets, and on the Internet) enable simple, Web-based access to information.
- **Ad-hoc analyses**
  The dynamic display of information, usually from a multidimensional model; such analyses permit the user to have a flexible and individual look at the data. Ad-hoc analyses can be implemented with either analysis tools or Web front ends.
- **Business planning and budgeting**
  Specific support for planning and budgeting processes with the availability of tools for data capture, quality assurance, workflow management, data distribution, forecasting, and simulation
- **Data mining**
  Complex and undirected analysis of very large quantities of data. The users here are highly qualified specialists who use various procedures—from statistics, machine learning, and artificial intelligence—to discover unknown structures and patterns. Data mining usually requires a specific data storage structure and a great deal of system resources.

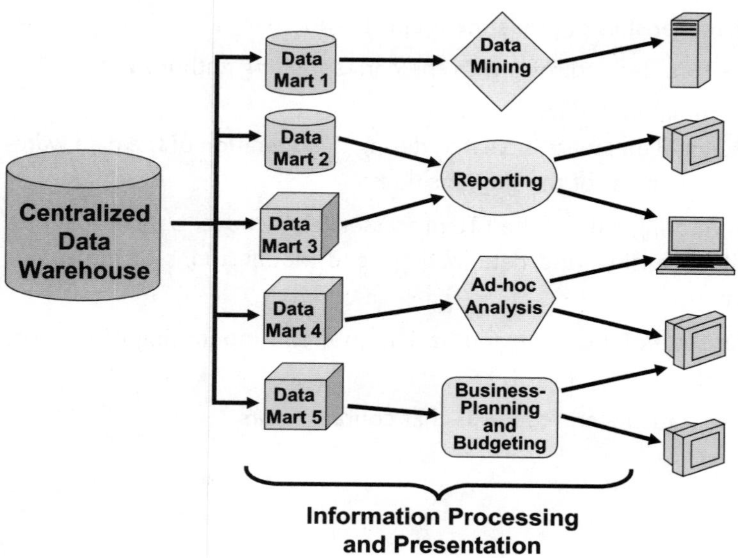

Figure 1.17 Various Target Groups and Their Influence on the Provision of Data

1.5.5 Administration

The core element of the administration of a data warehouse is a central metadata repository. The repository contains all the relevant information on the data stored in the data warehouse.

> In principle, metadata is data on data.

In general, two types of metadata are distinguished from each other:

Technical metadata
This type of metadata contains all the technical information required for the development, operation, and use of a data warehouse. This metadata can further be distinguished by the time of its creation.

- **Administrative metadata**
  This type of metadata contains all the information created during the development and use of the data warehouse. Examples include:
  - Definition of the data warehouse and OLAP schema with the corresponding key figures, characteristics, attributes, dimensions, and hierarchies
  - Description of the data sources, time of data loading, and data-cleansing and transformation rules
  - Description of the indices and aggregates used
  - Characteristics of predefined reports and queries
  - User profiles and roles with the corresponding authorizations
- **Operational metadata**
  Operational metadata is created during the operation of the data warehouse. Examples of this data include:
  - Monitoring data of the ETL processes (extractions, transformations, data cleansing, and data loading) and modifications of the source systems
  - The state of archiving and backup jobs and monitoring of memory usage
  - User statistics and requests that contain errors

Business metadata
This type of metadata contains all the required information on the business environment in the company. It includes the definition of field contents, nomenclature (synonyms and homonyms), and glossaries that are relevant here. It also stores the rules for semantic interpretation, derivations, and calculations.

Metadata repository

A central metadata repository is the precondition for efficient and user-friendly administration of a data warehouse. Until a few years ago, the lack of an appropriate standard was the reason for manufacturers of individual products to use individual repository models. In 2000, various attempts at standardization were merged by the Object Management Group (OMG) into an industry-wide standard that has since been widely accepted. The Common Warehouse Metamodel (CWM, see also *http://www.omg.org/cwm/*) brings us a step closer (a big step) to a central metadata repository that will enable seamless integration and the transparent exchange of metadata.

1.6 OLAP Designs

There are several approaches to, or designs for, storing multidimensional structures in a database. Note the distinction between multidimensional and relational databases: The first design is called multidimensional OLAP (*MOLAP*), and the second design is called relational OLAP (*ROLAP*). In addition to these two approaches, additional variants combine both designs: hybrid OLAP, or *HOLAP systems*. Figure 1.18 depicts all three designs, which are also examined more closely in the following sections.

1.6.1 Multidimensional OLAP (MOLAP)

MOLAP systems use Multidimensional Database Systems (MDDB) with true multidimensional memory structures to offer a multidimensional view of the data.

Advantages and disadvantages

Direct, multidimensional data mapping offers outstanding performance when executing queries. However, because query performance gets drastically reduced with growing memory volume, the high level of memory needed is a disadvantage of MOLAP systems.

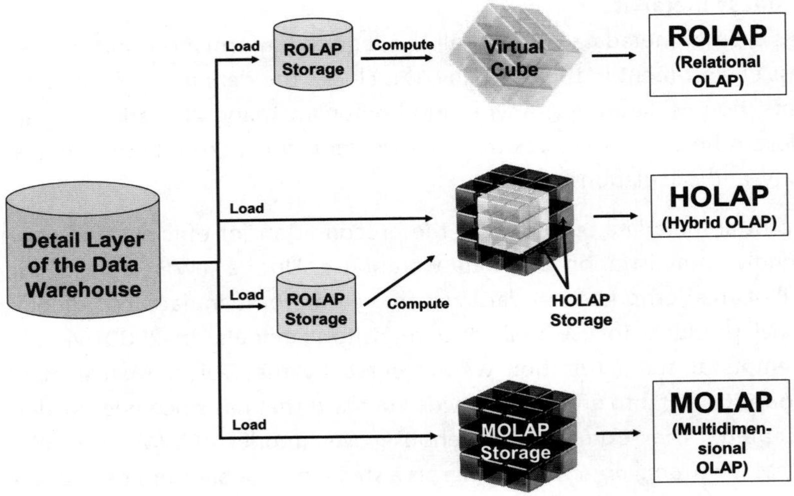

Figure 1.18 Comparison of the Three OLAP Designs

In addition, multidimensional structures usually fill cells only sparsely (*sparcity*). In older multidimensional databases, the empty cells still had to be stored, which resulted in a disproportionate use of disk space for many (poorly filled) cubes. However, most modern multidimensional OLAP systems are based on a multilevel memory structure. They can use compression to avoid storing empty cells. The use of MOLAP memory structures causes additional load time because the multidimensional data structures must be filled after the data warehouse is loaded. On the positive side, the greater portion of the data warehouse aggregation layer (see Section 1.5.3) is no longer necessary because the aggregates are implemented directly in the MDDB.

Because MOLAP systems are designed as pure retrieval database systems, they can function without some transactional database overhead (two-phase commit, recovery, versioning, and so on), which has a positive influence on performance.

The still missing standard for multidimensional databases can be seen as another disadvantage.

1.6.2 Relational OLAP (ROLAP)

ROLAP systems use a virtual, multidimensional data model to ensure transparent copying of multidimensional query structures into the relational data structures, which are used here as physical storage media.

Almost all ROLAP products use specific data structures, like star and snowflake schemas (see Sections 1.9–1.11). ROLAP data is usually maintained directly in the aggregation layer of the data warehouse, so you don't have to create additional databases.

Advantages and disadvantages

The metadata model contains all the information required to support the transition from the multidimensional structure to its relational representation.

But, it's also clear that the dynamic transformation of MOLAP query structures into ROLAP data structures slows down the response time for queries considerably. Manufacturers are trying to mitigate the problem with special optimization techniques such as the use of special indices, the use of aggregates, adjustment of the query optimizer, the use of Multipass SQL, and so on.

Because SQL doesn't offer comparable constructs for some important multidimensional operations (such as top-N and bottom-N queries), these must be calculated directly in the ROLAP engine later on.

Also note that ROLAP systems have shorter runtimes for loading than do MOLAP systems. ROLAP systems also require much less memory, because the cubes exist only virtually, and therefore the scalability is higher. And every advance in the technology of relational databases has a positive affect on ROLAP systems.

1.6.3 Hybrid OLAP (HOLAP)

HOLAP systems combine the advantages of multidimensional and relational memory structures. Depending on the aggregation level and frequency, data is stored in a MOLAP or a ROLAP model.

Advantages and disadvantages

Typically, the required aggregation levels are stored in a multidimensional memory structure. This approach significantly reduces the runtime of queries. Queries that require combinations or characteristics that rarely occur, or that demand a great deal of system resources, are calculated directly on the basis of the data warehouse (ROLAP).

The transparent fusion of both technologies offers optimal scalability, query runtime, and loading processes. Administration of HOLAP systems, however, involves more effort and requires specialized administration tools.

1.7 The Multidimensional Data Model

The OLAP model can be best described as a Rubik's Cube because data storage is multidimensional. In principle, the differentiation into qualitative and quantitative data can be seen as the foundation for multidimensional data structures. Quantitative data (revenue and sales, for example) has to be mapped based on various approaches and view points (qualitative data, such as sales organization, the product sold, and the point in time). The result is a multidimensional data structure, also called a *hypercube* or *data cube*:

Quantitative data

- The quantitative data (also described as *key figures*, *variables*, or *measures*) builds the cells inside the cube.

Qualitative data

- The desired approach (qualitative data) is mapped along the dimensions (axes) of the cube.

The following is a simple example of a multidimensional data model:

Example

> A company sells various products in a specific period of time through various organizational units: direct sales, indirect sales, telephone, Web, and so on. The company now wants to produce reports on its revenues and sales figures. The required data is stored in an OLAP cube (a cube with three dimensions in our example) whose axes are labeled "organization," "product," and "time" (see Figure 1.19). Every intersecting point in the cube is assigned business key figures of "revenue" and "sales" for a specific combination of "organization," "product," and "time."

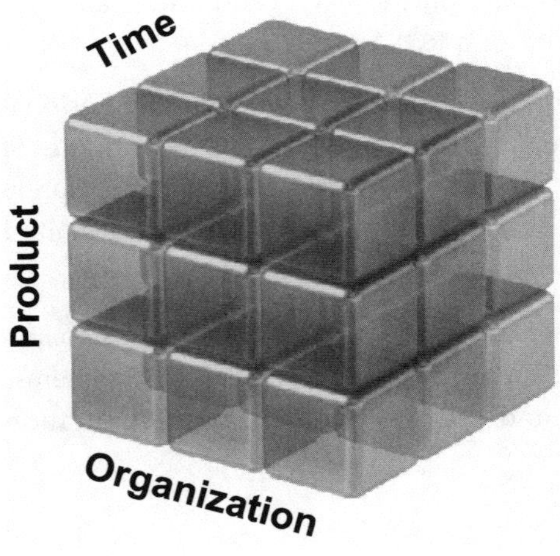

Figure 1.19 OLAP Data Model: Sample Cube

Even if, strictly speaking, the metaphorical use of the cube is valid for only a three-dimensional model, we still speak of a cube, even with "n" dimensions.

1.7.1 Key Figures and Fact Tables

Our sample cube maps two different key figures (revenue and sales) along three dimensions. The key figures define the type of data stored and form the basis for evaluations. Note the distinction between *basic values* (atomic figures and base factors) and *calculated values* (derived figures).

An "abnormality" can sometimes appear: a multidimensional structure that does not contain any true key figures. This case can occur when only the appearance of a specific event should be stored, for example, if all you want to know is that a certain subsidiary sold a specific product at a specific time.

Fact table

Key figures are usually stored in a *fact table*. The fact tables therefore form the foundation of an OLAP data structure.

1.7.2 Characteristics and Dimensions

Our sample cube has three dimensions: organization, product, and time. Therefore, it can manage key figures for the various combinations of these three dimensions. This cube cannot provide evaluations of customers or means of payment.

Each dimension has a number of characteristics derived from the dimension elements. For example, in addition to "product," the product dimension could contain the "vendor" and "storage location" characteristics, and the dimension elements "bread", "tomatoes", "microwaves", etc. for the product, and the elements "Web", "subsidiary A", "subsidiary B", "telemarketing", "inbound call center", "outbound call center", etc. for the organization.

The total of the cells in a cube is a result of the Cartesian product of the dimension elements of all the dimensions in a cube: one value can be stored for each key figure.

Dimension hierarchy

However, one important task of a data warehouse is to store aggregated data, such as the sales figures of specific product groups. That's why you can aggregate dimension elements at multiple levels and create *consolidation paths*.

In our example, the following applies: "product" resides at the lowest level of the product dimension: "product group" and "main product group" reside above it.

Normally, a *total aggregation* forms the highest level within a dimension. It allows you to evaluate key figures by organization and time, independently of the product. You can define various consolidation paths simultaneously for the same dimension. You can aggregate the revenues in individual organizational units according to both geography and organization.

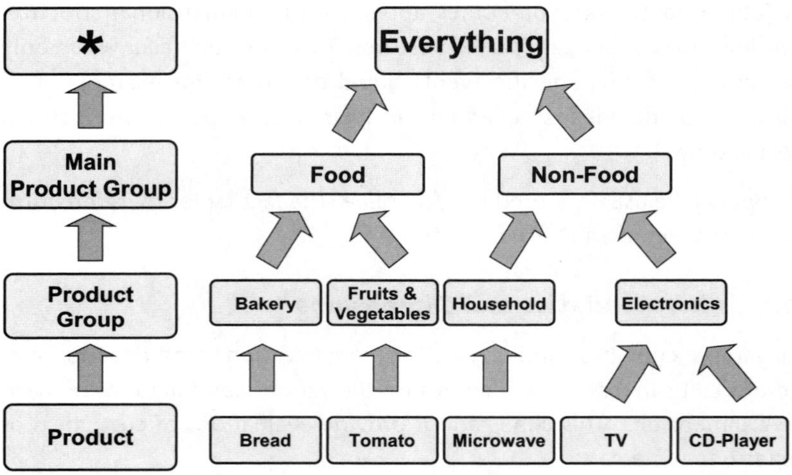

Figure 1.20 The Product Dimension (* Stands for Total Aggregation)

The individual characteristics within a dimension should exhibit a 1:1 or a 1:n relationship. For an n:m relationship, the affected characteristic is usually assigned its own dimension. In our example, the vendor that produced the product must be carried in a new dimension, because a product can be purchased from multiple vendors and one vendor can provide several products.

The lowest characteristic level within a dimension provides the granularity of the data and thus also determines the data set stored in the cube. Because the amount of storage space required directly affects performance (see Section 1.6.1), you must compromise between justifiable performance requirements and reporting requirements, without sacrificing either.

You define how aggregation is to occur individually for each key figure. In our example, we'll use the sum of the key figures along the dimensions.

In our day-to-day work, we often come across key figures whose totals don't lead to the desired results, or even results in an incorrect result. For example, stock key figures (such as inventory stock) cannot be totaled. Totaling cumulative value key figures along certain dimensions (such as a data type dimension with plan, budget, and actual figures) is not very sensible. The system must offer alternate aggregation forms here: "last value," "average," "maximum," "no aggregation," and so on.

1.7.3 Special Dimensions

Time dimension

The time dimension has a special place among the dimensions. It appears in almost every cube to enable mapping of the data over time. But it's quite possible that a source system does not deliver time data; it merely stores the current "state" of the company.

In this case, you can create the time characteristic when the data is loaded into the data warehouse, so that the granularity of the time dimension corresponds to the interval of the loading processes.

In our example, the time dimension does not contain a total aggregation: it does not store totaled, time-independent data. This data is calculated on the fly during execution of the corresponding reports—from the totals of the data at the annual aggregation level.

The various and partially incompatible dimension hierarchies (see Figure 1.21) are another special feature of the time dimension.

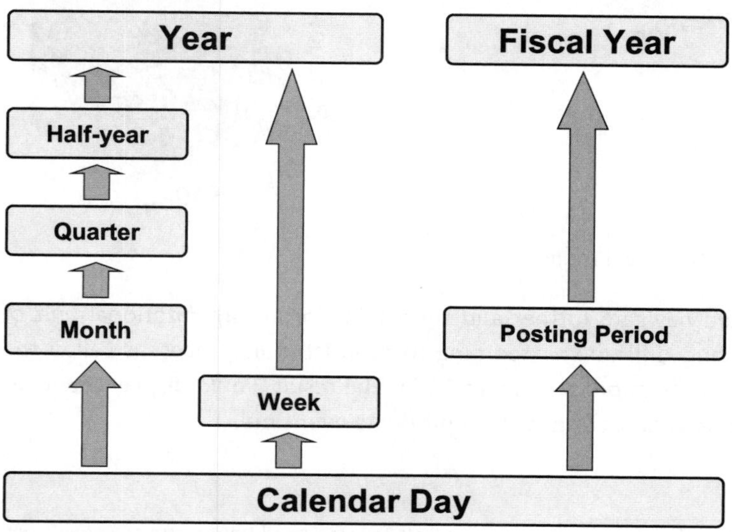

Figure 1.21 Time Dimension

Some specific OLAP implementations use additional special dimensions: unit, data package, and so on.

1.8 Navigation in Multidimensional Data Sets

An OLAP system should provide quick and intuitive navigation options. A visualization of the results of a query (a report) in two dimensions is a table (matrix); it uses a cube for three dimensions and (much more rarely), a tesseract for four dimensions.[6] The report can be manipulated further with the following four techniques.

1.8.1 Slicing, Dicing, Ranging, and Rotation

Slicing and dicing

Slicing and *dicing* essentially mean setting filters. In our example, setting a filter (for a specific product, for example) would cut a slice out of the cube (see Figure 1.22). The result would display the revenue of all organizations with this product over time.

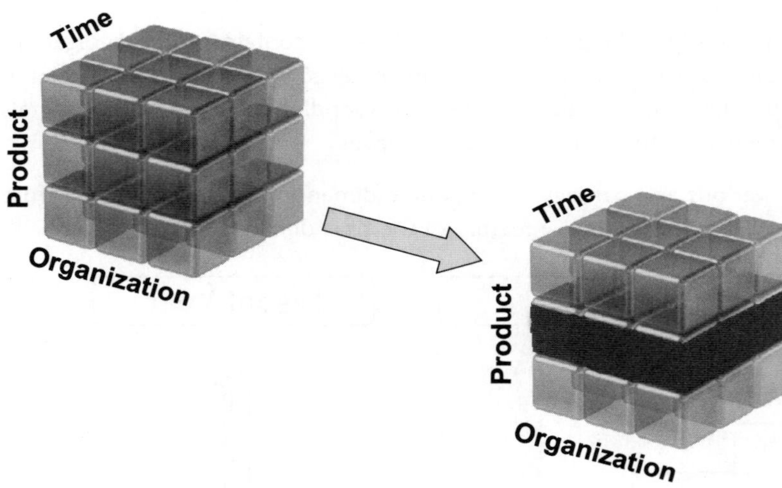

Figure 1.22 Slicing and Dicing

Rotation

You could navigate further and set a filter for an organizational unit of interest and drill down according to product. This process is called the *rotation* of the cube (see Figure 1.23). The result would display the revenue of this organization with all products over time.

6 See *http://www.geom.uiuc.edu/docs/holt/tesseract/top.html* or *http://pw1.net-com.com/~hjsmith/WireFrame4/tesseract.html*.

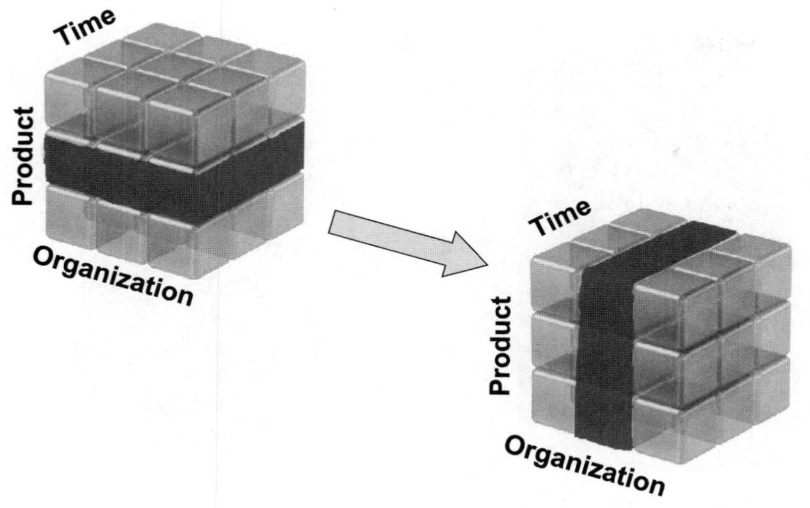

Figure 1.23 Rotation of the Cube

Rotation allows each user to display the data in the form that best meets his or her needs. The possible views of the data created by rotation rise exponentially. Three dimensions have six views. Five dimensions have 120 views. In theory, the number of possible views is equal to the factorial of the dimensions (3! = 6, 4! = 24, 5! = 120, 6! = 720, ...16! = 20'922'789'888'000). Even if many rotations don't appear to make sense, users should always be able to determine how they want to view their data.

> The need for a certain rotation might arise from the desired graphical visualization of the data.

Dicing and ranging

Dicing and *ranging* are special forms of the slice technique. These techniques reduce individual dimension to certain subsets: the discrete classification of the dimensions through setting intervals as filters.

This operation limits the data displayed to data that is only relevant to the user (see Figure 1.24). The result is a smaller cube that can be analyzed faster and that still offers all the operations of the original cube.

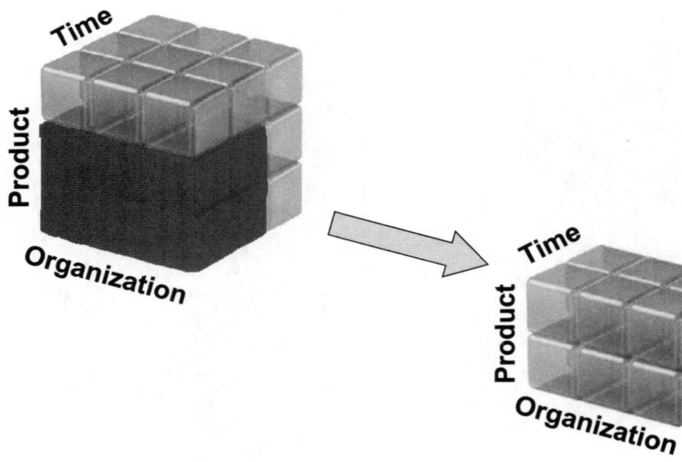

Figure 1.24 Dicing and Ranging

1.8.2 Drilldown and Rollup

Hierarchies can be defined for every dimension. The hierarchies can contain multiple levels. The higher the hierarchy level, the higher the aggregation level of the displayed data. The deeper a user goes into the hierarchy, or drills down into it, the more detailed the information becomes.

This process is called *drilldown*. It can occur within a dimension (by moving in the product hierarchy from main product groups, to product groups, and then to individual products) or by inserting characteristics from other dimensions. A *rollup* is the opposite of a drilldown.

1.8.3 Drill Across

Drill across usually means switching the X and Y axes of a report.

1.8.4 Drill Through

Several data warehouse systems offer an option for a report to include data that is not in the cube itself, but that is stored only in the detail layer of the data warehouse system or even in OLTP systems. A good example of this would be individual accounting documents. This ability is often called *drill through*.

> The professional literature does not offer a standard definition of these terms. The definitions given here reflect the majority of views cited in the literature.

1.9 The Classic Star Schema

The classic star schema is intended for the use of relational database systems at the physical design level. A drawing of the star schema looks like a star (see Figure 1.25) in which multidimensional data structures are mapped in two types of tables:

1. **In a single fact table**
   The fact table contains the key figures and a combined key with an element for each dimension.
2. **In dimension tables (one per dimension)**
   These tables are completely non-normalized and contain a compound primary key using all the attributes necessary for non-ambiguity, the hierarchical structure of the relevant dimension, and a level attribute that shows the hierarchy level of the individual entries.

To manage the relationship between the dimension tables and the related fact table, the primary key of the dimension tables is stored in the fact table as a foreign key (it forms the primary key of the fact table).

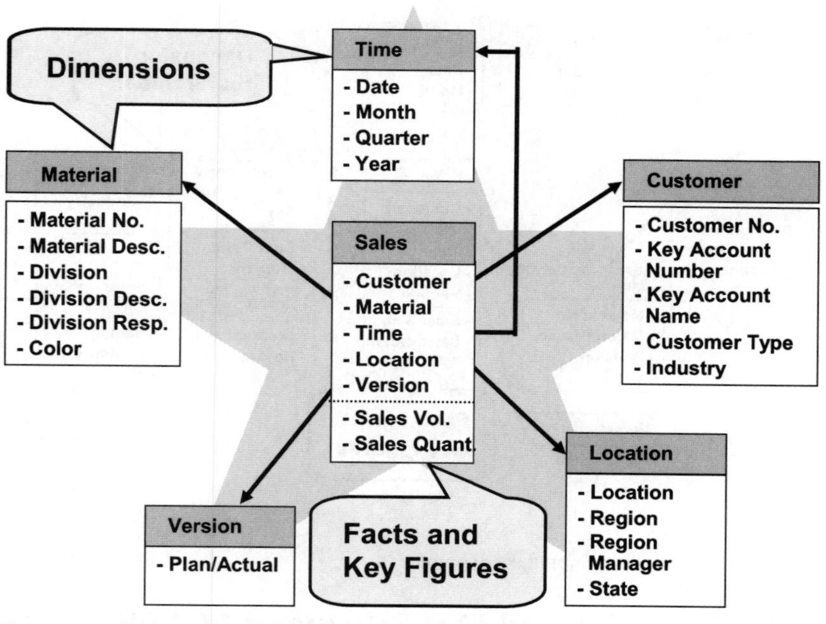

Figure 1.25 The Classic Star Schema

The storage of all the data belonging to a dimension, including the dimension hierarchies in a single, non-normalized table (the dimension table), allows a simpler connection between the fact and dimension table at the database level and therefore limits the number of required join operations.

But non-normalization causes a number of redundancies that can lead to problems during insert, update, and delete operation and that represent a challenge for each OLAP system.

1.10 The Classic Snowflake Schema

The classic snowflake schema (see Figure 1.26), however, stores the data in the dimension tables in a third normal form. Each hierarchy level of a dimension is stored in its own table (an implication of the normalization).

The relationships between the tables are mapped through foreign keys, as is the case with the star schema. Reports with multiple dimensions or dimension levels require many join operations, which can generate performance bottlenecks and nullify advantages such as the lower number of redundancies and the limited need for storage space.

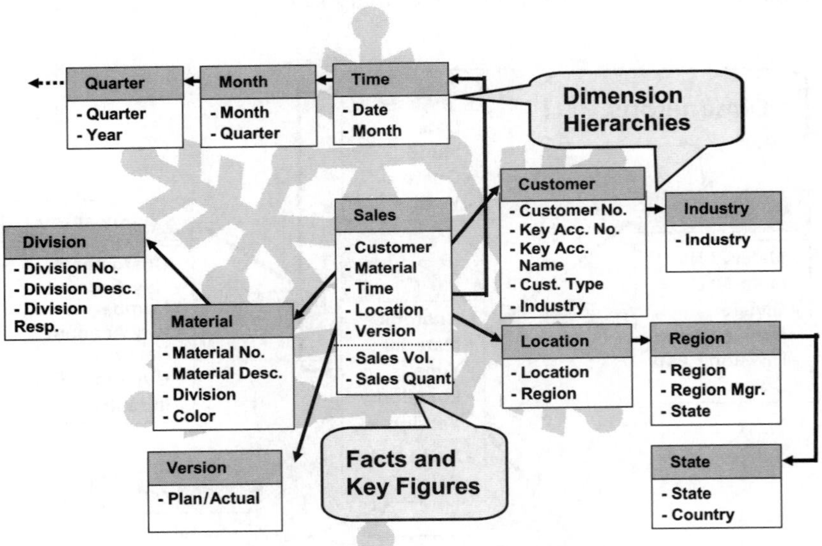

Figure 1.26 The Classic Snowflake Schema

1.11 The Enhanced Star Schema of SAP BW

For SAP Business Information Warehouse, SAP AG uses a *developed star schema*. The developed star schema is based on two basic components (see Figure 1.27):

1. The basic InfoCube star schema (an InfoCube can be compared with a multidimensional data cube). The design of the fact table and the dimension tables correspond to the classic star schema.
2. A portion independent of the InfoCube, the master data with attributes, texts, and hierarchies.

The basic InfoCube star schema

Unlike the classic star schema, the basic InfoCube star schema assigns the foreign keys of the dimension table artificially and they are not linked to real content, as a product number from a product dimension would be. These *surrogate keys* (four-byte integer values) are stored in the fact table where they form the primary key of the fact table.

The use of artificial keys enables the use of null values (empty cells) in some of the primary key fields. It thus allows n:m relationships and *unbalanced hierarchies* within a dimension. The dimension hierarchies are then carried as *characteristics* in the dimension tables.

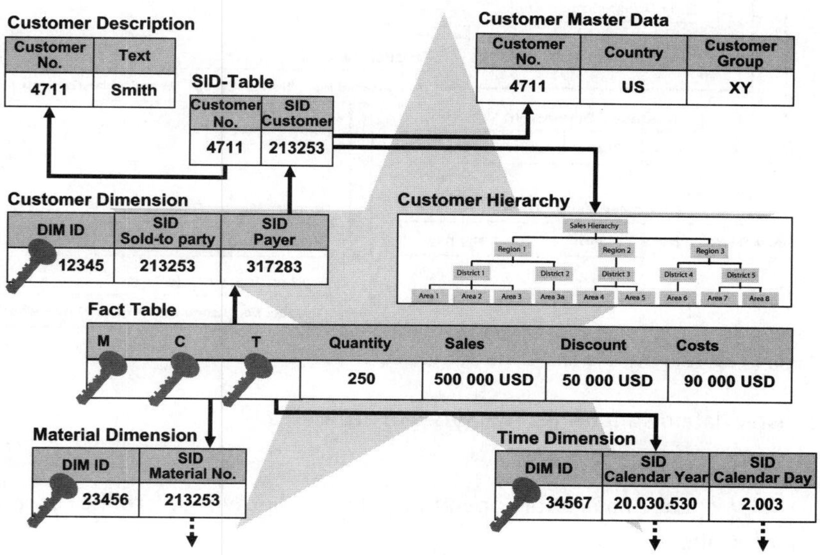

Figure 1.27 The Developed Star Schema from SAP

Predefined dimensions

Apart from the three predefined dimensions (time, unit, and data package), a maximum of 13 user-defined dimensions can be used in an SAP BW InfoCube.

Master data

The data in the tables that is independent of the InfoCube is the *master data*. It is defined once and then reused for the various InfoCubes as often as needed. Master data is physically present only once. The connection between the dimension tables and the master data occurs indirectly with artificial, system-assigned keys (*surrogate IDs* or *SIDs*) and requires its own SID tables.

Dimension hierarchies

The data of the dimension hierarchies is not stored within the dimension table, but in a *hierarchy table* (linked by a SID). The hierarchy tables are the precondition for the use of several external hierarchies for one characteristic.

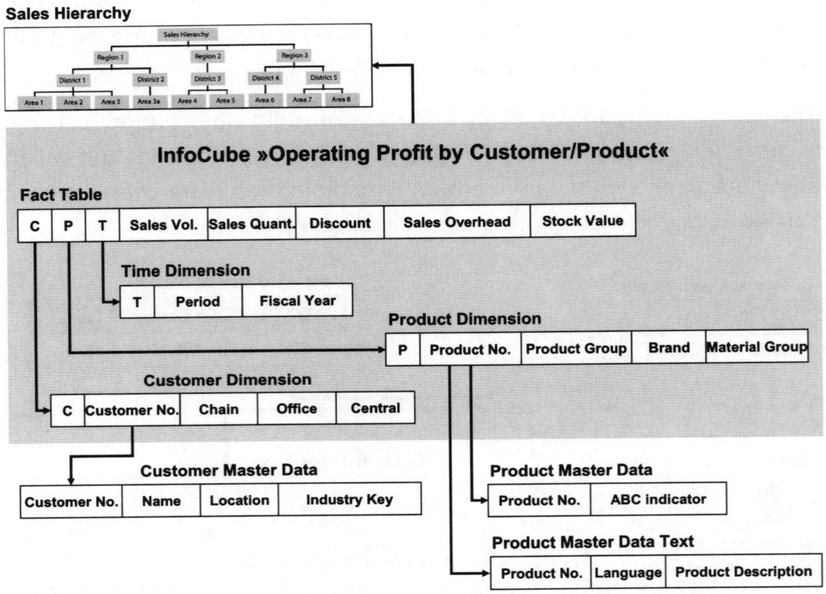

Figure 1.28 Master Data and Dimension Hierarchies

Master data distinguishes two types of attributes:

- **Navigation attributes**
  They enable navigation operations (like drilldown and rollup) in an InfoCube.
- **Display attributes**
  They can be displayed in reports but don't enable navigation.

Text descriptions of characteristics are stored in a separate table, the *text table*. This approach enables language-dependent descriptions of attribute values and support for several languages within an application. The use of SIDs also enables characteristics without a corresponding master data table.

The advantages of the developed star schema from SAP over the classic star and snowflake schemas are numerous. The following list summarizes the most important advantages:

- The use of automatically generated four-byte integer keys (SIDs and DIM IDs) enables much faster data access than that provided by long, alphanumeric keys.
- Storage of data outside the dimension tables with the SID technique makes it easy to implement the following modeling considerations:
    - Historicizing of the dimensions (time-dependent attributes)
    - Multilingual options
    - Reusing master data across basic InfoCubes
- Storing aggregated key figures in their own fact tables (*materialized aggregates*) significantly improves the performance of queries.

2 SAP Business Information Warehouse—Overview of Components

With SAP Business Information Warehouse 3.0, SAP offered for the first time a truly comprehensive tool for analytical applications that included all the required components of a data warehouse: tools for the ETL process, a flexible tool for data modeling, and high-performance reporting tools. SAP BW 3.5 has reached a new milestone—it includes significant innovations, extensions, and improvements, all of which are introduced to you in this chapter.

2.1 The Architecture of SAP BW

Comprehensive data warehouse solution

SAP Business Information Warehouse (SAP BW) is a comprehensive data warehouse solution (see Chapter 1, *Data Warehousing Concepts*) as defined by W.H. Inmon. Hence, it contains all the components required for the data warehousing process. The following list contains the core elements of SAP BW:

- Functions for the extraction, transformation, and loading (ETL) process (extraction of data from source systems and the corresponding data processing)
- Components for storing data (complex master and transaction data)
- Tools for analyses and reports (SAP Business Explorer with browser-based SAP Web reporting and the Excel-based Analyzer—BEx Web and BEx Analyzer)

Additional components

In addition to these core elements, SAP BW offers the required additional components. These components include tools for customizing (to set up and configure customer-specific applications), for administration, monitoring, scheduling, performance optimization, open-hub components, and so on. All elements of SAP BW are based on consistent metadata, and you can manage the metadata with the Administrator Workbench (see Figure 2.1).

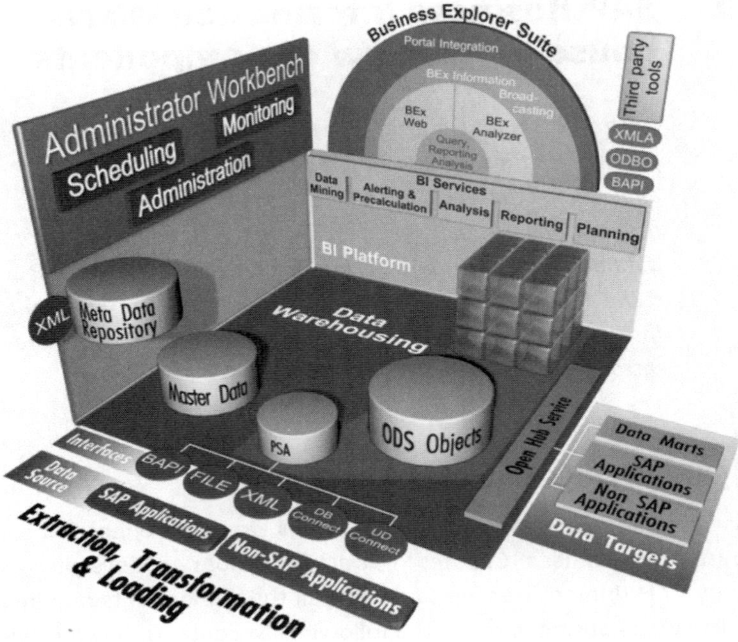

Figure 2.1 The Architecture of SAP Business Information Warehouse

Communication with other systems

SAP BW runs on its own installation. Actually, it usually runs on its own client/server architecture, which is why it contains functions to communicate with other systems. Various technologies are used for communication: Application Link Enabling (ALE, the proprietary SAP technology similar to EDI for communication between systems) for the exchange of metadata and data acquisition, and transactional Remote Function Calls (RFCs), the SAP interface protocol, for the extraction of data from SAP R/3.

SAP BW also handles connections to non-SAP source systems. Such connections can use the XML protocol or third-party extraction tools to exchange metadata. You can collect data with Universal Data Connect (UD Connect), interface files, third-party extraction tools, or the XML protocol.

Various technologies, such as OLE DB for OLAP (ODBO), XML for analysis (XMLA), or business application programming interfaces (BAPIs)—all standardized programming interfaces for access to the business processes and data of SAP systems—enable the connection of third-party tools for reporting.

SAP BW offers analytical applications as defined by data warehouse and OLAP concepts and it serves as the core of the business intelligence components of SAP NetWeaver.

2.2 Data Storage in SAP BW

2.2.1 InfoObjects as the Basis

InfoObjects provide the basis of the data model in SAP BW. You can edit InfoObjects under **InfoObjects** in the **Modeling** view of the Administrator Workbench, the SAP BW tool for the configuration, control, monitoring, and maintenance of all the processes involved in data acquisition, processing, and storage (see Figure 2.2). SAP calls these InfoObjects *business evaluation objects*.

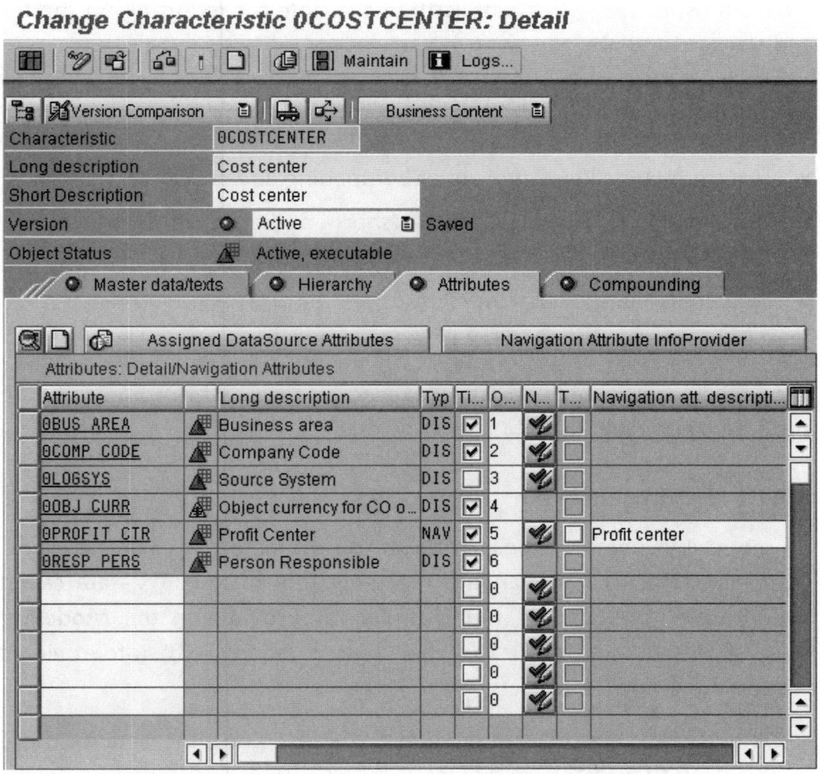

Figure 2.2 InfoObjects Provide the Basis of the SAP BW Data Model

InfoObjects are divided into *characteristics* and *key figures*:

Key figures

- *Key figures* provide the values (amounts, quantities, counters, dates, and time) to be analyzed.

Characteristics

- *Characteristics* represent the business events and create relationships. SAP provides the following types of characteristics:
  - Business characteristics (sold-to party, cost center, company code, and so on)
  - Units (currency and quantity)
  - Time characteristics (calendar day, calendar year, and fiscal year)
  - Technical characteristics (number of a data load procedure, for example)

Master data and texts

You can store master data, texts, and hierarchies for InfoObjects of the "characteristic" type. This data is then available for reporting on master and transaction data.

Complex key figures and characteristics

SAP BW enables you to map very powerful key figures and characteristics. Examples include:

- Non-cumulative key figures built by opening and supporting postings
- Complex, time-dependent texts (short- and medium-length texts), attributes (profit center and person responsible, for example)
- Hierarchies-based characteristics
- Characteristics compounded to a cost area

InfoObject-Catalogs and InfoAreas

InfoObjects are contained in *InfoObjectCatalogs*, which, in turn, are grouped by application area into *InfoAreas*.

2.2.2 InfoProviders

InfoProviders

All reportable objects—those that can be evaluated with *SAP Business Explorer (SAP BEx)*, the standard reporting tool of SAP BW—are called *InfoProviders*; they can be found under **InfoProvider** in the **Modeling** view of the Administrator Workbench (see Figure 2.3); InfoProviders include the following objects:

- Objects that physically contain data; SAP BW stores the data for these objects in their database tables.
- Logical views; objects whose data is stored in another system (such as SAP R/3) or in other physical objects.

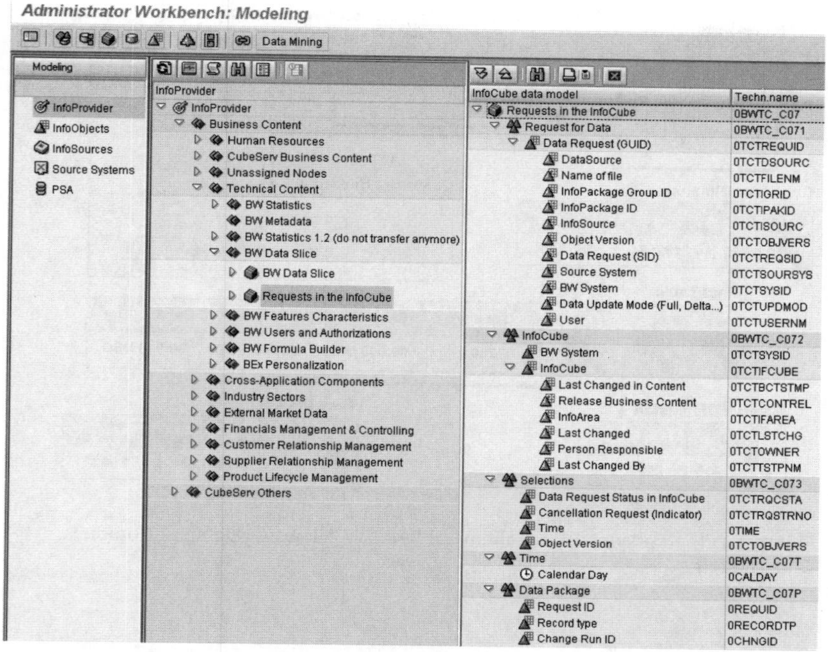

Figure 2.3 InfoCubes Create a Suitable Foundation for Queries with OLAP Functionality

BasicCubes

The group of objects that physically contains data includes InfoCubes, Operational Data Store (ODS) objects, and InfoObjects that contain master data. The group of logical views includes InfoSets, RemoteCubes, SAP RemoteCubes, virtual InfoCubes with services, and MultiProviders.

InfoAreas

Like InfoObjectCatalogs, InfoProviders are grouped into InfoAreas. The Basic InfoCubes that contain data consist of several relational tables that organize the InfoObjects they contain according to the enhanced star schema (see Section 1.11 and Figure 2.4 below).

ODS objects

Technically, *ODS objects* are simple tables that contain a number of key fields and a number of data fields. Note the following (possible) limitations to this approach: the number of key figures is limited to a maximum of 16. The arrangement of all key and non-key characteristics with the key figures in one data record can lead to extremely long records. The options for optimizing performance are much more limited here than they are with InfoCubes.

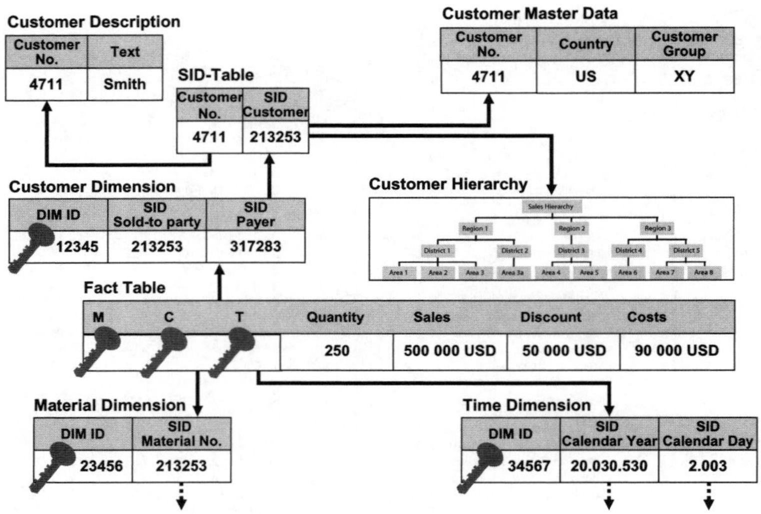

Figure 2.4 The Enhanced Star Schema of SAP BW Allows Mapping of Complex Data Models

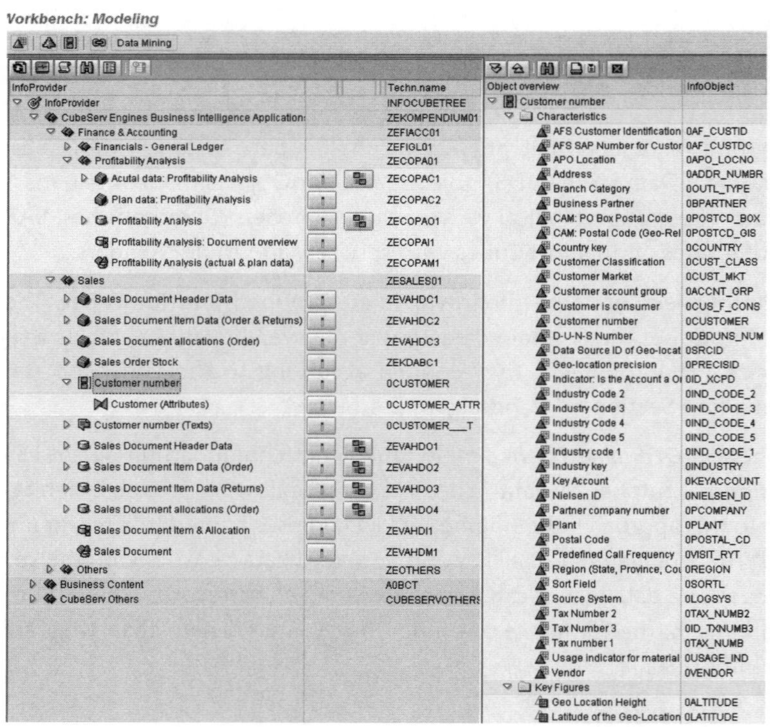

Figure 2.5 ODS Objects, InfoObjects, and InfoSets Supplement InfoProviders, thus Enabling the Mapping of Additional Reporting Requirements and Functions

InfoObjects as InfoProviders

Master-data-bearing characteristics as InfoProviders provide reporting with the master data tables of the attributes and texts of the particular characteristic involved.

MultiProviders

MultiProviders combine data from various InfoProviders. One possible use of a MultiProvider would be the combination of an InfoCube with sales data with an additional InfoCube with headcount data. This approach would enable reports that calculate per capita sales. Another possible use enables the combination of InfoCubes with sales with an InfoProvider type of **InfoObject Material** to display materials without sales. Note that MultiProviders are not based on a JOIN operation, but on a UNION operation (a union of the tables involved).

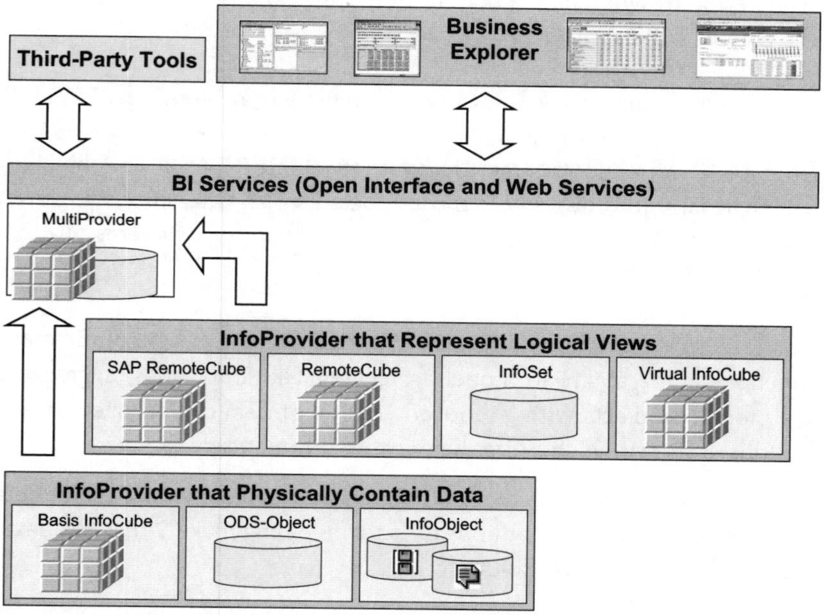

Figure 2.6 MultiProviders Make Objects That Physically Contain Data and Logical Views Available for Reporting

InfoSets

InfoSets form a semantic layer above the data sources, such as ODS objects and master data. With InfoSets, you can use all database techniques, including joins. The ability to use this technology greatly increases your flexibility in SAP Business Explorer.

SAP RemoteCube, RemoteCube, and Virtual InfoCube

Additional InfoProviders, objects in SAP BW that do not contain data, include the following: *SAP RemoteCubes* (access to transaction data in other SAP systems, based on an InfoSource with flexible update rules (see the following comments), *RemoteCubes* (access to data from another system over BAPIs), and *Virtual InfoCubes* (access to data from SAP and non-SAP data sources via a user-defined function module). All these InfoProviders enable flexible reporting.

For all objects, however, note that storing data in other systems and remote access generally precludes you from being able to influence system behavior, especially in terms of performance. Therefore, you should use these objects only after careful consideration. Data checking is one example where the use of these objects has proven to be particularly effective: an SAP RemoteCube enables access to a source system; a MultiProvider links the SAP RemoteCube to a BasicCube. A deviations analysis determines whether the data in the source system is consistent with the data in SAP BW.

In our experience, Basic InfoCubes combined with MultiProviders are the most important objects for reporting. Only these objects deliver the full performance optimization potential of SAP BW. Other objects, like virtual InfoCubes and RemoteCubes, can lead to serious performance problems, even with medium-sized quantity structures (10 to 100 million data records).

Performance optimization and aggregates

You can use various functions to optimize performance. One of the main functions is the ability to model *aggregates*. Like InfoCubes, aggregates are modeled objects with a reduced volume of data or improved access options; SAP BW synchronizes aggregates automatically.

Best-practice solution for data modeling

SAP BW has high-performance components to map complex data models and large sets of data. Its options for data modeling make SAP BW a best-practice data warehouse solution.

Innovations

Of course, versions of SAP BW prior to 3.0 could use SAP BEx to analyze InfoCubes and ODS objects along with InfoSet queries to analyze tables (master data, for example). However, users never accepted the InfoSet query tool because of its unusual handling and insufficient options. The new possibilities offered since SAP BW 3.x—to link all InfoProviders with MultiProviders, and to analyze all types of InfoProviders with the same reporting tool (SAP BEx)—are fundamental advances in SAP BW's development.

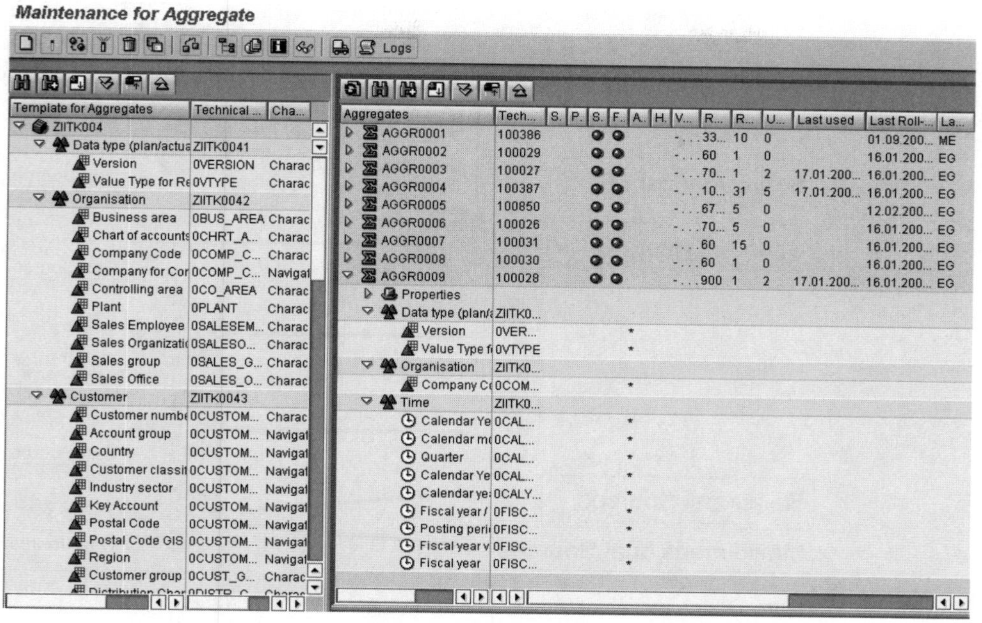

Figure 2.7 In Addition to Other Functions, Aggregates Offer Options for Optimizing Performance

2.3 Data Acquisition

2.3.1 Components of the Data Acquisition Process: Sources of Data and Their DataSources

SAP BW can extract data from almost any source. You can differentiate between the following main groups of source systems:

Types of source systems

- SAP systems: e.g., SAP R/3, SAP CRM, SAP APO, and SAP SEM
- Structured interface files: *flat files*
- XML data (through standard SOAP protocol): directly or by using SAP Exchange Infrastructure (SAP XI) to implement cross-system business processes. Within the overall architecture of SAP NetWeaver, SAP XI handles the task of process integration.
- Database systems that can be attached via DB Connect
- UD Connect permits access to practically all relational and multidimensional data sources.
- Third-party systems that can use staging BAPIs to load data and metadata into SAP BW (tools like Ascential DataStage and Informatica PowerCenter).

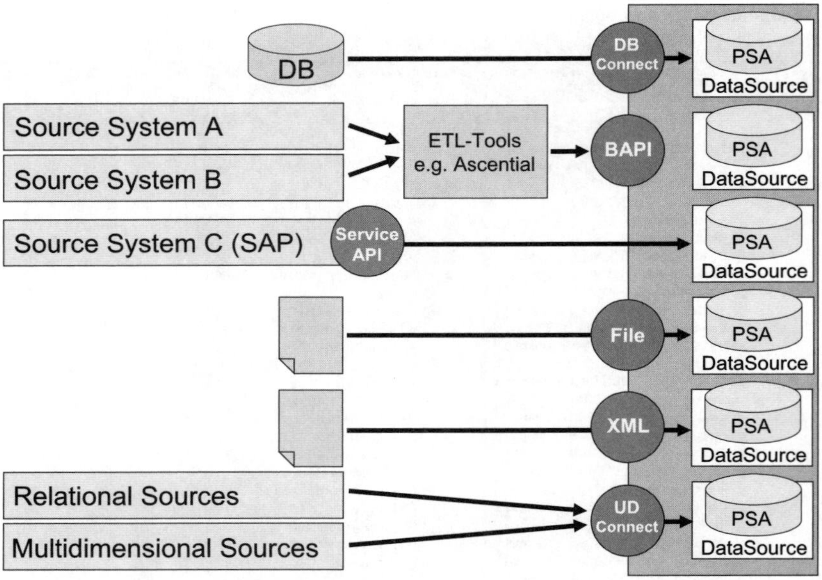

Figure 2.8 Integration of the ETL Process in the Architecture of SAP BW

In the end, the source systems just make the data available, usually through DataSources. Upon request, SAP BW starts to transfer the data. With source systems such as SAP systems, database systems (with UD Connect and DB Connect), and external systems (linked via BAPIs), the connection is highly integrated. SAP BW reads the data directly from the source system and imports it according to the selected procedure.

DataSources and transfer structure

You can maintain source systems under **Source Systems** in the **Modeling** view of the Administrator Workbench. For each source system, the known DataSources can be displayed. The structure for transferring data from a DataSource to SAP BW is called a *transfer structure*. If new DataSources are added later, they become available with a subsequent metadata upload. SAP R/3 systems provide a number of SAP Business Content DataSources that you can use immediately.

You can use DataSources for all objects that contain data: master data (texts, attributes, and hierarchies for InfoObjects) and transaction data.

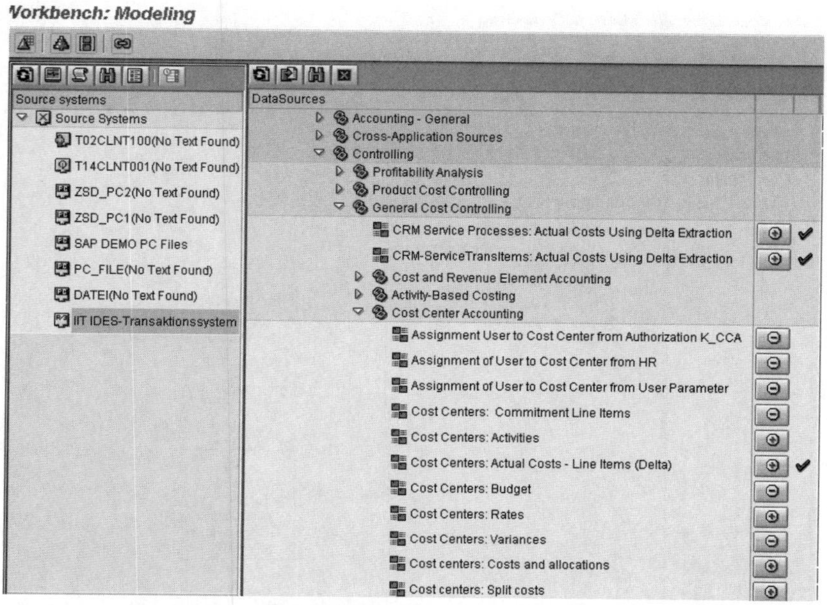

Figure 2.9 DataSources of SAP and Non-SAP Systems in the Administrator Workbench

2.3.2 Components of the Data Acquisition Process: InfoSources

Communications Structure

An *InfoSource* is a set of logically related information combined into a unit. A *communications structure* houses the InfoObjects into which an InfoSource is to transfer data (for master data, characteristic values, language key, and long text, for example).

You can maintain InfoSources under **InfoSources** in the **Modeling** view of the Administrator Workbench. DataSources (one or more) are assigned specifically to an InfoSource for each selected source system. Then, each DataSource makes available its transfer structure to the InfoSource.

Transfer rules

You use *transfer rules* to convert the data delivered in the transfer structure to a form appropriate to SAP BW in the communications structure. The transfer can occur in any of the following ways:

- Direct transfer (1:1 rule)
- Assignment of a constant value
- Routines (ABAP/4 program coding)
- Formulas

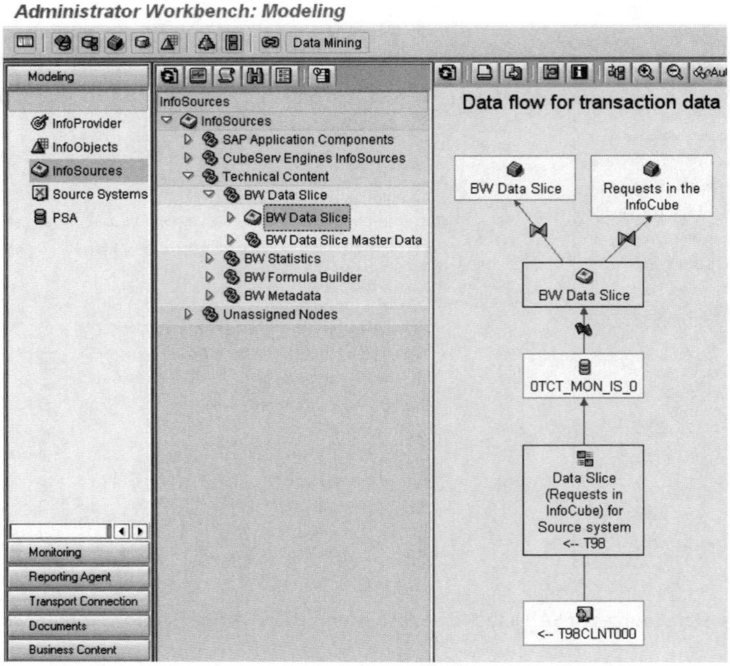

Figure 2.10 Configuration of Data Acquisition from Connecting the DataSource to Posting the Data to the Data Target (InfoCubes here) in the Administrator Workbench

You can use the mechanisms described here to update master data directly in the InfoObjects. For InfoProviders (transaction data and, as of SAP BW 3.0, InfoObjects), posting occurs in a second step, the *update rules*.

2.3.3 Components of the Data Acquisition Process: Update Rules

Update rules

In the *update rules*, you specify how the data from the communications structure of the assigned InfoSources is inserted in an InfoProvider. You can maintain update rules under **InfoProviders** in the **Modeling** view of the Administrator Workbench.

Processing occurs differently for the various types of InfoProviders: You must define an update rule for every key figure and the related characteristics for InfoCubes. For ODS objects, the same requirement applies to the data and key fields; for InfoObjects, this requirement applies to attributes and key fields.

The basic types of updates include the following:

Rules for each data field

- No update
- Addition, minimum, or maximum
- Overwrite (only for ODS objects)

You can set up the required rules for each key figure for key fields (such as characteristics in InfoCubes). Here, too, you can use the following processing methods:

Rules for each key field

- Direct transfer (1:1 rule)
- Assignment of a constant
- Routines (ABAP/4 program coding)
- Formulas

2.3.4 Components of the Data Acquisition Process: Requesting the Data Transfer and Monitoring

You use the scheduler to request the transfer of the data into SAP BW. Configuration occurs in InfoPackages that you maintain under **InfoSources** in the **Modeling** view of the Administrator Workbench.

InfoPackage

InfoPackages define the selection, processing and scheduling criteria for a DataSource assigned to an InfoSource. Customizing of the InfoPackages offers the settings required by the DataSources from various types of source systems: For interface files, you select the location of the flat files; for delta-capable SAP R/3 DataSources, you choose the full or delta upload option; for third-party tools, the parameters specific to the tool.

In SAP BW 3.0 and later versions, you can use process chains to configure complex processes: the sequence and criteria according to which the data requests are processed.

Process chains

You can keep an eye on the load in progress with the monitor. The monitor offers an overview screen and detailed information on the status and result of the load process.

Monitor

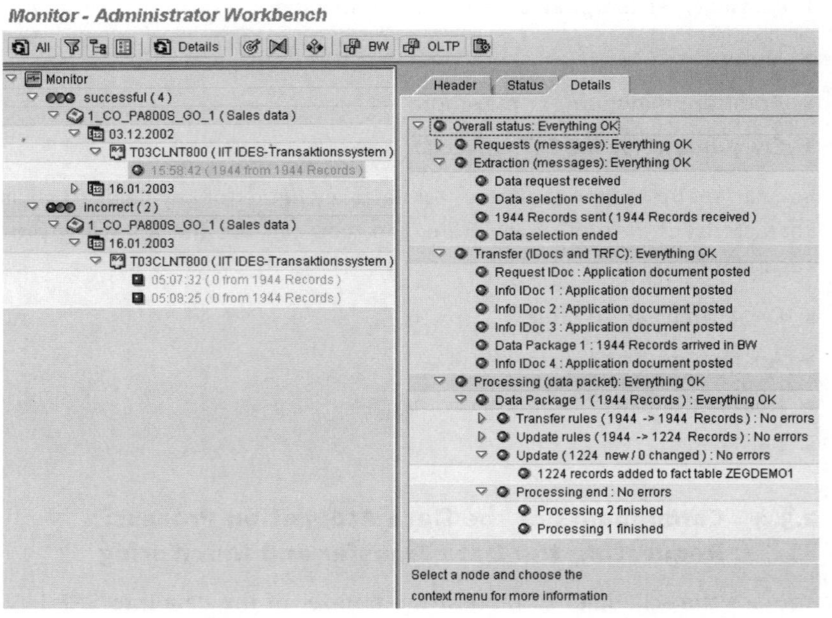

Figure 2.11 Monitoring Permits Cross-System Tracing of Data Acquisition and Supports Error Analysis

2.3.5 Components of the Data Acquisition Process: Persistent Staging Area (PSA)

PSA

When using the corresponding transfer methods, the *persistent staging area (PSA)* allows you to store the data in SAP BW as it was delivered by the source system (except for technical conversion, such as the *date* type). Transparent tables are used to store the data.

Recommendation: systematic reorganization of the PSA

Note that when you use the PSA transfer method, the data is stored in the PSA by default. This feature means that the PSA can quickly reach a size many times larger than that of the actual reporting-relevant objects. We therefore strongly recommend monitoring the size of the PSA and a corresponding reorganization of the PSA.

2.3.6 The ETL Process

As seen in the previous section, SAP BW offers a great deal of functionality and flexibility for the entire ETL process. Basically, however, we recommend that you use the transfer rules to create adequate cleanliness of the data and the update rules for logical transformations. Although SAP does not require this approach, it has the advantage of cleansing the data as soon as it *enters* SAP BW. It also allows you to dispense with (possibly) redundant cleansing functions and avoid the danger of not cleansing data at all the required locations, which would then lead to inconsistent and incorrect data for reporting.

2.4 Reporting and Analysis Tools

2.4.1 SAP BW Components and Third-Party Tools

Various reporting and analysis tools can be used with SAP BW. A basic differentiation exists between SAP tools and third-party tools.

SAP Business Explorer

SAP BW reporting and analysis tools are components of the SAP Business Explorer (SAP BEx), which consists of the following components:

- **Query Designer**
  Tool to define queries on SAP BW InfoProviders
- **Web Application Designer**
  Tool to create Web-reporting applications
- **Web Applications**
  The environment for running reports and analyses in a Hypertext Markup Language (HTML) browser
- **Analyzer**
  The environment for running queries in Excel
- **Information Broadcasting**
  The option to make objects with business-intelligence content available to a wide group of users
- **Additional functions**
  Personalization and mobile reporting components and functions to integrate SAP BEx Web applications into SAP Enterprise Portal (SAP EP)

Reporting Agent

The *Reporting Agent* supplements the functions of SAP BEx. The Reporting Agent offers background and additional functions:

- Evaluation of exceptions with alternate follow-up actions, such as sending messages (email) or creating entries in the Alert Monitor
- Printing queries
- Precalculation of Web templates and value sets for characteristic variables
- Managing bookmarks
- Functions for third-party tools

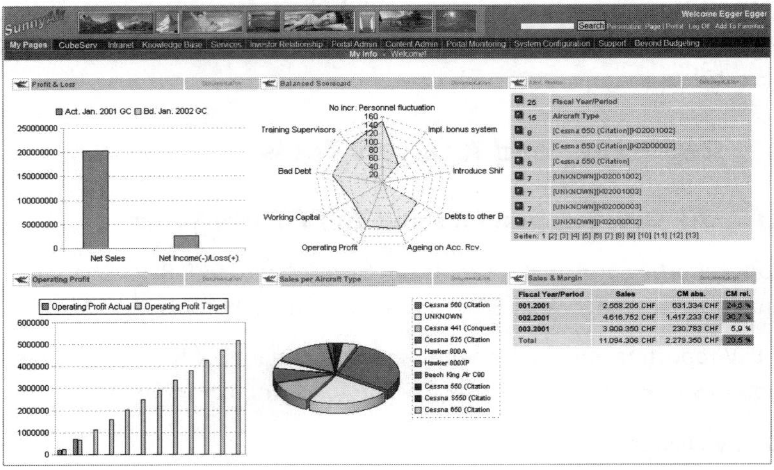

Figure 2.12 The Creation of Web Reports and Integration with SAP Enterprise Portal are Standard Functions of SAP BW

Third-party tools You can also use a variety of third-party tools to access data in SAP BW. For some time, the primary means of doing so has been to run an SAP BEx query from a front-end tool supplied by a third party. You can use various SAP interfaces to access queries:

- ▶ OLE DB for OLAP interface
- ▶ XMLA interface
- ▶ BAPI interface

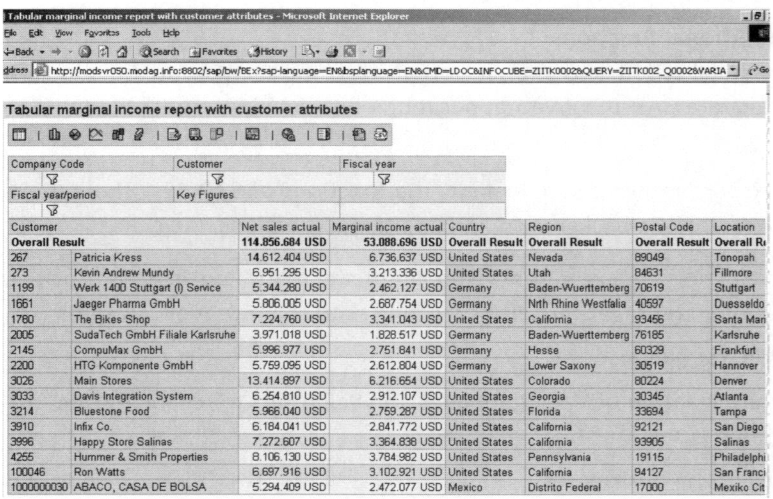

Customer		Net sales actual	Marginal income actual	Country	Region	Postal Code	Location
Overall Result		**114.856.684 USD**	**53.088.696 USD**	**Overall Result**	**Overall Result**	**Overall Result**	**Overall R**
267	Patricia Kress	14.612.404 USD	6.736.637 USD	United States	Nevada	89049	Tonopah
273	Kevin Andrew Mundy	6.951.295 USD	3.213.336 USD	United States	Utah	84631	Fillmore
1199	Werk 1400 Stuttgart (I) Service	5.344.280 USD	2.462.127 USD	Germany	Baden-Wuerttemberg	70619	Stuttgart
1661	Jaeger Pharma GmbH	5.806.005 USD	2.687.754 USD	Germany	Nrth Rhine Westfalia	40597	Duesseldo
1780	The Bikes Shop	7.224.760 USD	3.341.043 USD	United States	California	93456	Santa Mari
2005	SudaTech GmbH Filiale Karlsruhe	3.971.018 USD	1.828.517 USD	Germany	Baden-Wuerttemberg	76185	Karlsruhe
2145	CompuMax GmbH	5.996.977 USD	2.751.841 USD	Germany	Hesse	60329	Frankfurt
2200	HTG Komponente GmbH	5.759.095 USD	2.612.804 USD	Germany	Lower Saxony	30519	Hannover
3026	Main Stores	13.414.897 USD	6.216.654 USD	United States	Colorado	80224	Denver
3033	Davis Integration System	6.254.810 USD	2.912.107 USD	United States	Georgia	30345	Atlanta
3214	Bluestone Food	5.966.040 USD	2.759.287 USD	United States	Florida	33694	Tampa
3910	Infix Co.	6.184.041 USD	2.841.772 USD	United States	California	92121	San Diego
3996	Happy Store Salinas	7.272.607 USD	3.364.838 USD	United States	California	93905	Salinas
4255	Hummer & Smith Properties	8.106.130 USD	3.784.982 USD	United States	Pennsylvania	19115	Philadelphi
100046	Ron Watts	6.697.916 USD	3.102.921 USD	United States	California	94127	San Franci
1000000030	ABACO, CASA DE BOLSA	5.294.409 USD	2.472.077 USD	Mexico	Distrito Federal	17000	Mexiko Cit

Figure 2.13 Tabular Report in SAP BW 3.x

2.4.2 SAP Business Explorer Query Designer

The Query Designer enables you to define the components of an SAP BEx query: general properties, filters, free characteristics, rows, and columns.

Innovations

As of SAP BW 3.0, you can use the stand-alone tool, Query Designer to define queries on SAP BW InfoProviders. With the addition of InfoObjects (and their master data) to the reporting-relevant objects (see Section 2.2.2), SAP now offers reporting on transaction data and the analysis of master data. In addition, as of SAP BW 3.0, you can use tabular reporting as a new functionality in addition to the OLAP reporting available in earlier releases (see Figures 2.13 and 2.14).

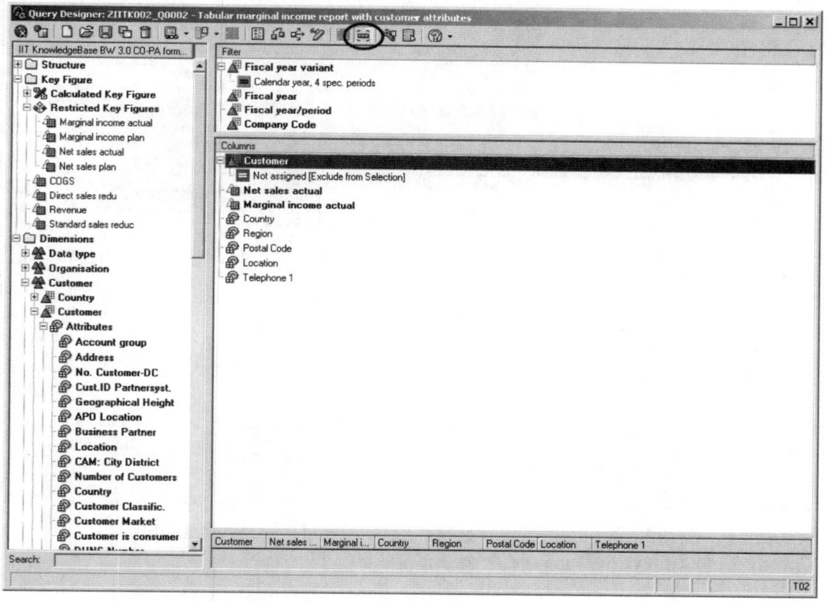

Figure 2.14 Creating Tabular Reports in the Query Designer

Building complex report elements

You can select and organize the objects of an InfoProvider in many different ways. For example, you can output the characteristics of an InfoCube as a list or a group change criterion; you can also use them as a selection or free characteristics for slice-and- dice or to build complex structures. The key figures of an InfoCube can be used for display as well as to build formulas and reusable, calculated key figures. With combinations of characteristics and key figures, you can configure reusable, restricted key figures and structures. In the query definitions, hierarchies can be flexibly displayed or used for a selection.

Variables

For an optimal selection, you can define variables that populate various query elements: You can use *Parameter Variables* (for selection of individual values), *Interval Variables*, or *Select Option Variables*, which support any selection on a characteristic, to select characteristic values.

You can select entire hierarchies (with *Hierarchy Variables*) or parts of hierarchies (with *Hierarchy Node Variables*) statically or dynamically. You can use *Formula Variables* for formula functions. *Text Variables* enable dynamic labeling of multilingual query elements, depending on the current selection, for example.

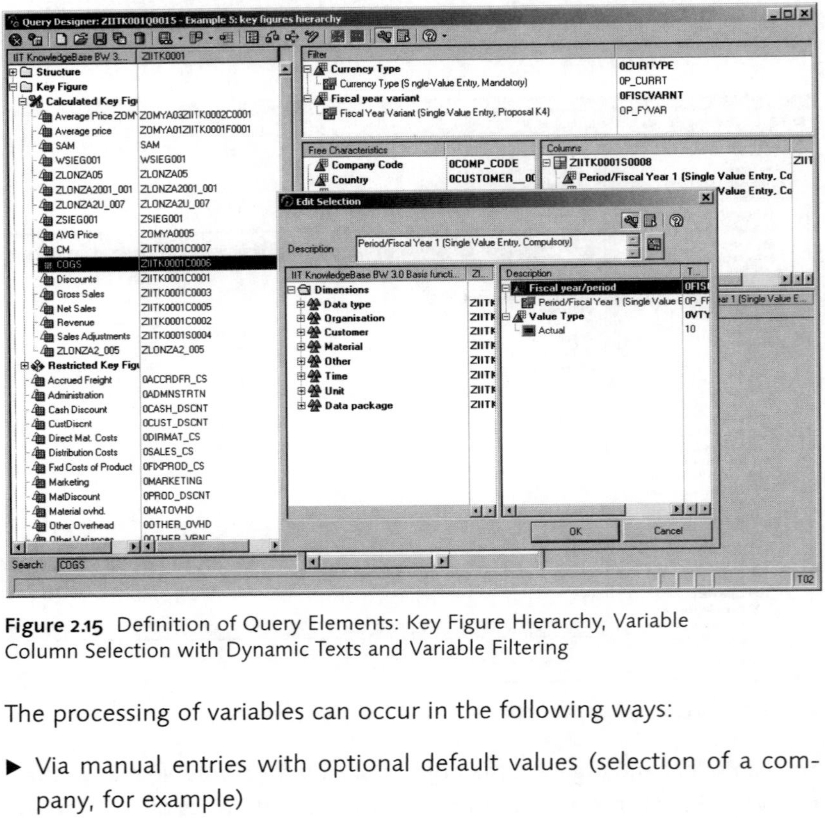

Figure 2.15 Definition of Query Elements: Key Figure Hierarchy, Variable Column Selection with Dynamic Texts and Variable Filtering

The processing of variables can occur in the following ways:

- Via manual entries with optional default values (selection of a company, for example)
- Via substitution paths (for example, a column header of **2003 Actual**, depending on the selection of the fiscal year and the value type **Actual**)
- Via SAP Exit or customer exit (with ABAP/4 coding flow logic to determine the values)
- Via authorization (automatic population of variables with the authorizations of the user performing the task)

The Exception functionality of the Query Designer enables you to highlight critical situations in color. Examples include a negative deviation in sales between the current year and the previous year or the budget or with a relative contribution margin lower than x%. You can use exceptions defined in the Query Designer in the reporting agent for the Alert Monitor (see Section 2.4.8).

Exceptions

The Query Designer also provides you with an option to define conditions. Conditions limit the results area with specific criteria. For example: Which customers have lower sales levels in the current year? SAP BW 3.0 vastly improved exception and condition functionality.

Conditions

You can run queries that have been defined in the Query Designer as soon as you have saved them. To start the query in a Web browser (such as Microsoft Internet Explorer), you can use the **Display query on the Web** button. Alternatively, you can also run queries in the SAP Business Explorer Analyzer.

2.4.3 Web Application Designer

Direct execution of queries uses a *Standard Web Template*. In this case, a systemwide template defines the functionality and layout of the query. This layout is usually only adequate for ad-hoc reports, which is why the BEx Web Application Designer enables you to implement the layouts and reporting functionalities of your choice.

The Web Application Designer supports all options, from creating OLAP reports according to targeted specifications to integrating a Business Intelligence Cockpit (BI cockpit) for management into the portal All the required functions are supported, including professional navigation components, selection and presentation objects, and the entire range of layout options of the HTML technology. Such reports are stored in SAP BW as Web templates in the form of HTML code. This feature also offers all the options of the Web technology, such as standard HTML functionality and the use of formulas, style sheets, Java Script, and so on.

Web templates and standard HTML functionality

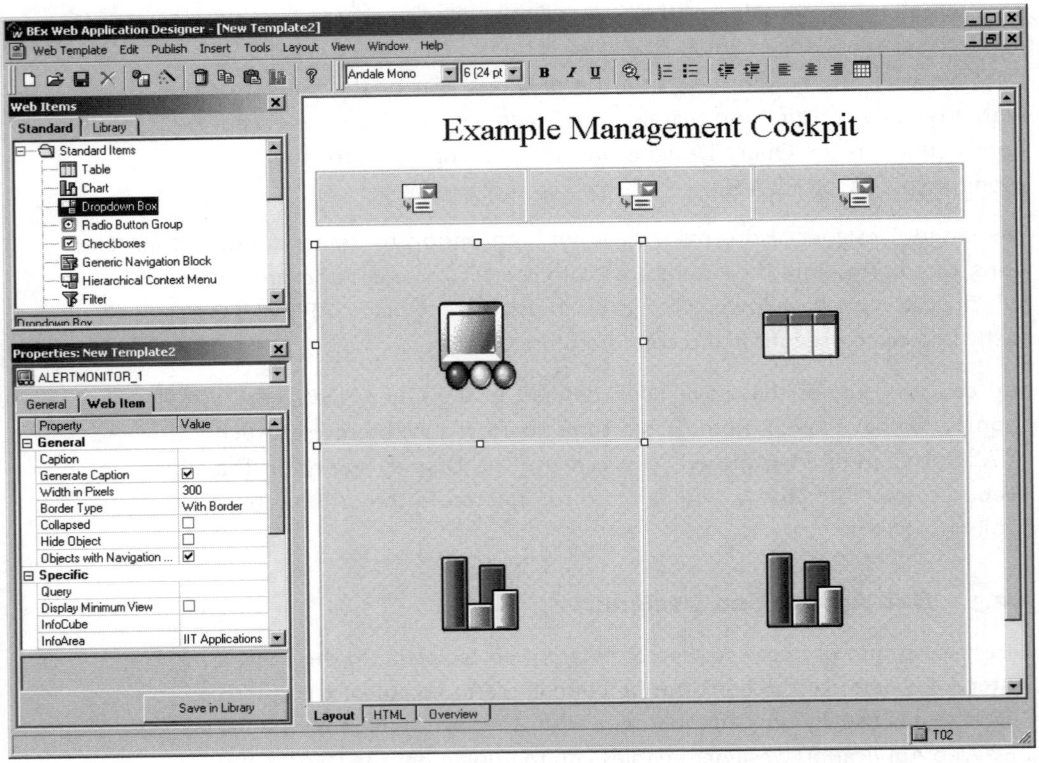

Figure 2.16 Web Templates are Defined in the Web Application Designer of SAP BW

The Web Application Designer will automatically insert all SAP BW objects as SAP-BW-specific object tags.[1] The tags represent control information for the following areas:

- ▶ Properties of Web templates
- ▶ Data providers
- ▶ Web items

Data providers

Data providers make available the specific SAP BW information—information that serves queries or query views (stored navigational states of an SAP BW query) as the data source in each Web template.

Web items

Web items are objects that display content specific to SAP BW, for example:

- ▶ **Tables**
  Display of the query results as tables

1 The assignment of control code occurs in tags in HTML. For example, <a href ...> ... </a> defines a hyperlink to another document or to a specific location in a document.

- **Charts**
  Display of the query results as navigable online graphics (bar charts, for example)
- **Dropdown boxes**
  Objects for filtering characteristics
- **Text elements**
  General query information, such as the timeliness of the data
- **Alert monitor**
  Lists of the exceptions calculated in the reporting agent
- **Role menu**
  SAP menu tree with Favorites and Roles
- **Maps**
  Map graphics populated with SAP BW data

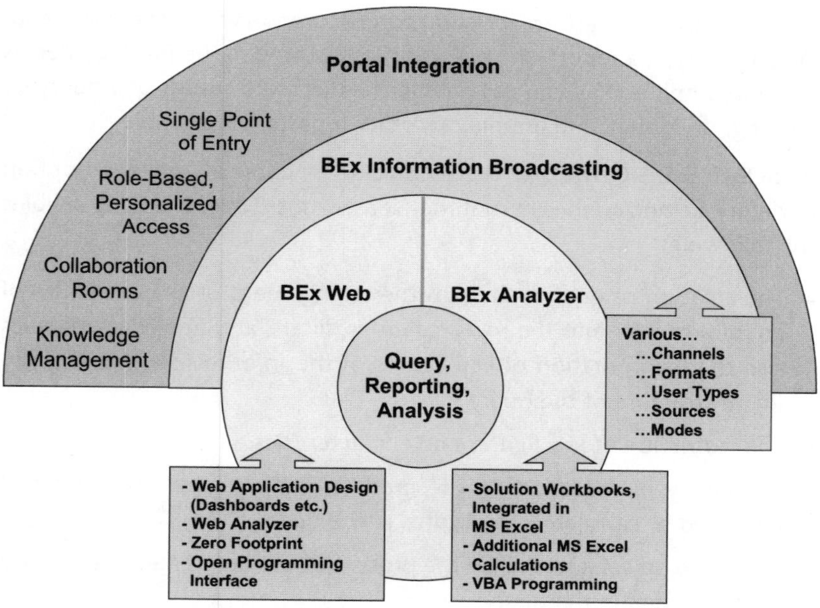

Figure 2.17 Architecture of the SAP BW Reporting Components

The Web Application Designer also offers a number of additional functions: these range from universal resource identifiers (URLs) specific to SAP BW (to call other Web templates or to insert language-dependent ABAP/4 text elements) to the Web Design Application Programming Interface (API), which offers ABAP/4 support for changing the display and functionality of tables and navigation blocks.

Innovations

As of SAP BW 3.0, the Web templates created with the Web Application Designer are stored on the SAP Web Application Server (SAP Web AS). This feature is a significant improvement over earlier releases because it makes obsolete the SAP Internet Transaction Server (SAP ITS) technology, which was not ideal for reporting. The technology of the SAP Web AS provides improved functions for SAP Web reporting, especially in terms of interactivity.

2.4.4 The Runtime Environment of Web Applications

Running Web reports

After you have defined queries or query views, you can run them immediately as Web applications. As of SAP BW 3.0, you can store queries directly in SAP roles. Accordingly, end users can run queries without performing additional tasks. The same holds true for Web templates created with the Web Application Designer. After you assign these items to roles, you can start high-performance and complex reports from the role menu. When you start a report, the reporting data stored in the InfoProviders is presented online. You can navigate in the displayed results of a query by filtering, drilldown, and jumping to other reports, for example.

The Ad-hoc Query Designer

As of SAP BW 3.0, the SAP Web reporting functionality offers an option to define ad-hoc queries at runtime. The Ad-hoc Query Designer enables the following:

- The creation of queries through the arrangement of characteristics of an InfoProvider into the rows, columns, filters, and free characteristics and the incorporation of key figures of the InfoProvider into the key figure structure of the query.
- The restriction of key figures and characteristics.
- The ability of the query to use predefined key figure structures and restricted or calculated key figures in the query.
- The ability to set and change the properties of queries, key figures, and characteristics in the query.
- The ability to create and change conditions and exceptions.

2.4.5 SAP Business Explorer Analyzer

The execution of queries and views from Microsoft Excel is called *Business Explorer Analyzer* by SAP, an SAP BW add-on that enhances Excel. SAP BEx Analyzer provides two basic options:

- Upon opening, the tool provides a toolbar specific to SAP BW that enables starting SAP Business Explorer queries that have already been defined. As noted with Web reporting, the query data is read from the InfoProviders online and is presented in Excel so that you can navigate through it.

Direct call of queries in SAP Business Explorer Analyzer

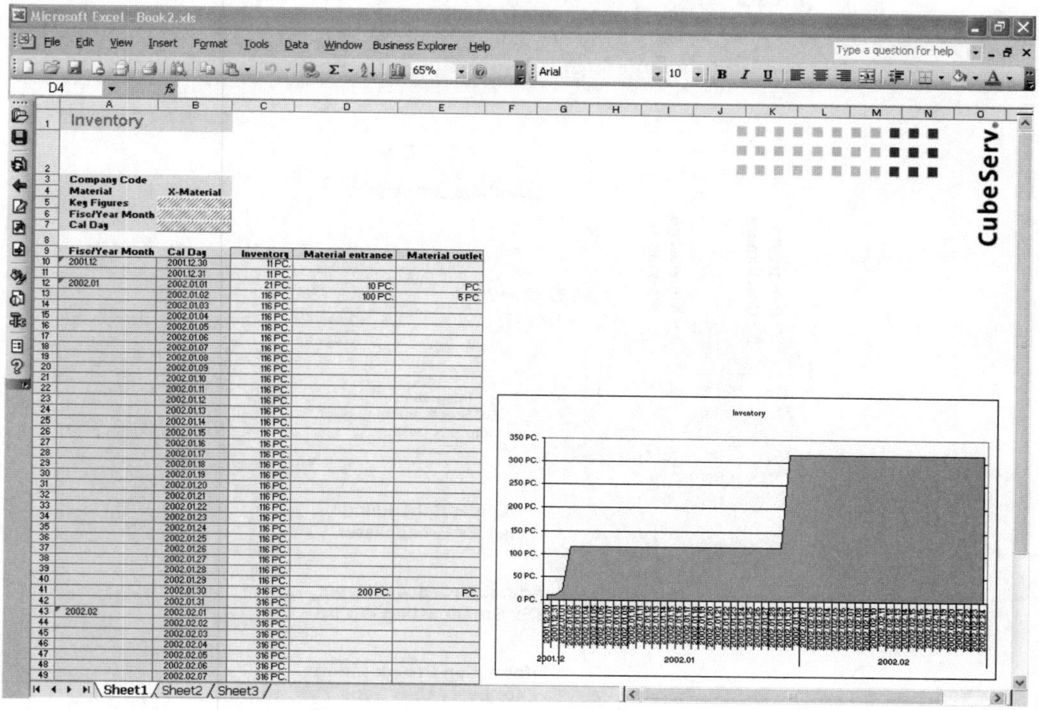

Figure 2.18 SAP Business Explorer Analyzer Combines Excel and OLAP Functionalities for Selected Tasks

- The second option is to open Excel workbooks that already contain embedded queries. This approach enables some report-specific formatting, linking graphics, and so on. You can also assign these workbooks to role menus so that they are directly available to end users. *SAP Business Explorer Workbooks* represent an alternate option for the presentation of queries to end users. However, the functionality and layout options of this option are limited when compared with SAP Business Explorer Web applications.

Queries in workbooks

2.4.6 SAP Business Explorer Information Broadcasting

Innovations

SAP Business Explorer (BEx) Information Broadcasting enables you to make objects with business-intelligence content available to a wide range of users according to the needs of customers. BEx Information Broadcasting is available in the various areas of SAP Business Explorer (BEx) (see Figure 2.19). It thus enables both the distribution of information to a large group of users and its consumption by these users.

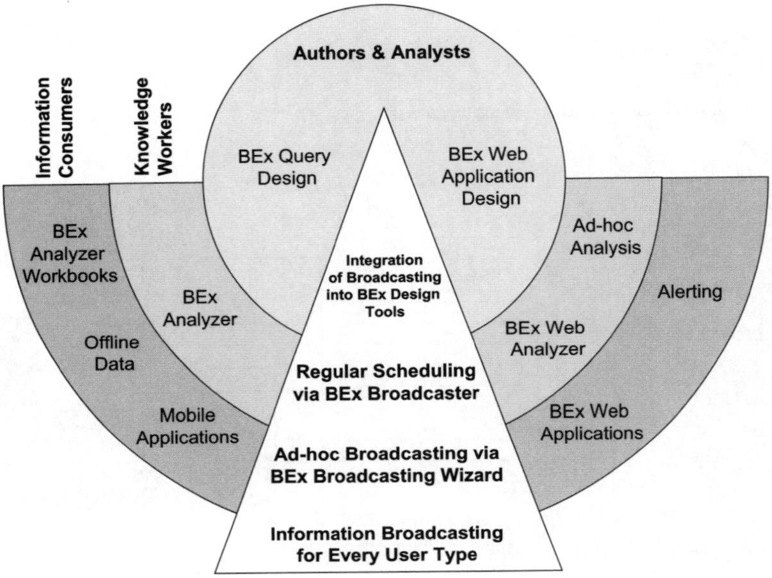

Figure 2.19 Overview of the Components of BEx Information Broadcasting

BEx Broadcaster

With the BEx Broadcaster, you can precalculate BEx Web applications, queries, and workbooks and then publish them in the SAP Enterprise Portal or distribute them via email. In addition to precalculated documents that contain historical data, you can also create online links to queries and Web applications. You can call the BEx Broadcaster from the following areas of the Business Explorer:

- BEx Query Designer
- BEx Web Application Designer
- BEx Analyzer
- BEx Web application
- Ad-hoc Analysis and BEx Web Analyzer

You can also embed the BEx Broadcaster in any Web application of your choice.

Furthermore, you can publish queries and Web templates to any SAP BW role or directly to the SAP Enterprise Portal from the design tools—*BEx Query Designer* and *BEx Web Application Designer*.

In the SAP Enterprise Portal, you would normally use a central entry point for business intelligence information (such as BEx Portfolio).

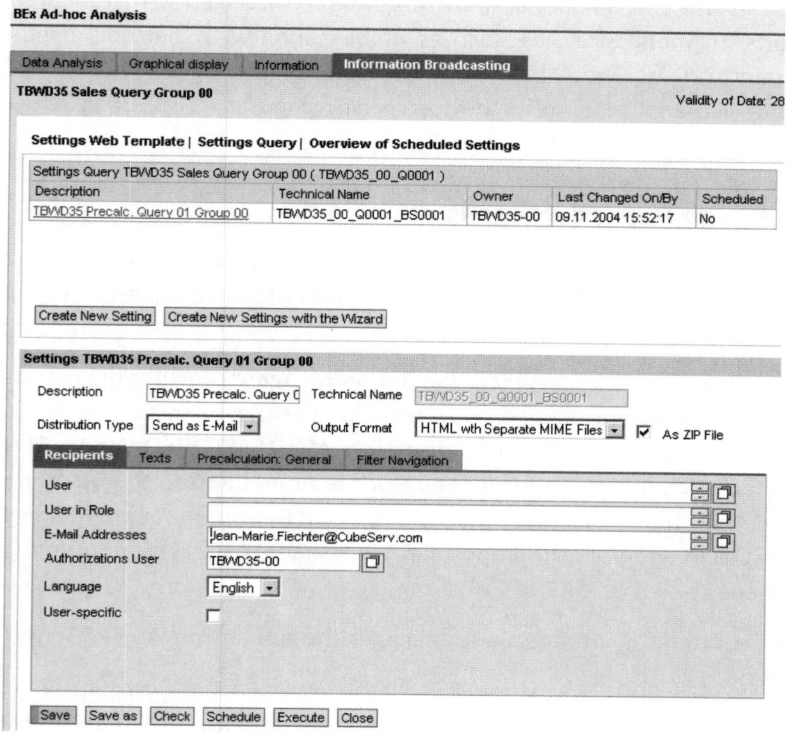

Figure 2.20 Configuration Options in BEx Broadcaster

2.4.7 Additional SAP BW Reporting Functions

SAP BW provides several additional functions for reporting.

Personalization

The most important reporting function is personalization, which is available as of SAP BW 3.0. The personalization function enables a user-specific population of variables and the storage of user-specific start views of Web applications. It also provides a user-specific history of the reporting objects opened last.

Integration with SAP Enterprise Portal

The integration of SAP BEx Web applications into the SAP Enterprise Portal reflects the increasing importance of portals. Currently, when you create Web templates, you can store them as an *iView*. An iView is a component of the portal solution that you can use to extract data from applications, documents, and the Internet and display it in the portal. These features enable you to use the Web-reporting functionality with the options provided by the portal technology (Single Sign-On or SSO and so on).

Mobile reporting

You can use the functionality of BEx Mobile Intelligence to run Web reports on mobile devices, such as mobile phones, or personal digital assistants (PDAs). The SAP BW server automatically recognizes the type of end device and generates a device-specific page in HTML or Wireless Markup Language (WML).

2.4.8 The Reporting Agent

The options provided by the Reporting Agent enhance SAP BW with background, administrative, and alert-monitoring functionalities, shown in Figure 2.21 and Figure 2.22.

Background functions

The background functionality of the Reporting Agent provides the precalculation of query results. For example, these results are also used when you run Web reports that use the DATA_MODE=STORED mode. This approach significantly reduces the response time, because the query no longer has to access the possibly huge dataset of the InfoProviders involved. In addition, the Reporting Agent enables background printing of queries based on SAP BEx Analyzer.

Administrative functions

The Reporting Agent stores and manages the bookmarks of all SAP BW users.

Exception reporting and monitoring alerts

Exception reporting and *monitoring alerts* are particularly important. These components evaluate exceptions in the background to trigger follow-up actions that you can configure to meet your requirements. Follow-up actions can include messages (email with information on the exception analysis) and alert-monitor entries (with traffic lights to display the entries and hyperlinks to the reports).

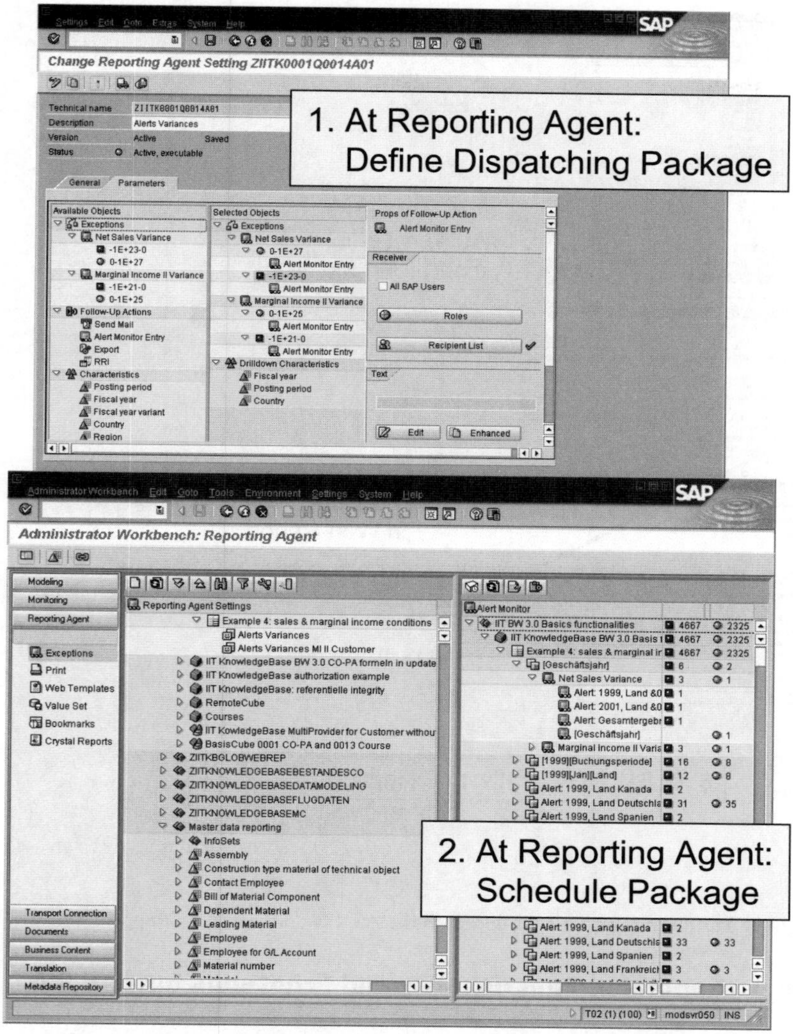

Figure 2.21 Information Distribution with the Alert Monitor in Web Reporting (1)

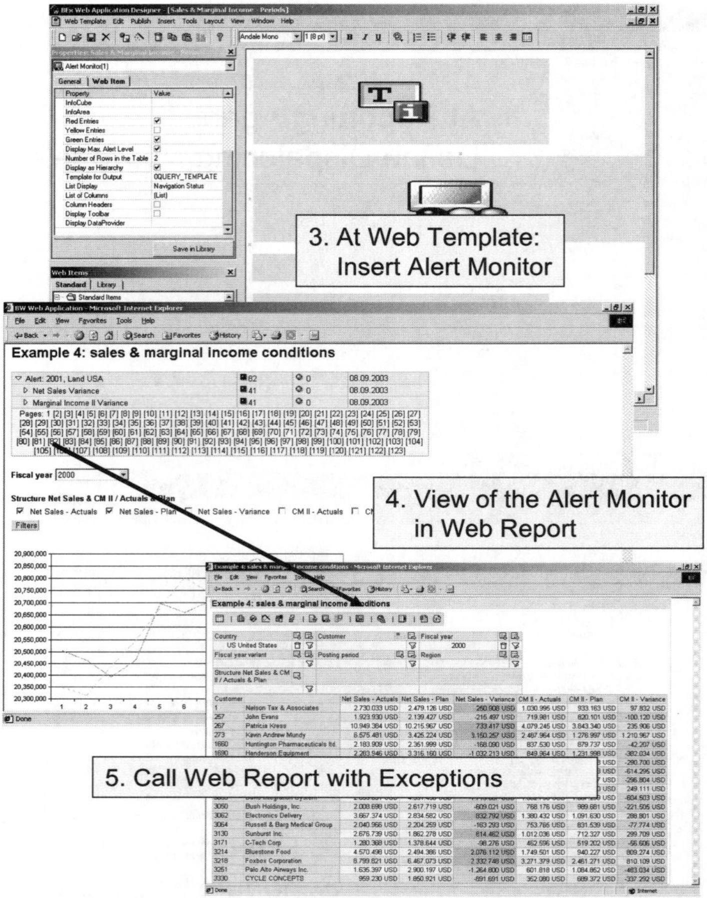

Figure 2.22 Information Distribution with the Alert Monitor in Web Reporting (2)

2.4.9 Reporting Functionality and Frontends for SAP BW

Innovations

As of SAP BW 3.0, the reporting functionality offers significant enhancements and improvements. Here too, SAP can be viewed as a best-practice OLAP and data warehouse solution.

Significant shifts have occurred within the reporting components provided by SAP. Up to SAP BW 1.2, SAP BEx Analyzer was the only standard tool that SAP provided for OLAP reporting. Even the appearance of Web reporting with SAP BW 2.0 did not produce any significant shift. With SAP BW 3.0, however, Web reporting clearly became the primary reporting technology in SAP BW. The following points illustrate its predominant position:

- Default execution of queries in the HTML browser instead of Excel
- Significant enhancements in the reporting functionality of SAP Business Explorer Web applications, especially when compared to the Excel-based SAP BEx Analyzer
- Earlier significance of third-party front-end tools
- Significantly greater functionality and extended options for Web reporting

The use of third-party front-end tools had an important place in the implementation of projects in earlier releases of SAP BW. Some 35 of the 40 projects that the CubeServ Group[2] was involved in (up to the release of SAP BW 1.2b) also used the third-party frontend *inSight/dynaSight* of *arcplan Information Services AG*. The remaining projects used SAP BEx Analyzer and products from *Cognos Incorporated* and *Business Objects*.

Proprietary SAP reporting tools were used in more than 50% of the 60 projects based on SAP BW 2.x in which the CubeServ Group was involved. In more than 10 projects, SAP Web reporting was used.

Reasons for the decreasing significance of third-party frontends

Our experience with projects based on SAP BW 3.x clearly shows a shift toward standard SAP functionality, specifically Web reporting. More than 70% of over 100 projects implemented on the basis of SAP BW 3.x also used SAP BEx Web applications.

From the perspective of protecting your investment, the search for reasons for this trend and probable future developments are of particular interest. While SAP had to work through all the development steps of an OLAP front-end tool with SAP Business Explorer, the development of SAP BW had reached the limits of Excel and the company had to shift the paradigm to Web technology. Simultaneously, other manufacturers already had mature products on the market. Partner companies were either unwilling or unable to keep up with the explosive development at SAP; therefore, when SAP BW 3.0 was introduced, no third-party tools provided anything like complete support of the reporting functions of SAP BW. Consequently, the outlook for third-party front-end tool for SAP BW is very bleak.

2 All authors of this book work for the CubeServ Group (*www.cubeserv.com*), which specializes in business intelligence solutions.

2.5 Open Hub Service

The Open Hub Service enables the distribution of data from an SAP BW system to SAP and non-SAP data marts, analytical, and other applications, ensuring the controlled distribution across multiple systems. The central object for data export is the *InfoSpoke,* which defines the object from which data is collected and into which target this data will be transferred.

The Open Hub Service makes SAP BW the hub of an enterprise data warehouse. Central monitoring in the SAP BW system makes distribution of the data manageable.

SAP BW objects such as *InfoCubes*, *ODS objects*, and *InfoObjects* (attributes or texts) can serve as open-hub data sources. You can select database tables or flat files as an open-hub destination. You can use both a full and delta-extract mode as an extraction mode.

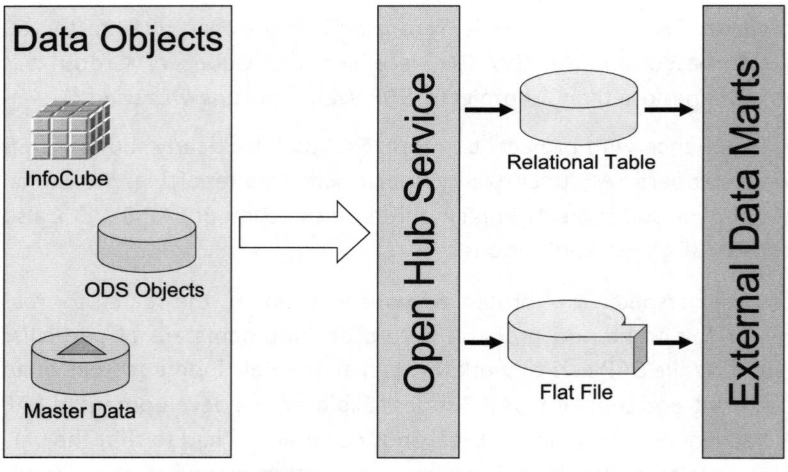

Figure 2.23 As of SAP BW 3.0, You Can Use Open Hub Services to Distribute Data from SAP BW into Other SAP and Non-SAP Systems

2.6 Additional Functions and Components

The functionalities of SAP BW described above are those of the key processes of analytical applications: data acquisition, data storage, and data presentation. Numerous other components are also available, but addressing them exceeds the scope of this introduction. We'd simply like to mention the following additional functions and components:

- The powerful and mature basic functions available as part of SAP R/3 Basis technology: job control, role and printing functionality, user management, and so on
- SAP BW components, such as SAP BW-specific functions to control authorizations, based on core functions in SAP R/3 or the integration of documents in the reporting

2.7 SAP Business Content

SAP Business Content assumes a preeminent place in the marketing of SAP Business Information Warehouse. In the documentation for SAP BW, SAP describes the Business Content as follows:

Definition of SAP Business Content

> *Business Content is a preconfigured set of role- and task-relevant information models based on consistent metadata in the SAP Business Information Warehouse. Business Content provides selected roles within a company with the information the company's employees need to carry out their tasks.*[3]

Note that unlike the application components of SAP R/3, the Business Content is expressly not positioned as the SAP standard.

Components of SAP Business Content

SAP Business Content contains all the components required for an analytical application. The components include extractors in SAP R/3, the required elements of the data model such as key figures, characteristics, InfoCubes, and ODS objects; components to load data into SAP BW, such as InfoSources and update rules; reporting components, such as queries, Web templates, and workbooks; and basic components, such as roles and types of currency conversion.

Because SAP Business Content is not set up as an SAP standard, the following applies:

- It can be used as-is.
- It can be tailored to the specific needs of SAP customers.
- It can be used as a template for customer-specific business content.

Advantages of SAP over its competitors

The scope of SAP Business Content is a performance feature that clearly places SAP ahead of its competitors. As the leading manufacturer of business software, SAP has a high level of knowledge that complements its ability to offer such solutions.

---

3 *SAP BW 3.5*, SAP AG 2004, section on BI Content: *http://help.sap.com/saphelp_nw04/helpdata/en/37/5fb13cd0500255e10000000a114084/content.htm.*

However, it's critical to use SAP Business Content carefully and with differentiation. Uncritical acceptance of the entire package can lead to unpleasant surprises: missing functionality, errors, or unacceptable handling (see Chapter 7, *SAP Business Content*). You should examine SAP Business Content in detail during a project's business blueprint phase. Perform a detailed comparison of the functions needed to the functionality available and undertake intensive quality control measures with tests during implementation.

Experience with SAP Business Content shows that there are two dimensions with different opportunities for use: the object type and analytical applications.

Object type

An examination of the core process of analytical applications shows that the SAP Business Content is clearly more usable in the first half of the process: data acquisition and data modeling. The extractors of SAP Business Content are usable to a great degree in transactional SAP components. Of the data model within SAP BW, a portion is still appropriate for productive use: the majority of InfoObjects and selected InfoProviders, such as InfoCubes and ODS objects.

The situation with the reporting components (queries, workbooks, and so on) is rather unpleasant. None of the 220 projects implemented by the CubeServ Group could use the reports in SAP Business Content.

Analytical application

An examination of the various analytical applications shows significant differences between the various business areas. For SAP BW applications in the areas of finance & accounting and financial controlling, SAP Business Content is at a qualitatively high level, so large portions of the extractors, data acquisition, and even the data model are frequently used. An appreciable percentage of projects could use SAP Business Content up to the level of (only insignificantly enhanced) InfoCubes.

However, SAP Business Content for logistics earns poor grades. The extractors are partially incorrect and the InfoCubes often too insufficient, so that customers often have to create their own data models. The same applies to the area of human resources, but to an even greater degree. Analytical applications that must be generated for the highest management level often have no SAP Business Content solutions at all. The reason for this situation is that, in our experience, the requirements of a company become more specific as the company perspective reflects the enterprise as a whole or looks beyond the boundaries of the enterprise.

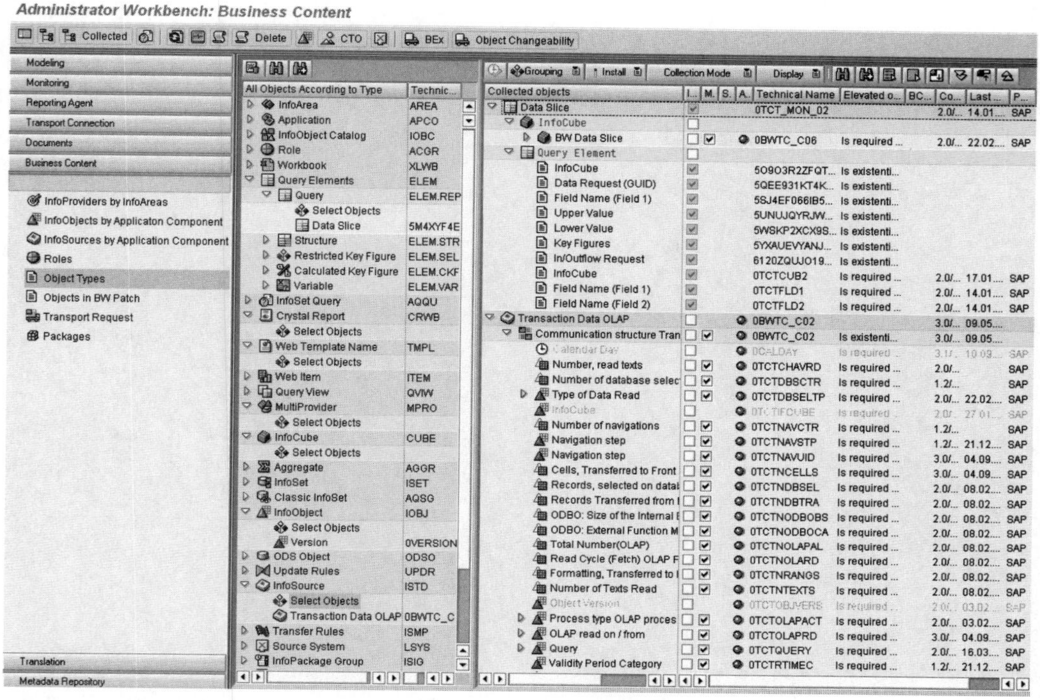

Figure 2.24 SAP Business Content Contains All the Components Necessary for an Analytical Application

2.8 The Position of SAP Business Information Warehouse

The aforementioned comments regarding individual components already resulted in an evaluation of SAP BW.

SAP BW as a best-practice solution

An overall evaluation shows that with SAP BW, SAP has for the first time offered a product that appropriately deals with the conceptual basics of both data warehousing and OLAP. According to our experience, SAP BW 3.x can truly be classified as a best-practice solution. From the viewpoint of reporting, for companies using SAP R/3, the effort required for implementation, operation, and enhancement of SAP BW is less than that required for reporting components in SAP R/3.

3 Introduction to Data Modeling

The quality of data modeling and the power of the underlying system determine the effectiveness and successful use of a data warehouse. In most cases, hierarchical dimension structures play a central role for navigating in analytical data sets and numerous Online Analytical Processing (OLAP) operations. This chapter provides an overview of the basic concepts of data modeling.

3.1 Introduction

A data model is a structured image of the data of a fixed and limited portion of the perceived reality that is relevant to a specific application or to specific users, including the relationships between them.[1]

Modeling designs

Several different modeling designs already exist for modeling informational systems, the majority of which were developed in the last 10 years. In terms of traditional operational Online Transaction Processing (OLTP) systems, the modeling community distinguishes three layers—the *conceptual*, *logical*, and *physical* design, and their corresponding design results: *conceptual*, *logical*, and *physical data models*.

In Section 1.5, we saw that this differentiation also applies to the architecture of a data warehouse (see Figure 3.1). In this chapter, the application of this differentiation to the modeling in the informational realm will help us organize the available modeling designs systematically (see Figures 3.2 and 3.3).

It's interesting to note that a relatively clear assignment of the existing modeling designs can be made to the individual layers. To date, no comprehensive design exists that completely covers all layers.

1 R. Maier, 1998.

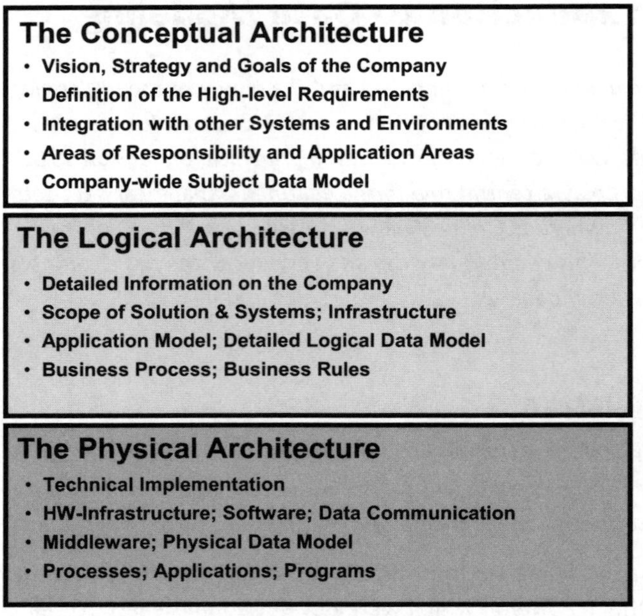

Figure 3.1 The Three Levels of the Data Warehouse Architecture

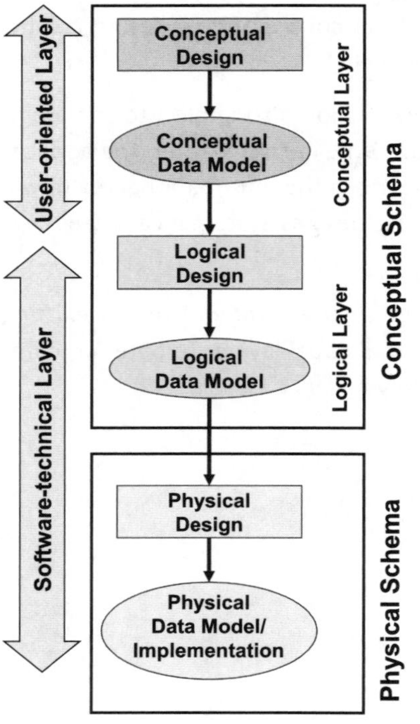

Figure 3.2 The Various Modeling Layers

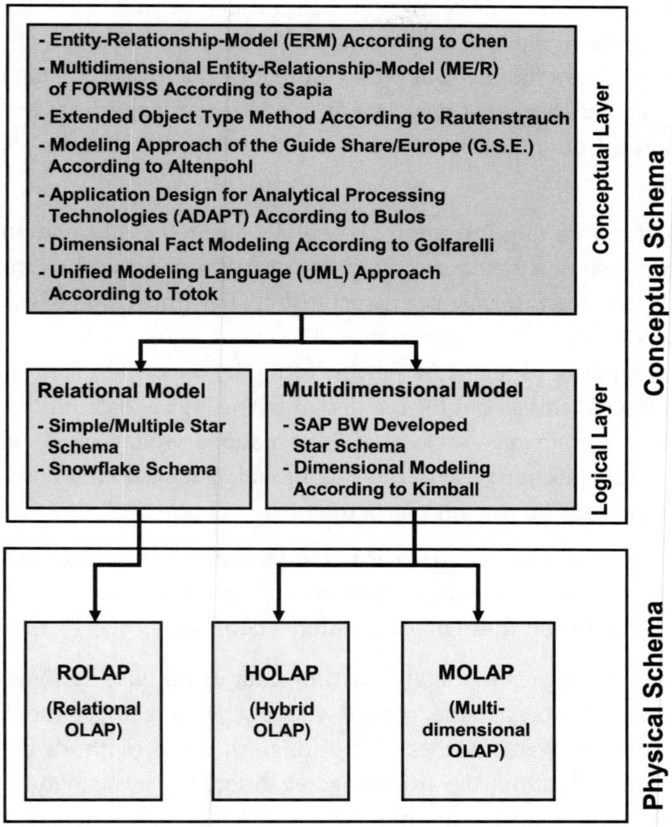

Figure 3.3 The Various Modeling Layers: Examples

3.2 Some Theory

Conceptual design

At the conceptual level, the design creates a data model that should be independent of the physical target data warehouse system.

The conceptual layer maps the interactions between business processes and agents (responsibilities, roles, actions, and messages) from a business perspective. Conceptual data models allow you to present the relevant facts of the real world without any loss of information. As the foundation for communication, and to discuss and validate the model with user representatives, a conscious orientation toward the needs of user departments (setting goals, identifying needs, and agreeing upon terminology) has a positive effect. Sadly, most of today's approaches to modeling still cater mainly to developers. Approaches to modeling in the conceptual area can be roughly divided into three categories (see Section 3.3 for more information).

Logical design While the conceptual data model is based on a user-oriented modeling approach, the logical and physical data models are based on a more technical, software-oriented modeling approach. The logical and physical data models are designed to increasingly forego the independence from the underlying systems and become more dependent on the specifics of those systems.

No current data warehouse system can handle arbitrary information structures. Each system is based on a specific database model and is limited to a specific set of performance characteristics. Transformation of the conceptual data model into an actual model for the planned data warehouse system establishes specific frameworks (the degree of standardization, type of schema, and so on) for the design of the logical data model. The frameworks can involve a loss of information, which must be weighed against the intended use of the data model. Details on the physical storage of the data do not yet play a role.

Conceptual schema Collectively, the conceptual and logical model form the conceptual schema, which is simply a catalog of the relevant information objects and the relationships between these objects within a company.

Several methods for logical modeling exist for data warehouse systems. They are based on the star schema, the snowflake schema, and variations of both. The primary characteristics that distinguish these methods are the degree of normalization, the use of aggregations, the availability of artificial key attributes, and the use of cubes.

At this point, we should also mention the following models: *dimension modeling* according to Kimball; *fact/constellation schema*, *galaxy schema*, *partial snowflake*, *simple star,* and *multiple star schemas* according to Poe; and the *starflake schema*. Section 1.11 used the *developed star schema* (as found in SAP Business Information Warehouse, SAP BW) as an example of a logical modeling method.

Physical design The physical data model deals ultimately with the blueprint—the implementation of the actual database schema—and the related system parameters. The performance considerations of the available hardware and operating systems are in the foreground here. Technically, the considerations here involve database tuning, denormalization, access mechanisms and paths, storage structures, indexing techniques (bitmap, B-tree, hybrid index, and so on), and partitioning (slice or dice precedence). You also decide which user requirements take precedence here in terms of performance.

No standard approaches to modeling exist today at the level of physical design. Tools to support modeling exist almost exclusively at the logical level of data modeling. This is in contrast to most of the methods, which usually include both the conceptual and logical levels. Kimball suggested using a holistic approach for business processes as early as 1997, but none of the approaches used today support his theory.

3.3 Conceptual Approaches to Modeling: Excursus

The *Entity Relationship Model* (ER model) by Chen has become both the theoretical and practical standard for conceptual modeling of operational systems (OLTP and ERP). However, the object-oriented approach that has undergone some standardization with the Unified Modeling Language (UML) has become increasingly more important in the last few years.

In data warehousing, this kind of standardization is still yet to be achieved. The following sections examine the most common approaches in conceptual modeling in more detail. The literature usually divides them into three categories:

- Designs based on the Entity Relationship (ER) model
- Designs based on the Object-Oriented (OO) model
- Designs without reference to these conventional models

3.3.1 Designs Based on the Entity Relationship Model

Entity Relationship Model

Starting from the standard ER model (see Figure 3.4), the basic types of this traditional form, such as entities, attributes, and relationships, were expanded over time with constructs to map complex structures. The extensions include elements for generalization to multidimensionality or for aggregations. Opinion is still divided on the appropriateness of the ER model for modeling multidimensional data structures. The primary problem areas include mapping of dimension hierarchies, the rules inherent to data structures, and the functions and views relevant to reporting.

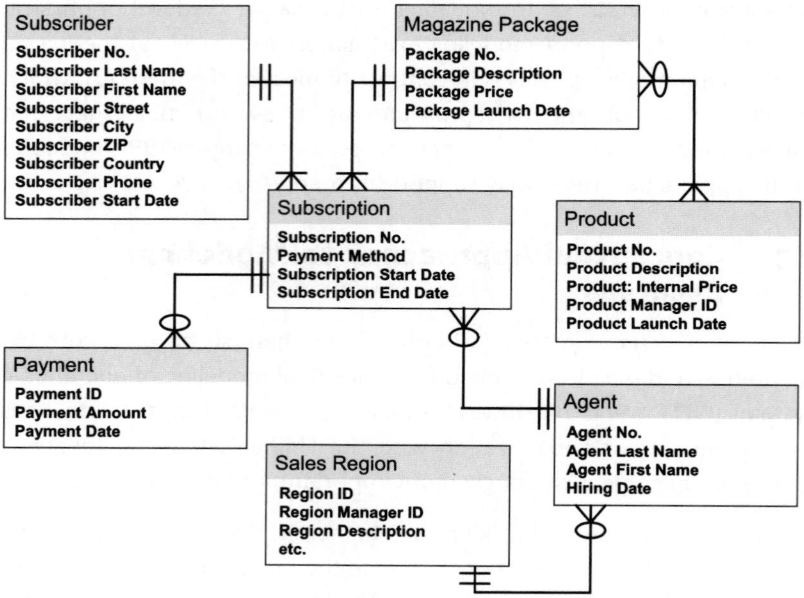

Figure 3.4 Example of Modeling with the Entity Relationship Model Design

Multidimensional E/R Model

Multidimensional Entity Relationship Model

C. Sapia developed the multidimensional entity relationship model (ME/RM) in 1998 (see Figure 3.5). The notation is based on the ER model, supplemented with three new notational elements: *fact relation*, *dimension level*, and *hierarchical relationship*. Fact relation and hierarchical relationship are specialized types of relationships. Dimension levels, however, are only a special type of entity.

This design is based on the principle of minimalism and deals with notation elements as economically as possible. Consequently, the search for elements for specific dimension types or dimension elements yields no answers. Instead of a traditional presentation with pound-sign (#) symbols, normal and hierarchical relationships are implicitly represented through the linking elements.

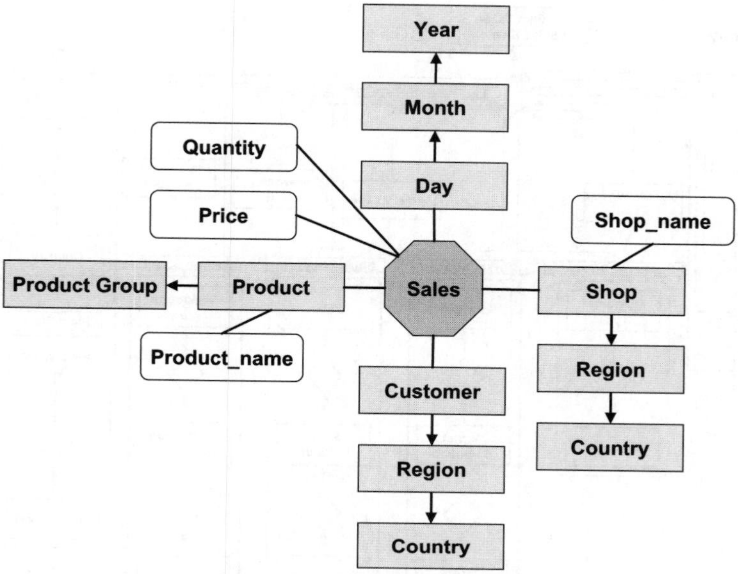

Figure 3.5 Example of Modeling with the Multidimensional Entity Relationship Model Design (according to FORWISS 1998)

Modified Object Type Method

Object Type Method

In 1997, C. Rautenstrauch modified the Object Type Method (OTM) for modeling data warehouses (see Figure 3.6). His goal was the creation of a formal terminology. The model uses the language constructs of *object type* (a synonym for entity type), *connection* (a relationship type for linking objects), and *aggregation* for multidimensional modeling. The novelty here is a complex object type that combines the dimension elements, which are hierarchically related to each other. Here too, there are no special symbols for certain data types nor a symbol for the central fact table.

The structure of the model follows star, snowflake, and multistar schemas. The use of event-condition activity rules support the modeling of integrity constraints.

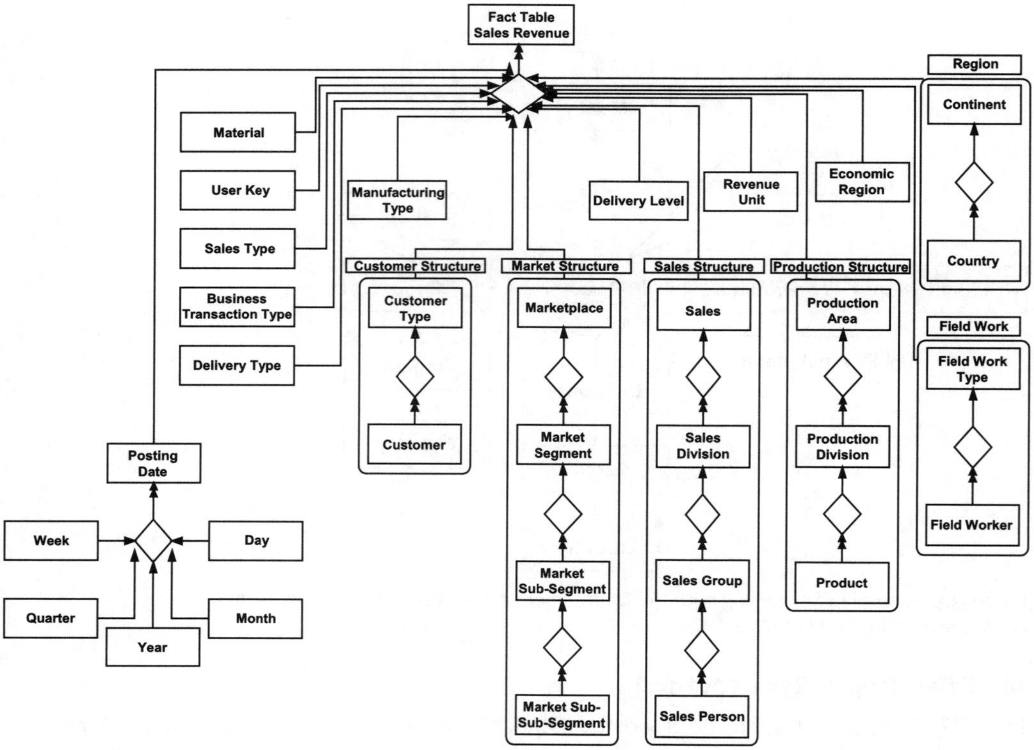

Figure 3.6 Example of Modeling with the Modified Object Type Method (Source: Rautenstrauch 1997)

Data Modeling Data Warehouse – A Solution Suggested by Guide/Share Europe

Data modeling DWH

The enterprise modeling group of Guide/Share Europe under the direction of U. Altenpohl developed this modeling design in 1997. It uses only entity and relationship types. As with the ME/R design, this design does not use the pound-sign (#) symbol. Double-sided arrows imply the relationship between entities.

The model focuses on the logical modeling of star and snowflake schemas, putting dimension hierarchies and central fact elements in the foreground. As is the case with the previous modeling designs, this approach makes no statements on dimension types or dimension elements.

Dimensional Fact Model (DFM)

Dimensional Fact Model

In 1998, M. Golfarelli suggested another design that contains a methodological approach in addition to a notation: the *Dimensional Fact Model*

(DFM) (see Figure 3.7). The DFM is a graphical form of notation that focuses on the requirements of data warehouse and OLAP structures. In this design, the conceptual model of a multidimensional information system consists of a set of fact tables subdivided into facts, dimensions, and hierarchies.

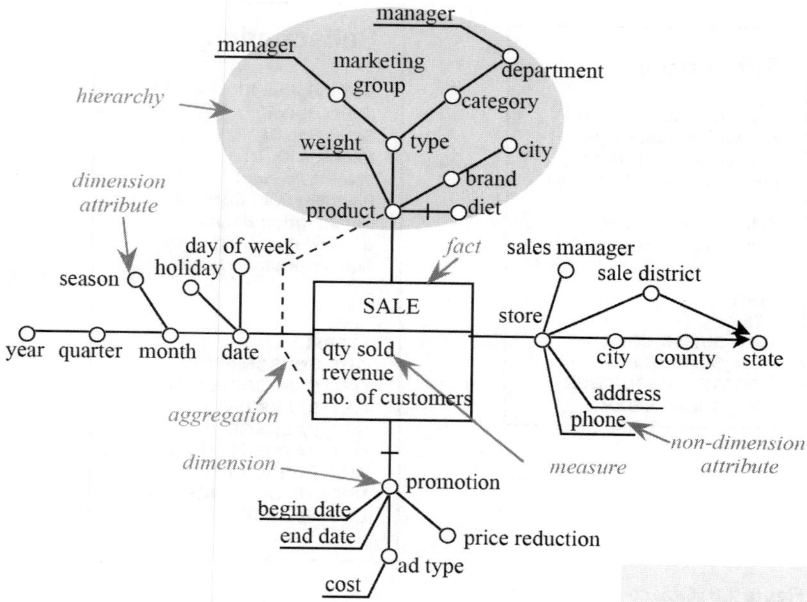

Figure 3.7 Example of Modeling with a Dimensional Fact Model (DFM) Design (Source: Golfarelli 1998)

Grey shadowing highlights hierarchies. As in other designs, additive key figures are represented by linking hierarchical dimension elements with solid lines along aggregation paths. Key figures that cannot be totaled along every dimension hierarchy are called *semiadditive*. Key figures that cannot be totaled along any dimension hierarchy are called *non-additive*. Accordingly, semiadditive or non-additive key figures can be assigned to only the lowest element of a dimension. Broken lines from the key figures to the proper dimension hierarchy (which cannot be used for totaling) are used as notation.

3.3.2 Designs Based on the Object-Oriented Model

Object-oriented models try to achieve an integrated coverage of the various phases of software development. The separation between a conceptual, logical, and physical model is much fuzzier here or even non-existent. Multidimensional applications must not only be *modeled* with an object orientation, but also *implemented* with an object orientation to take full advantage of the object-oriented model (class concept, encapsulation, multiple inheritance, and so on). Figure 3.8 shows an example that contains both data and functions to achieve the integration of the design.

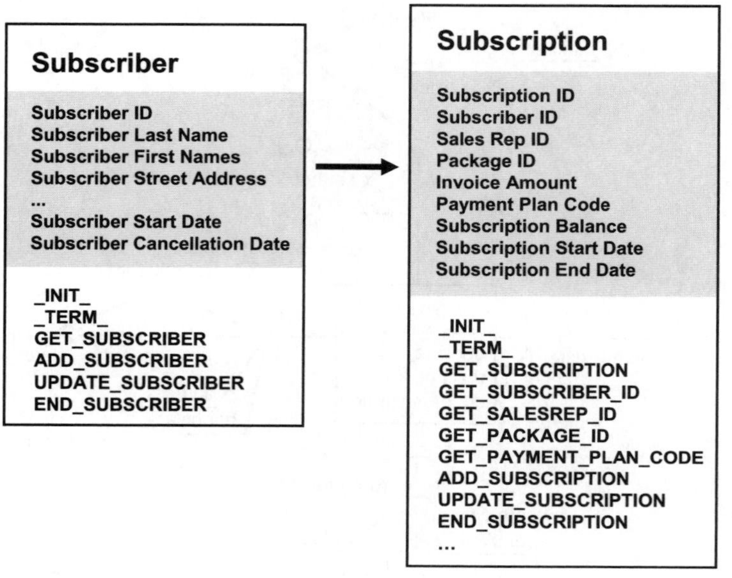

Figure 3.8 Object-Oriented Designs

Using Object-Oriented Analysis

Object-Oriented Analysis

The literature often suggests the use of Object-Oriented Analysis (OOA) by Coad and Yourdon for graphical modeling of data warehouse systems.

"Cube cell" class

The *cube cell* class is the central element of the design; its instances are linked to the dimensions relevant to it. The properties of the *cube cell* class are linked to the properties of the *characteristic* class by objects of the *atomic date*, so that the conceptual identification of an object is present in the database for every atomic multidimensional object. A special method indicates aggregations in the dimension class. The various dimensions inherit these methods, which can be overwritten in the dimensions.

This approach can be implemented in object-oriented database systems by linking the various instances with object identifiers.

Using the Object Modeling Technique

Object Modeling Technique

J. Holthuis suggested an OO approach to modeling in 1998; the approach differentiates between macro and micro views. Similar to the architecture of integrated information systems, the macro view is subdivided into a date, function, organization, and business process view. The micro views are a subdivision of the data view and help define static structures, functions, and behavior.

Object classes and class hierarchies are used to model dimensions with levels and aggregation layers that can be assigned directly to the micro-modeling view. In principle, key figures belong to the macro-data view; the method does not describe modeling key figures in any more details (the primary disadvantage of this approach).

The design is based on class and state diagrams and functional models to model multidimensional constructs according to the *Object Modeling Technique (OMT)*.

Using Unified Modeling Language

Unified Modeling Language

A. Totok developed a design for object-oriented, conceptual modeling of multidimensional information systems at the end of the 1990s. His design uses *Unified Modeling Language (UML)*, which has become a standard as graphical notation. The logical view of the UML can be called a conceptual view because it can describe both conceptual and logical aspects (see Section 3.2).

A class model for business key figures and for dimensions are each created with the functions required to manage the objects that will be generated later. Based on that foundation, dynamic aspects can also be considered. This approach is particularly appropriate to define requirements at the conceptual level and therefore for the creation of the business blueprint.

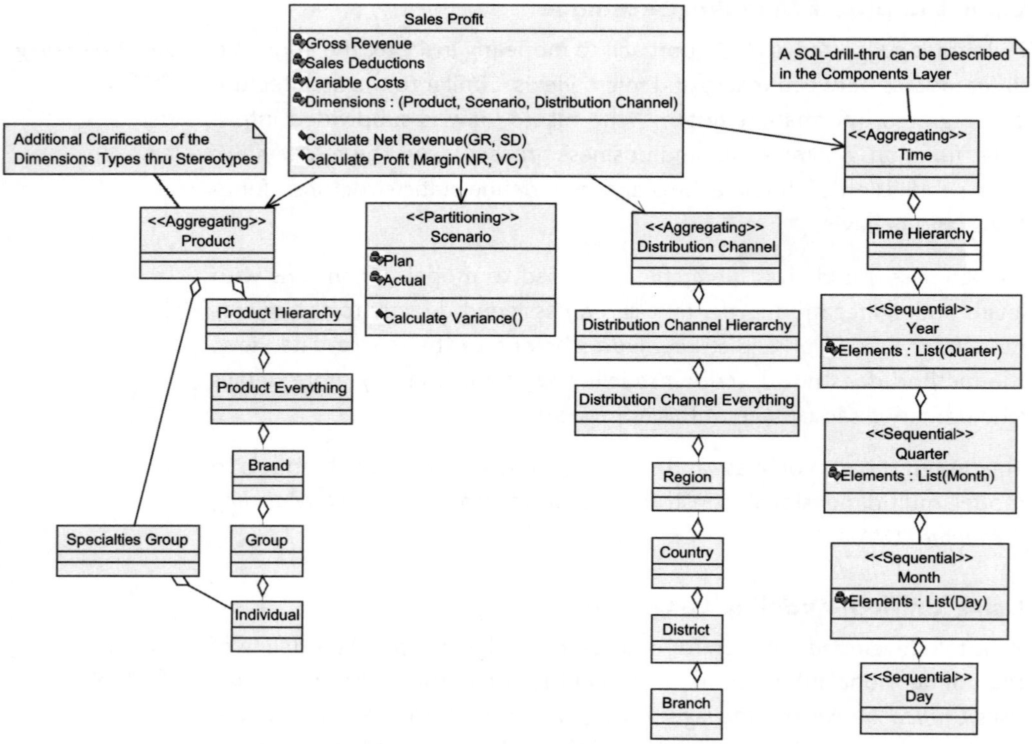

Figure 3.9 Example of Modeling with the Unified Modeling Language Approach (Source: Totok 2000)

3.3.3 Designs Without Reference to a Conventional Model

Application Design for Analytical Processing Technologies (ADAPT)

ADAPT

In 1996, D. Bulos developed a graphical modeling notation for multidimensional data structuring: the *Application Design for Analytical Processing Technologies (ADAPT)* was born. The origins of this notation are found in enterprise consulting.

ADAPT can be called an expanded conceptual notation because it contains both conceptual and logical aspects and even comprises some physical aspects.

The inadequacy of traditional modeling techniques triggered the development of this new notation. Bulos criticizes the ER model for not offering an option to map the processing logic for analytical processes. Data flow charts could, of course, display the dynamic aspects, but they are rarely adequate for representing calculations.

The design seeks to develop a modeling technique that can represent the processing logic (stored as update rules on the database server) for analytical processes in relation to multidimensional data structures.

But this requirement also identifies a weakness of ADAPT: Including implementation considerations in the conceptual modeling level blurs its boundaries. This blending occurs because even the conceptual data model affects the performance of the actual physical system.

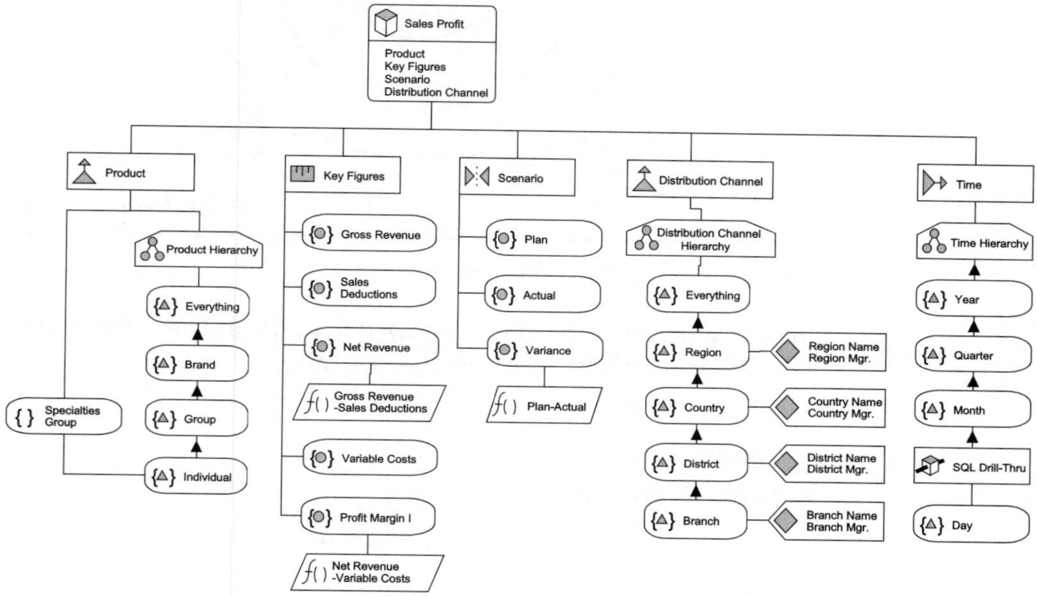

Figure 3.10 Example of Modeling with the ADAPT Approach (Source: Totok 1998)

3.4 Back to Practice: Procedures for DWH Projects

Regardless of the approach you use with data warehouse modeling, the procedures remain very similar. The implementation of a data warehouse solution requires intensive planning beforehand. The system must be modeled from the ground up before implementation.

Experience has shown the value of an iterative, phased top-down approach according to the motto "think big, start focused," to ensure efficient handling of a data warehouse project (see Figure 3.11). You look back at the end of each phase and check the project to implement any necessary corrections. Such careful structuring and planning eases the need to control and monitor the overall project and increases its flexibility.

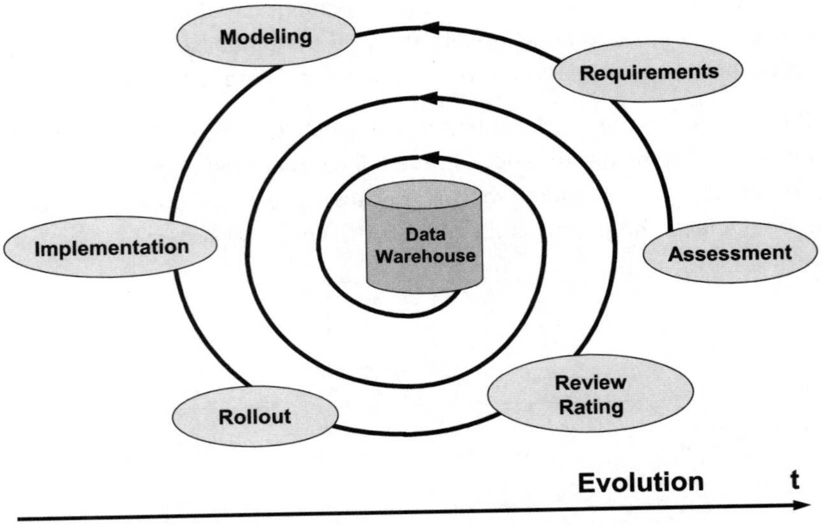

Figure 3.11 Iterative, Phased Top-Down Approach

The phase model used here is borrowed from the business dimensional lifecycle model of R. Kimball (see Figure 3.12) and is structured along the following main phases:

- Evaluation/Assessment
- Requirements analysis
- Conceptual, logical, and physical modeling
- Implementation
- Realization
- Evaluation and inspection

The following sections address the modeling phase in more detail.

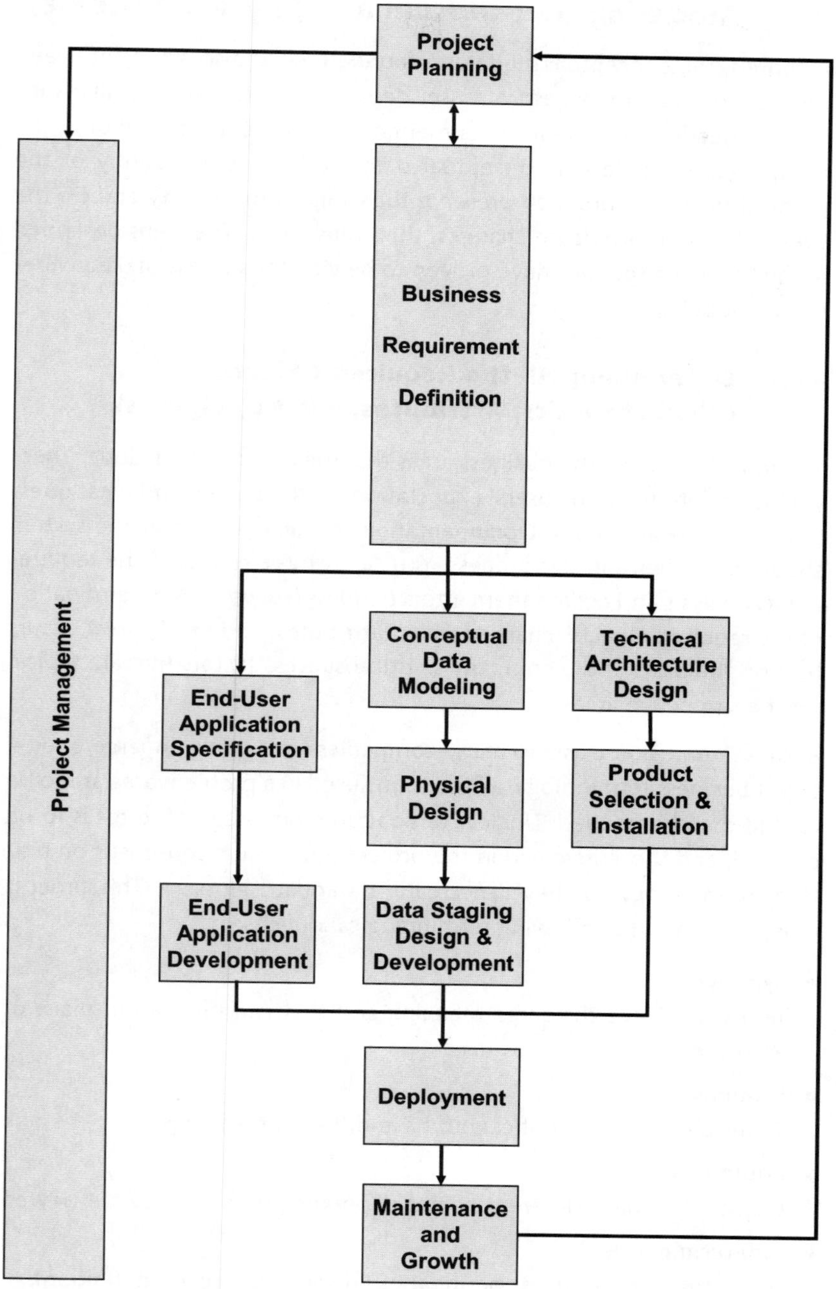

Figure 3.12 The Business Dimensional Lifecycle Model by R. Kimball

3.5 Modeling (Conceptual and Physical Schema)

As noted, the conceptual model is a foundation for discussions between developers and employees from user departments (terminological clarification, needs assessment, documentation, and data definition). It's advantageous to design conceptual data models independently of the physical system in order to preserve their long-term validity and, in the event of system or release changes, their reusability. The steps described in the following sections have proven to be vital for successful data warehouse modeling.

3.5.1 Determining All the Required Objects (Characteristics, Attributes, and Key Figures)

You must first clarify the business areas that the model is to include. Then, you must determine the users' expectations of the system and what questions must be answered. Documentation of the aspects that the system should cover helps in this process. You can use the results of the requirements analysis and collate them into a *business blueprint*. A determination of the required objects (characteristics, attributes, and key figures) occurs best on the basis of the company's critical success factors that are typical for the respective areas.

Standard glossary

Because confusion exists in many companies—especially in large ones—about business terminology, all the terms used in a problem area are to be captured and described. Unclear or contradictory usage of terms is to be clarified, and those involved in the project must reach consensus on uniform terminology so they can create a standard glossary. This process must eliminate the following terminological deficits:

- **Synonyms**
  Terms that have the same meaning and that can be used in place of each other
- **Homonyms**
  Terms that appear identical but have different meanings
- **Equipollences**
  Objects that have different names depending on how they are viewed
- **Indeterminacies**
  Terms that have no clear boundaries (absence of precise definition)
- **False identifiers**
  Terms whose meaning has changed over time

Based on this standard glossary, employees of business departments and application developers can communicate clearly with each other. In particular, developers can understand a given problem more quickly.

Since the collection of objects must occur systematically, a table can prove advantageous (see Table 3.1 for example).

Identification	Abbreviation	Format	Unit	Definition	Source of Data	Updating	Sample Data
Net Revenues	NR	DEC 8.3	Mio EUR	GR – DSD	SAP R/3 (P83)	Daily	123.456
Sales	A	INT 8	1000 pieces	CWS + AP – NWS	SAP R/3 (P83)	Daily	27
Sales Office	SO	CHAR 3	--	Smallest sales unit relevant to a profit center	SAP R/3 (P83)	As needed	PSG
Operating Hours	BS	INT 8	Hours	Hours that the motor operates	CSV by email	Weekly	18658
Location	LOC	TXT 25	--	Location of motor	CSV from customer services	As needed	San Lorenzo – Bldg. 1

Table 3.1 Systematic Collection of the Relevant Objects (Abbreviations: GR=gross revenue, DSD=direct sales deductions, CWS=current warehouse stock, AP=actual production, and NWS=new warehouse stock)

3.5.2 Displaying the Relations Between Individual Objects

After you define the relevant objects, you set the functional relationships between them. Variables (key figures imported directly from values in upstream systems) and formulas (mathematical links between key figures) are defined from the key figures. The other objects are subdivided into characteristics and attributes and the connections between them are made visible. These differentiations are essential to the data and interface requirements of the application.

3.5.3 Dimensioning of Key Figures

In an ideal world, you would be able to analyze key figures according to all possible dimensions for reasons of flexibility. In real life, however, factors like performance, memory, system limits, and so on limit the number of possible dimensions. The optimal need for dimensions is therefore a compromise between flexibility and speed.

The dimensions defined in this manner are then examined structurally; dimension elements and their granularity along with possible dimension hierarchies are set (see Figure 3.13).

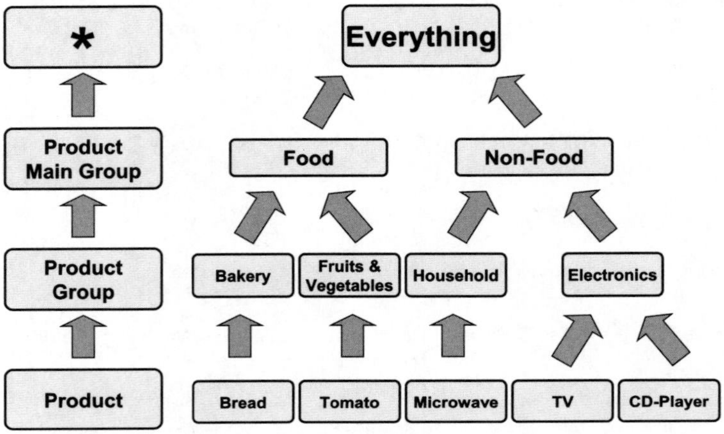

Figure 3.13 Dimension Elements and Hierarchies

You should then set the consolidation paths based on the aggregation rules of the dimension elements. It's not unusual for several consolidation paths to exist for some dimensions. See the example of a time dimension in Figure 3.14.

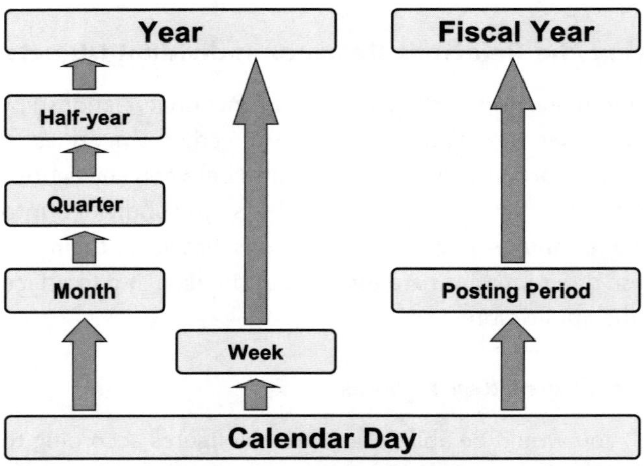

Figure 3.14 Various Consolidation Paths Based on the Example of a Time Dimension

3.5.4 A Step Toward a Physical Data Model: Determining the Objects Relevant to Reporting

> Assigning various dimensions (according to the need for dimensions determined previously) to the variables and formulas allows you to determine the reporting relevant objects: tables, cubes, views, and so on.

The question of how to design these objects always arises at this point. As with physical storage methods, you can follow any one of several approaches at the conceptual level. In principle, you must first decide about multidimensionality: tabular or multidimensional mapping. Multidimensional structures then raise the question of whether you should use a *HyperCube* (all key figures in one cube) or a *MultiCube* (each group of key figures in a separate cube) approach. Practical experience shows that when key figures are dimensioned differently, a separate cube must be generated for each group of key figures, however, you can always link individual cubes to each other over the common dimensions.

Key Figure Orientation Versus Characteristic Orientation

You must also make another fundamental decision regarding the cube architecture: Do you want a key figure-oriented data model or a characteristic-oriented one?

Key figure orientation

The key figure-oriented data model (also called *column-oriented data model)* has a variable (column) for each key figure. This approach keeps the number of data records small, but the length of the records grows considerably and can generate a significant number of empty cells (60–80 % empty cells is typical in real-world scenarios).

Characteristic orientation

The characteristic-oriented data model (also called *account-oriented data model)* has a variable (column) for each type of key figure (amount, quantity, and so on). The model is expanded with a dimension for the type of key figure; this dimension defines the content of the variable (account dimension, hour type, quantity type, and so on) unambiguously. With this approach, the number of data records grows considerably; however, the length of the records remains very short.

Case by case decision

With regard to the data model, it's impossible to give a blanket recommendation on the approach that you should adopt. You must simply examine the actual case. The decision is closely related to the question of physical storage in the data targets; the choice is inherently technical, not business-oriented:

- A key figure-oriented data model has advantages when the majority of key figures are filled for most properties (few empty cells appear).
- A characteristic-oriented data model has advantages when most of the key figures are often empty, or if you must later add or remove key figures.

The best solution often uses both approaches concurrently, depending on the contents of the data target. You can use views (or constructs such as a MultiProvider) to make this heterogeneity invisible to the end user.

3.5.5 The Golden Rules of Dimensional Modeling

That's enough theory for now. But we don't want to end this chapter without providing you with five rules we developed during our many years of working with data modeling.

When modeling a data warehouse, which differs from modeling an OLTP system, the following points have a critical and lasting influence on all the modeling techniques in use:

- "Dimensional thinking" is imperative when modeling multidimensional data structures. Setting the dimensions in terms of their purpose establishes the structure.
- Pay special attention to the hierarchies built within the dimensions. The hierarchies produce the aggregates that a data warehouse should provide to improve performance.
- Data is usually analyzed over a particular period of time. Modeling must consider the options for historicizing data warehouse data from the very beginning.
- Don't forget the mostly read-only access. The exclusive use of this type of data access influences the normalization of data (doing away with normal forms?).
- The volume of data to be processed often exceeds that of operational systems by several orders of magnitude. You should favor designs that allow for the reduction of the redundancy of data.

The following chapters describe in detail the application of this modeling theory to SAP BW.

4 Sample Scenario

This chapter introduces you to the case study that forms the basis for additional practical presentations in the following chapters. It describes the structure of CubeServ Engines, the model company, its analytical and planning requirements, and the SAP components included in the solution.

To enable easy access to the complex subject matter of SAP Business Information Warehouse (SAP BW), we've decided to work as authentically and with as many examples as possible in all volumes of the *SAP BW Library*.[1]

Therefore, the basis for our books is a uniform case study developed by the authors: a virtual company (CubeServ Engines). The case study will be used to present and communicate all the important requirements of business intelligence applications in a manner that is close to actual practice.

This chapter provides an overview of the basics of the case study. In light of the topic of this book, the chapter then addresses specific aspects of *data modeling* in detail.[2]

4.1 The Model Company: CubeServ Engines

4.1.1 Company Structure

Businesses and subgroups

The model company, CubeServ Engines, operates internationally: It includes various subsidiaries as legal units. Subgroups comprise the subsidiaries, and CubeServ Engines (Holding) runs the subgroups.

CubeServ Engines consists of the following subgroups (see Figure 4.1):

- The CubeServ Engines AMERICAS subgroup comprises the American subsidiaries.
- The CubeServ Engines ASIA subgroup comprises the Asian subsidiaries.
- The CubeServ Engines EUROPE subgroup comprises the European subsidiaries.

1 See Appendix L for an overview of the upcoming volumes in the *SAP BW Library*.

2 Upcoming volumes of the *SAP BW Library* will develop and modify the case study as needed to examine data retrieval, reporting and analysis, and business planning and simulation.

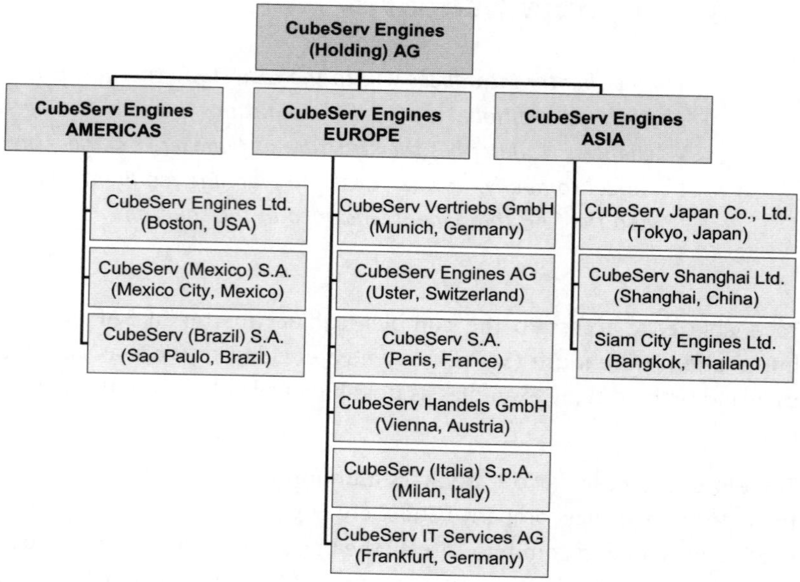

Figure 4.1 The Model Company: CubeServ Engines

4.1.2 Infrastructure

Specializations

The various elements of the company are specialized:

- The following list contains companies involved only in sales:
  - CubeServ Engines Ltd. (Boston, MA, USA)
  - CubeServ (Brazil) S.A. (Sao Paulo, Brazil)
  - CubeServ Vertriebs GmbH (Munich, Germany)
  - CubeServ Handels GmbH (Vienna, Austria)
  - CubeServ Japan Co., Ltd. (Tokyo, Japan)
  - Siam City Engines Ltd. (Bangkok, Thailand)
- The following list contains production companies that also perform sales tasks:
  - CubeServ (Mexico) S.A. (Mexico City, Mexico)
  - CubeServ Engines AG (Uster, Switzerland)
  - CubeServ S.A. (Paris, France)
  - CubeServ (Italia) S.p.A. (Milan, Italy)
  - CubeServ Shanghai Ltd. (Shanghai, China)

- The following businesses provide shared services:
  - CubeServ Engines (Holding) AG
  - CubeServ IT Services AG (Frankfurt, Germany)

Currencies

The Euro is the group currency. The various company codes use the following local currencies:

- US dollar
  CubeServ Engines Ltd. (Boston, MA, USA)
- Mexican peso
  CubeServ (Mexico) S.A. (Mexico City, Mexico)
- Brazilian real
  CubeServ (Brazil) S.A. (Sao Paulo, Brazil)
- Euro
  (CubeServ Vertriebs GmbH, Munich, Germany; CubeServ IT Services AG, Frankfurt, Germany; CubeServ Handels GmbH, Vienna, Austria; CubeServ S.A., Paris, France; and CubeServ (Italia) S.p.A., Milan, Italy)
- Swiss franc
  CubeServ Engines AG (Uster, Switzerland)
- Japanese yen
  CubeServ Japan Co., Ltd. (Tokyo, Japan)
- Chinese renminbi (yuan)
  CubeServ Shanghai Ltd. (Shanghai, China)
- Thai baht
  Siam City Engines Ltd. (Bangkok, Thailand)

Fiscal year variants

The model company's fiscal year corresponds to the calendar year with four special periods.

> In addition to calendar-based time characteristics (calendar day, calendar month, quarter, and calendar year, for example), SAP BW also supports parallel fiscal time characteristics.
>
> The *fiscal dimension* contains the fiscal year and its posting periods. Accordingly, a fiscal year can be identical to or deviate from a calendar year (example: a deferred fiscal year from April 1 of the calendar year to March 31 of the following calendar year).

SAP BW also supports *fiscal posting periods* that can correspond to or deviate from calendar months. This feature also enables the availability of special periods for closing activities. Fiscal year variants identify these settings for the fiscal year and the posting periods.

The standard settings in SAP BW define fiscal year variant K0 as a fiscal year (with two posting periods and no special periods) that corresponds to the calendar year. Fiscal year variant K4 also corresponds to the calendar year, but has four posting periods and four special periods. Fiscal year variant V3, however, defines a fiscal year deferred by three months (April to March); it also has four special periods.

IT systems CubeServ Engines uses four different operational systems: It uses SAP R/3 and the products of other software manufacturers for IT support of its transactional processes.

4.2 Requirements of the Case Study

CubeServ Engines plans to change its analytical applications. The existing analytical and planning applications (*MS Excel*, *Hyperion*, *Cognos*, and *Crystal Reports*) are to be replaced with a uniform and professional IT solution based on SAP NetWeaver, particularly SAP BW and SAP Enterprise Portal (SAP EP). Integration with legacy systems is not required. The transfer of data from legacy systems will occur over a file interface.

The need for coverage at CubeServ Engines involves sales, profitability analysis, and financial reporting (general ledger and consolidation). The company also requires mapping of comprehensive management reporting with data from all the analytical applications. Such mapping demands integration with a link to aggregated information from sales and profitability analysis, along with financial key figures.

4.2.1 Requirements of the Analytical Applications

Basic requirements The first step in implementing comprehensive business intelligence solutions includes mapping analytical applications (Sales & Distribution and Profitability Analysis), financial reporting for management, and operational processing.

All analytical applications must provide comparisons with the previous year and periods and time-series analyses. Both involve the use of hierarchies (characteristic and key figure hierarchies). A comprehensive consideration of the data requires currency conversion. All analytical applications contain tabular and graphical presentations.

Additional requirements

The following special requirements apply to individual analytical applications:

- **Sales & Distribution**
  Additional document reporting and automatic alerting (for late deliveries, for example)
- **Profitability Analysis and Financial Reporting**
  Additional plan-actual comparisons and structure analyses (the structure portion of profitability analysis items, for example)
- **Management Reporting**
  Additional plan-actual comparisons, geographical reporting (map graphics), and alerting (overviews according to information clusters, such as traffic lights for the analysis of goals reached)

Sales & Distribution

For the requirements from the Sales & Distribution area, the model company requires information from various sales documents (customer orders, deliveries, and invoices).

Lists of customers and customer orders must be mapped first to meet this requirement. This process contains data from the customer order (sold-to party, for example), the customer order item (material, order quantity, and value, for example) and delivery scheduling (confirmed quantity and dates, for example) at the document level.

Additional phases of the implementation will map the following additional information:

- **Deliveries**
  Data on the delivery (ship-to party, for example) up to the delivery item (such as material and delivery quantity) at the document level
- **Invoices**
  Billing data (such as payer) up to the invoice item (such as material, billed quantity, and value)

Profitability Analysis

The following levels of detailed key figures must be mapped to meet the requirements of profitability analysis.

- **Determining net revenue**
  Revenues minus revenue reductions
- **Determining the profit margin II**
  Net revenue minus full costs of production

- **Determining the profit margin III**
  Profit margin II plus or minus price and quantity deviations
- **Determining the profit margin IV**
  Profit margin III minus area fixed costs
- **Determining the profit margin (= operating profit) V**
  Profit margin IV minus company fixed costs

The analyses of profit margins must be enabled as local solutions (the non-consolidated view of individual entities in the company) and as consolidated solutions (with the elimination of revenues and costs between subsidiary companies).

Financial reporting

Information from the general ledger and consolidation is required to meet requirements in the area of financial reporting:

- Legal balance sheet and profitability accounting
- Consolidated balance sheet and profitability accounting

Management reporting

Data from all analytical applications is used to map comprehensive management reporting. The first step involves storing the complete data from the previous year and the periods of the current year. In the case study, this step includes the actual data of 2003 up to September 2004.

4.2.2 Planning Requirements

Rolling planning requires the integration of sales, revenue, and profit margin planning with plan profitability analysis. The plan data of sales, revenue, and full cost of manufacturing planning are to be transferred to plan profitability analysis.

Planning horizon

Plan data is also available as of 2003. Planning involves September 2004 as the current planning point with plan data from period October 2004 up to and including December 2005. Rolling planning occurs in quarters with planning period of 12 periods.

Planning functions

The planning process includes the transfer of actual data (sales quantities) with extrapolation to the entire year as an annual value. Distribution to the individual periods of the planning period is based on seasonal factors that you can enter. Variable, percentage-based revaluation must be available for selected key figures. Revaluation of the sales quantities occurs on the basis of plan prices and plan cost rates; revenue reductions should be planned as devaluation percentages. Aggregated key figures are to be mapped to meet the planning requirements:

- The key figures for sales, revenue, and the full cost of manufacturing are to be mapped to the level of product hierarchy 2, customer country, company code, currency type, version, value type, transaction type, and period/year.
- Plan prices are to be mapped to the level of product hierarchy 2, customer country, company code, currency type, version, value type, transaction type, and period/year.
- Plan CGM/FC are to be mapped as consolidated manufacturing costs at the level of product hierarchy 2, version, value type, and period/year.
- Plan Profitability Analysis is to be mapped at the level of the company code, plan item, period/year, currency type, version, and value type.

Key figures to be planned and granularity

4.3 Procedure and the SAP Components Involved

CubeServ Engines also requires coverage of the following SAP components:

SAP R/3 upstream systems

- **Sales & Distribution**
  SAP R/3 SD (Sales & Distribution)
- **Profitability Analysis**
  SAP R/3 CO-PA (Controlling—Profitability Analysis)
- **General Ledger Accounting**
  SAP R/3 FI-GL (Financial Accounting—General Ledger Accounting)
- **Consolidation**
  SAP R/3 EC-CS (Enterprise Controlling—Consolidation) and SAP SEM-BCS (Strategic Enterprise Management—Business Consolidation)

The project must implement the corresponding data targets (InfoCubes and InfoObjects, for example) and the ETL process for these components.

Components of SAP Business Content (SAP BCT) are also used as much as possible to improve understanding. If needed, the components of SAP BCT can be expanded and modified. The project must define its own objects if no components of SAP BCT are available.

Use of SAP Business Content

Integrated data retrieval with extractors is used to link upstream SAP R/3 systems. Four extraction methods are used for the ETL process from SAP R/3 upstream systems:

Extraction methods

- The transaction data of Profitability Analysis is retrieved with application-specific extractors of profit and market segment accounting at the level of individual items.
- The transaction data of Sales & Distribution is retrieved with an application-specific extractor of the *logistic extract structure customizing cockpit* at the document level.
- The transaction data of the General Ledger and master data are retrieved with SAP BCT extractors.
- SAP BCT and application-specific extractors map unmapped SAP R/3 source data with generic data sources.

Linking external systems

DB Connect will link external systems. File uploads and XML interfaces will retrieve additional data.

Use of SAP BW data targets

In general, the reporting components in SAP BW use InfoCubes and MultiProviders. The planning applications write their data back to transactional InfoCubes. An ODS layer is used to store document data. Other types of InfoProviders are used for dedicated applications in later steps of the implementation.

Reporting tools

Business Explorer (BEx) Web applications are used as the standard medium to map analytical requirements. The Business Explorer (BEx) Analyzer is used for specific requirements.

Planning interface

Web interfaces are generally used as the standard medium to map planning requirements.

4.4 Details on Data Modeling

SAP BW provides data for analytical applications with *InfoProviders* (see Section 2.2.2). CubeServ Engines requires InfoProviders that contain data (*InfoCubes*) and those that contain only reference to data (*InfoSets*).

In turn, all InfoProviders consist of *InfoObjects* (see Section 2.2.1), the basic carriers of information in SAP BW. To meet the requirements of the model company, we need various types of characteristics (company code, currency, and fiscal year) and key figures (revenues and revenue reductions).

4.4.1 InfoProviders

Types of InfoProviders used

The analytical and planning applications are primarily based on transaction data. InfoProviders store this information in SAP BW. The InfoProviders required to store the relevant data include the following:

- InfoCubes
- MultiProviders
- ODS objects
- Characteristics (as the data targets of SAP BW)

ODS objects and InfoCubes for customer orders

Various ODS objects help store document components for customer order header, customer order item, and distribution (of the customer order items). To use this document data in reporting applications, the data is stored in InfoObjects (master data attributes) and InfoCubes. Various InfoCubes that contain information on the same documents are made available to reporting as MultiProviders.

ODS objects and InfoCubes for profitability analysis

In addition to the analogous storage of individual item of Profitability Analysis in an ODS object, actual and plan data of this application is stored in various InfoCubes (actual data in non-transactional InfoCubes and plan data in transactional InfoCubes) because of the differing granularities. Actual and plan data InfoCubes are made available to reporting with MultiProviders. Plan prices, plan manufacturing cost rates, and revenue reductions are also stored in transactional InfoCubes.

ODS objects and InfoCubes for financial reporting

The data of the General Ledger and of consolidation are also stored in ODS objects and InfoCubes. The plan Profitability Analysis is stored in a transactional InfoCube. In Financial Reporting, a MultiProvider based on the actual and plan data InfoCubes of the consolidation structures is made available for plan-actual comparisons.

InfoObject data is used as a data target for the customer list required for master data reporting.

4.4.2 InfoObjects

As a rule, InfoProviders don't contain transaction data. InfoProviders consist of *facts* (key figures, revenues, and sales quantities, for example) and qualifying *characteristics* from these facts. Characteristics and key figures are called *InfoObjects*. They therefore help to implement characteristics and key figures in SAP BW.

General and application-specific InfoObjects for key figures and characteristics are necessary to meet the requirements of CubeServ Engines. Key figures, such as *revenues* and *sales quantity,* require additional units (currency and quantity unit). Analytical applications also need basic time characteristics, such as fiscal year and calendar day. SAP BW also uses technical characteristics, such as request numbers, to enable adequate management of the data warehouse.

Comprehensive InfoObjects

The technical data-modeling requirements of CubeServ engines require comprehensive InfoObjects:

- Mapping of the fiscal and calendar-based time dimension requires InfoObjects such as the following: "calendar day," calendar month," "quarter," "calendar year," "fiscal year variant," "fiscal year," "fiscal year/period," and "posting period."
- Mapping the amount key figures requires the "currency key."
- Organizational identification occurs in all applications with the "company code" characteristic.
- The differentiation of data from various sources occurs strictly via the "source system ID."
- The differentiation of plan and actual data occurs with "version" and "value type" in all applications.

Comprehensive InfoObjects are summarized along with application-specific InfoObjects in application-specific InfoObjectCatalogs (see Appendix B, *InfoObjectCatalogs*).

Application-specific InfoObjects

Application-specific InfoObjects are also required. They can be used anywhere, but are application-specific in this context:

InfoObjects for Sales & Distribution

- The analytical requirements from Sales & Distribution require InfoObjects used everywhere and InfoObjects specific to sales. These InfoObjects are characteristics such as "goods recipient," or "delivery status," or "actual delivered quantity in sales units" (see the InfoObject Catalogs specific to sales in Appendix B, *InfoObjectCatalogs)*.

InfoObjects for Profitability Analysis

- The analytical requirements of Profitability Analysis require that InfoObjects are used everywhere and that InfoObjects are specific to Profitability Analysis. These InfoObjects include characteristics, such as "transaction type" and the "reference document number of the profitability analysis line item" and key figures, such as "profit" or "variable production costs" (see the InfoObjectCatalogs specific to Profitability Analysis in Appendix B, *InfoObjectCatalogs*).

InfoObjects for Financial Reporting

- The analytical requirements of Financial Reporting need InfoObjects used everywhere and InfoObjects specific to the General Ledger. These InfoObjects include characteristics, such as the "chart of accounts" and "G/L account" and key figures, such as "cumulated balance" or "total of credit postings" (see the InfoObjectCatalogs specific to the General Ledger in Appendix B, *InfoObjectCatalogs*).

4.5 A Look Ahead: Additional Steps in the Implementation

As noted, the case study used in the first volumes of the SAP BW Library will undergo further development as needed for the various topic areas.

The first step of the implementation of our model company's requirements occurs in volumes 1–4 of the SAP BW Library. The following additional requirements will be developed for later implementation steps in the continuation of the SAP BW Library:

- HR reporting
- Logistics
- Competitors

5 InfoObjects of SAP BW

InfoObjects, characteristics and key figures form the foundation of the data model in SAP Business Information Warehouse. This chapter shows you how to use and modify the InfoObjects of SAP Business Content and how to define your own InfoObjects.

5.1 InfoAreas and InfoObjectCatalogs

5.1.1 Creating Structures and Hierarchies

Classification with InfoObject-Catalogs

InfoObjects are always stored in folders; the folders are called *InfoObject-Catalogs*. Note the distinction between InfoObjectCatalogs for characteristics and those for key figures (see Figure 5.1). SAP Business Information Warehouse (SAP BW) automatically assigns InfoObjects that have not been explicitly assigned to an InfoObjectCatalog to a default InfoObject-Catalog. The following default InfoObjectCatalogs are available:

- Unassigned units
- Unassigned key figures
- Unassigned characteristics
- Unassigned time characteristics

> **Using InfoObjectCatalogs systematically**
>
> Other than organizing InfoObjects, InfoObjectCatalogs have no other function. Nevertheless, we recommend the creation and use of logically grouped InfoObjectCatalogs. Doing so simplifies work with data modeling and data retrieval because it shortens the system response time during these activities.

Classification with InfoAreas

InfoObjectCatalogs are also stored in folders. These folders are called *InfoAreas* (see Figure 5.1). All InfoObjectCatalogs that are not explicitly assigned to an InfoArea are stored in the **Unassigned Nodes** InfoArea.

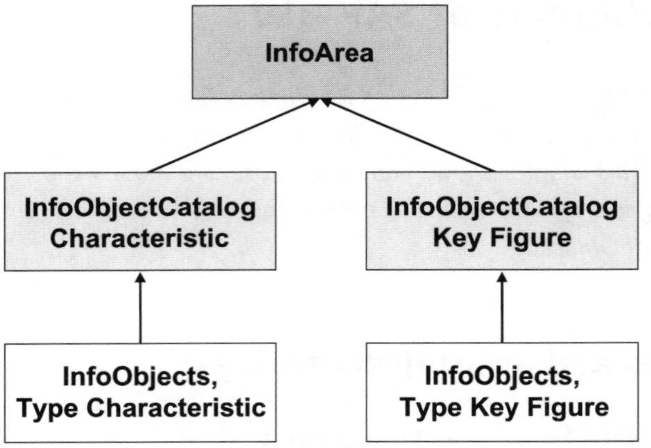

Figure 5.1 Classification Within InfoAreas

Hierarchical classification of InfoAreas

You can also classify InfoAreas hierarchically. In this manner, you can classify business-intelligence applications into various logical components.

Our model company, CubeServ Engines, uses the following levels of classification (see Figure 5.2):

- The highest level for all the analytical applications (here: "CubeServ Engines Business Intelligence Applications").
- A subordinate level for the application areas Finance & Accounting and Sales.
- If needed, another level for the individual analytical applications (Financials—General Ledger and Profitability Analysis) beneath the related application area (Finance & Accounting in the example).

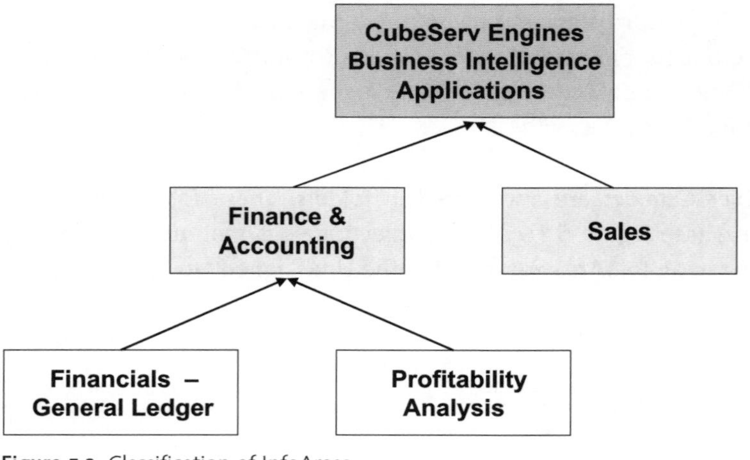

Figure 5.2 Classification of InfoAreas

Using InfoAreas systematically

Other than the classification of InfoObjectCatalogs and the grouping of subordinate InfoAreas, InfoAreas have no other function. Nevertheless, we recommend the creation and use of logically grouped InfoAreas. Doing so simplifies work with data modeling, data retrieval, and with the Business Explorer (BEx) because it's easier to find objects. This approach also shortens system response time during these activities.

InfoAreas in the Administrator Workbench

In the Administrator Workbench of SAP BW, InfoAreas are used in the **InfoProvider** and **InfoObjects** views, where they are the highest node of the hierarchy, corresponding to the view of the **InfoProvider** or **InfoObjects** nodes (see Figure 5.8).

An InfoObjectCatalog is a grouping of InfoObjects according to application-specific viewpoints. There are two types of InfoObjectCatalogs: characteristic and key figure. InfoAreas help classify the InfoArea, InfoProvider, and InfoObjectCatalog metaobjects in SAP Business Information Warehouse.

5.1.2 Setting Up InfoAreas

The following example sets up InfoAreas in the **InfoObjects** view of the Administrator Workbench. You can open this view from the role menu or with Transaction RSA14 (see Figure 5.3).

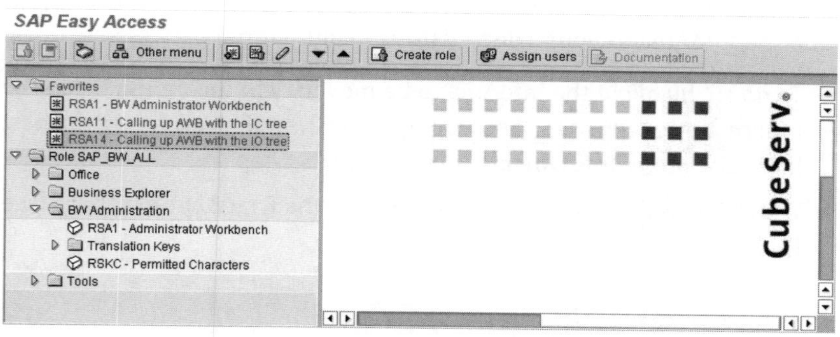

Figure 5.3 Opening the Administrator Workbench, InfoObjects View

Creating the Top-Level InfoArea

- To create InfoAreas, highlight the uppermost node of the **InfoObjects** hierarchy node in the **InfoObjects** view of the Administrator Workbench. Right-click to open the context menu.

- In the context menu, select the entry **Create InfoArea** (see Figure 5.4, Step 1).
- Enter the technical name and a description of the InfoArea in the **Create InfoArea** popup (Step 2).
- Click **Next (Enter)** to create the InfoArea (Step 3).

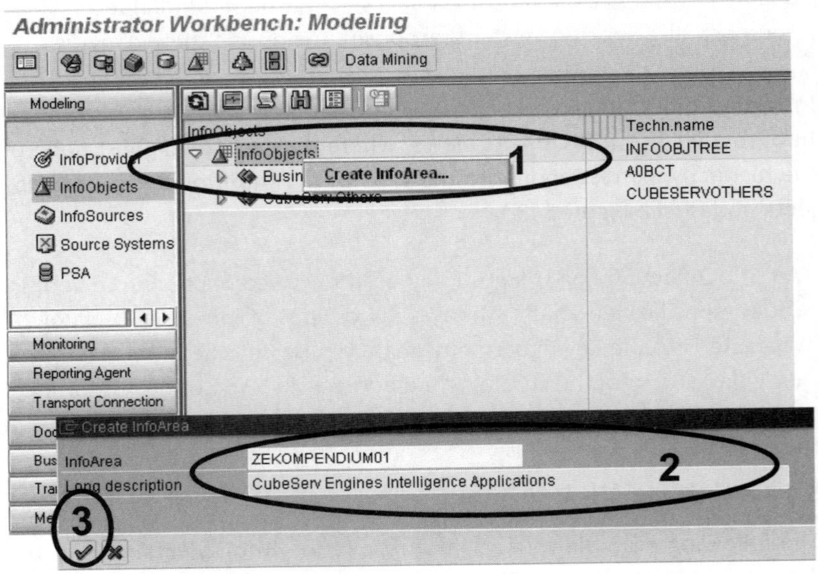

Figure 5.4 Creating the Top-Level InfoArea

Repositioning an InfoArea

The InfoArea you just created is shown last in the display. You can position the InfoArea to your liking by using Drag&Drop:

- To do so, highlight the InfoArea to be moved with the mouse, keep the mouse button pressed, and simply drag the InfoArea to the highest hierarchy node, **InfoObjects** (see Figure 5.5, Step 1).
- The object is then positioned according to the Drag&Drop settings (see Figure 5.5, Step 2).

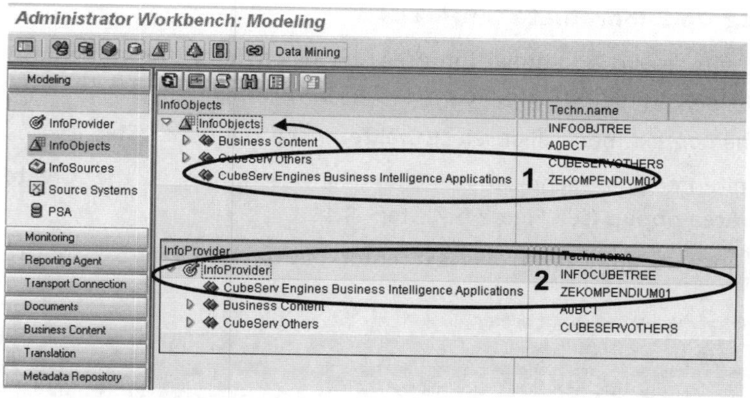

Figure 5.5 Placing or Moving an InfoArea

Activating Drag&Drop

In some cases, the **Drag&Drop** function might be switched off. If it is and you attempt to move an object, an **Information** popup appears (see Figure 5.6, Step 1); confirm the popup with the **Next (Enter)** button (see Figure 5.6, Step 2). If you want to permit the function, proceed as indicated by the popup information:

- Use Transaction SM30 to start maintenance of the table view for table RSADMINSV.
- Deactivate the **Drag&Drop off** option (see Figure 5.6, Step 3).
- Save this setting (Figure 5.6, Step 4).
- When you restart the Administrator Workbench of SAP BW, the **Drag&Drop** function will be active.

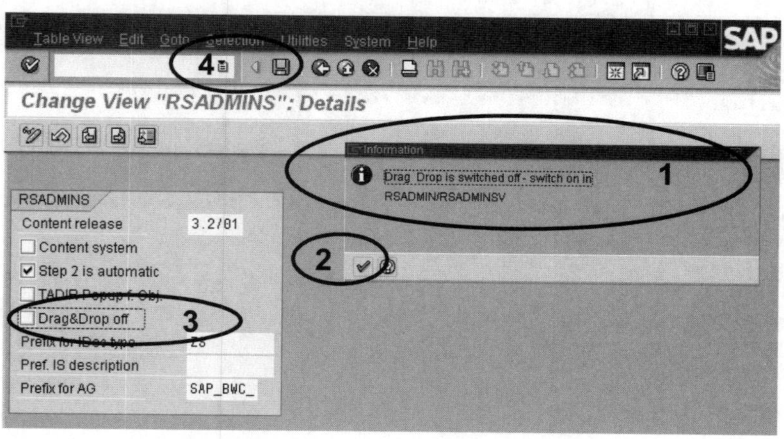

Figure 5.6 Activating Drag&Drop for the Administrator Workbench

Setting Up Subordinate InfoAreas

- You can set up additional InfoAreas by highlighting the uppermost InfoArea and right-clicking to open the context menu.
- In the context menu, first select **Create...** (see Figure 5.7, Step 1).
- Then enter the technical name and a description in the **Create InfoArea popup** (see Figure 5.7, Step 2).
- Confirm your entries with the **Next (Enter)** button (see Figure 5.7, Step 3).

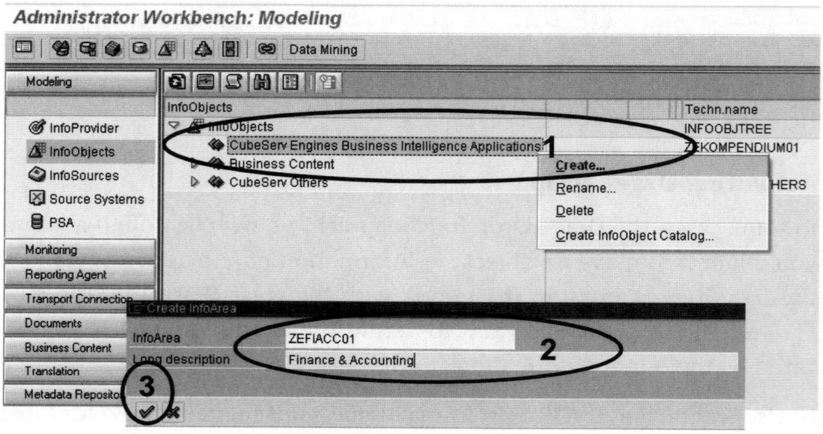

Figure 5.7 Creating Subordinate InfoAreas

Proceed similarly until you have created the desired InfoArea hierarchy (see Figure 5.8).

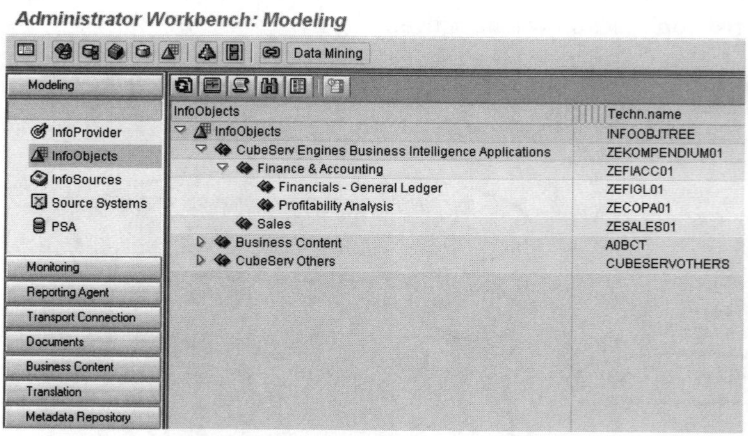

Figure 5.8 InfoArea Hierarchy

5.1.3 Setting Up InfoObjectCatalogs

Based on the InfoArea hierarchy, you set up the required InfoObjectCatalogs in the **InfoObjects** view of the Administrator Workbench of SAP BW.

Setting Up an InfoObjectCatalog for Characteristics

- To create an InfoObjectCatalog, select the InfoArea to be assigned to the catalog in the **InfoObjects** view of the Administrator Workbench (see Figure 5.9, Step 1).
- Right-click to open the context menu. Then click to select the menu entry **Create InfoObjectCatalog...** (see Figure 5.9, Step 2).
- In the **Edit InfoObjectCatalog** popup, enter the name and a description of the InfoObjectCatalog (see Figure 5.10, Step 1).
- You can retain the default setting **Characteristic** (see Figure 5.10, Step 2).
- Click on the **Create** button to create the InfoObjectCatalog (see Figure 5.10, Step 3).

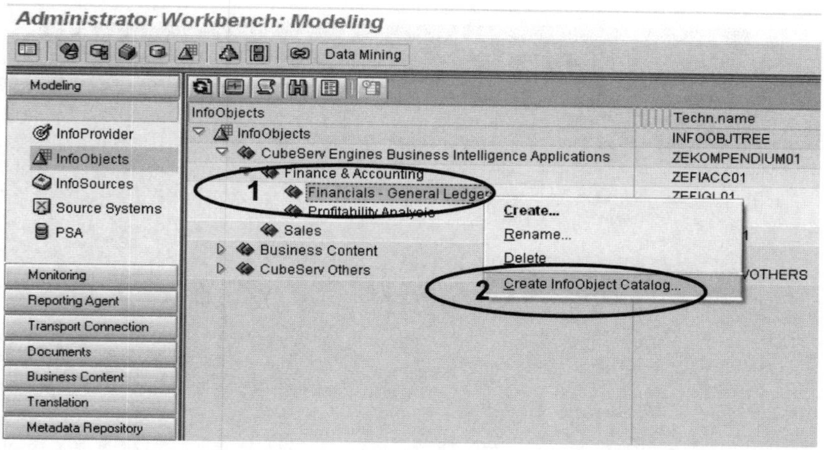

Figure 5.9 Creating an InfoObjectCatalog

Activating the object

- You can activate the object in the **Edit InfoObjectCatalog** dialog (see Figure 5.11, Step 1).
- Return to the **InfoObjects** view of the SAP BW Administrator Workbench with the **Back** button (see Figure 5.11, Step 2), which will display the catalog beneath the InfoArea (see Figure 5.11, Step 3).

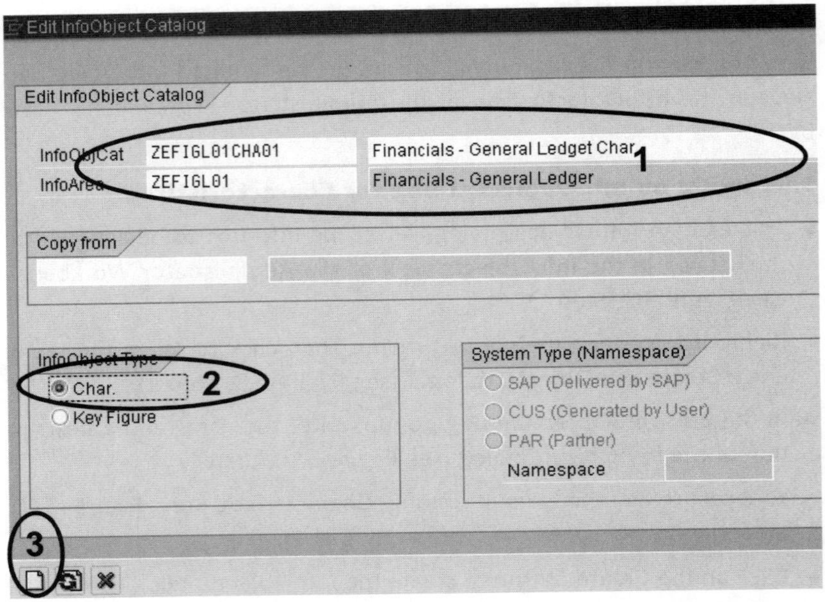

Figure 5.10 Entering the Technical Name, Description, and the "Characteristic" Type

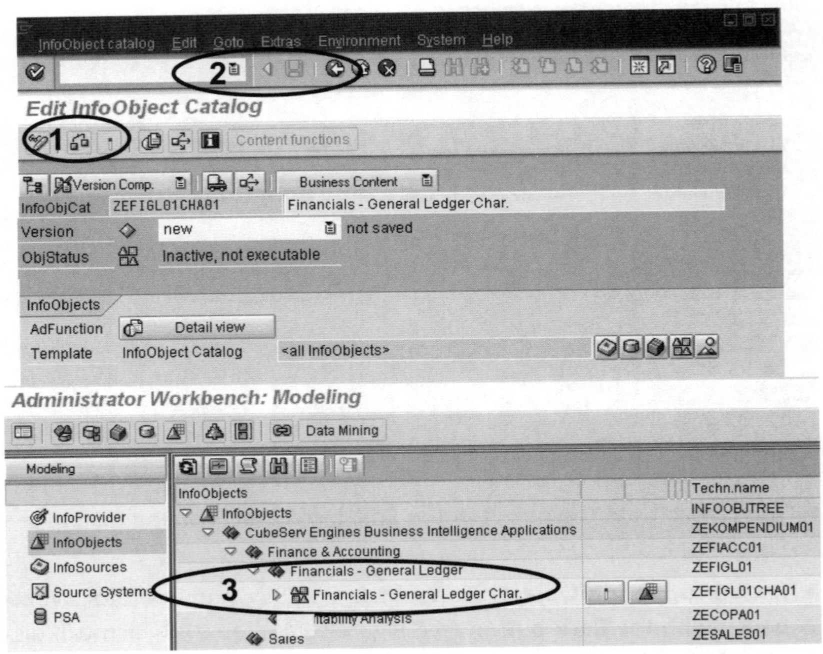

Figure 5.11 Activating the Characteristics InfoObjectCatalog and Display in the InfoObjects View of the Administrator Workbench

Setting up an InfoObjectCatalog for Key Figures

The creation of an InfoObjectCatalog for key figures is similar to the creation of InfoObjectCatalogs for characteristics (see Figure 5.12, Step 1 and Step 2). The only modification is the selection of the **Key Figure** type in the **Edit InfoObjectCatalog** popup (see Figure 5.12, Step 2).

Proceed accordingly until you have created all the required InfoObjectCatalogs for the desired InfoAreas (see Figure 5.13).

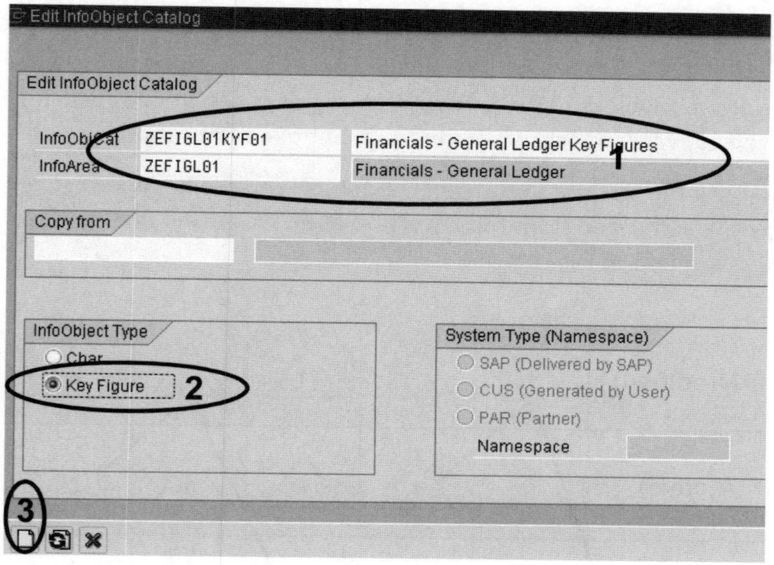

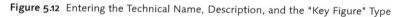

Figure 5.12 Entering the Technical Name, Description, and the "Key Figure" Type

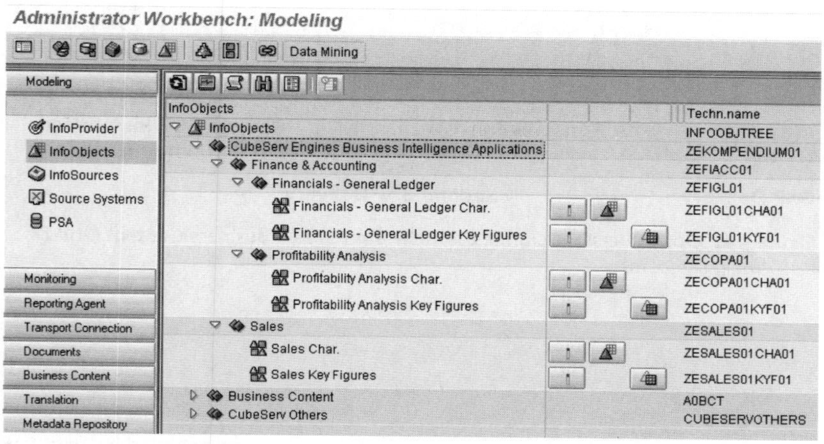

Figure 5.13 InfoAreas and InfoObjectCatalogs

5.2 InfoObjects of SAP Business Content

Object versions

SAP Business Content provides objects for direct use. As explained extensively in Section 2.7, SAP Business Content involves preconfigured, role- and task-related information models based on consistent metadata in SAP BW. SAP Business Content contains all the components necessary for an analytical application.[1]

Excursus

> **Activating the objects of SAP Business Content**
>
> The objects provided in SAP Business Content are available in a D(elivery) version. Activation of these objects converts them into an A(ctive) version (see Table 5.1). Note that SAP also generates an intermediate M(odified) version that remains in the event of a termination.
>
> If you want to activate SAP Business Content, you should note that its objects are changed from the D version to an M version and then to the A version (see Figure 5.14).

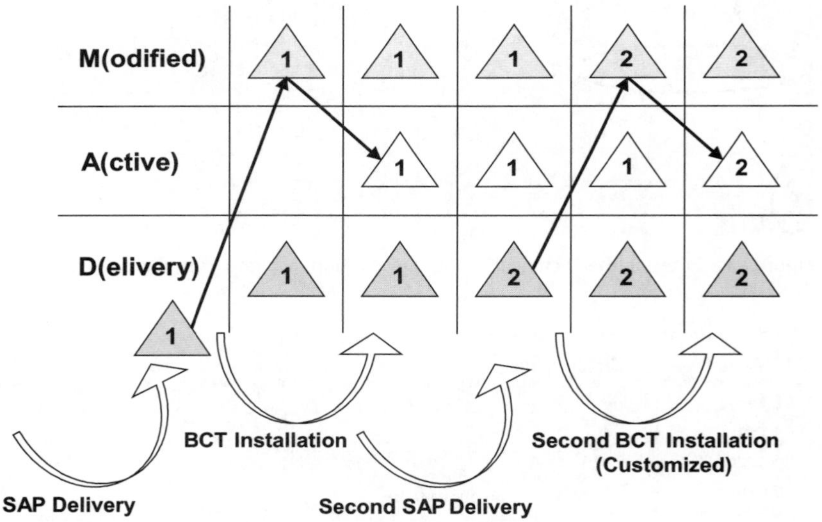

Figure 5.14 Object Versions During the Activation of SAP Business Content (Source: http://help.sap.com)

1 See Chapter 7 for additional notes and suggestions on using and working with SAP Business Content.

5.2.1 Activating an Individual InfoObject of SAP Business Content

The InfoObjects of SAP Business Content that can be used are made available by selective or comprehensive activation of SAP Business Content. The following sections examine both variants in more detail.

Grouping with SAP Business Content Activation

- First change to the **Business Content** view of the Administrator Workbench (Transaction RSA1: see Figure 5.17, Step 1).
- Ensure that the grouping setting corresponds to the proper procedure. You can use the **Grouping** button to choose among the following variants (see Figure 5.17, Step 2):
  - **Only Necessary Objects**
    This variant activates only the dependent objects of SAP Business Content required for successful activation of the selected objects.
  - **In Data Flow Before**
    This variant activates all the dependent objects of SAP Business Content required for successful activation of the selected objects and those that deliver data to a collected object (see Figure 5.15).

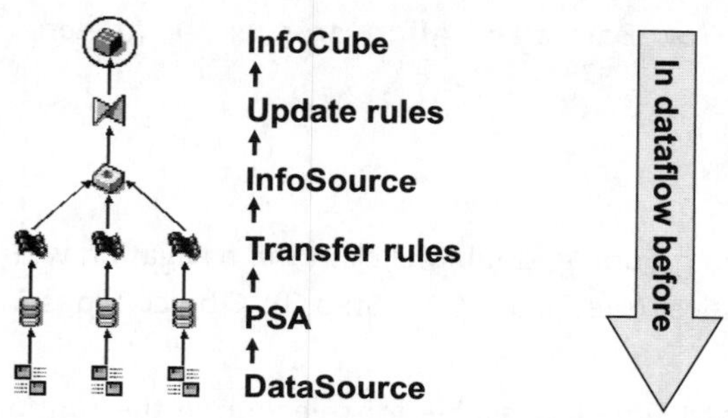

Figure 5.15 In Data Flow Before (Source: http://help.sap.com)

  - **In Data Flow Afterwards**
    This variant activates all the dependent objects of SAP Business Content required for successful activation of the selected objects and those received from a collected object (see Figure 5.16).

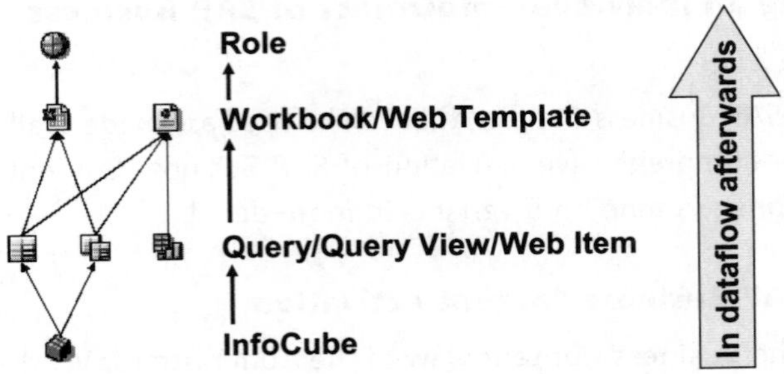

Figure 5.16 In Data Flow Afterwards (Source: http://help.sap.com)

- **In Data Flow Before and Afterwards**
  This variant activates all the dependent objects of SAP Business Content required for successful activation of the selected objects, those that deliver data to a collected object, and objects that receive data from a collected object.

> - For a minimal activation, select the **Only Necessary Objects** grouping when activating SAP Business Content.
> - A selective activation (characteristics with their data retrieval, for example) ideally occurs with the **In Data Flow Before** option.
> - You can use **In Data Flow Before and Afterwards** for comprehensive activations.

Selecting InfoObjects

- After setting the desired grouping, double-click in the navigation window on the selection level (see Figure 5.17, Step 3): **Object Types** in our example.
- **All Objects According to Type** is available for selection in the central frame (Step 4).
- Open the **InfoObject** folder in this frame. The **Select Objects** entry is displayed (if SAP Business Content has been activated and the objects are inserted in your personal list of values, InfoObjects might be listed under the **Select Objects** entry).
- You can then double-click on the **Select Objects** entry to begin the selection (Step 5).
- The **Input Help for Metadata** provides the InfoObjects for selection, sorted alphabetically by technical name (Step 6).

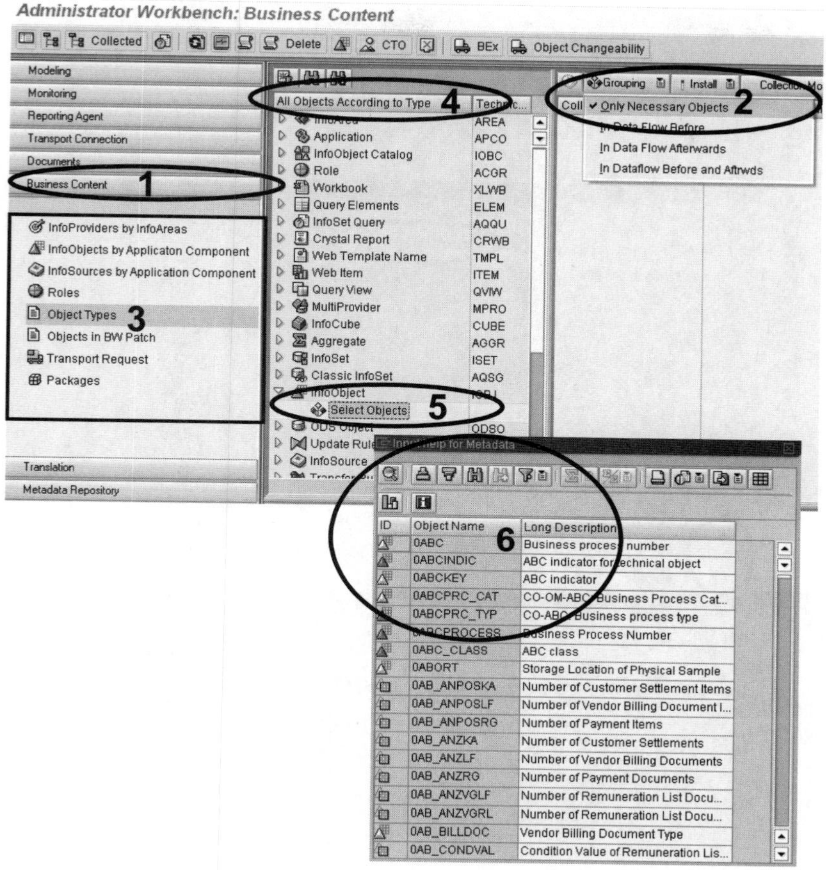

Figure 5.17 Selecting SAP Business Content InfoObjects, Part 1

- To make a specific selection, simply select the **Object Name** column in the popup (see Figure 5.18, Step 1) and click on the **Filter** button (see Figure 5.18, Step 2).
- In the **Determine Values for Filter Criteria** popup, you can specify your desired selection (one or more InfoObjects, generic selection, or lists of InfoObjects): in our example the InfoObject 0VERSION is specified (Step 3).
- After you confirm your selection (Step 4), the InfoObject you selected is displayed in the **Determine Values for Filter Criteria** popup.
- When you click to mark an object in the corresponding line of the list of values (Step 5) and select the **Copy Selection** button (Step 6), the process of collecting the required objects begins according to the grouping option.

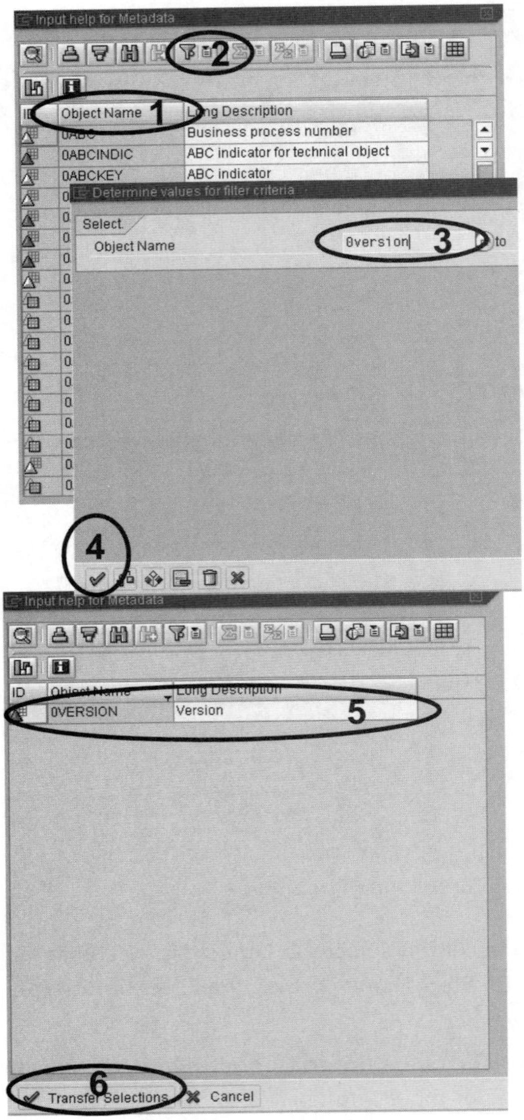

Figure 5.18 Selecting SAP Business Content InfoObjects, Part 2

Activating Objects of SAP Business Content

- At the end of the collection process (our example uses the grouping option **Only Necessary Objects**), the collected objects are displayed in the **Collected Objects** frame (see Figure 5.19, Step 1).
- The activation process begins when you click on the **Install** button (see Figure 5.19, Step 2).

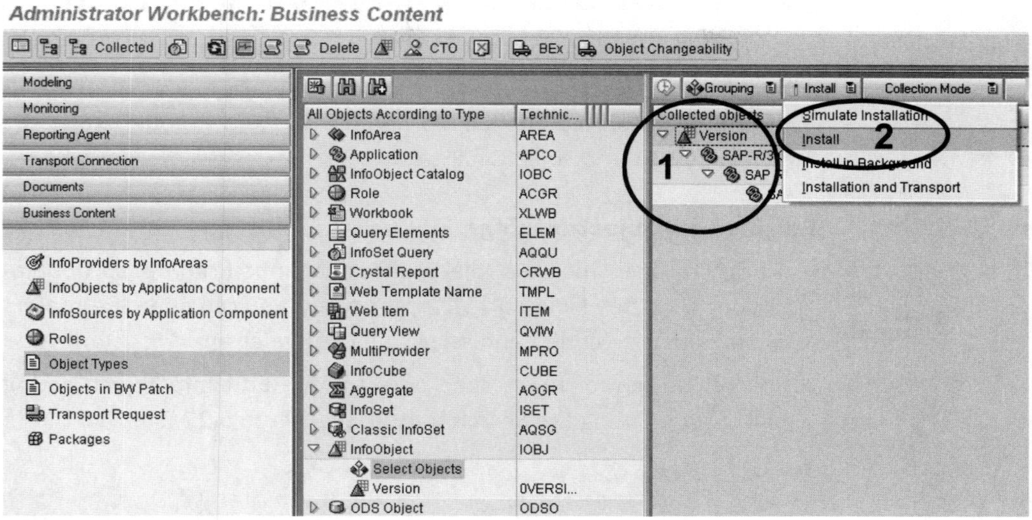

Figure 5.19 Activating SAP Business Content InfoObjects

When the activation ends, two frames display a log of the results (see Figure 5.20). If the log entries have a green information icon, no further steps are necessary. The InfoObject is available for work with SAP BW.

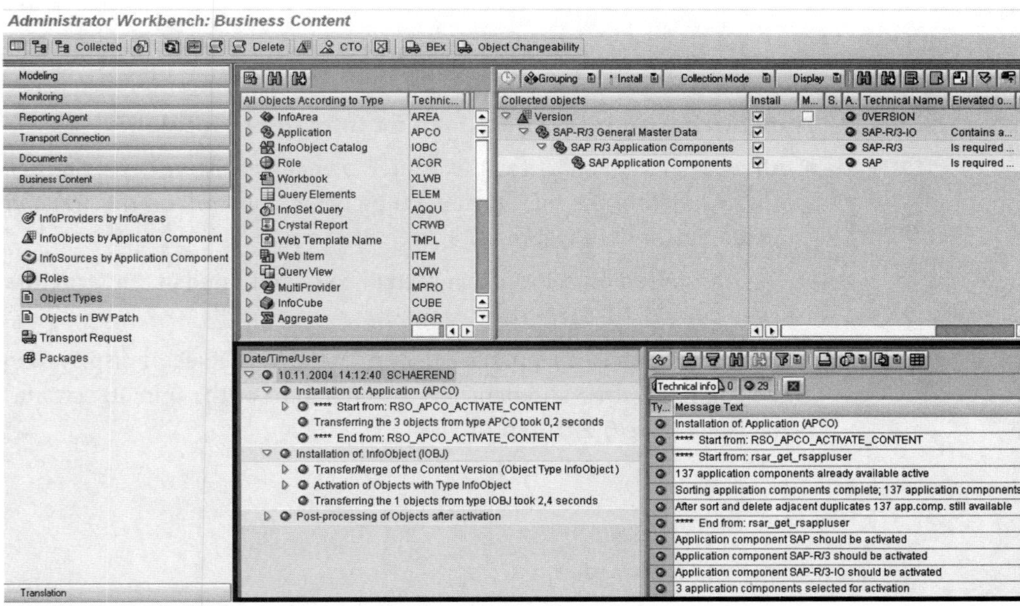

Figure 5.20 Results Log of SAP Business Content Activation

5.2.2 Transferring an SAP Business Content InfoObject into an InfoObjectCatalog

Activated InfoObjects are available in the **InfoObjects** view of the SAP BW **Administrator Workbench**. As noted earlier, you should group the InfoObjects into InfoObjectCatalogs.

Editing InfoObjectCatalogs

- To do so, open the InfoObjectCatalog for modifications by double-clicking on it (see Figure 5.21). Alternatively, you can open the context menu with a right-click and select the **Change** entry.
- You can search for the desired object in the **Edit InfoObjectCatalog** dialog (or by using the **Search** button: see Figure 5.22, Step 1).

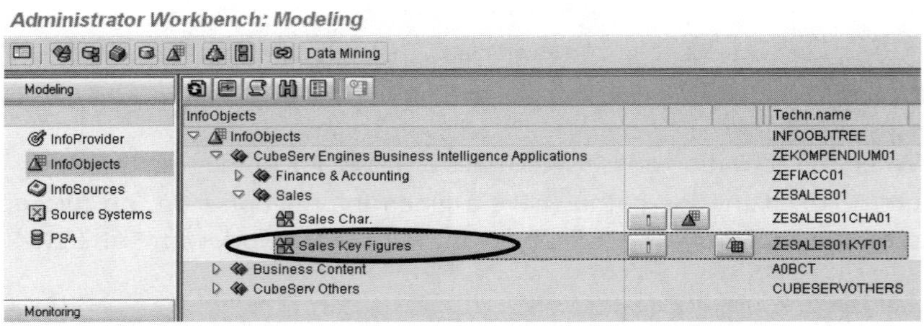

Figure 5.21 Selecting an InfoObjectCatalog for Editing

Transferring an InfoObject into an InfoObjectCatalog

- After you have highlighted the desired object (see Figure 5.22, Step 2), it is included in the InfoObjectCatalog when you click on the **Transfer Fields** button (see Figure 5.22, Step 3).
- The transferred object is highlighted in color and listed in the **Structure** (see Figure 5.23, Step 1 and Step 2).
- After activation (see Figure 5.23, Step 3), the InfoObject is displayed in the Administrator Workbench as a component of the InfoObjectCatalog (see Figure 5.23, Step 4).

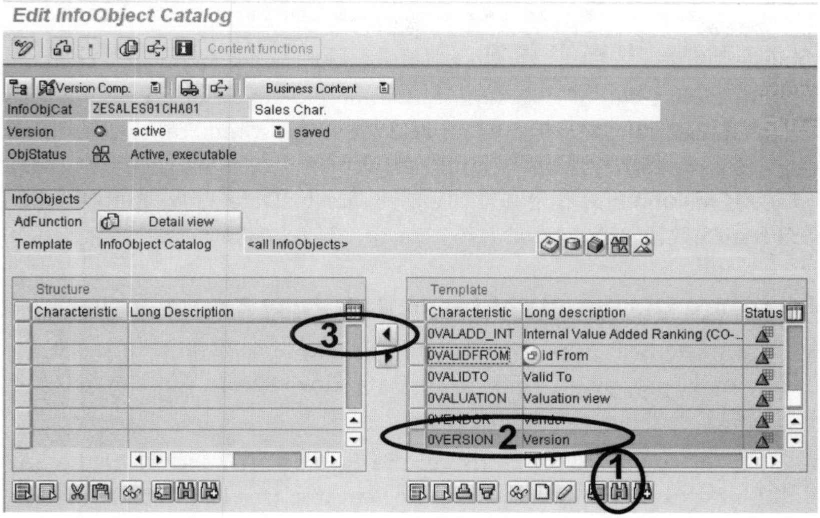

Figure 5.22 Selecting an InfoObject for Transfer into the InfoObjectCatalog

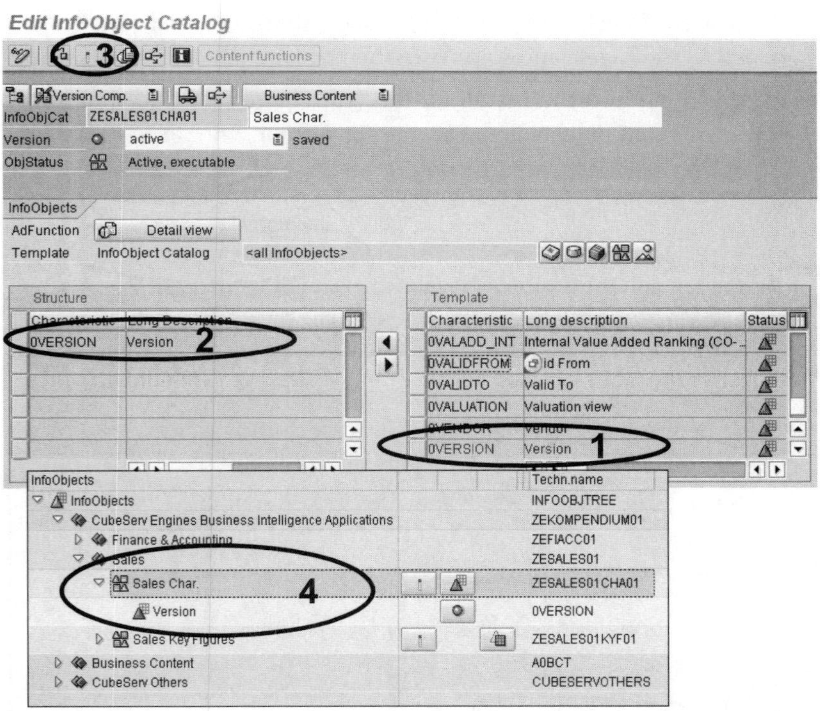

Figure 5.23 Results of the Transfer and Activation of the InfoObject in the InfoObject-Catalog

5.2.3 Transferring an SAP Business Content InfoObject In Data Flow Before

Comprehensive activation of SAP Business Content

SAP Business Content offers more than ample coverage for InfoObjects (characteristics and key figures). It also meets most requirements for data retrieval (master data, texts, and hierarchies) for characteristics. That's why we recommend that you also activate **In Data Flow Before** when you transfer characteristics.

Procedure and Results of the In Data Flow Before Activation

- To activate SAP Business Content In Data Flow Before, first set the groupingGgrouping option to **In Data Flow Before** (see Figure 5.24, Step 1).
- Then select (as indicated above: see Figures 5.17 and 5.18) the SAP Business Content InfoObjects to be activated (see Figure 5.24, Step 2).
- For the selected objects, the related and required objects (compoundings and attributes, for example) and the elements of the upstream ETL (Extraction, Transfer, and Loading) process (transfer structures, transfer rules, InfoPackages, and so on) are then collected.
- After you click on the **Install** button (see Figure 5.19 and the related comments), all objects are available for further work in SAP BW provided they were activated without errors.

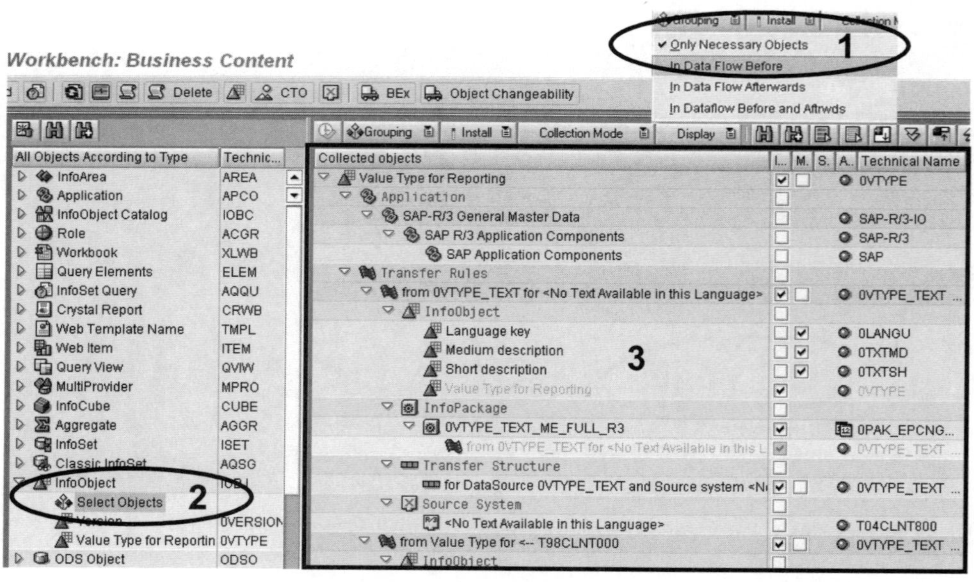

Figure 5.24 Collecting Objects In Data Flow Before

Errors when activating SAP Business Content

If errors occurred during the activation of SAP Business Content (see Figure 5.25, Steps 1 and 2), you must deal with them systematically. In our example, the key field is missing in the transfer structure.[2]

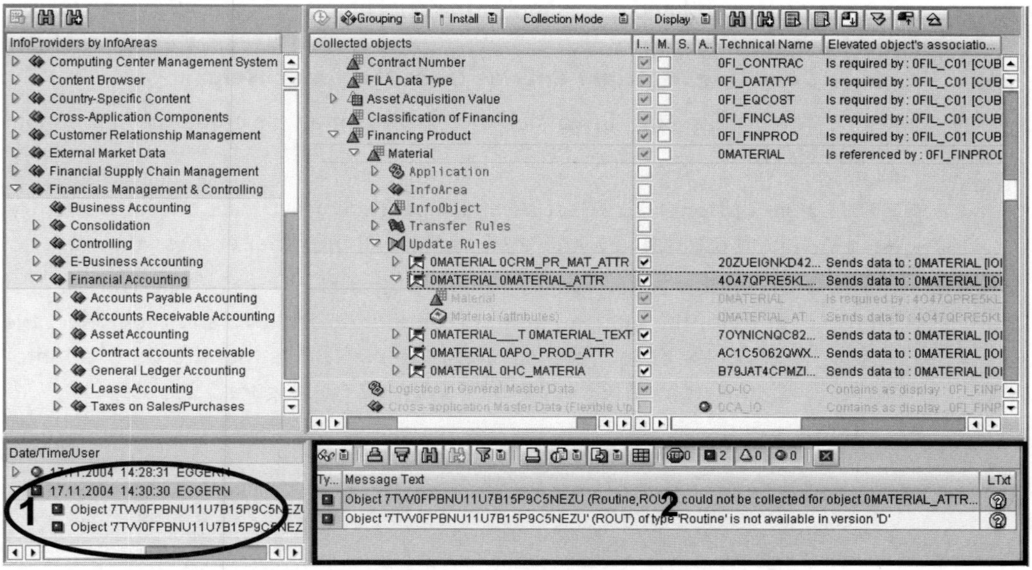

Figure 5.25 Errors When Activating SAP Business Content

5.2.4 Transferring SAP Business Content InfoObjects by Selecting InfoCubes In Data Flow Flow Before

Activation to collect Info Objects

In general, the effort involved in step-by-step activation is too great. That's why you can analyze SAP Business Content and activate targeted InfoCubes with the grouping option **In Data Flow Before** to make the InfoObjects available to an analytical application. In our model company, CubeServ Engines, we want to implement Financial Reporting (general ledger with profitability analysis and balance sheet). To do so, we select InfoCubes 0FIGL_*.

Selecting SAP Business Content InfoCubes

- To do so, proceed as you did with the selection of InfoObjects. Simply select the InfoCubes that you want in the InfoCube folder of the **All Objects According to Type** frame by opening the InfoCube folder with

2 See Volume 2 of the SAP BW Library (forthcoming). Egger et al.: *SAP BW Data Retrieval*. SAP PRESS, 2005.

a click. Double-click on the **Select Objects** entry to start the selection (see Figure 5.26, Step 1).

- Select the InfoCubes in the **Input Help for Metadata** popup. You can also use filtering to simplify the selection (see Figures 5.17 and 5.18).

Selecting Multiple Entries from the Input Help

You can use one of two methods to select multiple entries from the Input Help:

- In **option 1**, to select several separate entries, click on the first entry, hold the **Ctrl** key, and then click on all the other entries you want.
- In **option 2**, to select a coherent interval of entries, click on the first entry of the interval, hold the **Shift** and **Ctrl** keys, and then select the last entry of the interval. The example selects the interval of all InfoCubes from 0FIGL_C01 to 0FIGL_VC2 (see Figure 5.26, Step 2).

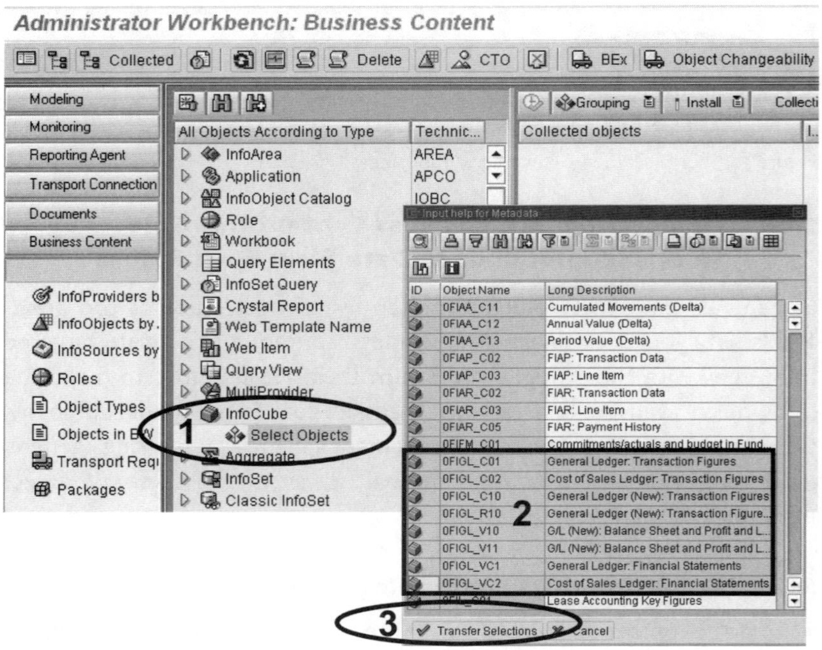

Figure 5.26 Collecting InfoObjects via InfoCubes

- After you click the **Transfer Selections** button (Step 3), SAP BW starts to collect all the related InfoObjects and ETL components. See the comments above on the activation of individual InfoObjects **In Data Flow Before**.

Merging the Active Version and the Content Version

In some circumstances, portions of the SAP Business Content that you want to activate are already active. In this case, the system merges the active version with the content version.

- In our example, the system first requests confirmation to overwrite the transfer routine for InfoObject 0SOURSYSTEM.
- After you confirm the query (see Figure 5.27, Step 1), a **Merge InfoObject...** dialog offers you an option to overwrite all transfer routines with the Content version without further queries. To do so, simply click on the **Transfer All Without Dialog** button (Step 2).

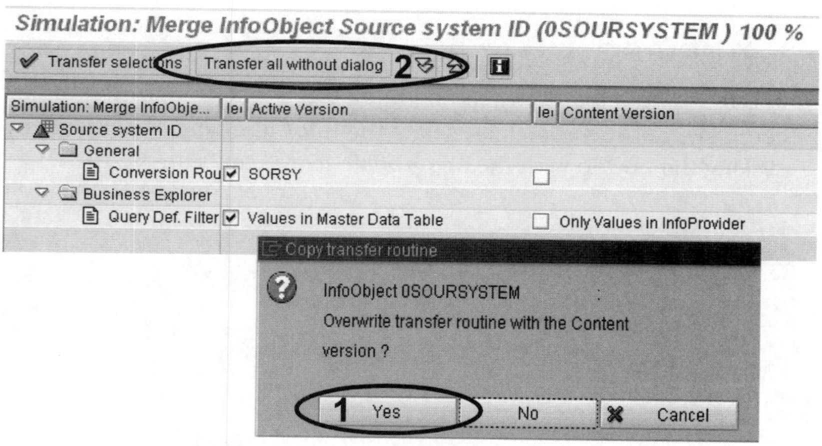

Figure 5.27 Query: Overwrite the Active Version with the SAP Business Content Version

With the initial activation of SAP Business Content in several steps, the option to overwrite the active versions without dialog (i.e., without further queries) is usually doable. However, if you've made customizing settings (and especially if productive analytical applications already exist in SAP BW), you should use this option only with great caution.

5.2.5 Simultaneous Transfer of Several SAP Business Content InfoObjects into an InfoObjectCatalog

After you've activated the InfoCubes and the related InfoObjects, you can assign several InfoObjects to an InfoObjectCatalog in one step. To do so, open an InfoObjectCatalog in the **InfoObjects** view of the **Adminis-**

trator Workbench with a double click (or use the right mouse button and select the **Modify** entry in the context menu of an InfoObjectCatalog) to edit it.

Selecting a Template

- In the **Edit InfoObjectCatalog** dialog, you can select one of the following buttons to select the type of template:
  - InfoSource
  - ODS object
  - InfoCube
  - InfoObjectCatalog
  - All InfoObjects
- In our example that transfers the InfoObjects available for the model company, CubeServ Engines, select the **InfoCube** type of template by clicking the button with the appropriate icon (see Figure 5.28).

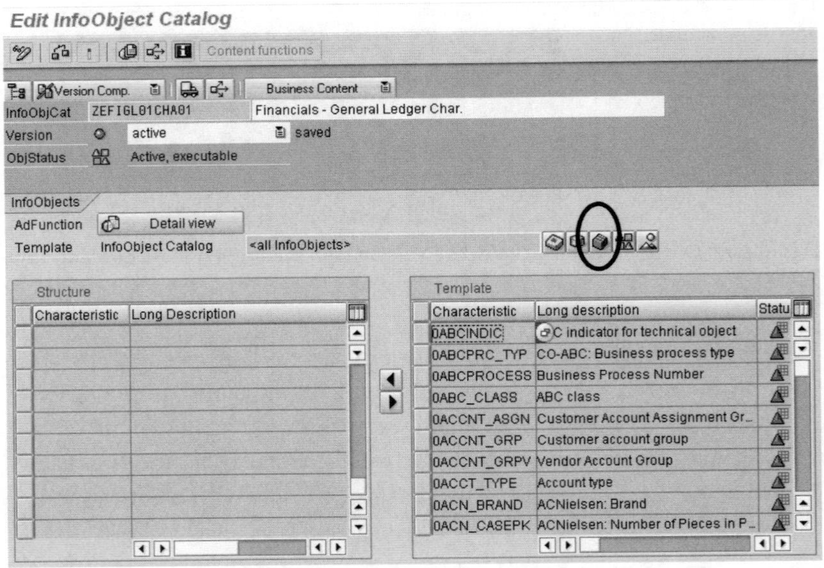

Figure 5.28 Selection of the InfoCube Type of Template to Transfer InfoObjects into the InfoObjectCatalog

- When you select the InfoCube type of template that you want, the **Select InfoCube** popup appears. Click the **All InfoCubes** button to display a list of all active InfoCubes (see Figure 5.29, Step 1).

- Double-click (or use a single click and confirm the selection with the **Next (Enter)** button) to make the InfoObjects of the selected InfoCubes available as a template (Step 2). The **Transfer Fields Automatically** popup prompts you to transfer all the InfoObjects of the corresponding catalog type (characteristics or key figures).

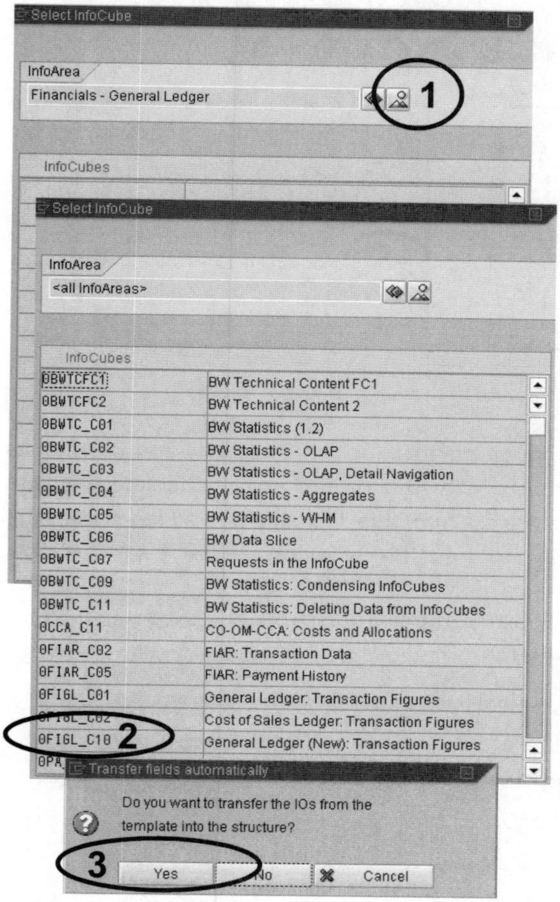

Figure 5.29 Selection of an InfoCube as a Template to Transfer InfoObjects into the InfoObjectCatalog

- Confirm this option (see Figure 5.29, Step 3) to include all the InfoObjects of the corresponding type in the InfoObjectCatalog automatically (see Figure 5.30, Step 1).
- If you don't accept this option, you can only transfer the InfoObjects in the **Edit InfoObjectCatalog** dialog into the template (Step 2).
- Then activate the InfoObjectCatalog (Step 3).

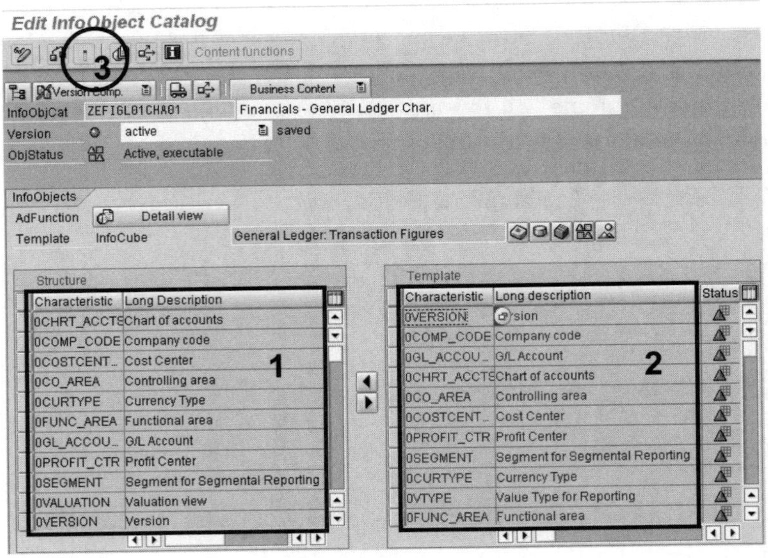

Figure 5.30 Results of the Copy and Activation of the InfoObject

Characteristics and key figures

You can proceed in the same manner for characteristics and key figures (see Figures 5.29 and 5.30). With this procedure, all characteristics are transferred into a characteristics InfoObjectCatalog and all key figures are transferred into a key figures InfoObjectCatalog. Figure 5.31 illustrates the results.

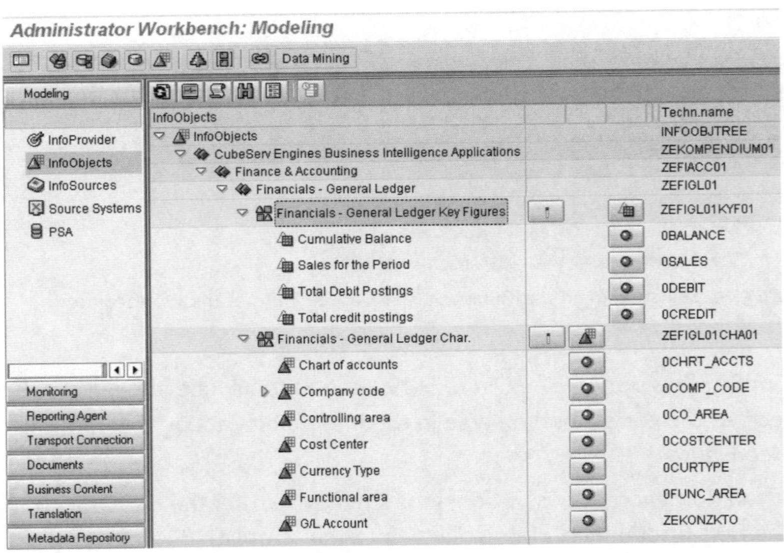

Figure 5.31 InfoObjectCatalogs for Characteristics and Key Figures

5.3 Configuration of Your Own InfoObjects Based on SAP Business Content InfoObjects

5.3.1 The Need for Configuration of Your Own InfoObjects: Example

As noted above, the InfoObjects of SAP Business Content often cover most of the requirements. However, the InfoObjects do not map all the relevant elements in majority of projects, so the need to supplement or modify SAP Business Content with your own objects arises.

Missing attribute: "Group G/L account"

The **General Ledger Account** InfoObject (0GL_ACCOUNT) is critical for financial reporting. But SAP BW does not contain attributes for this InfoObject, although the attributes are very important in the OLTP system (such as SAP R/3).

Integrated reporting on the **group G/L account** attribute should occur for our model company, CubeServ Engines (see Figure 5.32). But SAP Business Content does not contain this attribute (see Figure 5.33). Therefore, you must create your own InfoObject and insert it into the **General Ledger** InfoObject in SAP Business Content.

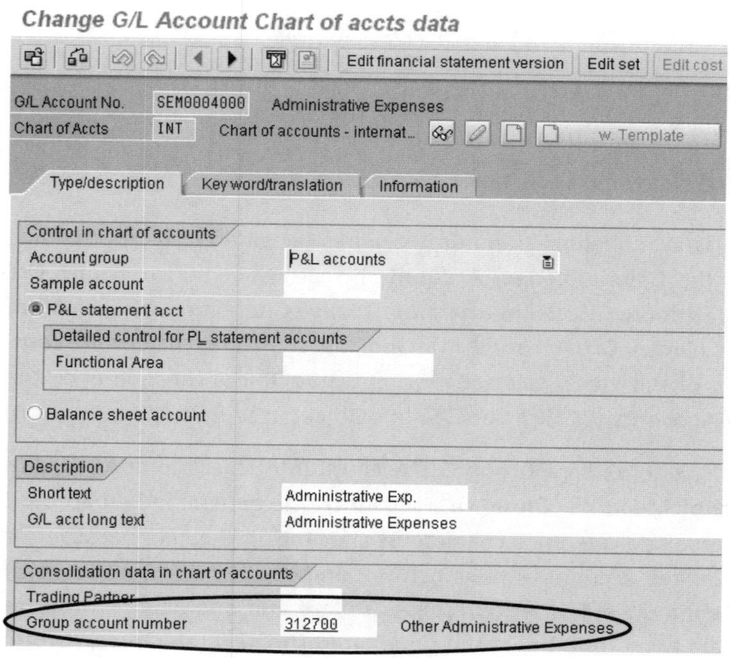

Figure 5.32 The Group G/L Account Number in SAP R/3 as an Attribute of the "General Ledger Account" InfoObject

Compounding to various chart of accounts properties

The general ledger account is then compounded to the chart of accounts (in SAP BW: InfoObject 0CHRT_ACCTS). In the example of our model company, the **Administrative Expenses** account (SAP R/3 key SEM0004000) of the **International Chart of Accounts** (SAP R/3 key INT) is assigned in SAP R/3 to the **Other Administrative Expenses** group account (SAP R/3 key 312700) (see Figure 5.32).

The menus in the OLTP system, SAP R/3, show the deviating chart of accounts for the group G/L accounts with the SAP R/3 key of CONS (see Figure 5.34, Steps 1 and 2).

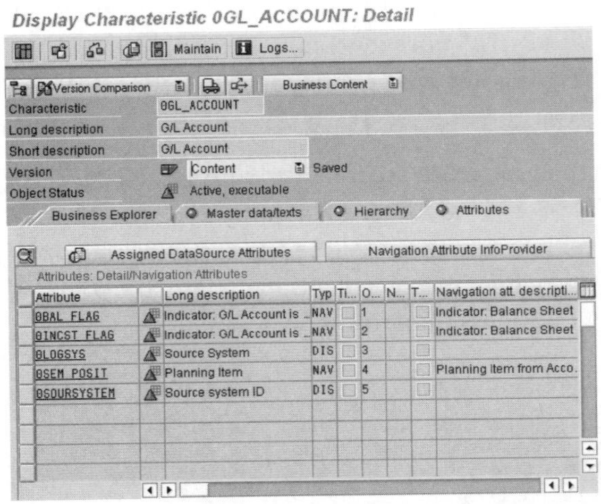

Figure 5.33 The SAP Business Content Version of the "General Ledger Account" InfoObject Does Not Contain a "Group G/L Account" Attribute

InfoObject to be defined

Correct data modeling therefore requires a different compounding between the **General Ledger Account** characteristic and the **Group G/L Account** attribute. Modeling therefore requires definition of a **Chart of Accounts (Group G/L Account)** InfoObject that enables the correct compounding of the group G/L account. This InfoObject can reference the **Chart of Accounts** (0CHRT_ACCTS) InfoObject in SAP Business Content.

You also have to define a **Group G/L Account** InfoObject compounded to the **Chart of Accounts (Group G/L Account)**. The **general ledger account** cannot serve as a reference characteristic for this InfoObject because the general ledger account InfoObject is compounded to the **Chart of Accounts** InfoObject of SAP Business Content and one data record cannot contain two properties at the same time. The new InfoObject, **Group G/L Account**, will be a navigation attribute for the **General Ledger Account** InfoObject.

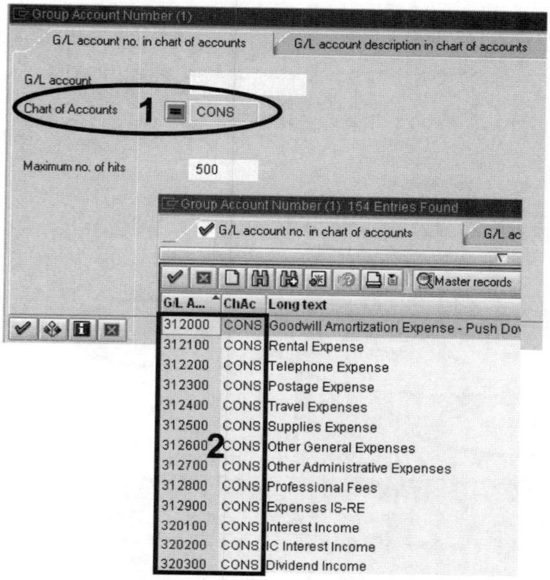

Figure 5.34 Deviating Chart of Accounts of the Group G/L Accounts

5.3.2 Creating Your Own InfoObject with Reference to an InfoObject of SAP Business Content

You can create your own InfoObjects in SAP BW (view: **Administrator Workbench**).

Creating a Referenced InfoObject

- First select the InfoObjectCatalog that you want (see Figure 5.35, Step 1).
- Right-click to open the context menu and select **Create InfoObject...** (Step 2).
- Enter the technical name of the characteristic (ZECHRTACC in the example), the description (Step 3), and the reference characteristic (Step 4) in the **Create Characteristic** popup.
- After you confirm your entry (Step 5), the screen displays information on using the attributes of the reference characteristic (as long as the reference characteristic has attributes). Confirm the information (Step 6).
- After activation of the InfoObject in the **Change Characteristic...** dialog (see Figure 5.36), the object is available for additional work.

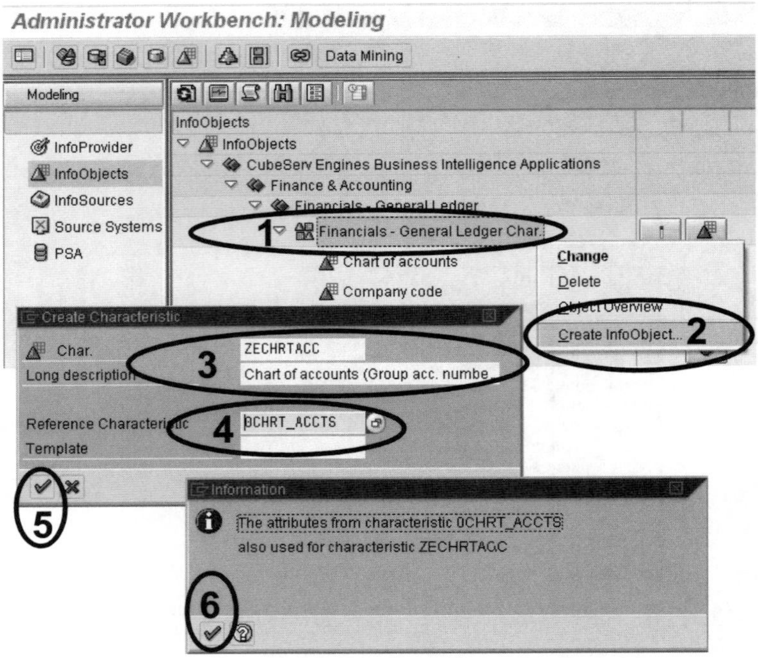

Figure 5.35 Creating Your Own InfoObject with Reference

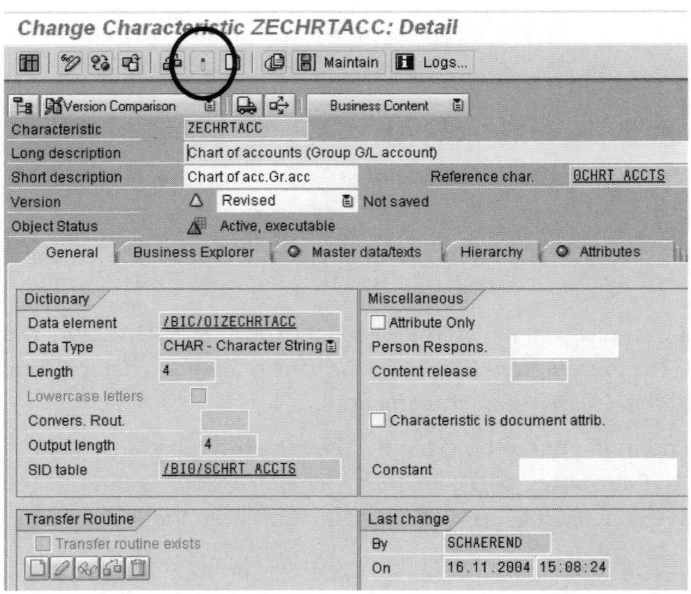

Figure 5.36 The "Chart of Accounts (Group G/L Account Number)" InfoObject

5.3.3 Creating Your Own InfoObject Based on InfoObjects of SAP Business Content with a Template

As noted, the **Group G/L Account** InfoObject cannot be created as a referenced InfoObject. But because all settings must be identical to the **General Ledger Account** InfoObject (except for compounding), this InfoObject is created with a template.

Creating an InfoObject with a Template

- The dialog for creating the InfoObject is started similarly to the description in Section 5.3.2 (see Figure 5.35, Steps 1 and 2).
- Enter the technical name and a description of the InfoArea in the **Create Characteristic** popup (see Figure 5.37, Step 1).
- Define the template InfoObject (Step 2).
- After confirmation (Step 3), the **Create Characteristic...** dialog screen is displayed.
- Because different compounding must be entered for the group G/L account, you must use the navigation menu (or the scroll function in the tabs) to access the **Compounding** tab.

Modifying the compounding

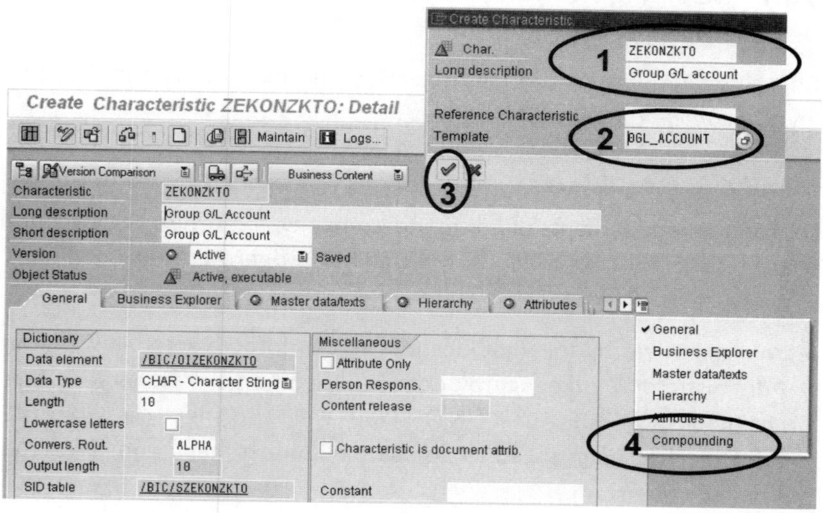

Figure 5.37 Creating an InfoObject with a Template

- Here you replace the original compounding with the **Chart of Accounts (Group G/L Account)** InfoObject (see Figure 5.38, Step 1) and activate the InfoObject (Step 2).

The object is then available for additional work.

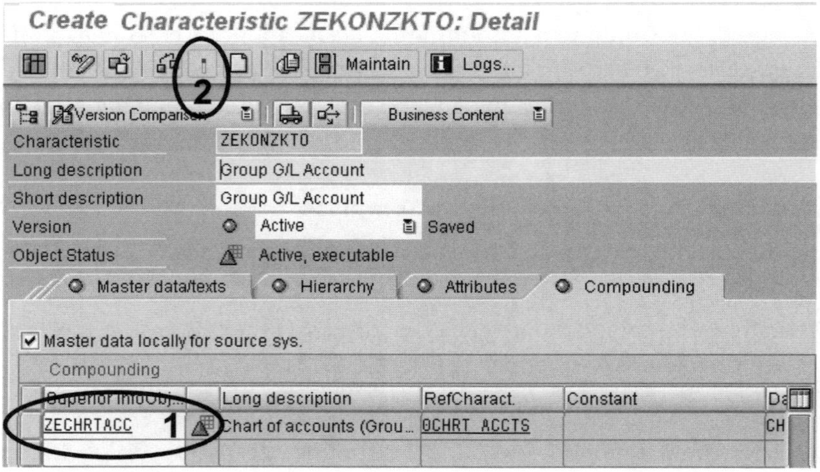

Figure 5.38 Modifying the Compounding

5.4 Modifying SAP Business Content InfoObjects

5.4.1 Inserting Attributes into SAP Business Content InfoObjects

Changing SAP Business Content objects is a normal activity and does not involve a *modification* as SAP defines it.

Modifying InfoObjects

To map the requirements of our model company, the **Group G/L Account** characteristic must be added to the **General Ledger Account** InfoObject as a navigation attribute.

- You can perform the modification in the **InfoObjects** view of the Administrator Workbench by double-clicking on the **General Ledger** characteristic (0GL_ACCOUNT). (You can also right-click on the InfoObject to be changed to display the context menu and select the **Change** entry.)

Inserting an attribute

- Navigate to the **Attributes** tab in the **Change Characteristic...** dialog (see Figure 5.39).
- There you can supplement the definition of the InfoObject as an attribute (Step 2). You can make the entry manually by specifying the technical name or use SAP menus.

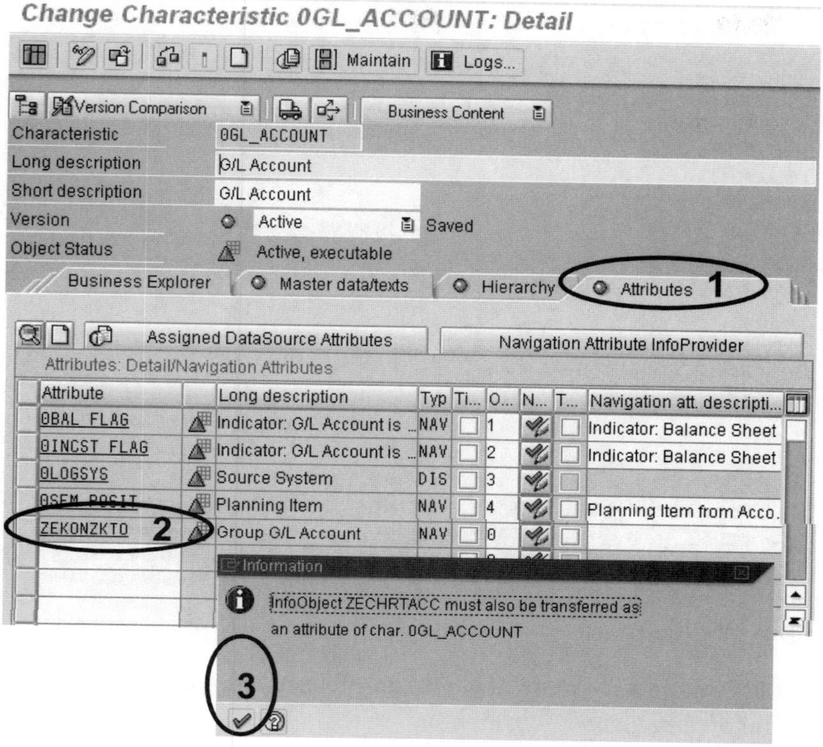

Figure 5.39 Inserting Attributes in the Change InfoObject Screen

System behavior with compounded attributes

In our example, the characteristic to be inserted is compounded to the **Chart of Accounts (Group G/L Account)** as a characteristic. When attributes are themselves compounded characteristics, SAP BW expects the compounded characteristic to be contained in the compounding of the InfoObject, or to be an attribute itself.

If neither case is true, the compounded characteristic is automatically converted into an attribute. This system behavior is reflected in our example, which is why you are alerted of this situation by the **Information** popup.

- After you have confirmed the information (see Figure 5.39, Step 3), the screen displays the **Group G/L Account Number** as a usable attribute of the **General Ledger Account** characteristic (see Figure 5.40, Step 1).

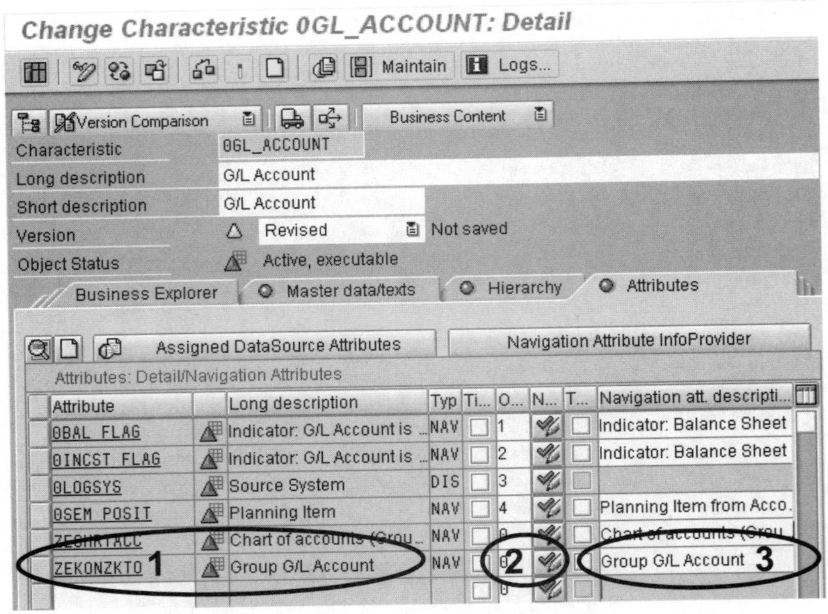

Figure 5.40 Activating the Group G/L Account Number as a Navigation Attribute

Switching on a navigation attribute

- Click on the **Navigation attribute on/off** button to turn this feature on and off (see Figure 5.40, Step 2).
- Then, enter the description of the Navigation attribute (Step 3), or click on the **Texts of Characteristic** column header to copy the description of the characteristic as the description of the navigation attribute.

We generally recommend an unambiguous description of navigation attributes because many of them occur in various InfoObjects. If you use only the description of the characteristic, you make it difficult to employ such navigation attributes in reporting. The **country key** InfoObject (0COUNTRY) is a navigation attribute for the **sold-to** characteristic (0SOLD_TO) and a navigation attribute for the **ship-to** characteristic (0SHIP_TO) with the same description. In reporting, you cannot tell which navigation attribute is involved because both have the same description.

Activating the Modified InfoObject

- When you click on the **Activate** button (see Figure 5.41, Step 1), the screen displays a **Log** popup that contains information on the navigation attributes that have been turned on (Step 2). You must confirm the information (Step 3).

- When you confirm the final **Save** popup (Step 4), the activation procedure is complete and the characteristic that has been enhanced with the navigation attribute is available for further use.

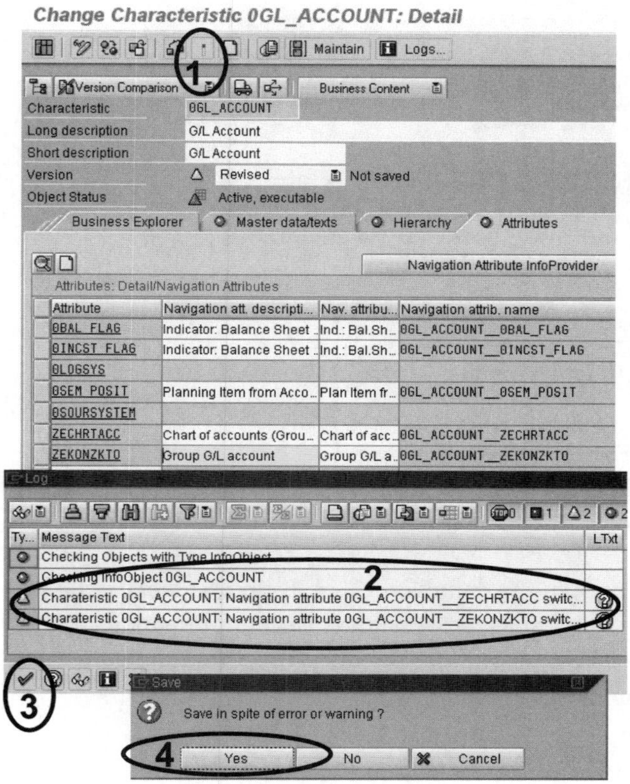

Figure 5.41 Activating the Modified InfoObject

5.4.2 Modifying the Properties of SAP Business Content InfoObjects

The properties of SAP Business Content InfoObjects should be scrutinized systematically and critically in terms of end user requirements and adjusted as necessary. This level of scrutiny applies to the properties of both key figures and characteristics.

Presentation and display of decimal places

SAP has not defined the presentation of key figures (such as amount key figures) in Business Explorer (see Figure 5.42). Therefore, key figures appear in reporting with the maximum number of decimal paces (two for most currencies). Legibility therefore suffers with key figures in the amount of millions or even billions.

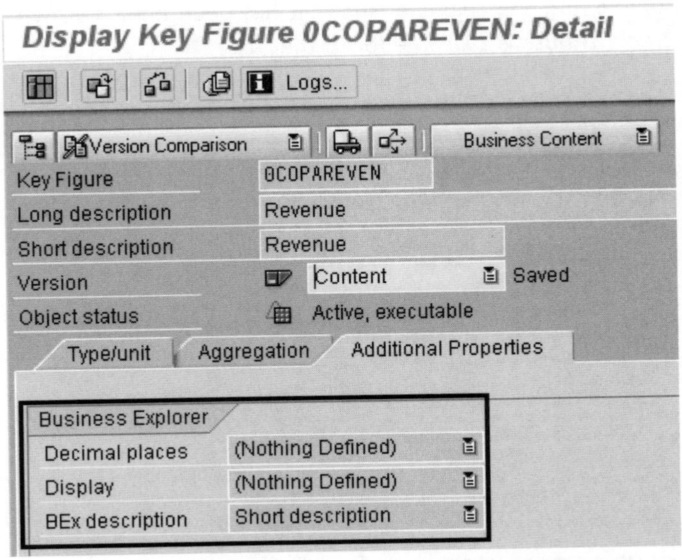

Figure 5.42 SAP Business Content Key Figures Without Definitions for Presentation and Decimal Places

If no setting is made in the definition of key figures, a direct setting is often made in queries to provide the desired presentation. This approach requires a significant maintenance effort that should not be underestimated.

Modifying the Presentation of Key Figures

For these reasons, it is often helpful to make explicit settings for the presentation of decimal places when maintaining key figures in the SAP BW Administrator Workbench. Our model company, CubeServ Engines, wants *Presentation in 1* without decimal places.

- To make this setting, start with the modification of InfoObjects.
- Make the desired settings in the **Change Key Figure...** dialog (see Figure 5.43, Step 1).
- Then activate the InfoObject (Step 2).

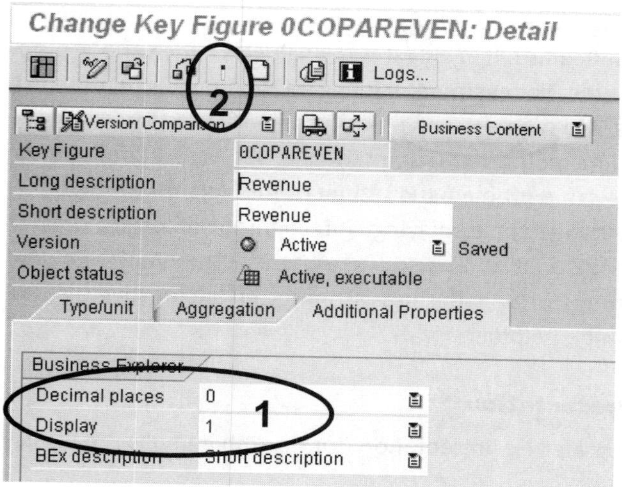

Figure 5.43 Changing the Presentation and the Display of Decimal Places

Coded presentation and impermissible summation

In some cases, you may also have to change the settings of SAP Business Content for characteristics. The default presentation setting of the **Value Type for Reporting** (0VTYPE) characteristic is a **key** (see Figure 5.44, Step 1). This setting means that a user sees only the technical key (010 and 020, for example) when drilling down, which makes the data difficult to interpret.

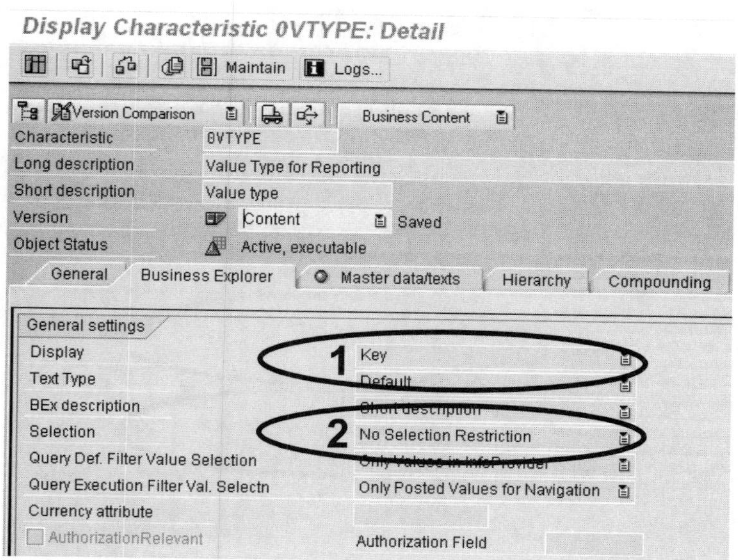

Figure 5.44 Coded Presentation and Impermissible Summation for the "Value Type for Reporting" Characteristic

The selection setting **No Selection Restriction** (see Figure 5.44, Step 2) poses even more difficulties. It aggregates the values for the various properties of the value type. For example, this aggregation means that the values for actual data and plan data of all keyfigures—figures for which the standard aggregation method of **summation** is set—are added. When combined with the same problematic setting of the **Version** (0VERSION) characteristic, the danger of displaying unrecognized incorrect data to Business Explorer (BEx) users exists. Therefore, we generally find that modifying the settings of SAP Business Content characteristics 0VTYPE and 0VERSION can be helpful.

User-Friendly Presentation

For end users, the preferred presentation (for no ambiguity) is the display of the texts.

Avoiding an impermissible summation

- We therefore recommend that you change the **Display** setting for the characteristics noted above to **Text** (see Figure 5.45, Step 1).
- To avoid the likelihood of incorrect information, we recommend that you change the setting for **Selection** to **Unique for Every Cell** (Step 2).
- Then activate the InfoObject (Step 3).

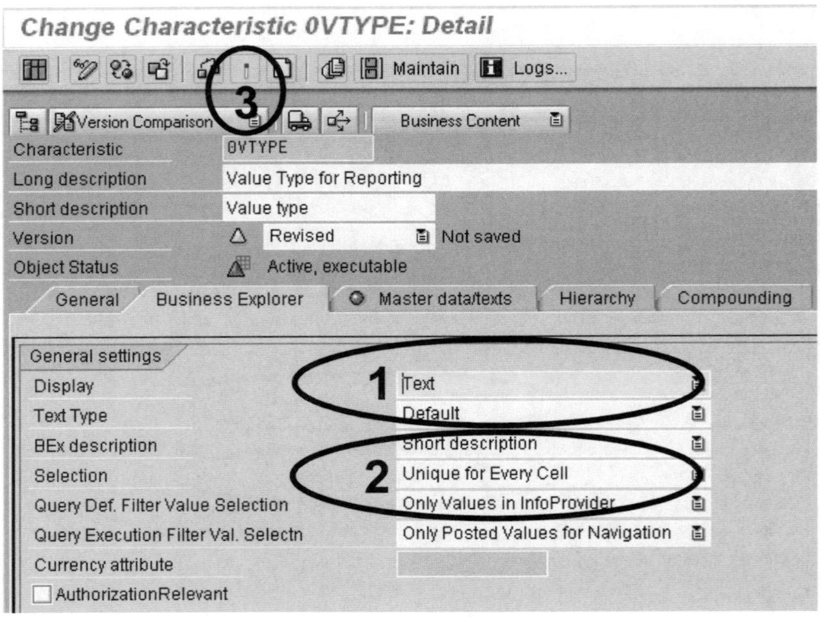

Figure 5.45 Correction of SAP Business Content Settings

5.4.3 Source System Compounding

The problem of mismatched master data

When the ETL process stores data from upstream systems (usually OLTP systems) in a data warehouse, the data must be delivered in a non-ambiguous state (harmonized), or edited in the context of the transformation process.

Non-ambiguous in this context means that the same key values have the same meaning and that the different key values also have different meanings. As soon as data from various source systems is delivered to a data warehouse, this state does not usually exist. For example, it can contain different vendor numbers for the same vendor and various upstream systems might use one key value for various vendors.

Source system compounding

The traditional approach to converting keys in the transformation process is generally not optimal because it is reactive and demands a great deal of effort. In SAP BW, SAP and other data warehouse tools allow you to transform data with source system compounding and an additional proactive way in which to handle non-harmonized key values. With the latter approach, you can compound all characteristics with non-ambiguous keys to a **source system ID** (0SOURSYSTEM) provided by SAP. Doing so provides non-ambiguity by supplementing the leading key field **source system ID** for all key values.

Grouping source systems

The **source system ID** is assigned to the **source system** characteristic (0LOGSYS), which enables you to group various source systems. For example, systems OLTP 1A and OLTP 1B contain harmonized data but are not harmonized with systems OLTP 2A and OLTP 2B. The data of the latter two systems is harmonized.

You can use the **source system ID** to summarize systems 1A and 1B (**source system ID O1**, for example). The same applies to systems 2A and 2B (**source system ID O2**, for example).

One of the key values delivered by each source system group (4711 in the example) is therefore sufficiently qualified by the leading key **source system ID** (O1 or O2). At the same time, the master data is not stored in parallel for the four source systems, but is stored once in SAP BW for each source system group.

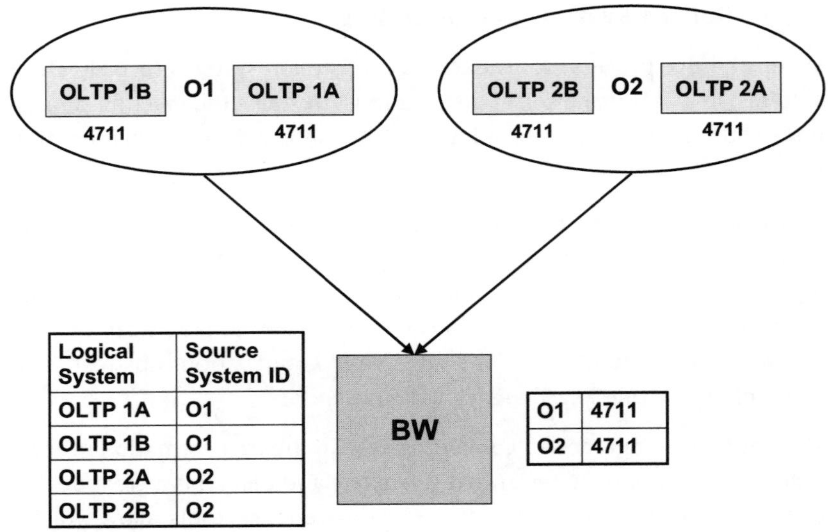

Figure 5.46 Source System and Source System ID

Source system and report-to-report interface

As of SAP BW 3.x, the report-to-report interface (RRI) and Drag&Relate functionality of SAP Enterprise Portal make additional demands on the source system logic. To ensure that you can check the source system with the RRI, the characteristic **source system** (0LOGSYS) attribute should contain all the characteristics that can be traced in the original system with the RRI.

Setting Up Source System Compounding

You can change the source system compounding in the **Change Characteristic...** dialog.

- Navigate to the **Compounding** tab (see Figure 5.47, Step 1).
- Select the option **Master Data Locally for Source System** (Step 2).
- The 0SOURSYSTEM characteristic is transferred as a superordinate (compounded) characteristic (Step 3).

Automatic consistency check

Depending on the scope of the activated and used SAP Business Content, recording the source system compounding can require some follow-up work:

- As part of activation, the modified InfoObjects are checked (see Figure 5.47, Steps 4 and 5).

- If the activity results in an inconsistency of customizing, the **Log** displays the inconsistency (see Figure 5.48). You must resolve any inconsistencies before activation.
- After you have resolved the inconsistencies (in this case, recording characteristic 0SOURSYSTEM in the communications structures and the resulting follow-up activities), you can activate the InfoObject with source system compounding.

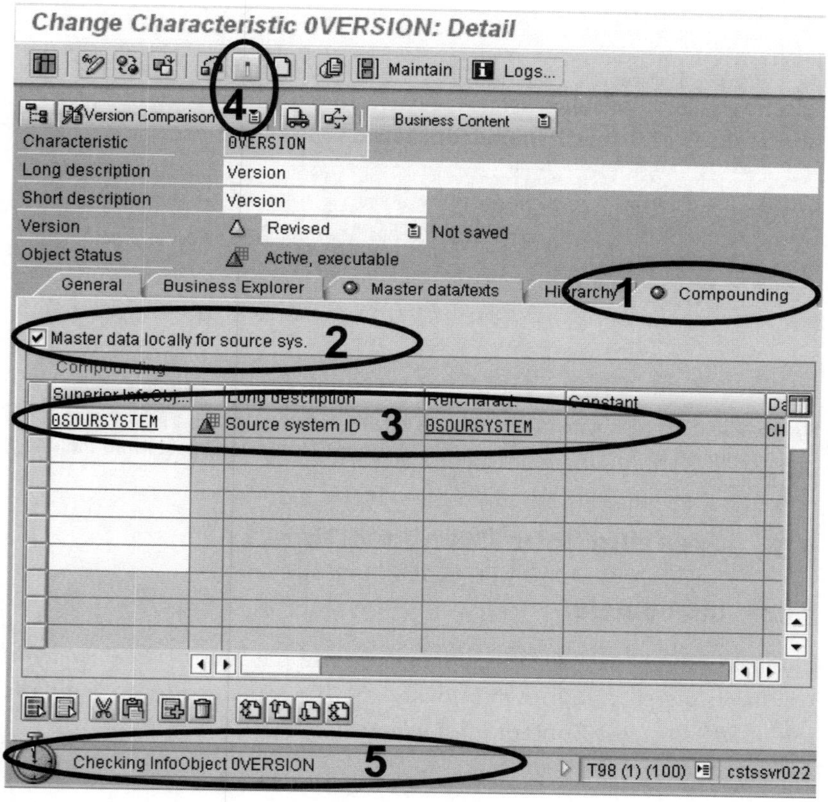

Figure 5.47 Setting Up Source System Compounding

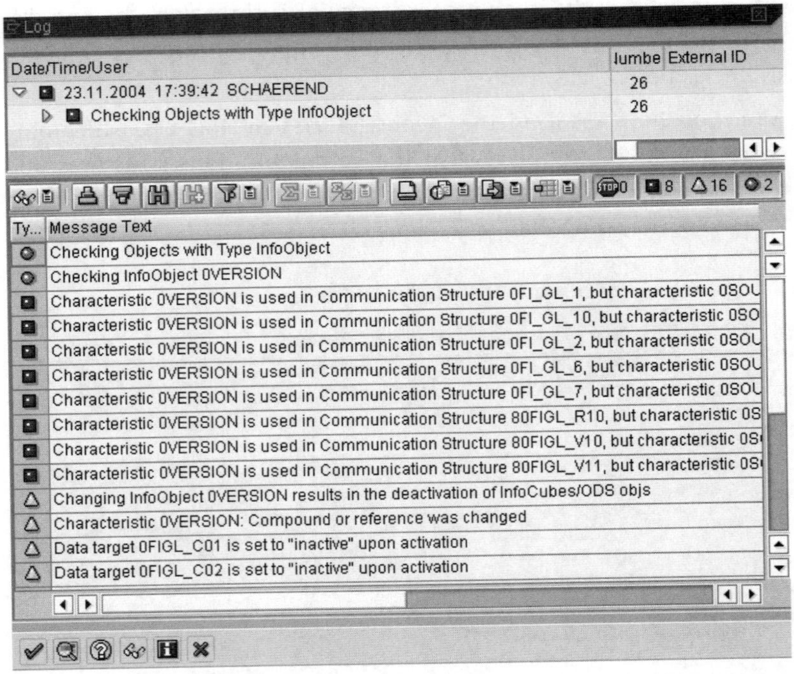

Figure 5.48 Source System Compounding Results in Inconsistencies in SAP BW Customizing. You Must Resolve the Inconsistencies Before You Can Activate the InfoObject.

5.5 Creating Your Own InfoObjects

5.5.1 Introduction

In most of the implementations of analytical applications in SAP BW, you will have to create your own InfoObjects. The same applies to the basic use of SAP Business Content InfoObjects.

The need to create your own InfoObjects is also required in the following cases:

- When SAP Business Content contains information from upstream systems (and SAP R/3).
- When you need company-specific information objects for which no supplier provides business content.
- When business content is present, but cannot be used because of problems in the upstream systems or, the modeling of the business content itself is insufficient. See the next section for a description of such a case.

5.5.2 Creation of an InfoObject—"Characteristic" Type: The Harmonized Version

Data fields to differentiate plan-actual

The differentiation of the various plan and actual data occurs in transaction data tables of SAP R/3-based upstream systems with the **version** and **value type** fields (also sometimes known as **plan-actual ID**). As long as they are contained in SAP R/3 tables (which is certainly not always the case for all application components in the same manner), these fields are made available in the various DataSources for transfer into SAP BW and are stored there in the InfoObjects **version** (0VERSION) and **value type** (0VTYPE).

Non-harmonized version of actual data from the upstream system

However, problems can develop with the use of these SAP Business Content objects and the data that belongs to them. Although actual data of version **001** was copied from the *financial accounting (general ledger)* application component, the actual data from the *controlling* application *(overhead cost management/cost center accounting)* application component is identified as version **000**. The actual data from the *controlling (profitability analysis)* application component is identified as version " " (blank).

Consequences and problems

If you now create a MultiProvider that makes all the data of these application components available for reporting, the intersection for actual data is empty (blank). To further complicate matters, various SAP R/3 application components (human resources and sales & distribution, for example) do not deliver the InfoObjects **version** and **value type** via DataSources, and the SAP Business Content InfoProviders of the application components either do not contain these InfoObjects or only partially contain them.

Variation 1: Recoding (Not Recommended)

One approach to dealing with the problem is to recode the data, which we do not recommend.[3]

Variation 2: Creating Your Own InfoObjects

The need therefore arises to create your own InfoObject that—regardless of the source—contains uniform coding of actual and plan data in terms of the source system and source system components. For the SAP BW solution of the model company, CubeServ Engines, we therefore need to create a characteristic: ZEVERSION.

---

3 See the related sections of Volumes 2 and 3 of the SAP BW Library: Volume 2: Egger et al.: *SAP BW Data Retrieval*, SAP PRESS, 2005. Volume 3: Egger et al.: *SAP BW Reporting and Analysis*, SAP PRESS, 2005.

Creating an InfoObject

You can begin the creation of your own InfoObject in the **InfoObjects** view of the Administrator Workbench.

- First select the desired InfoObjectCatalog (see Figure 5.49, Step 1).
- Right-click to open the context menu and select the **Create InfoObject...** entry (Step 2).
- Enter the desired technical name and the description of the InfoObject in the **Create Characteristic** popup (Step 3).
- After confirmation of the entry (Step 4), the **Create Characteristic...** dialog screen is displayed.

Text, type, and length

- You must make at least the following entries:
  - The short description. If you do not enter one, the long text is copied and abbreviated automatically (see Figure 5.50, Step 1).
  - The **Data Type** (here CHAR) in the **General** tab (Step 2).
  - The **Length** of the key value (here 10 characters) (Step 3).

Lowercase letters

- If the key value must contain uppercase and lowercase letters, activate the **Lowercase Letters** flag (Step 4). If you don't set the flag, all values entered via a screen template will automatically be converted to uppercase letters.

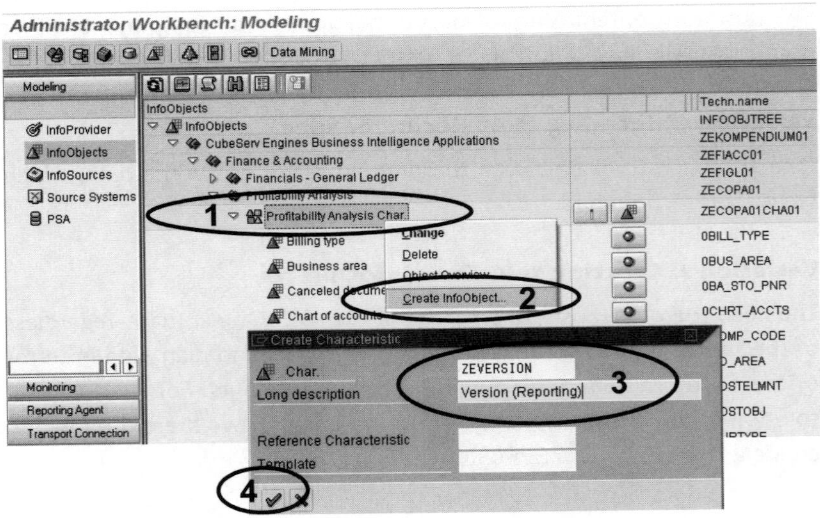

Figure 5.49 Creating Your Own InfoObject—"Characteristic" Type

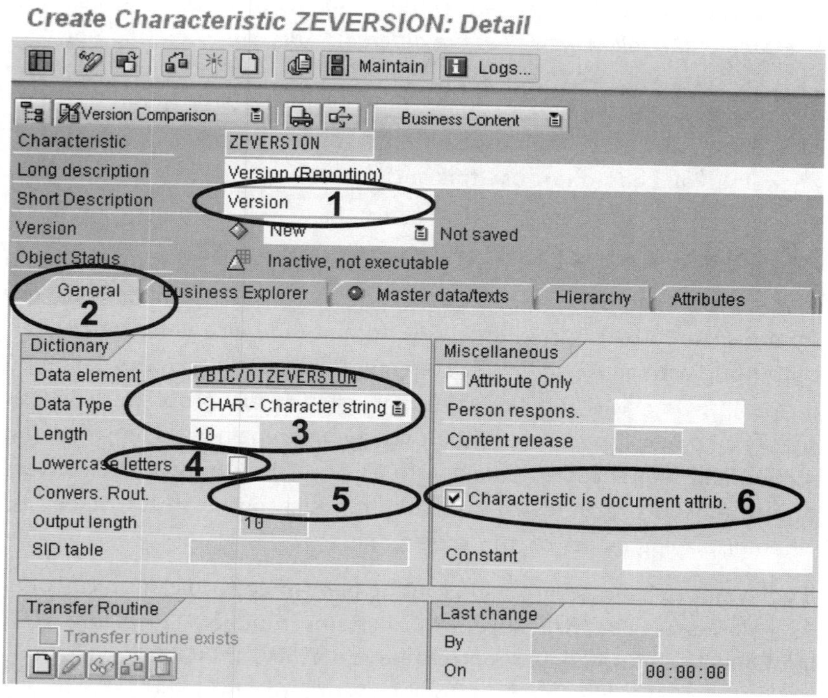

Figure 5.50 Definition of the General Settings of the Characteristic

The problem with lowercase letters

The activation of **Lowercase Letters** is somewhat difficult. The problem becomes clear in the warning displayed when the flag is set and the InfoObject is to be activated (see Figure 5.51).

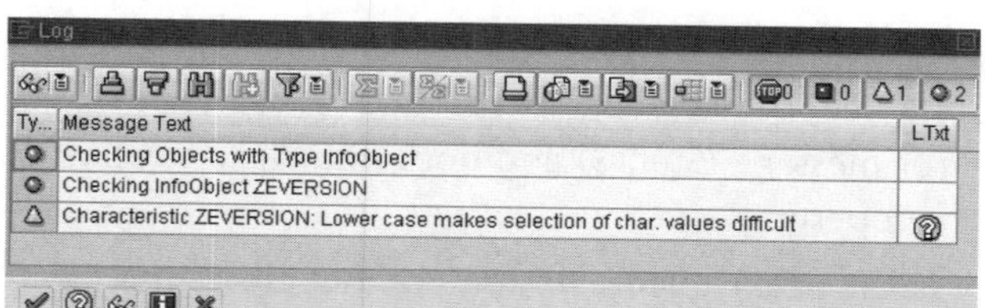

Figure 5.51 Warning When Activating an InfoObject with the "Lowercase Letters Allowed" Setting

The long text of the warning explains the problem:

> *Lowercase letters are permitted for the values of the characteristic ... The characteristic ... is not an exclusive attribute. In other words, it can be used in InfoCubes, ODS objects, and as a navigation attribute. It can also be used to select data on the values of the characteristic with the help of variables. ... The values of the characteristic are found only when upper-*

case and lowercase letters are entered exactly in the entry screen. For example, the following values are different: ABC, aBC, Abc, and AbC.[4]

> Use this setting only when the various characters (as noted above: ABC, aBC, and so on) are used to differentiate various key values. **In general, you should not use this setting.**

InfoObject—General Settings: Conversion Routine

A conversion can occur when converting the content of a screen field from display format into internal SAP format (and vice versa) and when outputting with an ABAP WRITE statement—depending on the data type of the InfoObject. If the standard conversion is inappropriate, you can specify a conversion routine in the underlying domain to use instead. If a screen field references a domain with a conversion routine, the conversion routine is executed automatically for each entry on the screen or when displaying values on this screen field.

Suggested conversion routines

If you want to have a conversion routine performed, you can specify one. As a standard value, SAP suggests conversion routine ALPHA for CHAR InfoObjects and no conversion routine for NUMC InfoObjects. No conversion routine is possible for InfoObjects of type DATS and TIMS.

Example: ALPHA conversion

The following example shows the difference between characteristics with ALPHA conversion and characteristics without conversion:

- Figure 5.52, Step 1, illustrates the display of data in master data maintenance. The characteristic property 2 was created with a leading zero (as 02). But master data maintenance shows it left-aligned.
- If you now create a new characteristic property 01 (Step 2), SAP BW reacts with an error message (Step 3) and does not allow creation of this characteristic property.
- The table display of the data explains why you cannot create this property: ALPHA conversion stores both numeric characteristic properties as right-aligned and fills them with leading zeros (Step 4). That makes characteristic properties 1 and 01 identical and therefore not permitted.

4 SAP BW Message No. R7424.

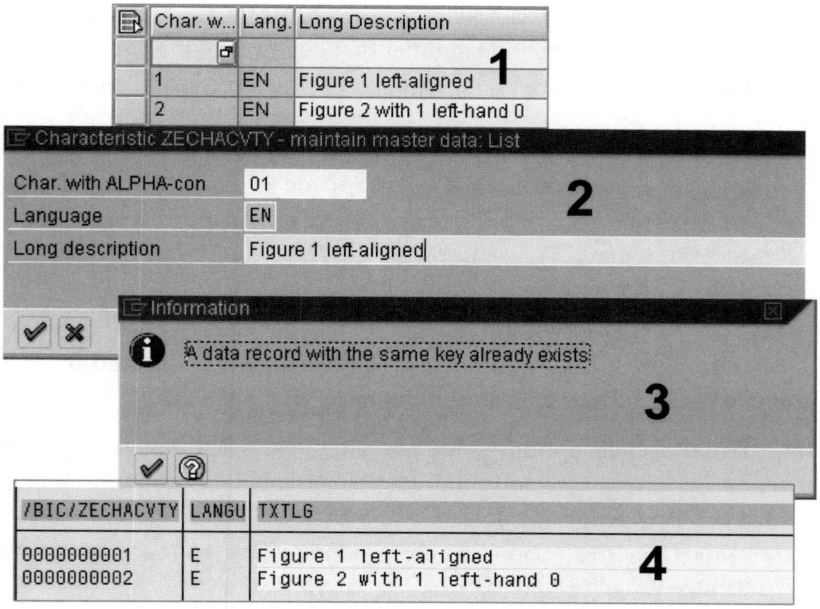

Figure 5.52 Characteristic with ALPHA Conversion

Example: without conversion routine

But the characteristic without a conversion routine differs:

- ▶ Characteristic properties 1 and 01 can be created and are visible in master data maintenance as created (see Figure 5.53, Step 1).
- ▶ The table display shows how the data is stored (Step 2).

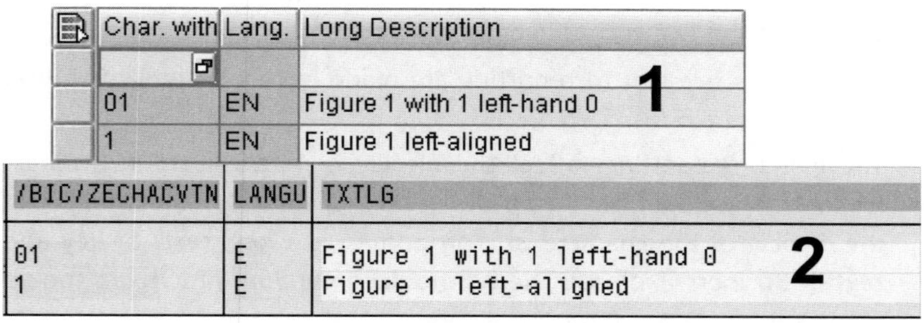

Char. with | Lang. | Long Description
01 | EN | Figure 1 with 1 left-hand 0
1 | EN | Figure 1 left-aligned
1
/BIC/ZECHACVTN | LANGU | TXTLG
01 | E | Figure 1 with 1 left-hand 0
1 | E | Figure 1 left-aligned
2

Figure 5.53 Characteristic Without Conversion Routine

Consequently, the intended use forces or forbids the use of conversion routines: The **customer number** must be stored only with the correct number of places, right-aligned, and with leading zeros so that it can be sorted correctly—with ALPHA conversion); the **telephone number** characteristic must be stored with an exact number of leading zeros.

Consider the following example. The existence of a German area code (04101) and a Swiss telephone number that begins with the country code (004101) forbid any conversion, as long as the country code must begin with 00.

> Review your requirements for the conversion of key fields and copy only the standard settings: conversion routine ALPHA for InfoObjects of the CHAR type.

Depending on the conversion requirements, you must remove, enter, or select a conversion routine from the list (see Figure 5.50, Step 5). The example uses the **harmonized version** of our model company.

Creating an InfoObject: Characteristic is only an attribute

The **Attribute Only** option is not relevant for the **harmonized version** characteristic. This characteristic should be available for proper presentation of the data types in InfoCubes as a basic characteristic for analysis and planning. For this reason, the corresponding flag is not activated (see the default setting in Figure 5.50).

Creating an InfoObject: Characteristic is Document Attribute

However, the **Characteristic is Document Attribute** characteristic is relevant. You must activate this option because the meaning of the various version and the value type characteristics, the meaning of the individual properties of the harmonized version, and the meaning of the transaction data must be commented on.

- Simply set the flag accordingly (see Figure 5.50, Step 6).
- The settings relevant to reporting are made in the **Business Explorer** tab (see Figure 5.54, Step 1).

Display

- The first three settings affect the display of InfoObjects in Business Explorer. The uppermost drop-down box, **Display**, enables you to set the display of the characteristic properties as a **key**, **text**, or **key and text** in Business Explorer. The **harmonized version** InfoObject should be presented as text (Step 2).

Text Type

- The next drop-down box, **Text Type**, determines the type of text to be displayed for the characteristic properties, depending on the selected display. For example, if you select **Text** as the display, you can display the long text by selecting it in the drop-down box (Step 2).

"Default" setting

Select **Default** to have a variable display. If you selected **Key and Text** or **Text and Key** with the **default** text type, the shortest available text is used. If you selected **Text with the default text type**, the longest available text is used.

The long texts are to be output for the characteristic properties of the **harmonized version**. Accordingly, set the text type to long text in this drop-down box (Step 2).

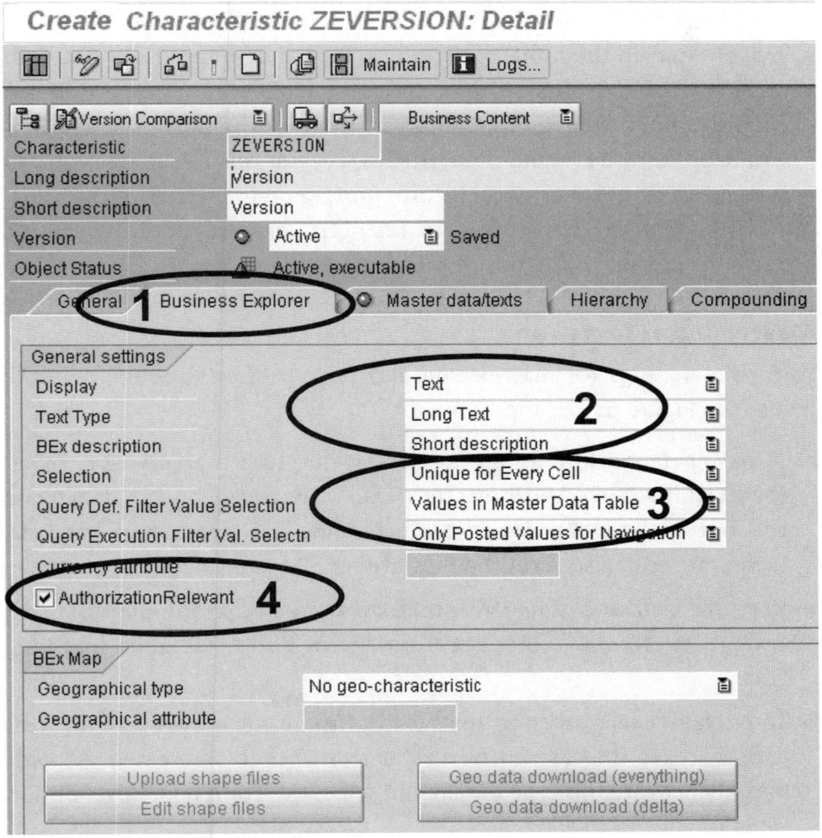

Figure 5.54 Reporting-Relevant Settings in the InfoObject

- **BEx Description** You can describe the InfoObject with a short or long text in Business Explorer. Make the setting in the **Description** drop-down box in **BEx**. In our example, select **Short Description** (See Figure 5.54, Step 2).
- **Selection** Similar to the procedure with the **value type** InfoObject (see Figure 5.44 and the related comments), aggregation over the various properties of the version does not make sense and should be prevented even when defining the InfoObject. To do so, select **Unique for Every Cell** in the drop-down box with the same name (Figure 5.54,Step 3).

Filter selection

- Set the behavior of the system in regard to the selection of characteristic properties in **query definition** or **query execution** in the corresponding drop-down boxes: **Query Def. Filter Value Selection** and **Query Execution Filter Val. Selectn.**

  In our example, all the existing properties in the master data table are to be permitted for query definition, but only the actual values posted for navigation should be allowed for query execution (Step 3).

Authorization Relevant

- Not all users in the model company will be allowed to use the various versions. You must therefore create preconditions to set up the appropriate authorization control. To do so, activate the **Authorization Relevant** option (see Figure 5.54, Step 4). When this flag is set, you can generate authorization objects for reporting on the related characteristic. This feature enables you to restrict query execution to specific users for certain properties of this characteristic.

Master Data/Texts Tab

You make settings for master data and texts in the tab with the same name (see Figure 5.55, Step 1).

- If master data attributes are to be assigned to a characteristic, retain the default setting, **With master data.** Otherwise, you can deactivate this option (Step 2). Deactivation reduces the number of database tables. You can also reset the flag later on, which is helpful.
- Keep the default setting **With texts** to keep an option open to assign texts (Step 3). You can select from among short, medium, and long texts.
- The default value for short texts is insufficient for the **version** InfoObject, as is also the case for other characteristics to be created. Accordingly, deactivate this type of text and select the **Long text exists** option (Step 4).
- Texts in each logon language are also required. Accordingly, keep the **Texts language dependent** option as is (Step 5).

Authorization check for master data maintenance

- When you set the **MstDataMaint with Authorization** flag (Step 6), you can use authorization to protect maintenance of master data and texts for the corresponding characteristic at the level of the individual record.

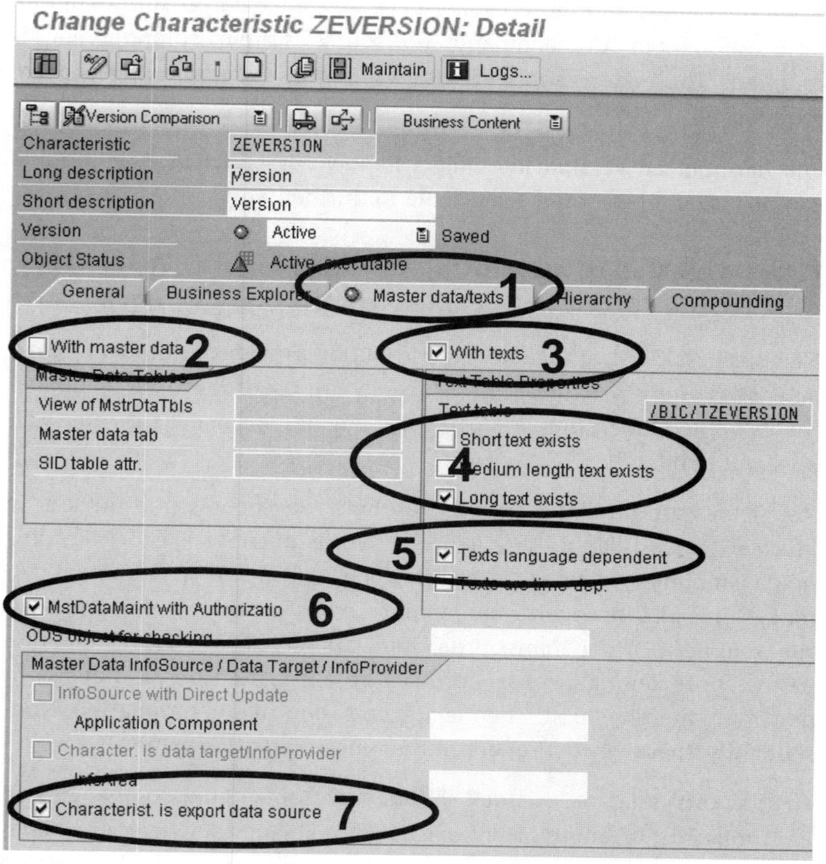

Figure 5.55 Definition of the Settings for Master Data and Texts

If this option is activated, you can use the profile generator (Transaction PFCG) and authorization object S_TABU_LIN to enter characteristics values for each key field of the master data table for which the user has authorization. If the flag is not set, you can only enable or forbid master data maintenance in general for all characteristic values.

Export DataSource

- In some cases, you should copy data from one SAP BW system to another system, or redirect characteristics and InfoProviders within an SAP BW system. To permit these actions, activate the **Characterist. is export data source** option (Step 7).

Setting the Hierarchy and Compounding Tabs

The **reporting version** characteristic does not require any hierarchies, therefore, do not change the default settings in the **Hierarchy** tab.

Compounding is also unnecessary. Because the characteristic should be used throughout the company, no source system compounding is required. For that reason, no settings in the **Compounding** tab are required.

The **harmonized version** InfoObject is now completely configured and can be activated so that it is available for further work.

5.5.3 Creation of an InfoObject—"Key Figure" Type: Sales Order Stock in Document and Group Currency

SAP Business Content for Sales & Distribution provides a number of characteristics and key figures. These objects are used to map the requirements of the model company, CubeServ Engines, insofar as they are available and usable.

Cumulative values

Key figures are provided, including counter key figures (the number of invoice items), quantity key figures (invoice quantity in stock keeping units), amount key figures (net value of the invoice item in document currency). This feature covers requirements to analyze the number and average volume of order items, order item quantities, and values of order items. These key figures can normally be aggregated on all dimensions (including the time axis): The main aggregation rule is **summation**. Consequently, these key figures are of the type **cumulative value**.

Inventory values

The value of sales order stock should serve our model company as an early indicator of future revenue. CubeServ Engines defines these values as the sum of incoming orders minus the sum of invoices. Analysis should occur in the company code and group currency.

Excursus: Peculiarities of Inventory Values

In terms of the time axis, inventory values behave differently than do cumulative values. First, inventories cannot be totaled like cumulative values along the time axis. Over a series of points in time (x-1, x, and x+1 to x+n), the value at point x+n represents the current inventory, which can be determined at any point in time as the difference from a previous point in time: increased by goods received and decreased by goods issued. Secondly, the inventory at point x without actual values (inventory changes) does not have to be 0 (as is the case with cumulative values). It is equal to the inventory at the previous point in time (see Figure 5.56).

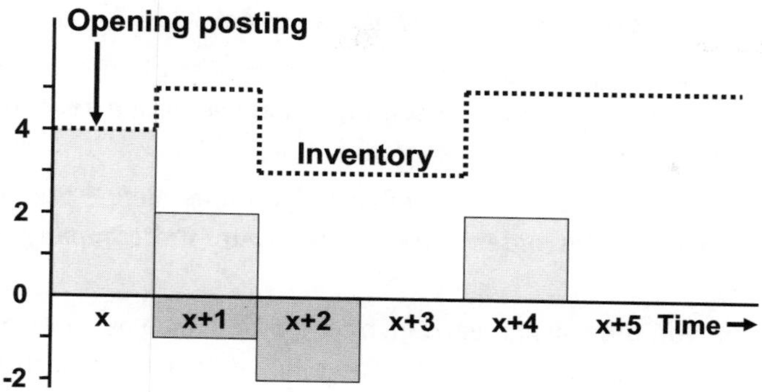

Acquisition	4	2	0	0	2	0
Retirement	0	1	2	0	0	0

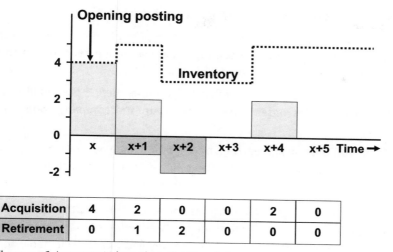

Figure 5.56 Inventory Values Along the Time Axis

Dedicated inventory key figures in SAP BW

SAP Business Information Warehouse offers an outstanding option to configure dedicated inventory key figures that completely correspond to the requirements of inventory management.

The basis for determining the sales order stock is formed by the SAP Business Content key figure **Net value of the order item in document currency** (0NET_VALUE) and the new value of the invoice item in the document currency (0NETVAL_INV). The cumulative values make available the amount of inventory increases (net value of the order item) and decreases (net value of the invoice item). Note that these key figures are present in the document currency (0DOC_CURRCY), according to their origin in SAP R/3 document tables).

Reporting in the company code and group currency

However, reporting should (also) occur for incoming orders and revenues and thus for sales stock in the company code currency and the group currency. In principle, this reporting can occur based on a currency conversion during query execution or by using currency conversion during the update. This case uses currency conversion during the update.

Customer-specific InfoObjects

Because SAP Business Content does not provide any objects here, you must implement customer-specific InfoObjects of the **key figure** type for inventory changes and for sales order stock with an appropriate currency key. The number of InfoObjects to be defined depends on the selected approach to data modeling.

Variation 1: Column-oriented data model

- If you select the column or key figure-oriented approach, you must define both key figures (**incoming order value** and **revenue**) in the company code and group currency.
- In addition to these four key figures, you must define two additional key figures: **sales order stock in the group** and **company code currency**.
- Then, you must assign each incoming order value as an incoming key figure (and the revenue as an outgoing key figure) to each inventory key figure of the corresponding currency.

Thus, you must define six key figures for a column-oriented approach. This approach is not optimal from the viewpoint of data modeling, because it doubles the number of physical key figures in the fact table and can produce numerous empty cells.[5] The following does not address this approach.

Variation 2: Account-Oriented Data Model

- If you choose the account-oriented approach, you must define an amount key figure of the **cumulative value** type that stores the value of the incoming order and revenues.
- The differentiation of the values in terms of the document type occurs based on a qualifying characteristic (Transaction type 0REC_TYPE).
- The differentiation of the currency (company code and group currency) occurs based on another qualifying characteristic (Currency type 0CURTYPE).
- A neutral currency InfoObject (InfoObject 0CURRENCY) is assigned.
- Finally, you must define an inventory key figure that is assigned to the amount key figure as InfoObject as a inventory-changing key figure. As with the related cumulative value, a neutral currency InfoObject is assigned.

Because we find the advantages of the account-based approach overwhelming, in the following section, we will implement this approach for our model company.

---

5 See the comments in: Egger: *SAP BW Professional*, Chapter 4: *Data Modeling and Converting a Column-Oriented InfoSource into an Account-Oriented InfoCube*. SAP PRESS, 2004.

Defining a Cumulative Value

You must first define the amount key figure of the **cumulative value** type.

- To do so, select the **Create InfoObject** function in the Administrator Workbench of SAP BW (see Section 5.3.2) and then enter the technical name and description in the **Create Key Figure** popup. Confirm your entry.
- In the **Create Key Figure...** dialog, enter a **short description** that differs from the **description** and then select the **Type/unit** tab (see Figure 5.57, Step 1).

Type/Unit

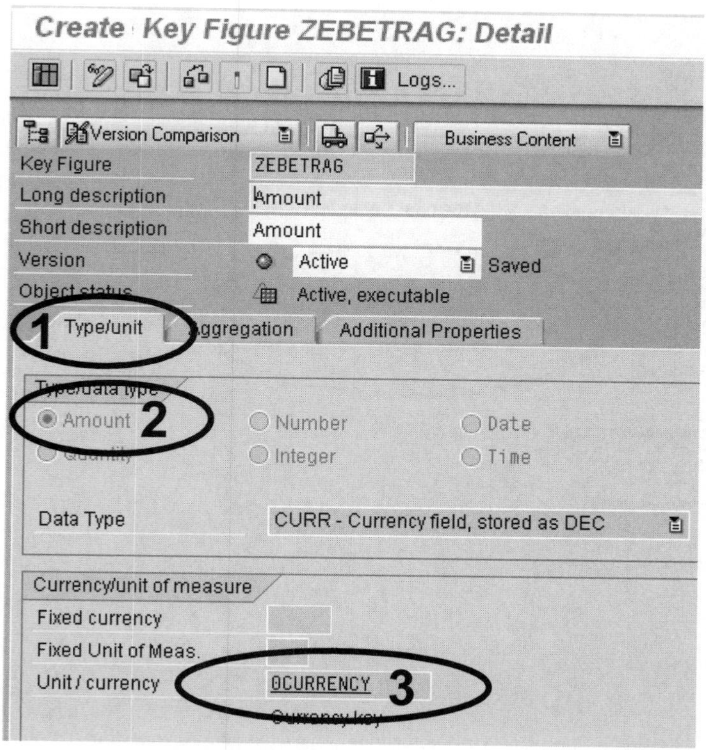

Figure 5.57 Creating a Cumulative Value for Inventory Changes: Type/Unit

- Select the **amount** data type (Step 2) and enter the InfoObject **0CURRENCY** as the **Unit/currency** (Step 3).
- Then, go to the **Aggregation** tab (see Figure 5.58, Step 1).
- The settings for aggregation, with **Summation** as the default (Step 2) and the type of **Cumulative value** (Step 3), remain unchanged.

Aggregation: Cumulative value

Additional properties

- Similar to the situation with key figure 0COPAREVEN and in light of the comments above (see Section 5.4.2), the setting for **decimal places** is 0 and the setting for **Display** is 1. To make these settings, select the **Additional Properties** tab.

After you activate the InfoObject, the key figure for the assignment to the inventory key figure is available.

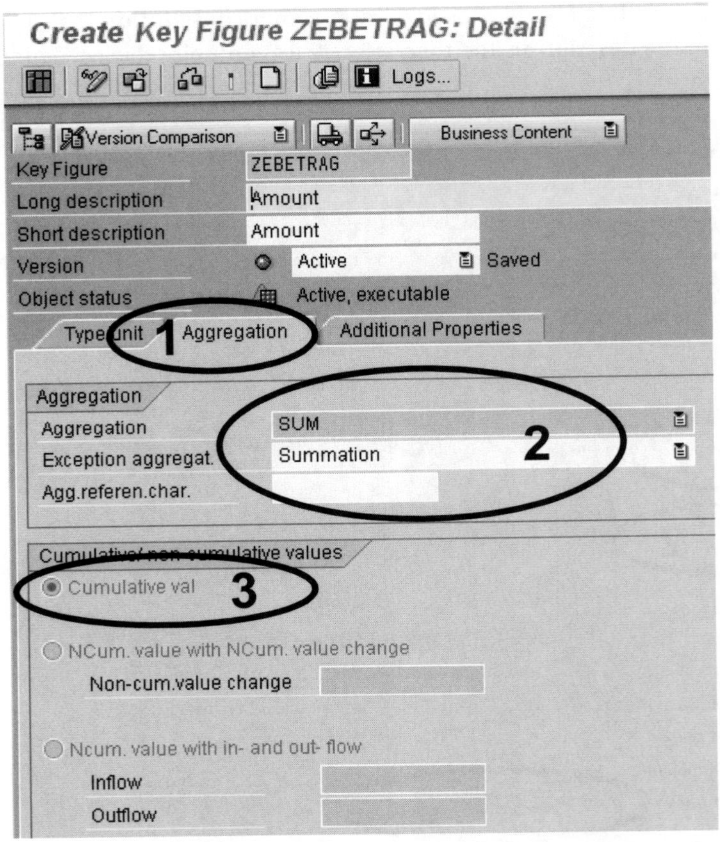

Figure 5.58 Creating a Cumulative Value for Inventory Changes: Aggregation

Defining an Inventory Key Figure

- To create the inventory key figure, select the **Create InfoObject** function in the Administrator Workbench of SAP BW (see Section 5.3.2 and the following).
- Enter the technical name and description in the **Create Key Figure** popup and confirm your entry.

- In the **Create Key Figure** dialog screen, navigate to the **Type/unit** tab and make the same settings for **Data Type** and **Unit/currency** that you did for the cumulative value created earlier.
- Then, select the **Aggregation** tab (see Figure 5.59, Step 1).

Aggregation Inventory key figure

- Select the key figure type of **Non-Cumulative Value Change** and enter the cumulative value as the key figure for inventory changes (Step 2).
- The specification of the key figure as an inventory key figure automatically sets the (standard) **Aggregation** to **SUM**. Set the **Exception Aggregation** to **Last value** (Step 3).

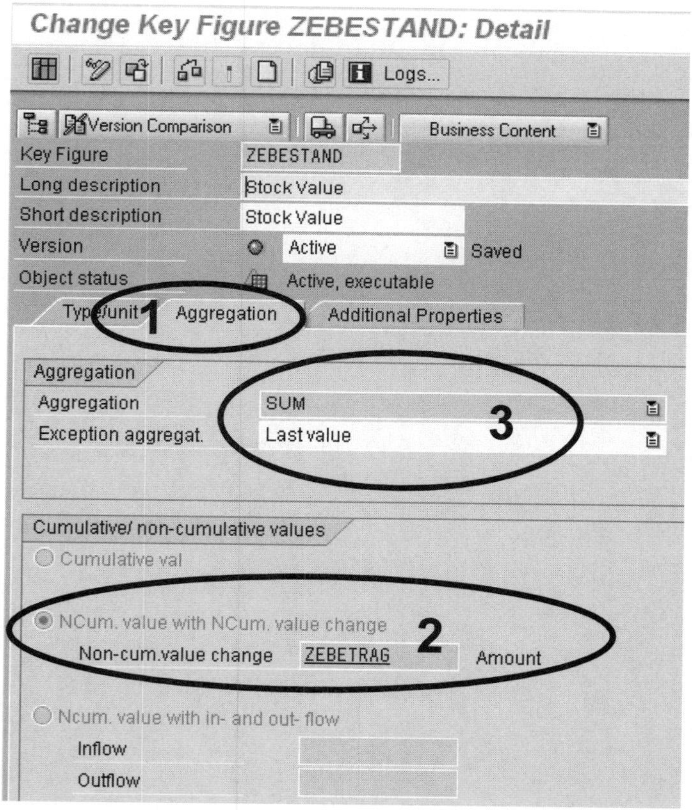

Figure 5.59 Creating an Inventory Key Figure: Aggregation

Additional properties

- Then, navigate to the **Additional Properties** tab and make the same settings for **Decimal Places** and **Display** that you did for the cumulative value.

After you activate the InfoObject, the key figure is available for additional work (see Chapter 6).

6 InfoProviders of SAP BW

In SAP BW, all those objects are called InfoProviders for which SAP Business Explorer Queries can be generated. These objects contain physical data and logical views to stored data. This chapter sets up the InfoProviders of our case study step by step. It also examines the individual types of InfoProviders. Here, examples are used to show you how to create InfoProviders and to shed light on which distinctive features you should take into account.

6.1 Selective Approach

In Section 2.2.2, you were introduced to the various types of InfoProviders. Some of them will be addressed in more detail in this chapter (examples of *data targets*).

- InfoCubes
- ODS objects
- InfoObjects (Characteristics with attributes, texts, or hierarchies)
- MultiProviders

The following additional types of InfoProviders, however, are not considered in this book:[1]

- InfoSets
- RemoteCubes
- SAP RemoteCubes
- Virtual InfoCubes with services

6.2 Characteristics as a Basis for Master Data Reporting

It is intended to enable the **General Ledger Account** (0GL_ACCOUNT) characteristic for master data reporting, which means that the characteristic needs to be inserted as an InfoProvider.

1 These InfoProvider types will be dealt with in future volumes of the *SAP BW Library* (see Appendix L).

Inserting a Characteristic as a Data Target

- You can insert a characteristic as a data target by selecting **Modeling**, view **InfoProvider** in the Administrator Workbench of SAP BW.
- Then select the InfoArea in which you want to insert the characteristic as a data target by clicking the left mouse button (see Inserting a Characteristic as a Data Target, Figure 6.1, Step 1).
- Activate the context menu by clicking the right mouse button and select **Insert Characteristic as Data Target...** (Step 2).
- In the **Assign InfoArea to an InfoObject** popup, you can then enter the relevant InfoObject (Step 3) and confirm this by clicking on the **Enter (Next)** button (Step 4).

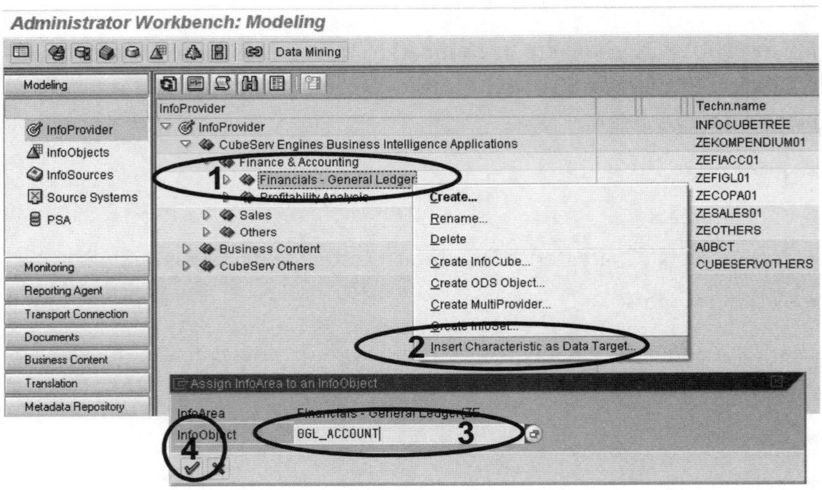

Figure 6.1 Inserting a Characteristic as a Data Target

Displaying characteristics as data targets

- The selected characteristic has now been included into the **InfoProvider** view and can be used for reporting with SAP Business Explorer (BEx) (see Figure 6.2).

Provision for query creation

- After you have saved the aforementioned settings, the new characteristic will be listed among the InfoProviders available for the creation of queries (see Figure 6.3).

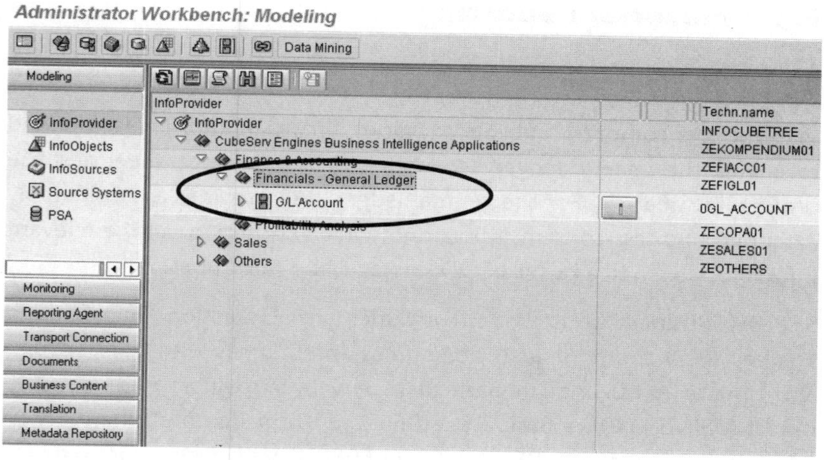

Figure 6.2 Displaying Characteristics as Data Targets

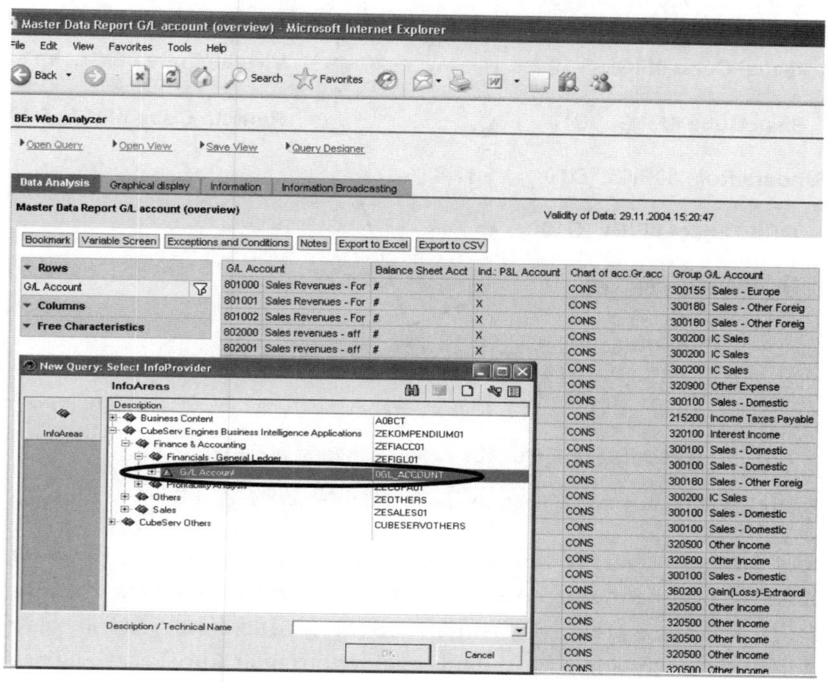

Figure 6.3 Master Data Query for the G/L Account Characteristic

The details on updating and reporting will be addressed in later volumes of the SAP BW Library.[2]

---

2 Cf. the relevant sections in volumes 2 and 3 of the SAP BW Library (see Appendix L).

6.3 Financial Reporting

6.3.1 Introduction

Using SAP Business Content

In our model company, CubeServ Engines, financial reporting is intended to enable the general ledger accounting for the balance sheet and the profitability analysis. For the general ledger, SAP provides a considerably extended business content, the core of which consists of all the relevant InfoObjects as well as a set of ODS objects and InfoCubes.

New Business Content components

SAP BW Business Content 3.5.1 includes new Extraction, Transfer, and Loading (ETL) components (DataSources, InfoSources with transfer rules and update rules) and, in particular, new InfoProviders with an ODS object (0FIGL_O10), a BasicCube (0FIGL_C10) or RemoteCube (0FIGL_R10), and virtual cubes (0FIGL_V10 and 0FIGL_V11) (see Figure 6.4).

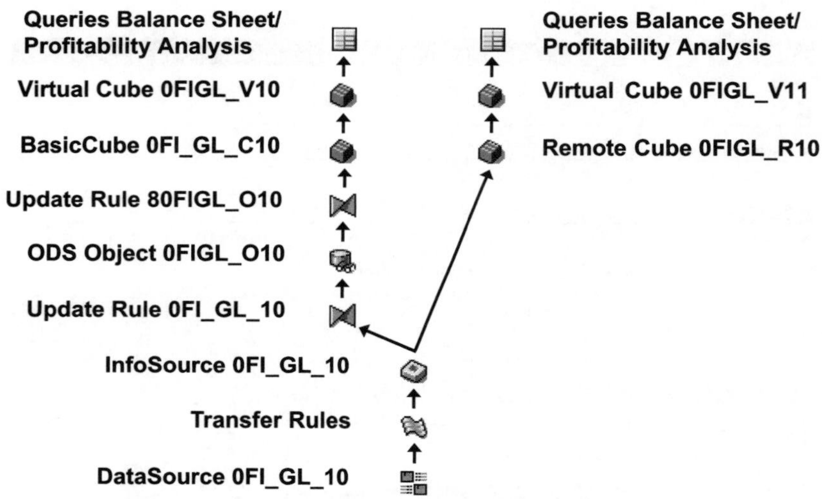

Figure 6.4 SAP Business Content Components for General Ledger Data

Problem areas

SAP Business Content can be used to a far-reaching extent. However, both the non-harmonized version and the dimension modeling that is far from ideal cause problems that must be solved. Therefore, we will create our own InfoProviders for the financial reporting at CubeServe Engines; these InfoProviders are modified and extended copies of the SAP Business Content InfoProviders. In this book, we'll first create the ODS object, BasicCubes, and a necessary MultiProvider.[3]

3 Virtual cubes will be used only for further enhancements of the application, therefore, they will be discussed in later volumes of the SAP BW Library (see Appendix L).

The application's InfoObjects are located in the **Finance & Accounting** InfoArea of the **CubeServ Engines Business Intelligence Applications**. The **InfoObjects** view of the SAP BW Administrator Workbench contains the InfoObjectCatalogs for the key figures and characteristics of the general ledger (see also Chapter 5, *InfoObjects of SAP BW*). The application's ODS objects and InfoCubes are created in the InfoProvider view.

Structure of the application

6.3.2 The Components of an ODS Object

An ODS object consists of the following components:

- **Status information**
  The status information items **Version, Backup,** and **Status** provide information about the current status of the ODS object and are administered automatically.
- **Settings**
  You can change the settings of an ODS object either by changing the relevant checkbox or via the context menu of the relevant setting you would like to modify. The individual settings of an ODS object have the following meanings:
  - **BEx Reporting**
    If this feature is set, then reporting is permitted for this ODS object. Please note that in this setting, the characteristics with all their values are stored in the respective tables as required by OLAP. However, you may not always want this default setting.
  - **Type ODS Object**
    You can change the **Standard** setting to **Transactional** via the context menu. Everything in this book that we have described so far refers to a standard ODS object because the transactional ODS object contains the following special features:
  - It is not updated via the usual SAP BW loading process, but transactionally via service application programming interfaces (APIs). Therefore, it is primarily used in the SAP SEM environment.
  - Because direct reporting with SAP BEx is not possible, you must define an InfoSet—a method that may prove to be quite cumbersome.
  - It consists of a table with only *active* data.
  - The data can be unloaded via a downloading function in the ODS administration.

- **Unique data records**
  If you use this feature, you must determine whether only unique key combinations can be loaded into the ODS.
- **Check table for InfoObject**
  Here the name of the InfoObject—for which an ODS object was created as a check table—is displayed.
- **Set quality status to OK automatically**
  If this flag is set, the quality status of a loaded request is automatically set to green. Select this setting whenever the data should not be checked and released manually.
- **Activate data of the ODS Object automatically**
  With this flag, the automatic activation of loaded requests is controlled. If this flag is set, the updating of the active data and the change logs in tables occurs automatically in the course of a new job.
- **Update data targets from the ODS Object automatically**
  Typically, data from the ODS is updated in subsequent data targets. This flag enables you to determine whether the updating process should be done automatically, or scheduled manually. In our example, the flag is set. If the data loading processes were controlled via process chains, setting this flag wouldn't be necessary.

- **Key fields**
  With complex data structures, the technical limit of 16 key fields per ODS object can quickly be reached. However, experience shows that it is often difficult to determine which fields of a DataSource are the key fields. A proven method to substantiate this is to analyze the data source at the table level and then to define the key fields of the DataSource as such in the ODS object. For customer order header data, this can be done rather easily as the source of this data—DataSource 2LIS_11_VAHDR—refers to SAP R/3 data from Table VBAK. For example, for the header data, a key field would be the unique order number from the DataSource.
- **Data fields**
  Additional fields of an ODS object that are not key fields.
- **Navigation attributes**
  The navigation attributes of selected InfoObjects are displayed automatically and can be enabled or disabled via a flag. **On** means that the navigation attribute is available in Business Explorer and that it can also be selected when you define MultiProviders for navigation.

- **Indices**
  It is possible to define tables and secondary indices in addition to the primary index of the ODS object. You can do this via the corresponding context menu, and it can have a positive effect on the reporting performance.

6.3.3 Configuring an ODS Object to Consolidate the Actual Data on the Basis of an SAP Business Content ODS Object

Our objective is to collect the data of the transactional source systems in a single ODS object.

Calling Up the ODS Object Creation

- To create an ODS object, start the **InfoProvider** view of the SAP BW Administrator Workbench.
- Highlight the InfoArea for which you want to create the ODS object (see Figure 6.5, Step 1), and open the context menu with the right mouse button. Select **Create ODS Object...** (Step 2).

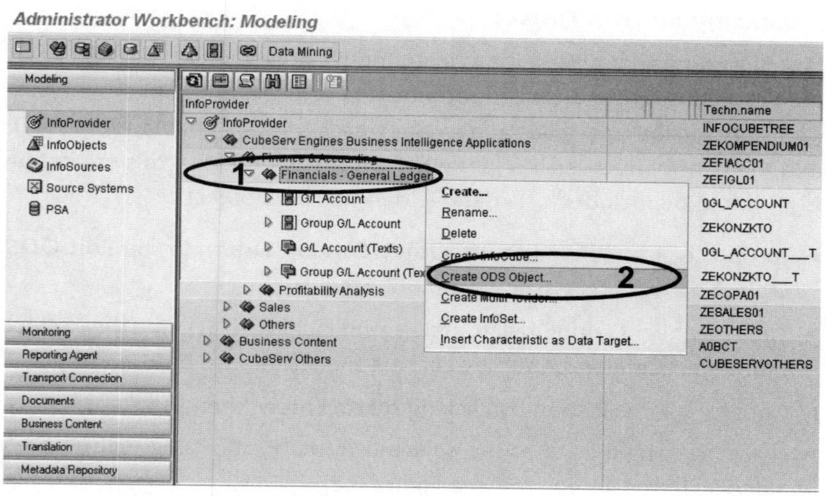

Figure 6.5 Calling the Create ODS Object Function

- In the **Edit ODS Object** popup, enter the SAP Business Content ODS object template (see Figure 6.6, Step 1) as well as the technical name and the description for the ODS object to be created (Step 2).
- Click the **Create** button to confirm (Step 3).

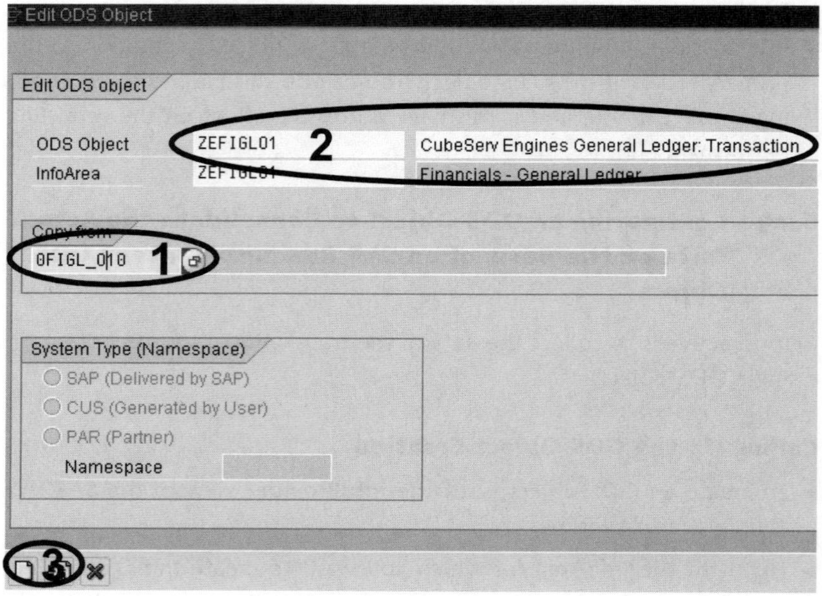

Figure 6.6 Creating an ODS Object with a Template

Enhancing an ODS Object

You must now adapt the settings in your ODS object, which has been created as a copy of the Business Content. To avoid the problem of non-harmonized version and value type values described in Chapter 5, we will add the harmonized version in the ETL process. Therefore, this characteristic should be included as a data field in the ODS object.

- To do this, first select the **InfoObjectCatalog** button in the **Edit ODS Object** dialog screen (see Figure 6.7, Step 1).
- Then highlight InfoObjectCatalog **ZEFIGL01CHA01** in the **Select InfoObjectCatalog** popup by clicking the left mouse button (Step 2).
- Confirm your selection by clicking **Next (Enter)** (Step 3).

Including the InfoObject into the ODS object

- Now the InfoObjects of the selected InfoObjectCatalog will be provided as template objects (see Figure 6.8).
- To transfer the InfoObjects, highlight them by clicking the left mouse button (see Figure 6.8, Step 1) and Drag&Drop the objects to the **Data Fields** folder (Step 2).

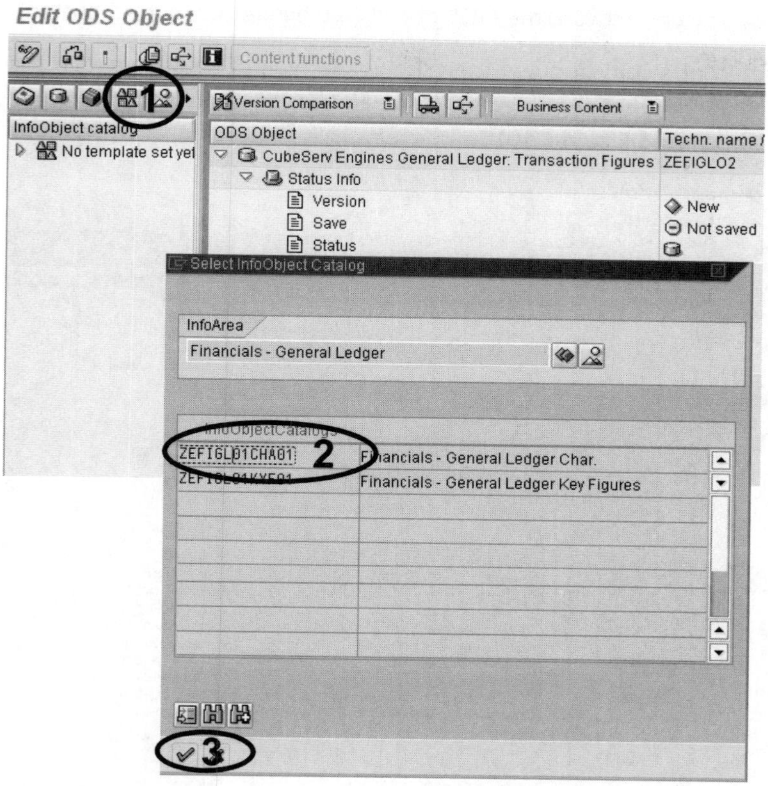

Figure 6.7 Selecting an InfoObjectCatalog

- As a result, the InfoObject is displayed in the InfoObjects list of the ODS object (Figure 6.8, Step 3).

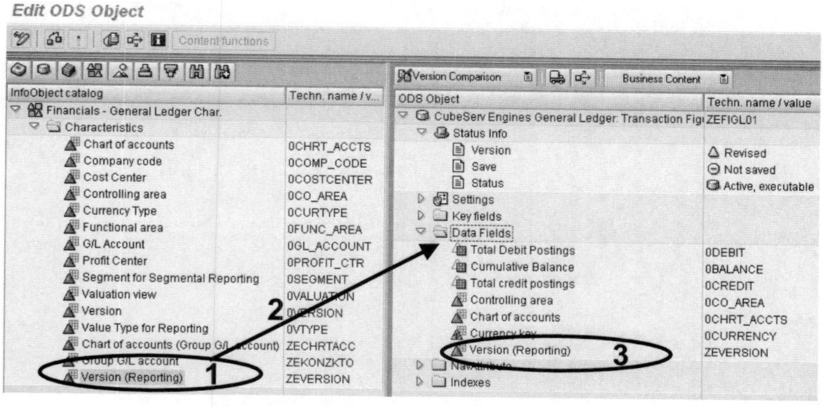

Figure 6.8 Transferring an InfoObject into the ODS Object

▶ Now you can activate the ODS object (see Figure 6.9, circled button).

The result of a control query then shows the type of data storage in the ODS object **CubeServ Engines General Ledger: Transaction Figures** (ZEFIGLO1) (see Figure 6.10).

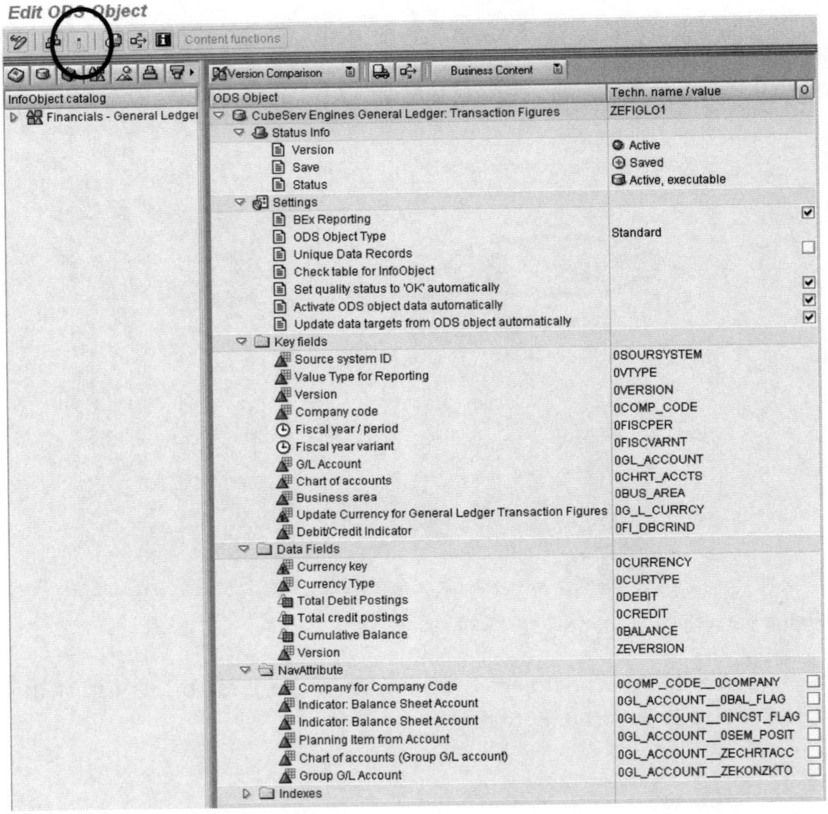

Figure 6.9 Settings of the Customer-Specific ODS Objects

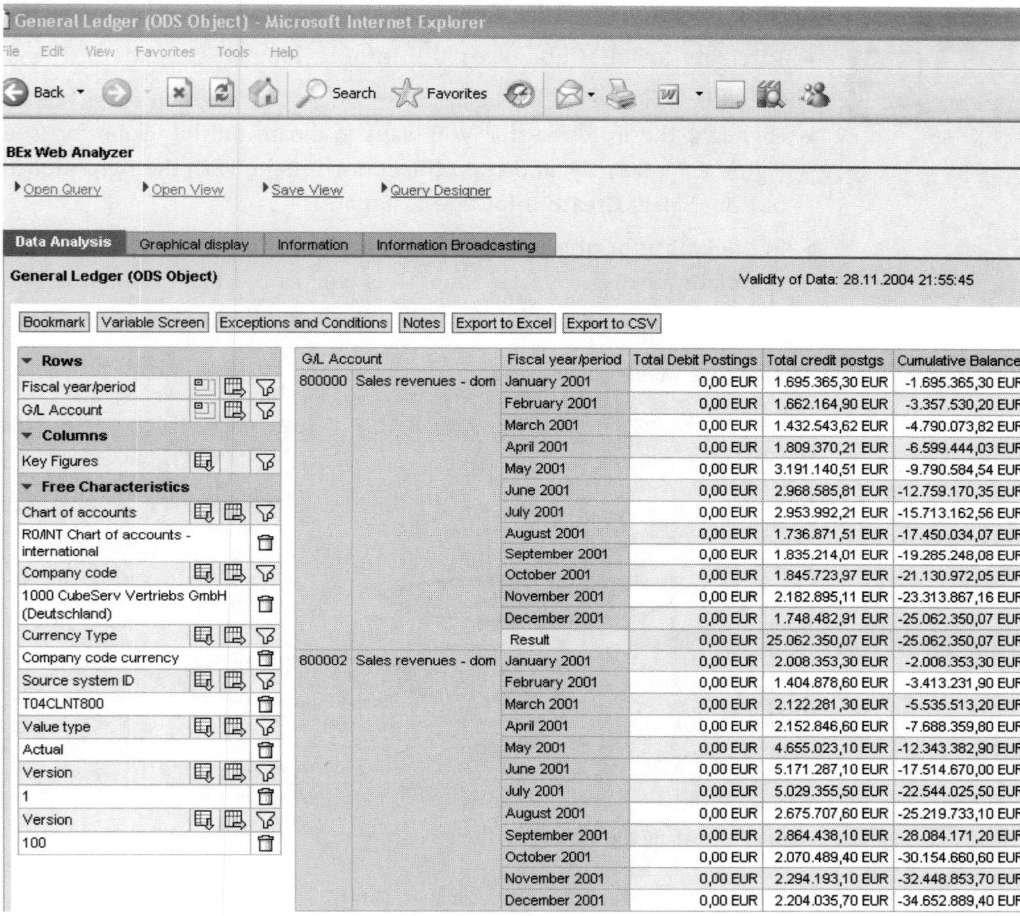

G/L Account		Fiscal year/period	Total Debit Postings	Total credit postgs	Cumulative Balance
800000	Sales revenues - dom	January 2001	0,00 EUR	1.695.365,30 EUR	-1.695.365,30 EUR
		February 2001	0,00 EUR	1.662.164,90 EUR	-3.357.530,20 EUR
		March 2001	0,00 EUR	1.432.543,62 EUR	-4.790.073,82 EUR
		April 2001	0,00 EUR	1.809.370,21 EUR	-6.599.444,03 EUR
		May 2001	0,00 EUR	3.191.140,51 EUR	-9.790.584,54 EUR
		June 2001	0,00 EUR	2.968.585,81 EUR	-12.759.170,35 EUR
		July 2001	0,00 EUR	2.953.992,21 EUR	-15.713.162,56 EUR
		August 2001	0,00 EUR	1.736.871,51 EUR	-17.450.034,07 EUR
		September 2001	0,00 EUR	1.835.214,01 EUR	-19.285.248,08 EUR
		October 2001	0,00 EUR	1.845.723,97 EUR	-21.130.972,05 EUR
		November 2001	0,00 EUR	2.182.895,11 EUR	-23.313.867,16 EUR
		December 2001	0,00 EUR	1.748.482,91 EUR	-25.062.350,07 EUR
		Result	0,00 EUR	25.062.350,07 EUR	-25.062.350,07 EUR
800002	Sales revenues - dom	January 2001	0,00 EUR	2.008.353,30 EUR	-2.008.353,30 EUR
		February 2001	0,00 EUR	1.404.878,60 EUR	-3.413.231,90 EUR
		March 2001	0,00 EUR	2.122.281,30 EUR	-5.535.513,20 EUR
		April 2001	0,00 EUR	2.152.846,60 EUR	-7.688.359,80 EUR
		May 2001	0,00 EUR	4.655.023,10 EUR	-12.343.382,90 EUR
		June 2001	0,00 EUR	5.171.287,10 EUR	-17.514.670,00 EUR
		July 2001	0,00 EUR	5.029.355,50 EUR	-22.544.025,50 EUR
		August 2001	0,00 EUR	2.675.707,60 EUR	-25.219.733,10 EUR
		September 2001	0,00 EUR	2.864.438,10 EUR	-28.084.171,20 EUR
		October 2001	0,00 EUR	2.070.489,40 EUR	-30.154.660,60 EUR
		November 2001	0,00 EUR	2.294.193,10 EUR	-32.448.853,70 EUR
		December 2001	0,00 EUR	2.204.035,70 EUR	-34.652.889,40 EUR

Figure 6.10 Control Query on the Basis of the ODS Object Data

6.3.4 Creating an InfoCube to Store the Actual Data on the Basis of an SAP Business Content BasicCubes

The actual data of the transactional source systems is to be provided for reporting via an InfoCube. To do this, we want to use a copy of the SAP Business Content InfoCubes 0FIGL_C10. This copy should contain the following:

- An optimal modeling of the InfoCube's dimensions
- Navigation attributes
- The harmonized version

Calling up the InfoCube Creation

- To create an InfoCube, start the **InfoProvider** view of the SAP BW Administrator Workbench.
- Highlight the InfoArea that you want to create the InfoCube for (see Figure 6.11, Step 1), and open the context menu with the right mouse button. Select **Create InfoCube...** (Step 2).
- In the **Edit InfoCube** popup, enter the SAP Business Content InfoCube Template (see Figure 6.12, Step 1) as well as the technical name and the description for the InfoCube to be created (Step 2).

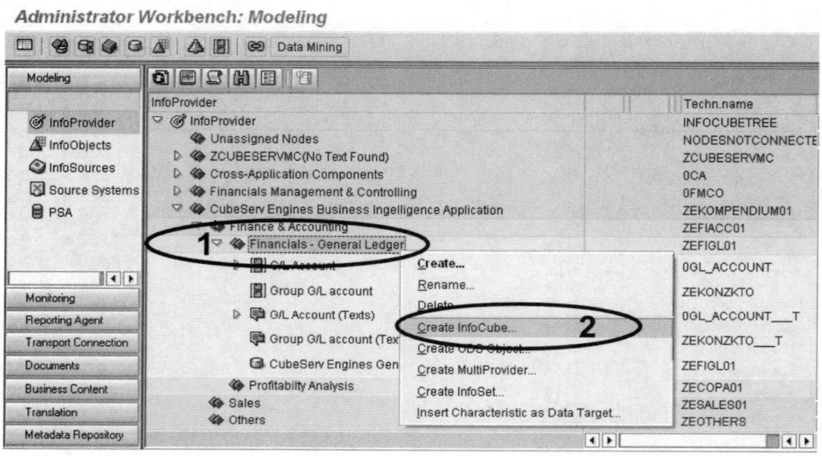

Figure 6.11 Calling the Create InfoCube Function

- Click the **Create** button to confirm (Step 3).
- For the actual data, the specifications for the InfoCube type remain **BasicCube** and **Non-Transactional** as the data will be physically provided via an ETL process.

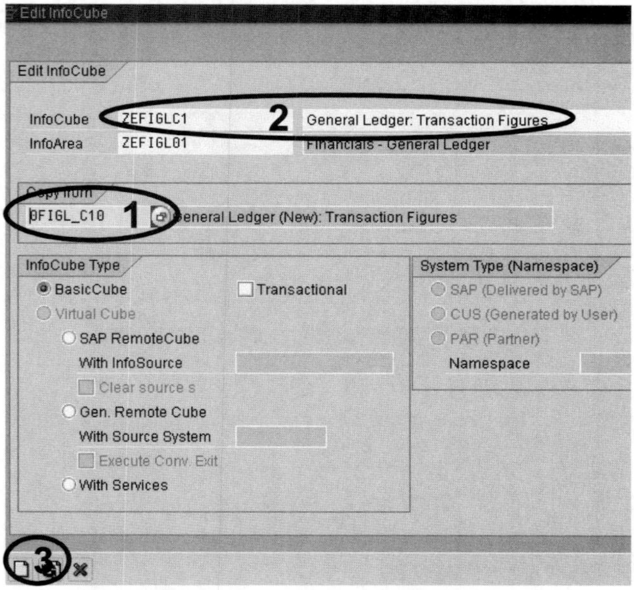

Figure 6.12 Creating an InfoCube with a Template

Selecting an InfoObjectCatalog Template

- First, you must add the **Harmonized Version** characteristic to the InfoCube. To do this, click on the **InfoObjectCatalog** button in the **Edit InfoCube: Characteristics** dialog screen (see Figure 6.13, Step 1).
- Then, highlight catalog **ZEFIGL01CHA01** in the **Select InfoObjectCatalog** popup by clicking the left mouse button (Step 2).
- Confirm your selection by clicking **Next (Enter)** (Step 3).
- In the **Transfer fields automatically** popup, click on **No** (Step 4).

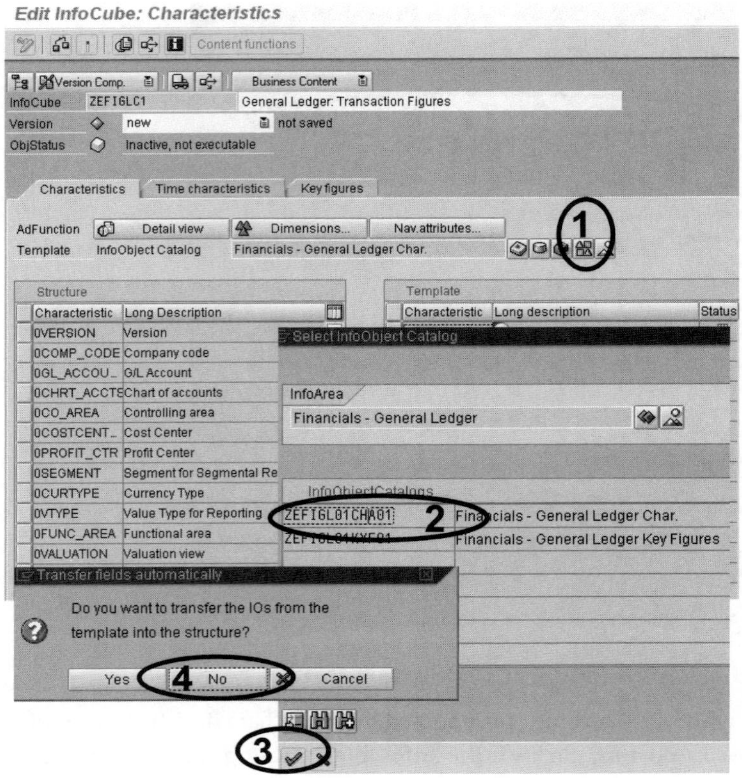

Figure 6.13 Selecting an InfoObjectCatalog Template

Including a Characteristic with the InfoCube

The InfoObjects of the selected InfoObjectCatalog are now listed in the template.

- Use the left mouse button to highlight InfoObject ZEVERSION which we want to include (see Figure 6.14, Step 1).
- Then click on the **Transfer fields** button (Step 2).

The newly transferred InfoObject is now included in the structure of the InfoCube and highlighted in the template.

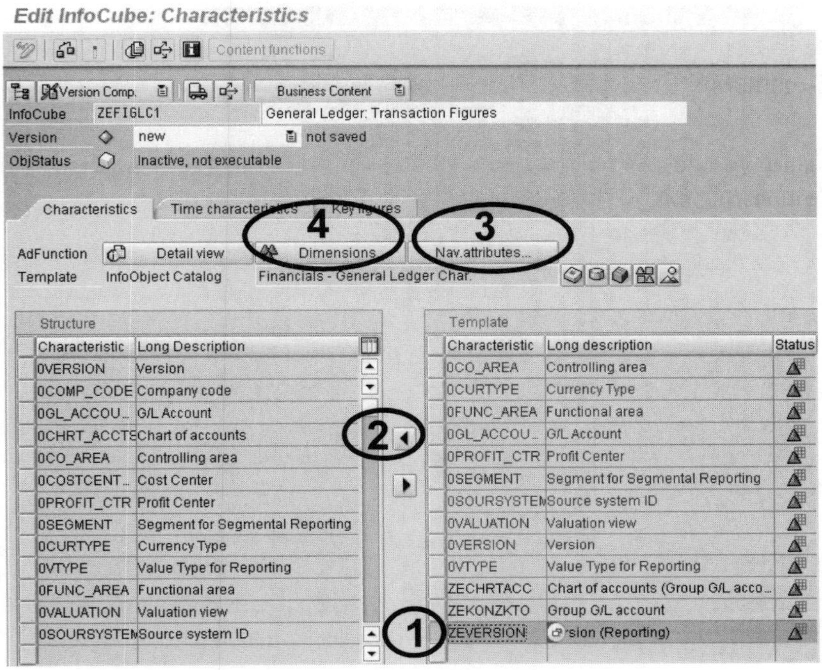

Figure 6.14 Including a Characteristic with the InfoCube

Customizing Navigation Attributes

- By clicking on the **Nav.attributes** button (see Figure 6.14, Step 3), you can open the **Switch On/Off Navigation Attribute** (see Figure 6.15).
- Here you can activate the required navigation attributes by checking the **I/O** flag (see Figure 6.15, Step 1).
- Confirm the settings by clicking on the **Next (Enter)** button (Step 2).

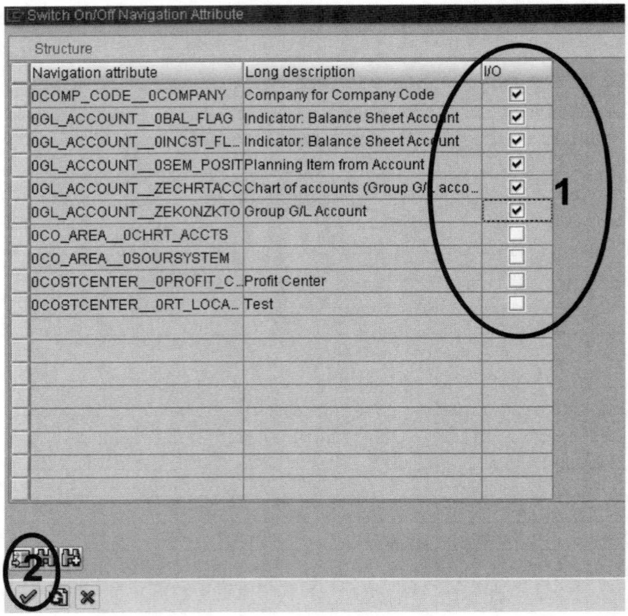

Figure 6.15 Activating and Deactivating the Navigation Attributes

Optimizing Dimensions

- By clicking on the **Dimensions** button (see Figure 6.14, Step 4), you can open the **Define Dimensions** dialog screen (see Figure 6.16).
- First, create the required dimensions in the **Define** tab. To do this, click on the **Create** button repeatedly until there is a sufficient number of dimensions available (see Figure 6.16, Step 1).
- Then, you can enter the appropriate descriptions for the dimensions (Step 2).

Assigning characteristics to dimensions

- Now switch to the **Assign** tab (see Figure 6.17, Step 1).
- Here you can either assign the characteristics directly or use graphical assignment. Due to the large number of characteristics to be assigned, we would recommend the latter.
- Therefore, you should use the **Graphical assignment** button (Step 2).
- Click **Next (Enter)** when you see the following information dialog screen ("Characteristics without assignment can be assigned graphically to dimensions!").

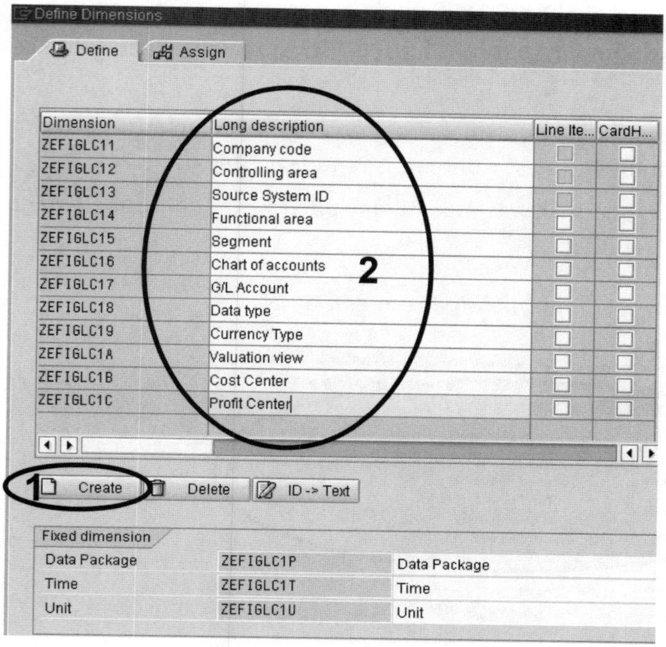

Figure 6.16 Defining Dimensions

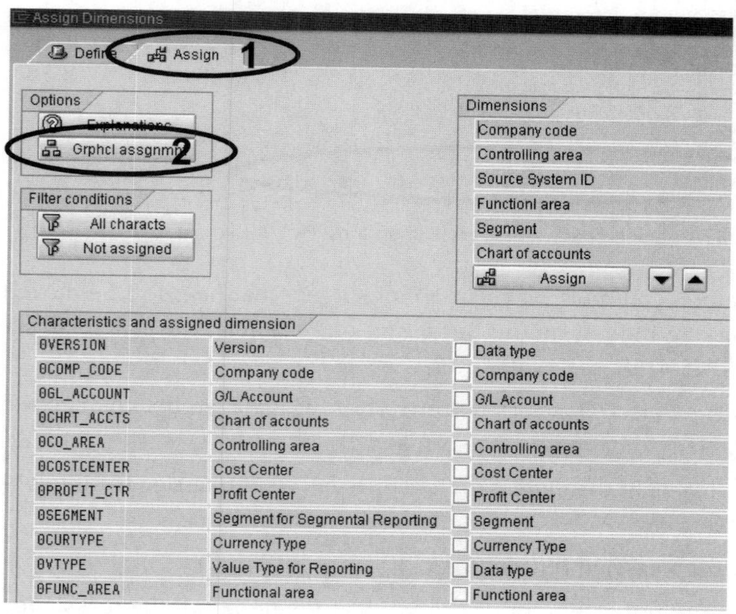

Figure 6.17 Call: Assigning Characteristics to Dimensions

- For the actual assignment, we will now open the **InfoProvider: Tree Display (Assignment of New Characteristics)** dialog screen (see Figure 6.18).
- It soon becomes apparent that the grouping of characteristics, which derives from the Business Content, is not ideal (Step 1).
- The characteristic that was recently included in the InfoCube has no assignment yet (Step 2).

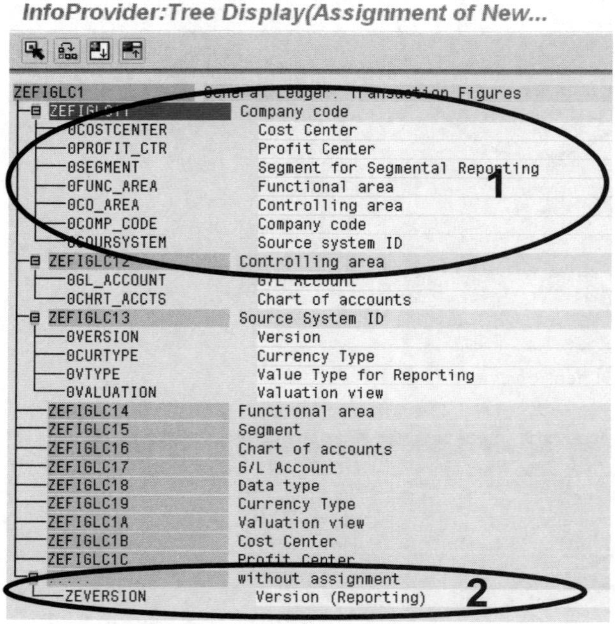

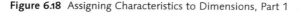

Figure 6.18 Assigning Characteristics to Dimensions, Part 1

- Therefore, you must highlight an InfoObject that needs to be moved by clicking the left mouse button (in our example, this is InfoObject 0COSTCENTER, see Figure 6.19, Step 1).
- Click the **Select/Deselect** button, which will change the color of the InfoObject to be moved (Steps 2 and 3).
- Then, highlight the dimension to which you want to assign the InfoObject (Step 4).
- Click the **Reassign** button (Step 5).
- When prompted, you must confirm that the node is to be **reassigned to a Lower Level position** to the dimension (Steps 6 and 7).
- Finally, the assignment will be displayed (Step 8).

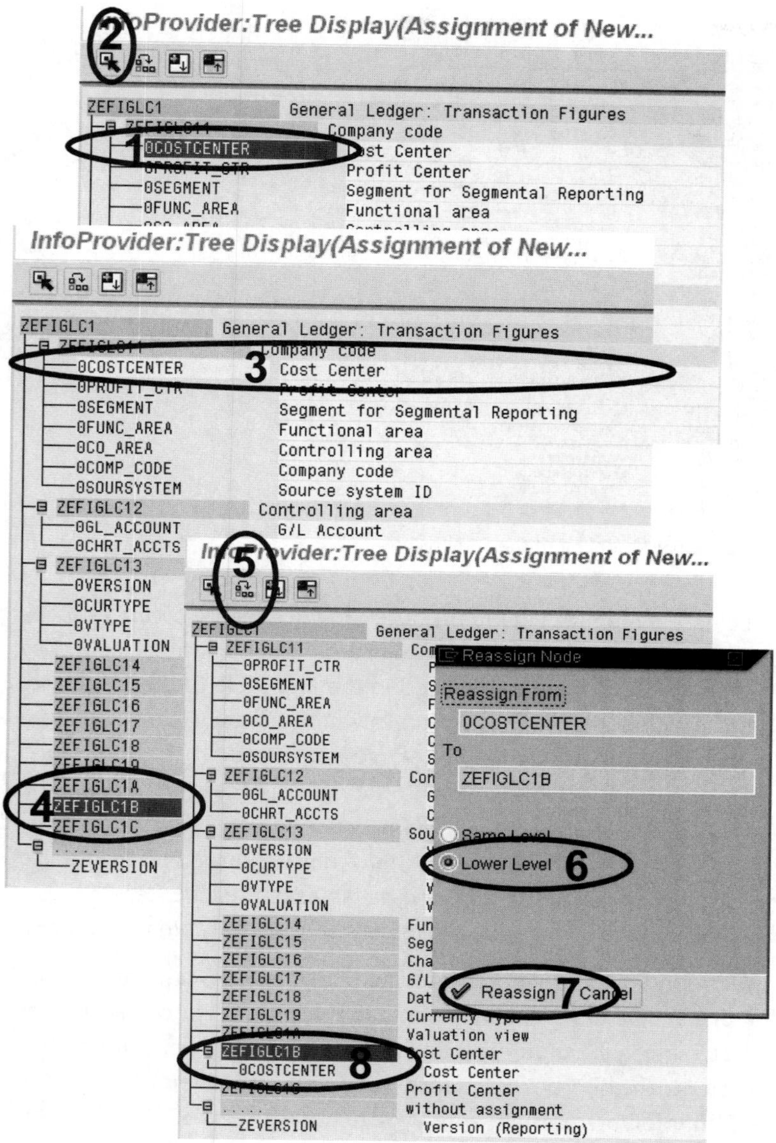

Figure 6.19 Assigning Characteristics to Dimensions, Part 2

- Repeat this procedure until you have reached the required dimension modeling (see Figure 6.20).
- Having returned to the **Define Dimensions** dialog screen, you can now set the line item settings of the required dimensions (see Figure 6.21, Step 1).

Setting line item settings

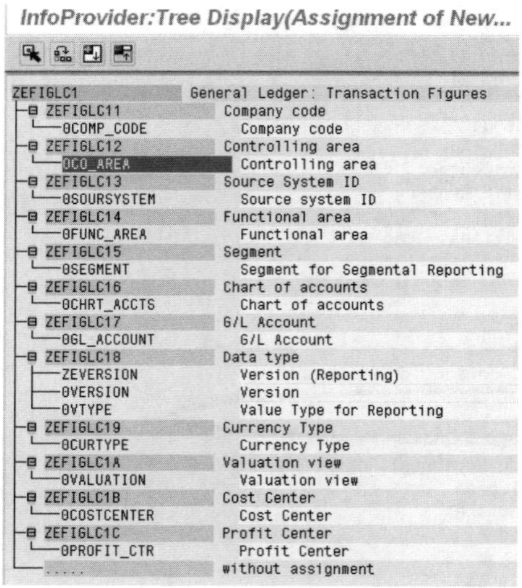

Figure 6.20 Final Modeling of the Dimensions

In the context help for Line Items, SAP provides the following description: A Line Item is an InfoObject such as an order number for whose values one or several facts are listed in the fact table of the InfoCube. This means that the dimension table which contains the Line Item InfoObject becomes considerably large compared to the fact table. This, in turn, leads to problems with the query processing because the use of such Line Items results in joins between very large tables (particularly between fact and Line Item dimension tables, but also between the latter and the master data tables of the Line Item InfoObjects), which can no longer be processed by using star-join techniques.

Consequently, performance problems occur. In the case of such an InfoObject, that is, if the dimension table becomes almost as large as the fact table, you should mark the dimension as a Line Item. This dimension can then be assigned exactly one InfoObject, that is, the Line Item InfoObject. Then, when you activate the InfoCube, no database table will be created for this dimension; instead, a field with data element RSSID will be written into the fact table that points directly to the SID table of the InfoObject (see the context help in the Define Dimensions dialog screen).

- Then confirm your entries by clicking the **Next (Enter)** button (see Figure 6.21, Step 1).

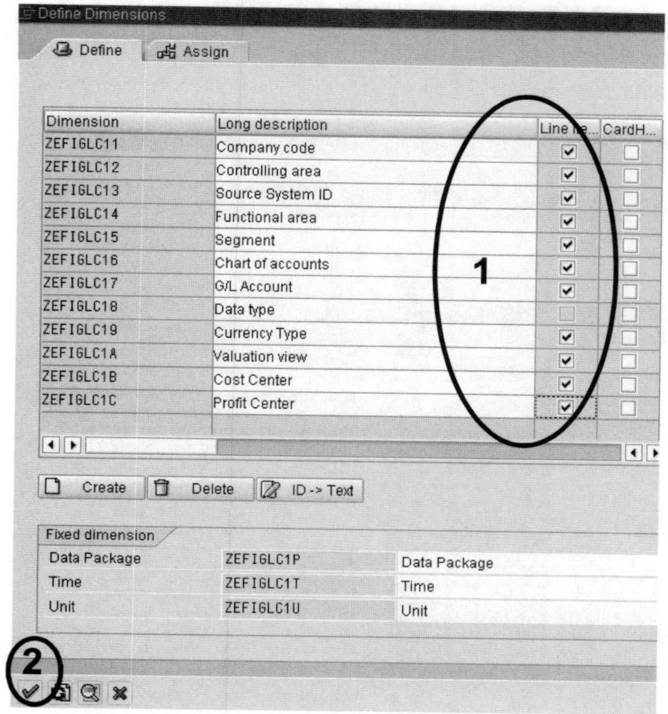

Figure 6.21 Defining Line Item Settings of Dimensions

- Lastly, you must activate the InfoCube (see Figure 6.21, Step 2, and Figure 6.22).

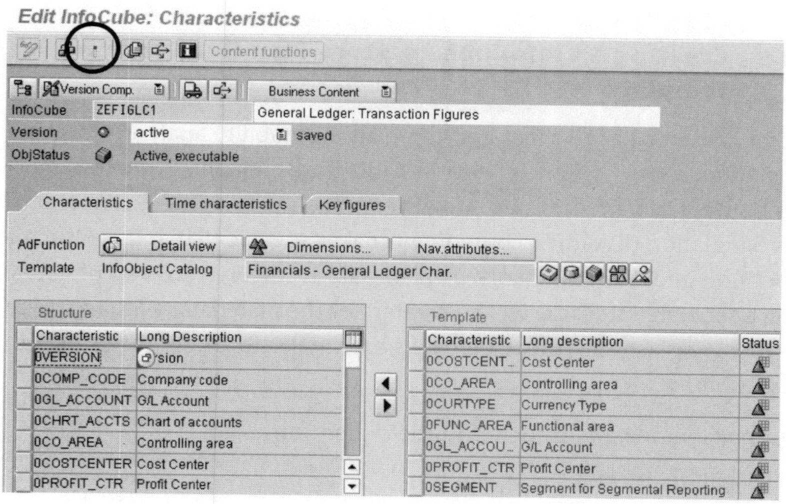

Figure 6.22 Activating the InfoCube

The sample query displays data from the SAP R/3 general ledger of the InfoCube **General Ledger: Transaction Figures** (ZEFIGLC1) via G/L Account Hierarchy (see Figure 6.23).

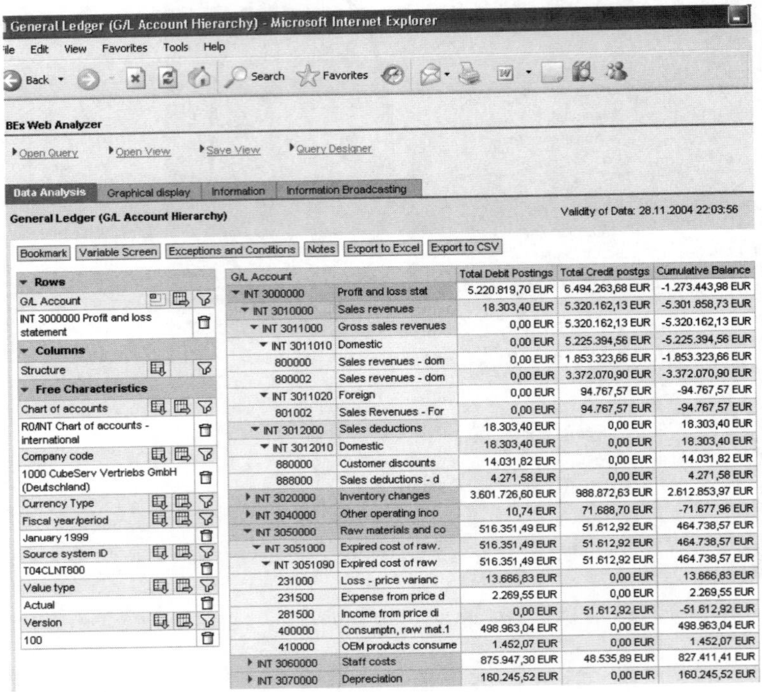

Figure 6.23 Displaying Data from the SAP R/3 General Ledger in the Actual-Data InfoCube via G/L Account Hierarchy

6.3.5 Creating an InfoCube to Store Plan Data with a Template

Requirements to a dedicated Plan-data InfoCube

The budgeted balance sheet and the plan profitability analysis that were generated in the context of the BW-integrated planning process must also be stored in an InfoCube. However, since the SAP BW-Business Process Simulation (BW-BPS) component makes specific demands on such a BasicCube and the granularity of plan data is lower than that of actual data, a separate InfoCube will be created for the plan data. With regard to the following aspects, these demands are similar to those of the Actual-data Cube:

- Optimal modeling of the InfoCube dimensions
- Navigation attributes
- Harmonized version

Therefore the Actual-data Cube will be used as a template. Planning is carried out with the granularity of year, period, accounting sector, and planning item. Thus, for the Plan-data InfoCube, you can do without the characteristics **Controlling Area, Source system ID, Functional Area, Segment, Chart of Accounts, General Ledger Account, Cost Center** and **Profit Center.**

Creating the Plan-Data InfoCube

- ▶ To create the InfoCube, start the **InfoProvider** view of the SAP BW Administrator Workbench.
- ▶ At the beginning, you should proceed as you did when you created the Actual-data InfoCube (see Section 6.3.4).
- ▶ In the **Edit InfoCube** popup, enter the Actual-data InfoCube as a template (see Figure 6.24, Step 1) as well as the technical name and the description for the InfoCube to be created (Step 2).
- ▶ Set the InfoCube Type to **Transactional** (Step 3) and confirm it by clicking the **Create** button (Step 4).

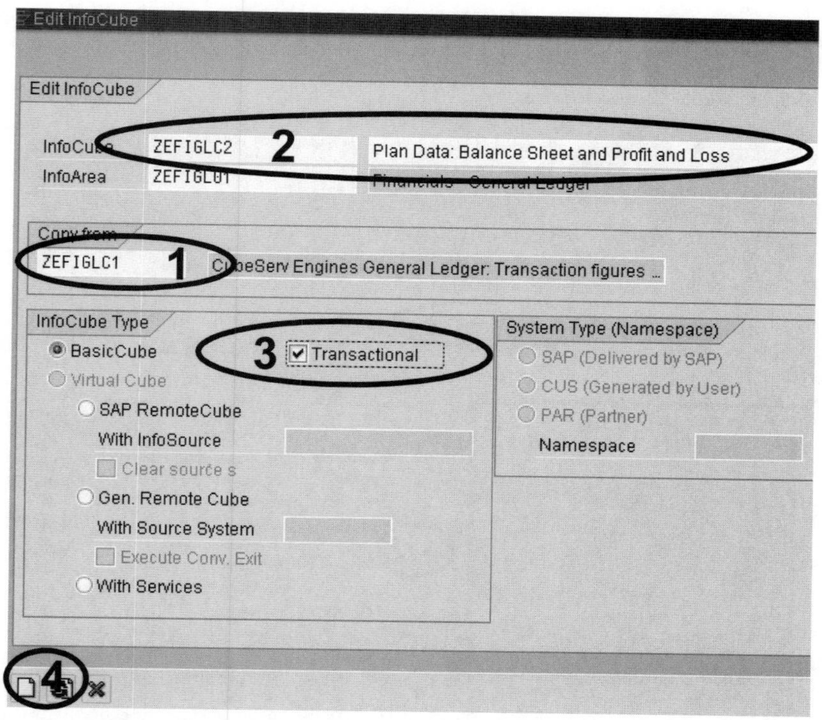

Figure 6.24 Creating the Transactional InfoCube for Planning Using the Actual-Data InfoCube as a Template

> **Transactional InfoCubes**
>
> Transactional InfoCube data is accessed in a transactional manner: Data is written to the InfoCube (sometimes by several users simultaneously) and might be read immediately. Contrary to non-transactional InfoCubes, the request management for transactional InfoCubes is different: BW-integrated planning writes data into a data request of the transactional InfoCube. Once the number of sets in this data request exceeds a certain threshold value, the request is closed and a rollup of this request into defined (asynchronous) aggregates is carried out. With transactional InfoCubes, a reduced read performance is accepted in order to enable parallel (transactional) writing and an improved write performance.

Removing Superfluous InfoObjects

- In the **Edit InfoCube: Characteristics** dialog screen, highlight all InfoObjects that you don't need for the planning (see Figure 6.25, Step 1).
- Then click the **Retransfer fields** button (Step 2).

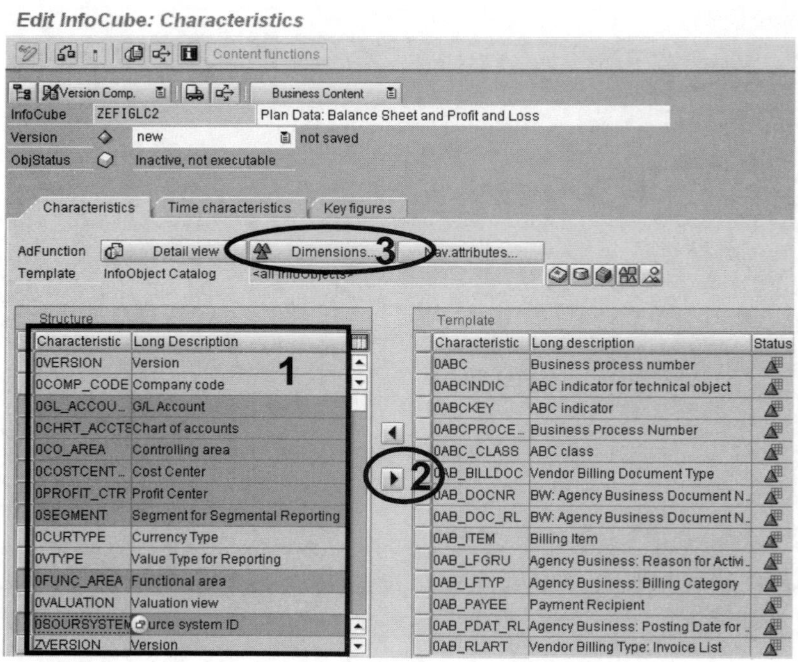

Figure 6.25 Removing Superfluous InfoObjects from the Template

Deleting Unused Dimensions

- Since the **G/L Account** characteristic has been removed, the planning item is no longer available. However, the planning must be based on the basic characteristic **Planning Item,** therefore, you must include this characteristic in the InfoCube by deleting the unused dimension. To do this, search for InfoObject 0SEM_POSIT in the template.
- Click the **Find** button in the template (see Figure 6.26, Step 1).
- Specify the desired InfoObject in the **Determine Search Criterion** dialog screen (Step 2) and click **Next (Enter)** (Step 3).
- The InfoObject-List template will be positioned to the specified InfoObject. Then transfer the InfoObject into the structure adhering to the previously described procedure (see Figure 6.14).

Deleting Dimensions

- Because you must delete unused dimensions, click on the **Dimensions** button (see Figure 6.25, Step 3).

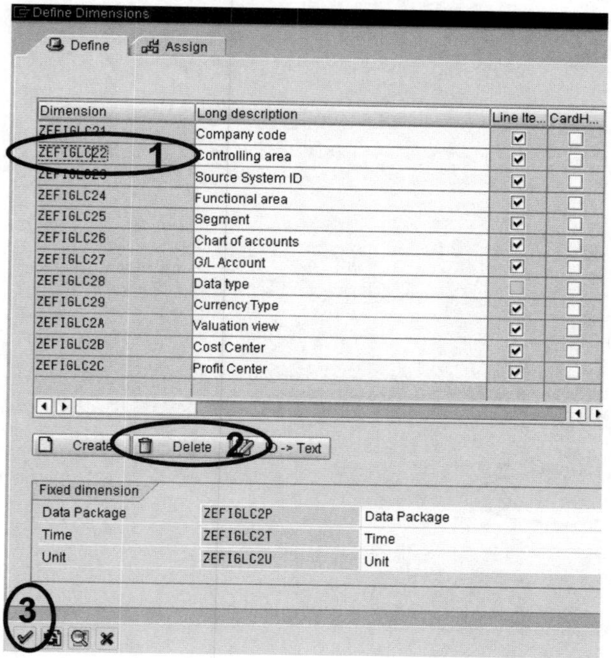

Figure 6.26 Transferring the Planning Item into the InfoCube Structure

- In the **Define Dimensions** dialog screen, highlight a dimension that is not needed (see Figure 6.27, Step 1) and click on the **Delete** button (Step 2). Repeat this procedure for each dimension that you want to delete.

- The name of the **G/L Account** dimension will be changed to **Planning Item.**

Assigning a characteristic

- Switch to the **Assign** tab. Select the **Planning Item** characteristic, which hasn't been assigned to any dimension yet by clicking the left mouse button (see Figure 6.28, Step 1).
- Assign the characteristic to the desired dimension by double-clicking the left mouse button (Step 2).
- Confirm your entries by clicking **Next (Enter)** (Step 3).
- Switch on the navigation attribute **Item Type** (see Figures 6.14 and 6.15).
- Lastly, activate the Plan-data InfoCube.

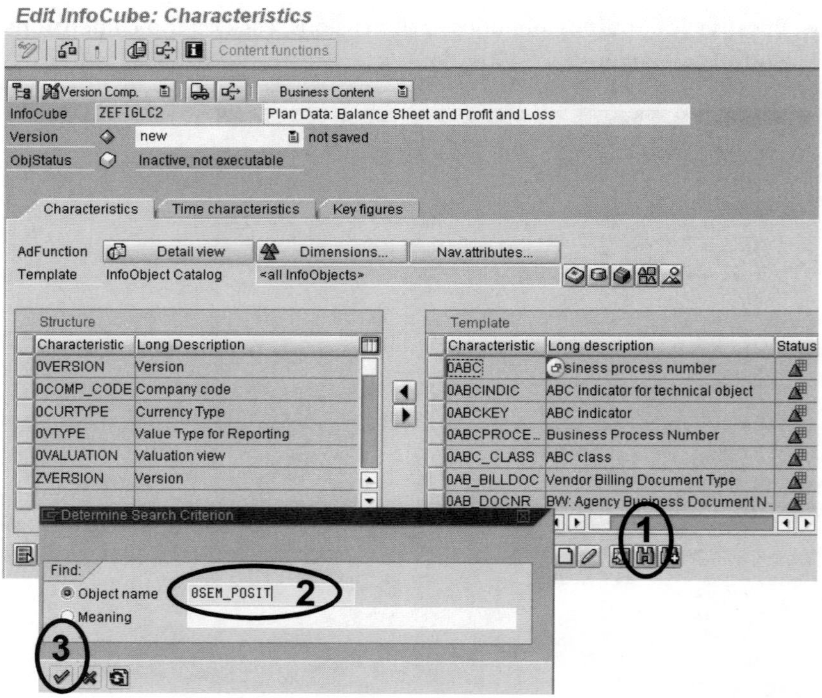

Figure 6.27 Deleting Unused Dimensions

Figure 6.29 shows the planned revenues in InfoCube **Plan Data: Balance Sheet and Profit and Loss** (ZEFIGLC2).

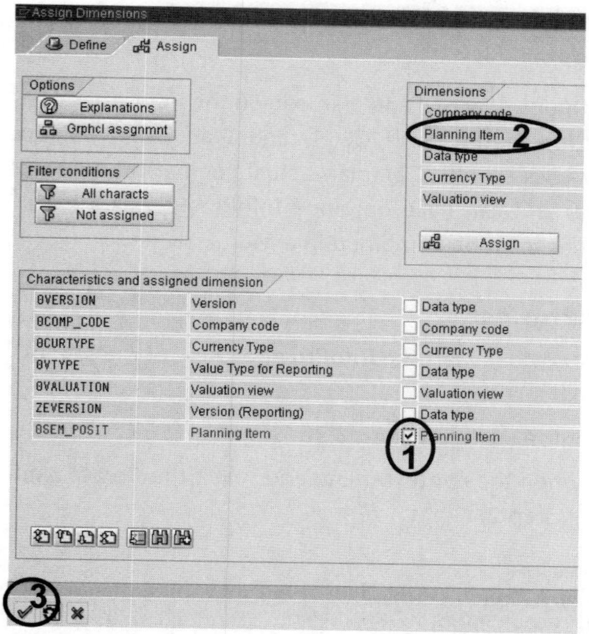

Figure 6.28 Assigning the Planning Item Characteristic to the Corresponding Dimension

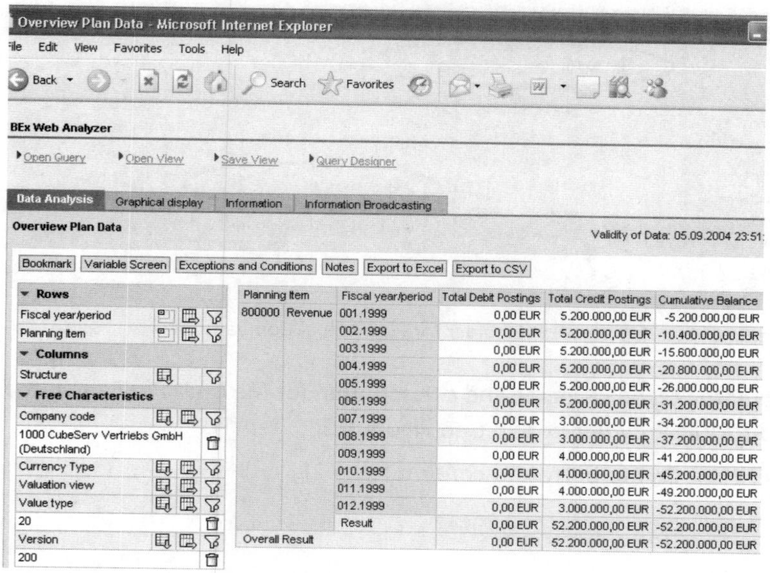

Figure 6.29 Planned Revenues in InfoCube Plan Data: Balance Sheet and Profit and Loss (ZEFIGLC2)

6.3.6 Creating a MultiProvider as a Basis for Plan-Actual Comparisons

Due to the separate storage of actual and plan data in the InfoCubes **General Ledger: Transaction Figures** (ZEFIGLC1) and **Plan Data: Balance Sheet and Profit and Loss** (ZEFIGLC2), plan-actual comparisons are not yet possible as queries and can have only one InfoProvider as a basis.[4] Therefore the InfoCubes must be combined in a MultiProvider.

Creating the MultiProvider

- To create the MultiProvider, start the **InfoProvider** view of the SAP BW Administrator Workbench.
- Select the desired InfoArea (see Figure 6.30, Step 1).
- Then right-click to open the context menu and select the **Create MultiProvider** function (Step 2).

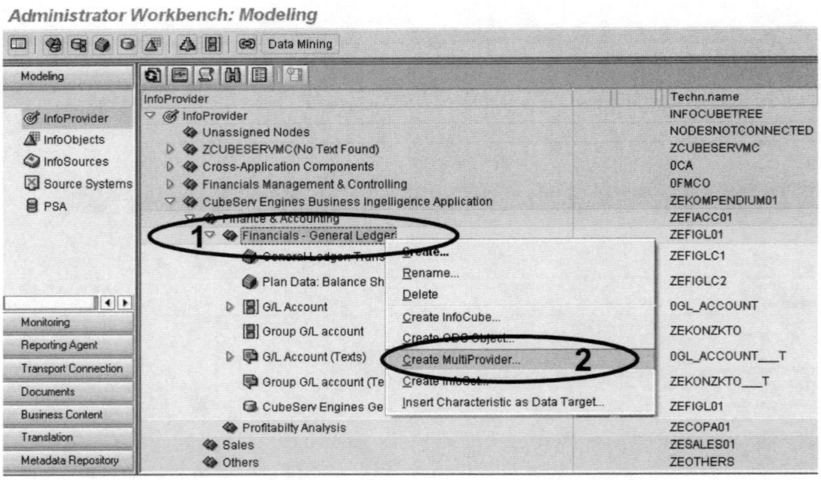

Figure 6.30 Creating the MultiProvider for Plan-Actual Comparisons

- Enter the technical name and a description for the MultiProvider in the **Edit MultiProvider** popup (see Figure 6.31, Step 1).
- Click the **Create** button to confirm (Step 2).

4 See also Volume 3 of the SAP BW Library (see Appendix L): Egger et al.: *SAP BW—Reporting and Analysis*. SAP Press, 2005.

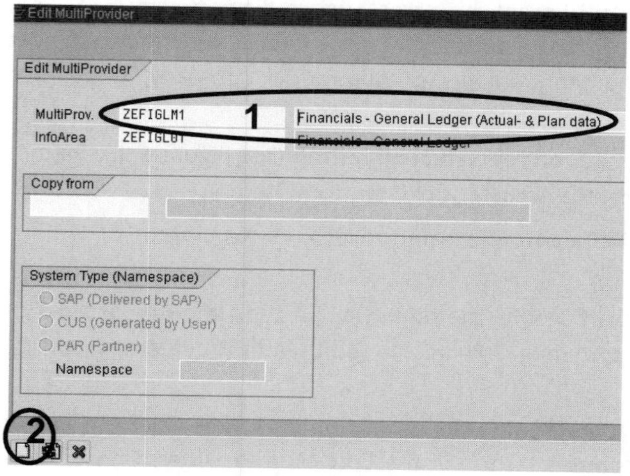

Figure 6.31 Specifying the Name and Description of the MultiProvider

Selecting InfoCubes

- In the **MultiProvider: Relevant InfoProviders** popup, select the previously created InfoCubes in the **InfoCubes** tab (see Figure 6.32, Step 1) by highlighting them in the **InfoProvider** column (Step 2).
- Click **Next (Enter)** to confirm the entries (Step 3).

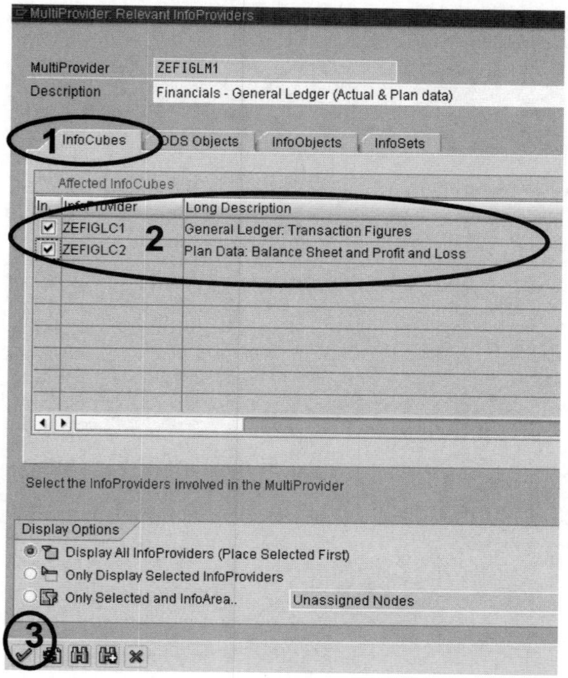

Figure 6.32 Selecting the Relevant InfoCubes

Selecting fields

- Now the **Edit MultiProvider: Characteristics** dialog screen is started. Here we'll select all characteristics from the InfoCubes in order to meet all the reporting requirements of our model company, CubeServe Engines.
- To do this, first click on the **Select all** button (see Figure 6.33, Step 1) and then click on the **Transfer fields** button (Step 2).
- The characteristics are now transferred into the structure of the Multi-Provider (Step 3).
- Then, you must proceed in the same way for the **Time Characteristics** (see the corresponding tab in the **Edit MultiProvider: ...** dialog screen).

Selecting navigation attributes

- You now have to determine the navigation attributes. To do this, click on the **Nav.attributes** button in the **Edit MultiProvider: Characteristics** dialog screen (Step 4).

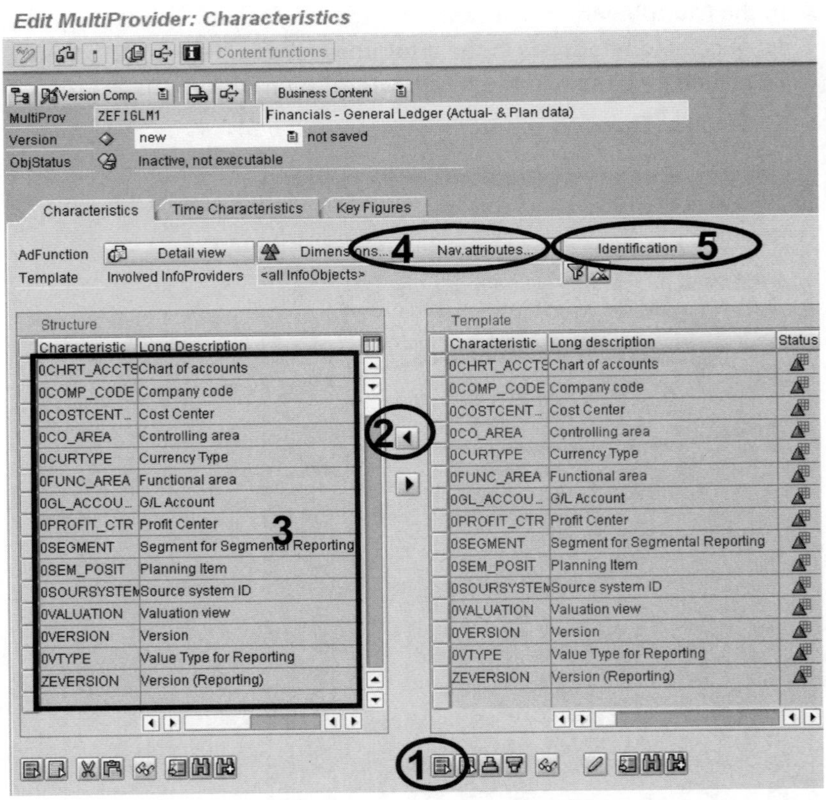

Figure 6.33 Transferring the Characteristics of the InfoCubes Which Serve as a Basis for the MultiProvider

- Since all permitted navigation attributes are necessary in order to meet the reporting requirements of the model company, you should switch on all navigation attributes available by clicking into the I/O column in the **Switch On/Off Navigation Attribute** popup (see Figure 6.34, Step 1).
- Click the **Next (Enter)** button to confirm (Step 2).

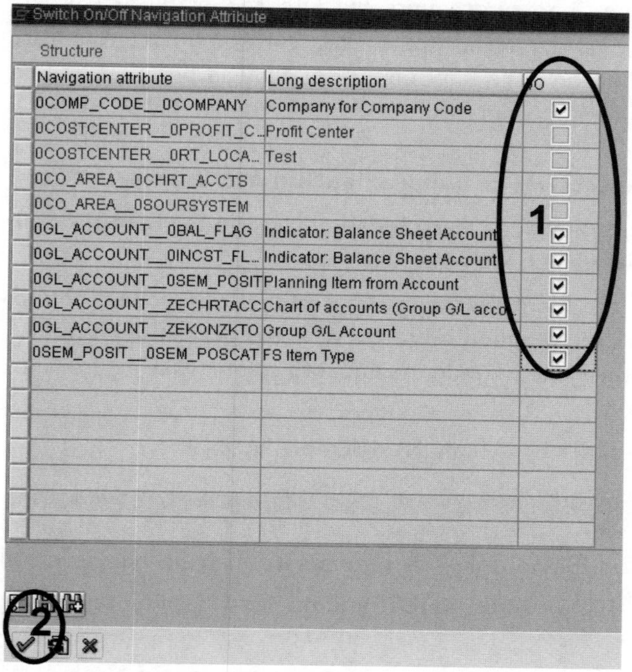

Figure 6.34 Switching On/Off the Navigation Attributes

Identification Procedure

To be able to access the data contained in the InfoCubes you must now identify the characteristics and navigation attributes according to their origins. The identification determines which characteristic and navigation attribute is to be linked to which other characteristic or navigation attribute. For example, the following items are supposed to correspond to each other:

- The **accounting sector** characteristic of the Actual-data InfoCube should correspond to the **accounting sector** of the Plan-data Info-Cube.

- The **Planning Item** characteristic of the Plan-data InfoCube should correspond to the **Planning Item** navigation attribute of the Actual-data InfoCube (this is because the planning item is not available as a basic characteristic in the Actual-data InfoCube whereas the **Planning Item** attribute of the **General Ledger Account** in the Actual-data InfoCube has the same meaning).

A link between the **Chart of accounts** characteristic of the Actual-data InfoCube and the navigation attribute **Chart of accounts** (group G/L account number) of the same InfoCube is not allowed because the two don't have corresponding contents.

Identifying Characteristics and Navigation Attributes

- In the **Edit MultiProvider: Characteristics,** click on the **Identification** button (see Figure 6.33, Step 5).
- This will open the **Identification of Characteristics Involved** popup. Here you select the required characteristics and navigation attributes by clicking on the checkboxes in the **Equal to** column (see Figure 6.35, Step 1).
- Confirm your entries by clicking **Next (Enter)** (Step 2).

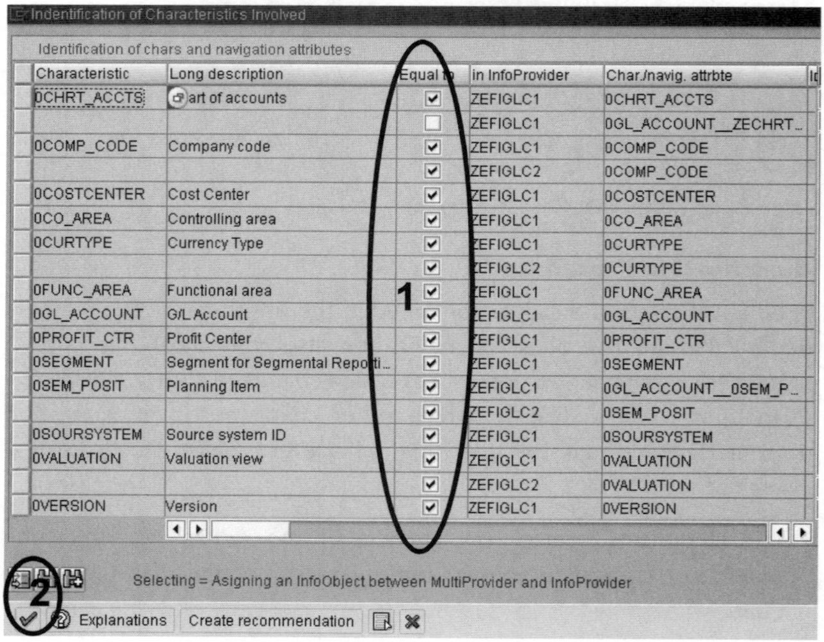

Indentification of Characteristics Involved
Identification of chars and navigation attributes
Characteristic
Long description
in InfoProvider
Char./navig. attrbte
0CHRT_ACCTS
art of accounts
ZEFIGLC1
0CHRT_ACCTS
ZEFIGLC1
0GL_ACCOUNT__ZECHRT...
0COMP_CODE
Company code
ZEFIGLC1
0COMP_CODE
ZEFIGLC2
0COMP_CODE
0COSTCENTER
Cost Center
0COSTCENTER
0CO_AREA
Controlling area
0CO_AREA
0CURTYPE
Currency Type
0CURTYPE
0FUNC_AREA
Functional area
0FUNC_AREA
0GL_ACCOUNT
G/L Account
0GL_ACCOUNT
0PROFIT_CTR
Profit Center
0PROFIT_CTR
0SEGMENT
0SEGMENT
0SEM_POSIT
Planning Item
0GL_ACCOUNT__0SEM_P...
0SEM_POSIT
0SOURSYSTEM
Source system ID
0SOURSYSTEM
0VALUATION
Valuation view
0VALUATION
0VERSION
Version
0VERSION
1
2
Selecting = Asigning an InfoObject between MultiProvider and InfoProvider
Explanations
Create recommendation

Figure 6.35 Identifying Characteristics and Navigation Attributes Involved

Creating dimensions

Now you must define the dimensions. Because the MultiProvider contains a reference to only the data of the InfoCubes involved, you can group these dimensions logically.

- To do this, click on the **Dimensions** button in the **Edit MultiProvider** dialog screen. When defining the dimensions, proceed as described in Section 6.3.4, Figures 6.18 and 6.19.
- You should strive for the results illustrated in Figure 6.36.

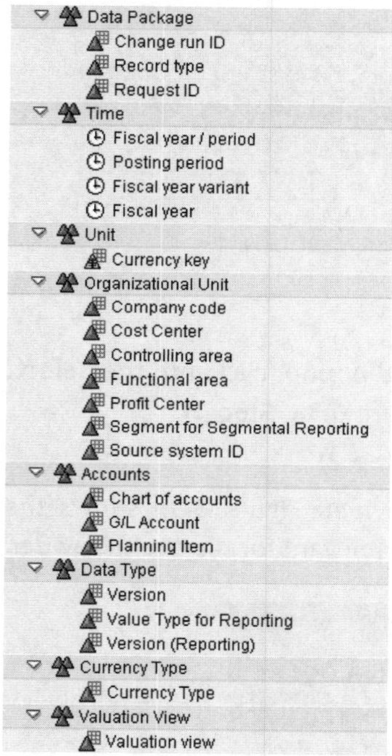

Figure 6.36 The Dimensions of MultiProvider ZEFIGLM1

Selecting the key figures

Finally you must select the necessary key figures. In our example the key figures of all the involved InfoCubes are necessary.

- To select them, switch to the **Key Figures** tab and proceed in the same way as you did when transferring the characteristics in Figure 6.33.
- So first click on the **Select all** button, and then click on the **Transfer Fields** button (see Figure 6.37, Steps 1 and 2).
- The key figures are now transferred into the structure of the MultiProvider (Step 3).
- To identify the origin of the key figures, click on the **Selection** button (Step 4).

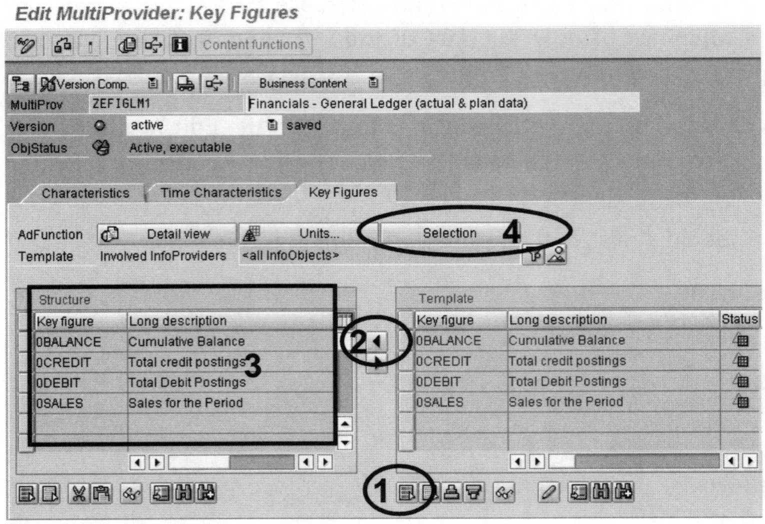

Figure 6.37 Transferring the Key Figures

- In the **Selection of Key Figures Involved** popup, click into the **Select.** column to select all key figures (see Figure 6.38, Step 1).
- Confirm this by clicking **Next (Enter)** (Step 2).
- Lastly, you must activate the MultiProvider. Figure 6.39 shows the storage of data in the InfoCubes that are relevant for the MultiProvider.

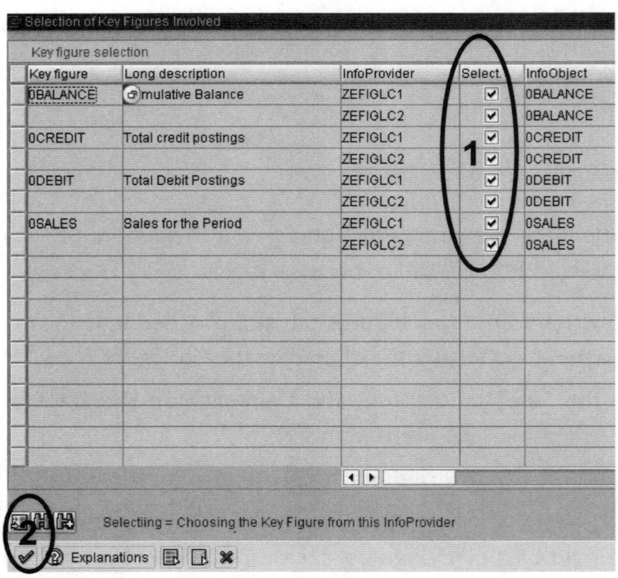

Figure 6.38 Selecting Key Figures Involved

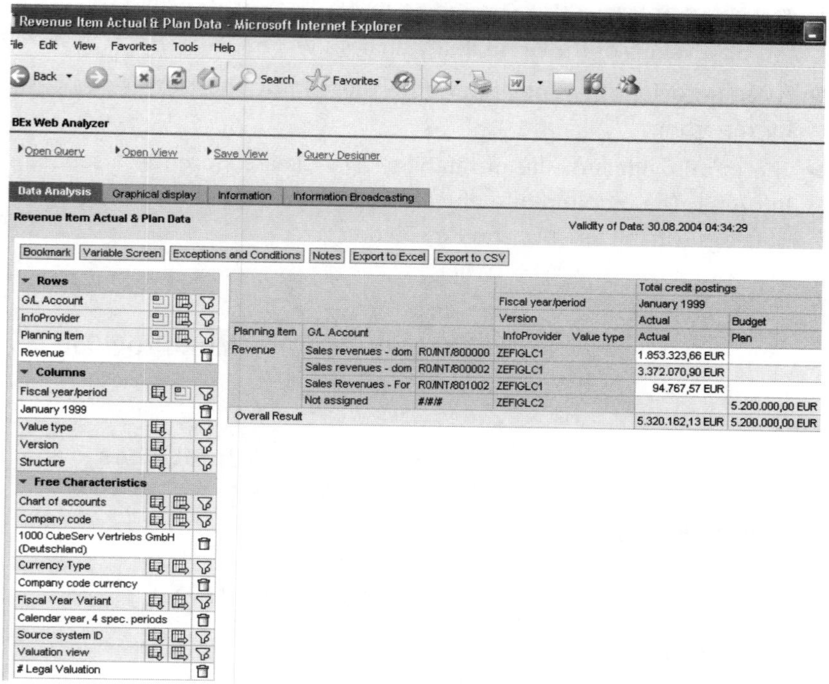

Figure 6.39 Results of a Query on the Financial Reporting MultiProvider

6.4 Profitability Analysis

6.4.1 Data Model and Data Flow: Overview

The profitability analysis is supposed to provide detailed information on a company's revenues and costs. In our example, the source of this information is, among others, the profit and market segment accounting in SAP R/3. On the basis of this, data model and data flow for the profitability analysis are as follows (see Figure 6.40): DataSource.

- In the SAP R/3 upstream systems, individual DataSources are generated for the data of the CO-PA module. The data is then extracted into SAP BW via this interface definition. This procedure should be carried out on a daily basis. To do this, you should use the delta procedure so only the data that has accumulated since the last extraction is loaded.
- First the data is loaded into an operational data source (ODS) object down to the document level; from the ODS object, the key figures will be updated and further aggregated into an InfoCube.

ODS
InfoCube

- To store the data of the planning process, a transactional InfoCube for the plan values of the profitability analysis will be created.

MultiProvider

- A MultiProvider that integrates both these InfoCubes serves as a basis for reporting.

Additional objects

- The InfoProviders of the profitability analysis are stored in a separate InfoArea. The required InfoObjects were combined in two InfoObject-Catalogs (Characteristics and Key Figures).

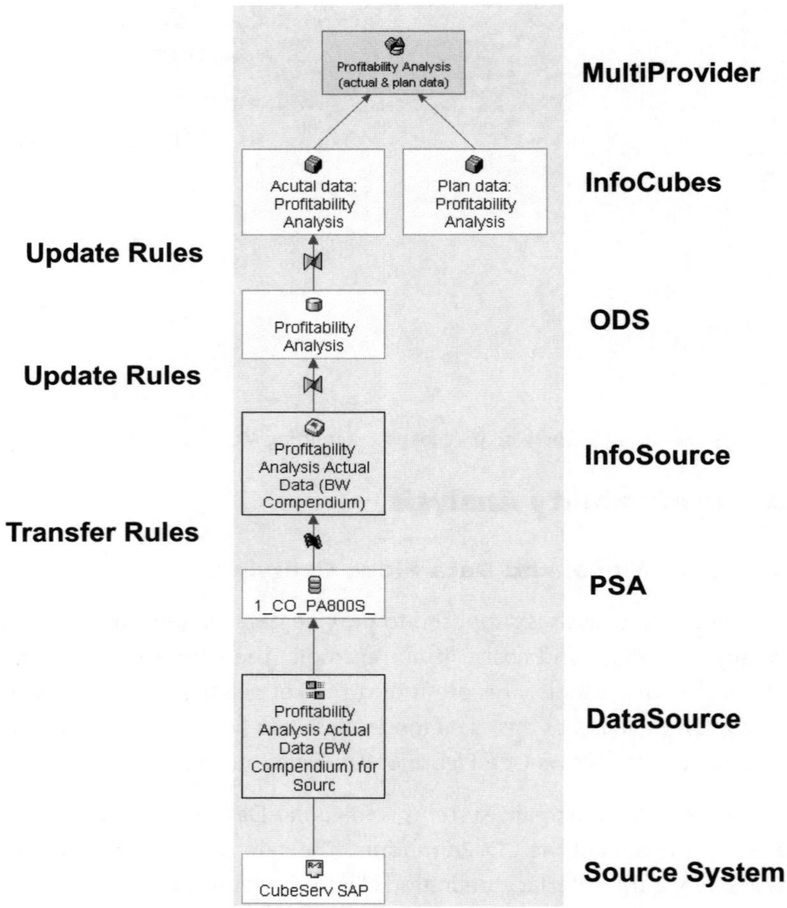

Figure 6.40 Data Flow of the Profitability Analysis

6.4.2 ODS: Profitability Analysis—Actual Data

For the actual data of the profitability analysis, an ODS object, which is supposed to contain data at the lowest document level, is created. Therefore, all fields of the DataSource must be assigned to the corresponding

InfoObjects of the ODS object. Because usually more than one source system is linked to an SAP BW system, the data is stored in an ODS object in a consolidated but not yet aggregated form.

Creating an ODS Object

You can create an ODS object for the Actual-data profitability analysis in a similar manner as it is described in Section 6.3.2 (see Figure 6.41, Steps 1 to 4). The list of the ODS InfoObjects results from the data source (e.g., the InfoSource).

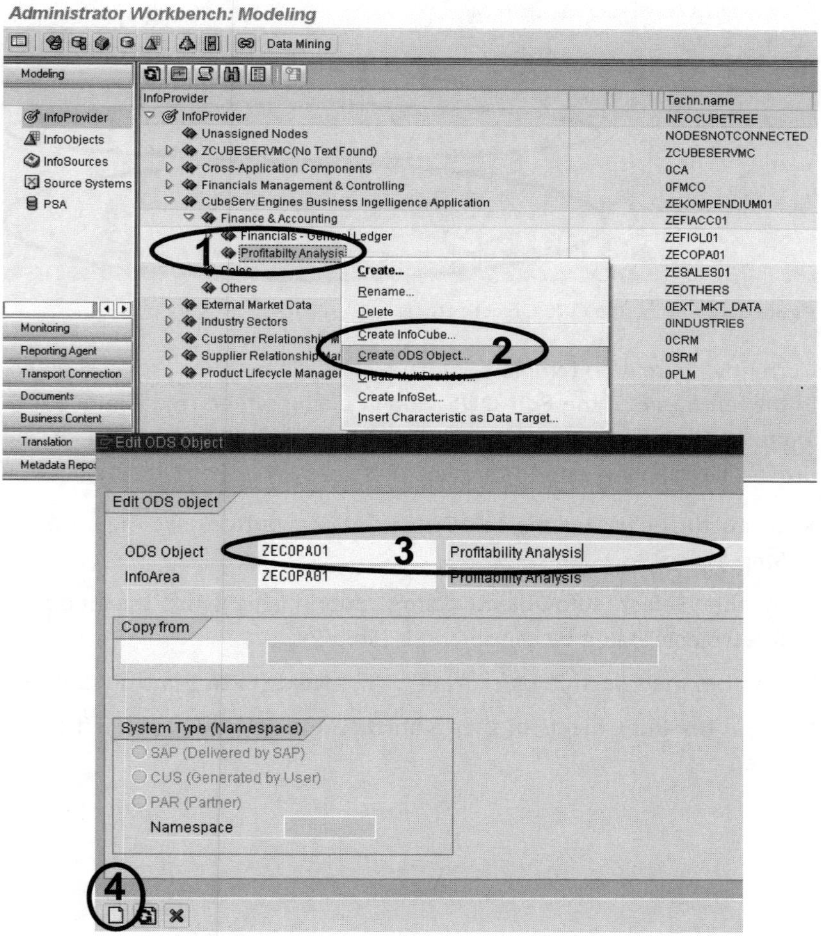

Figure 6.41 Creating ODS Object ZECOPAO1, Part 1

Settings of the ODS object

First, you should set the basic settings of the ODS object. We don't recommend that you permit (default) BEx Reporting for the ODS object;

however, the ETL Process should be carried out automatically as much as possible.

Therefore you set the flags **Set quality status to 'OK' automatically**, **Activate ODS object data automatically**, and **Update data targets from ODS object automatically** (see Figure 6.42, Steps 1 and 2).

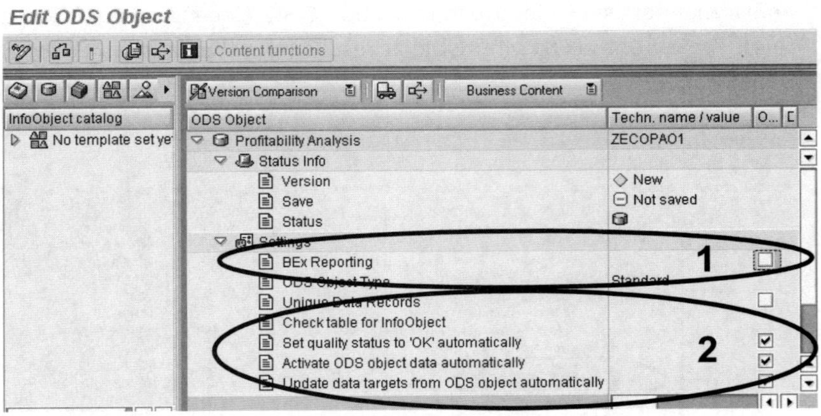

Figure 6.42 Setting the ODS Object Settings

Template for InfoObject selection

Currently, there is no template displayed to further define the ODS object in the left frame of the **Edit ODS Object** dialog screen (see Figure 6.43). Therefore, we first select the characteristics InfoObjectCatalog of the profitability analysis as our template.

- To do this, click on the **InfoObjectCatalog** button (see Figure 6.43, Step 1).
- In the **Select InfoObjectCatalog** popup, highlight the required InfoObjectCatalog by clicking on it (Step 2).
- Confirm the selection by clicking on the **Next (Enter)** button (Step 3).
- Then, the InfoObjects of the template are displayed in the left frame (Step 4).

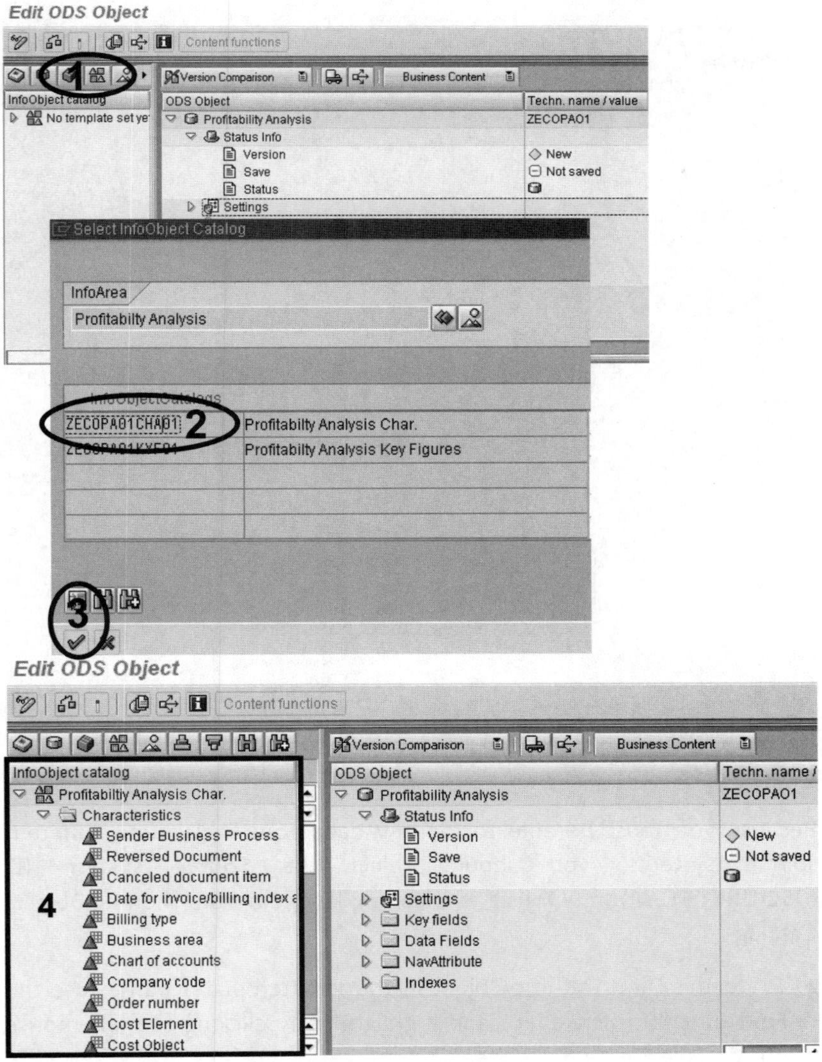

Figure 6.43 Selecting the Characteristics InfoObjectCatalog as a Template

Key Fields

Now you must select the key fields for the document ODS object. For the profitability analysis, specify all available key fields of the source table CE1xxxx of profitability analysis (see Figure 6.44).

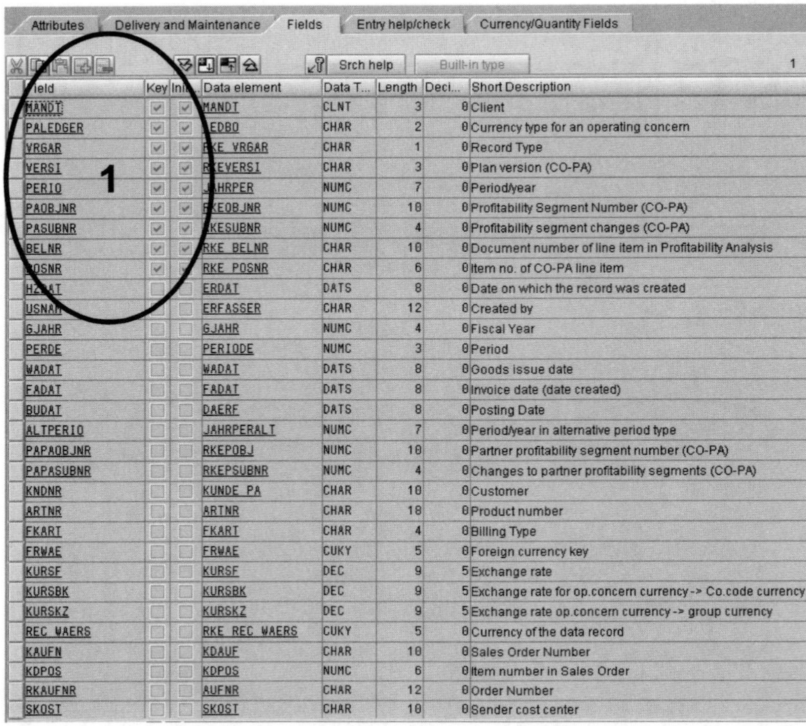

Attributes | Delivery and Maintenance | Fields | Entry help/check | Currency/Quantity Fields

Srch help | Built-in type | 1 /

ield	Key	Ini..	Data element	Data T...	Length	Deci...	Short Description
MANDT	☑	☑	MANDT	CLNT	3	0	Client
PALEDGER	☑	☑	EDBO	CHAR	2	0	Currency type for an operating concern
VRGAR	☑	☑	KE_VRGAR	CHAR	1	0	Record Type
VERSI	☑	☑	RKEVERSI	CHAR	3	0	Plan version (CO-PA)
PERIO	☑	☑	JAHRPER	NUMC	7	0	Period/year
PAOBJNR	☑	☑	KEOBJNR	NUMC	10	0	Profitability Segment Number (CO-PA)
PASUBNR	☑	☑	KESUBNR	NUMC	4	0	Profitability segment changes (CO-PA)
BELNR	☑	☑	RKE_BELNR	CHAR	10	0	Document number of line item in Profitability Analysis
DSNR	☑		RKE_POSNR	CHAR	6	0	Item no. of CO-PA line item
HZ AT	☐	☐	ERDAT	DATS	8	0	Date on which the record was created
USNA	☐	☐	ERFASSER	CHAR	12	0	Created by
GJAHR	☐	☐	GJAHR	NUMC	4	0	Fiscal Year
PERDE	☐	☐	PERIODE	NUMC	3	0	Period
WADAT	☐	☐	WADAT	DATS	8	0	Goods issue date
FADAT	☐	☐	FADAT	DATS	8	0	Invoice date (date created)
BUDAT	☐	☐	DAERF	DATS	8	0	Posting Date
ALTPERIO	☐	☐	JAHRPERALT	NUMC	7	0	Period/year in alternative period type
PAPAOBJNR	☐	☐	RKEPOBJ	NUMC	10	0	Partner profitability segment number (CO-PA)
PAPASUBNR	☐	☐	RKEPSUBNR	NUMC	4	0	Changes to partner profitability segments (CO-PA)
KNDNR	☐	☐	KUNDE_PA	CHAR	10	0	Customer
ARTNR	☐	☐	ARTNR	CHAR	18	0	Product number
FKART	☐	☐	FKART	CHAR	4	0	Billing Type
FRWAE	☐	☐	FRWAE	CUKY	5	0	Foreign currency key
KURSF	☐	☐	KURSF	DEC	9	5	Exchange rate
KURSBK	☐	☐	KURSBK	DEC	9	5	Exchange rate for op.concern currency-> Co.code currency
KURSKZ	☐	☐	KURSKZ	DEC	9	5	Exchange rate op.concern currency-> group currency
REC_WAERS	☐	☐	RKE_REC_WAERS	CUKY	5	0	Currency of the data record
KAUFN	☐	☐	KDAUF	CHAR	10	0	Sales Order Number
KDPOS	☐	☐	KDPOS	NUMC	6	0	Item number in Sales Order
RKAUFNR	☐	☐	AUFNR	CHAR	12	0	Order Number
SKOST	☐	☐	SKOST	CHAR	10	0	Sender cost center

Figure 6.44 Key Fields of the Profitability Analysis Line Item Table in the SAP R/3 Source System

Because you must be able to identify data from the various different source systems, you should select the **Source system ID (0SOURSYSTEM)** InfoObject as a leading key field from the InfoObject-Catalog .

- ▶ To do this, find the InfoObject in the left (template) frame (use the **Find** function, if needed) and highlight it by clicking the left mouse button (see Figure 6.45, Step 1).
- ▶ Keep the mouse button pressed and move the selected characteristic to the **Key fields** folder in the right frame (Step 2). Release the mouse button (Drag&Drop).
- ▶ The **Source system ID** InfoObject has now been transferred as a key field into the ODS object (Step 3).
- ▶ Repeat these steps for other InfoObjects until the ODS object key has been completely defined.

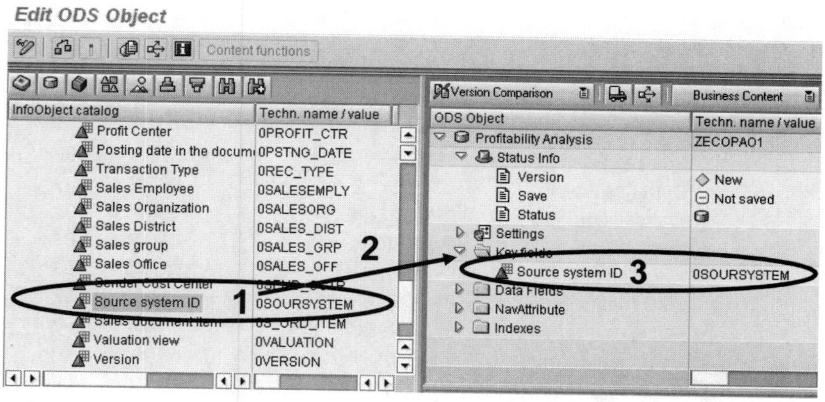

Figure 6.45 Transferring an InfoObject as a Key Field into an ODS Object

Including time characteristics

- To select the time characteristics in the key, switch to the **All InfoObjects** template. With this template, you can include the **Fiscal year variant** and **Fiscal year/period** InfoObjects into the ODS object key (see Figure 6.46, Steps 1 to 3).

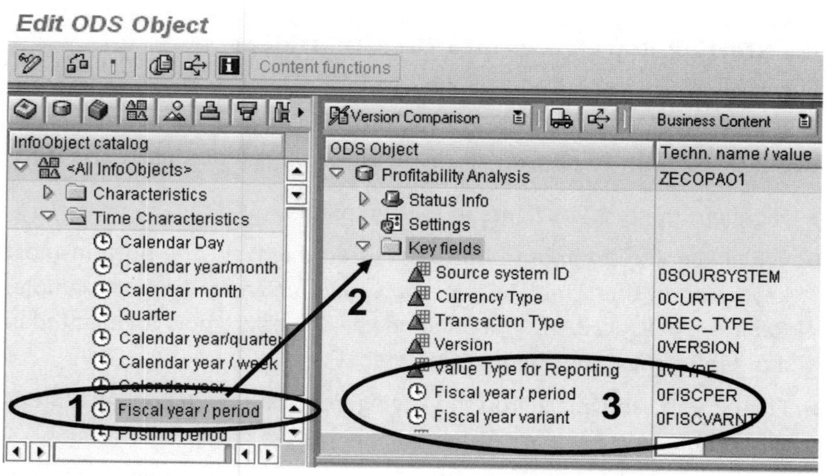

Figure 6.46 Including Time Characteristics into the ODS Object Key

- Assign the remaining key fields to the profitability analysis on the basis of the characteristics InfoObjectCatalog (see Figure 6.47).

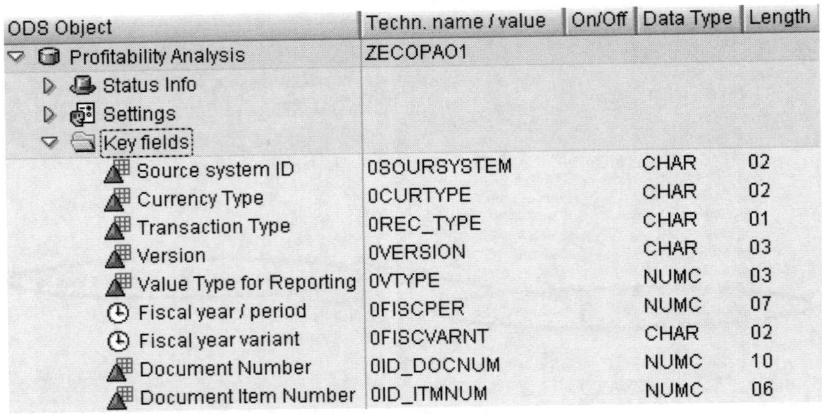

Figure 6.47 Complete ODS Object Key

The remaining characteristics are transferred into the data fields of the ODS object via Drag&Drop. If you want to include additional time characteristics, proceed in the same way as you did when you transferred time characteristics into the key.

Transferring Key Figures into the ODS Object

To transfer key figures into the ODS object, select the key figures InfoObjectCatalog (ZECOPA01KYF01) of the profitability analysis as a template. Because you want to transfer all key figures, you can do this in one step:

- Highlight the first key figure in the template.
- While keeping the mouse button pressed, highlight the bottom-most key figure in the template that you want to transfer (in our example: Rebate, 0VOL_REBATE). All selected key figures are now highlighted in a different color (see Figure 6.48, Step 1).
- Finally, you can Drag&Drop the key figures into the ODS object (Steps 2 and 3).

Navigation attributes

- Because you should not use the ODS object for BEx Reporting, you don't need to switch on any navigation attributes (see the highlighted section in Figure 6.49).

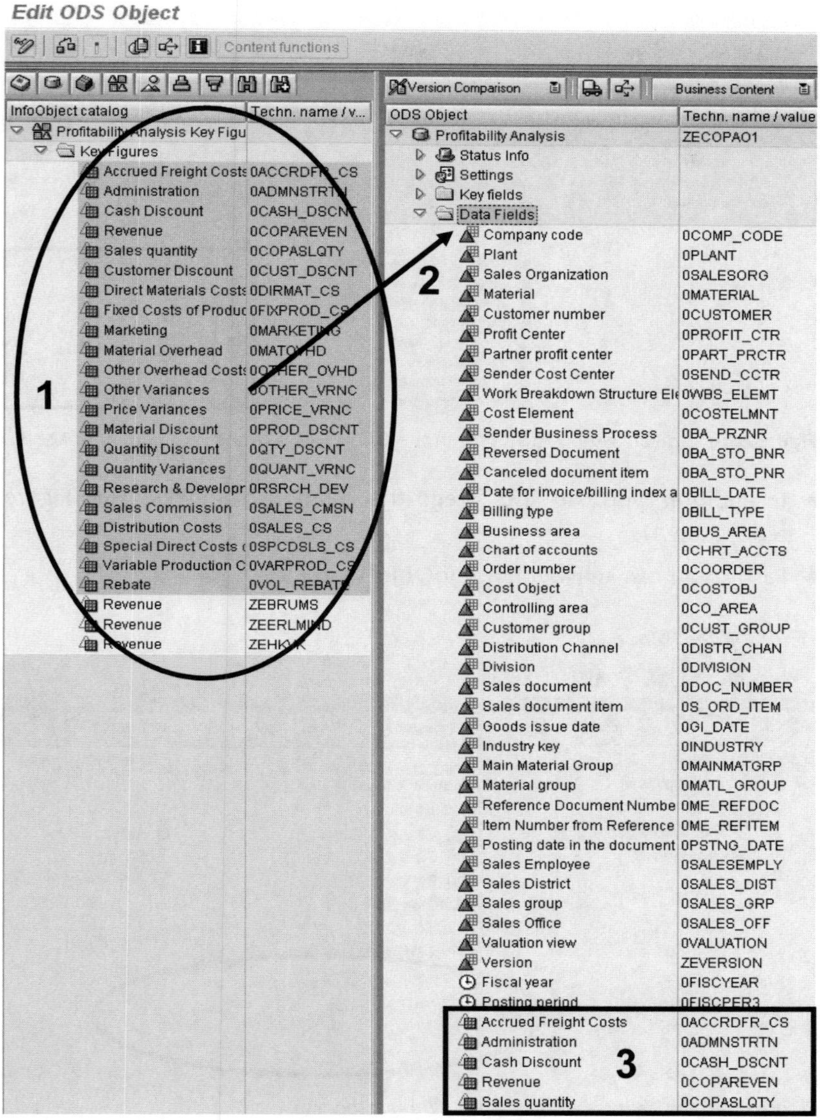

Figure 6.48 Transferring Key Figures as Data Fields of the ODS Object

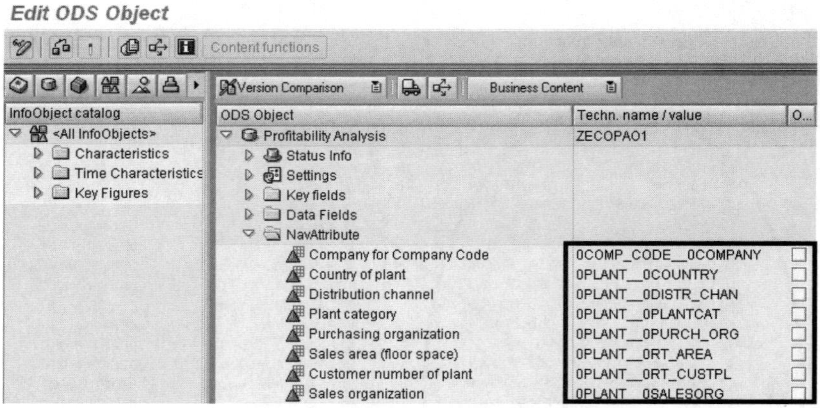

Figure 6.49 No Navigation Attributes in the ODS Object of the Profitability Analysis

Activating indexes

- In addition, you can also forego the creation of indexes (see Figure 6.50, Step 1).
- Lastly, you can activate the InfoObject (Step 2).

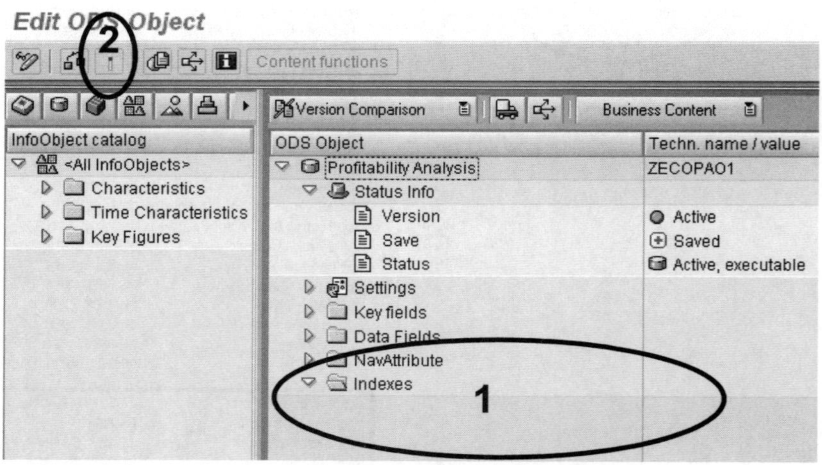

Figure 6.50 Activating the InfoObject Without Indexes

For the ODS object that is not used for BEx Reporting, you must permit analyses on the basis of an InfoSet.

6.4.3 Creating an InfoSet for Document Reporting in the Profitability Analysis

In contrast to the InfoProvider types *InfoCube* and *ODS object*, which were introduced earlier in this book, the *InfoSet* is a semantical layer above data sources and is itself not a data target. (*Note:* Since the introduction of SAP BW 3.0, you should not interchange this InfoSet with the *Classic InfoSet* in SAP R/3). Contrary to the *MultiProvider*, the InfoSet enables joins via ODS objects and InfoObjects (characteristics). SAP BEx queries can be defined on the basis of InfoSets.

Creating a Simple InfoSet

The creation of InfoSets is similar to the creation of InfoCubes and ODS objects.

- Start the **InfoProvider** view in the Administrator Workbench.
- Select the desired InfoArea by clicking on it and click the right mouse button to open the context menu (see Figure 6.51, Step 1).

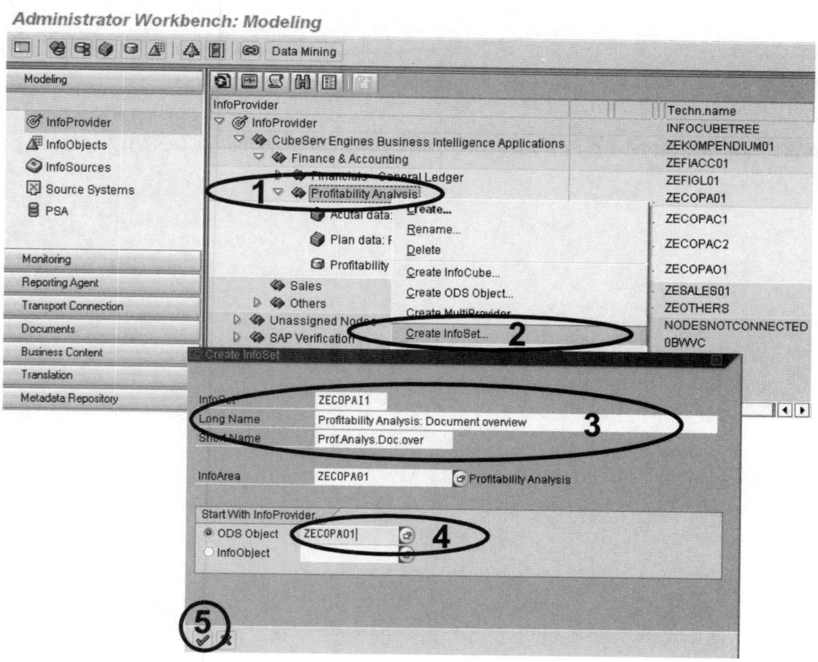

Figure 6.51 Creating an InfoSet

- In the context menu, select **Create InfoSet** (Step 2).
- In the **Create InfoSet** popup, enter the technical name and descriptions (Step 3), and in the **Start With InfoProvider** field, enter the ODS object from Section 6.4.2 (Step 4).
- Confirm this by clicking on **Next (Enter)** (Step 5).
- The InfoSet is now displayed in the **Change InfoSet...** dialog screen (see Figure 6.52).

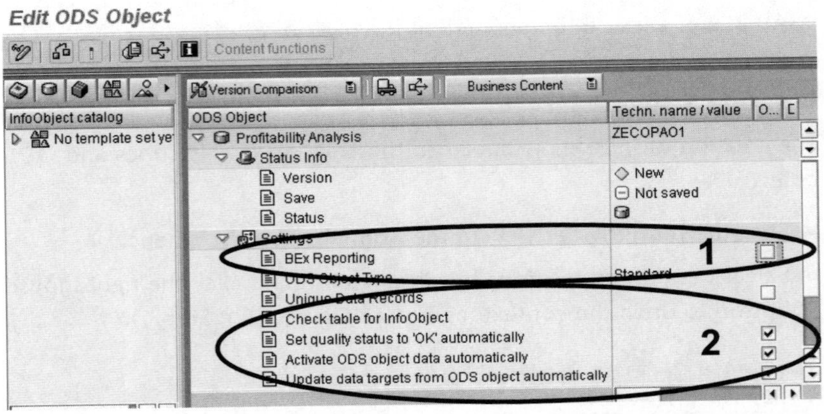

Figure 6.52 InfoSet for Document Reporting in the Profitability Analysis

- It still needs to be activated to make it available for reporting (see Figure 6.53).

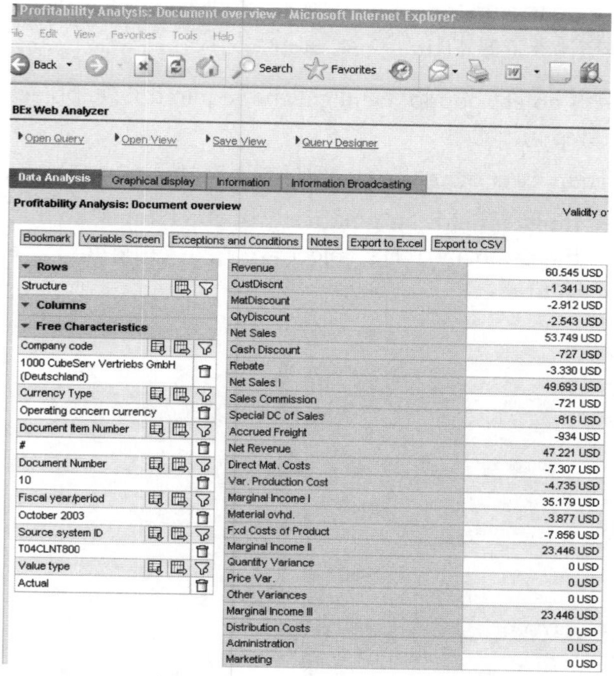

Figure 6.53 Line Items of the Profitability Analysis on the Basis of an InfoSet Query on the ODS Object "Profitability Analysis" (ZECOPAO1)

6.4.4 Creating an InfoCube for Actual Data of the Profitability Analysis

The actual data of the transactional source systems must be provided for reporting via an InfoCube. To do this, you must create an InfoCube.

Non-transactional BasicCube

To create an Actual-data InfoCube for the profitability analysis, you can first proceed as you did when you created the Actual-data InfoCube for the financial reporting general ledger (see Section 6.3.4). For that reason, the Actual-data InfoCube of the profitability analysis must also be defined as a non-transactional BasicCube.

Choosing a Template for Selecting InfoObjects

Transferring InfoObjects from template ODS

After specifying the name, the technical description, and the type of InfoCube, you must select the InfoObjects of the InfoCube. Since the InfoCube of the profitability analysis should contain the same InfoObjects as the ODS object **Profitability Analysis** (ZECOPAO1) but without the document information, select this ODS object as a template.

- To do this, click on the **ODS object** button in the **Edit InfoCube: Characteristics** dialog screen (see Figure 6.54, Step 1).
- In the **Choose ODS object** popup, highlight the required ODS object by clicking on it (Step 2).
- Confirm the selection by clicking the **Next (Enter)** button (step 3).
- Click on **Yes** in the **Transfer fields automatically** popup (Step 4) so that all InfoObjects of the template ODS object are transferred into the structure of the InfoCube.

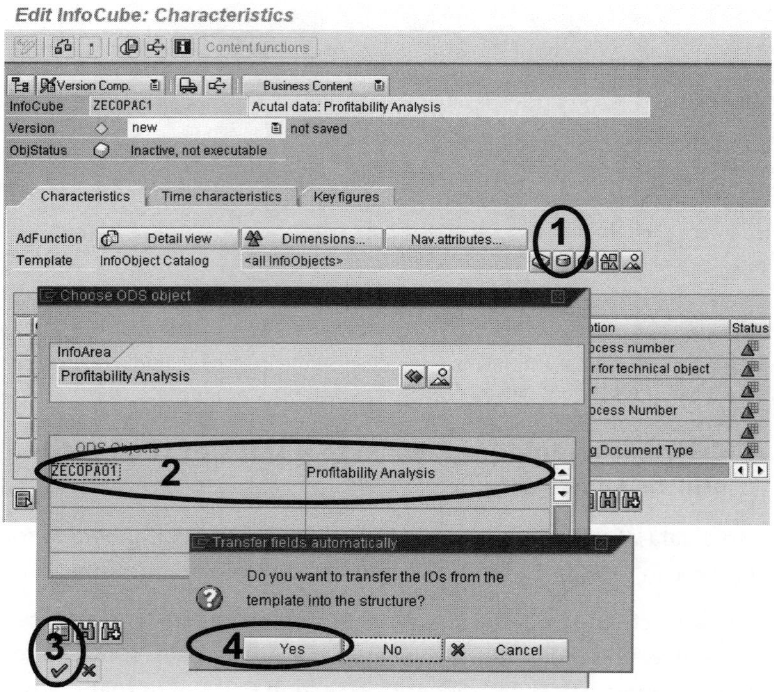

Figure 6.54 Choosing the ODS Object as a Template for the InfoObject Selection and Transferring the InfoObjects

Retransferring document characteristics

- You must now eliminate unused InfoObjects, because all fields have been transferred into the structure of the InfoCube, including the following:
  - **Document Number** (0ID_DOCNUM)
  - **Document Item Number** (0ID_ITMNUM)
  - **Cancelled Document** (0BA_STO_BNR)
  - **Cancelled Document Item (0**BA_STO_PNR)

- **Sales Document** (0DOC_NUMBER)
- **Sales Document Item** (0S_ORD_ITEM)
- **Reference Document Number of the Profitability Analysis Line Item** (0ME_REFDOC)
- **Item Number** of the reference document (profitability analysis) (0ME_REFITEM) of the ODS object

- To do this, highlight the unused InfoObjects by clicking on them (see Figure 6.55, Step 1).

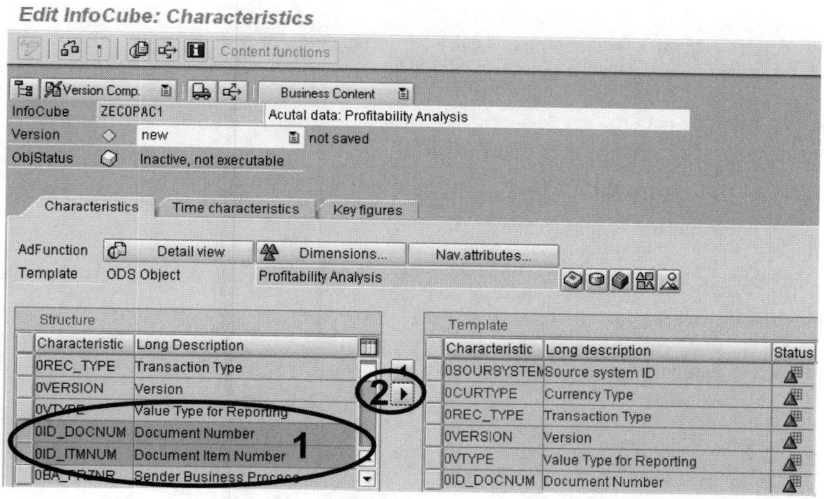

Figure 6.55 Retransferring Unused InfoObjects of the Template

- Then click on the **Retransfer fields** button (Step 2).

Navigation attributes instead of basic characteristics

In addition to the document characteristics, other basic characteristics that are irrelevant for reporting were transferred into the InfoCube with the template: The **Industry key** (0INDUSTRY) and **Material group** (0MATL_GROUP) characteristics are provided for reporting via a navigation attribute for the basic characteristics **Customer** (0CUSTOMER) and **Material** (0MATERIAL). The Main Material Group can be used via Attribute or Hierarchy. Therefore, you must also retransfer these InfoObjects.

Customizing Navigation Attributes

- Click on the **Nav. attributes** button in the **Edit InfoCube: Characteristics** dialog screen to open the **Switch On/Off Navigation Attribute** popup.

- Here you can activate the required navigation attributes by checking the **I/O** flag (see Figure 6.56, Step 1).
- Confirm the settings by clicking on the **Next (Enter)** button (Step 2).
- In particular, you must switch on those characteristics, namely, industry key and material group, that, according to the current assignments, are to be used as navigation attributes instead of basic characteristics in reporting (industry key and material group).

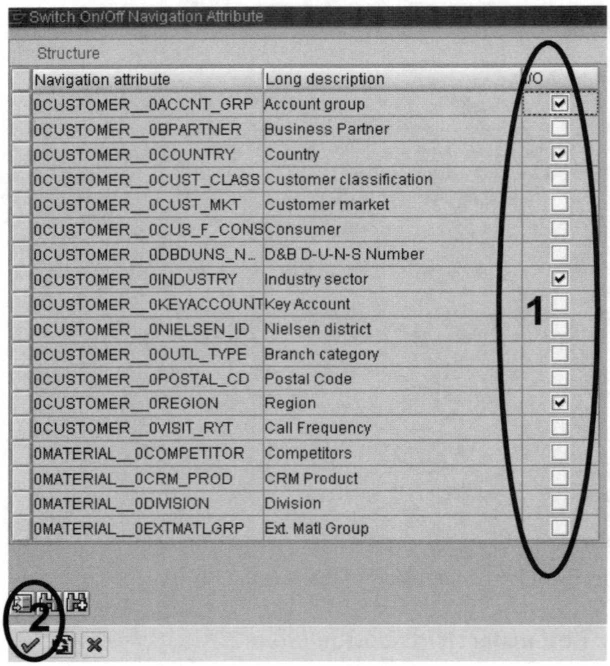

Figure 6.56 Selecting the Required Navigation Attributes

Defining Dimensions

- When you click on the **Dimensions** button in the **Edit InfoCube: Characteristics** dialog screen, in the following **Create Dimensions** popup you will be asked if you want to create dimensions from a template. Click on **No** (see Figure 6.57, Step 1).
- This opens the **Define Dimensions** popup (see Figure 6.57).
- Create the required dimensions in the **Define** tab. To do this, just click on the **Create** button repeatedly until there is a sufficient number of dimensions available (Step 2).
- Next, enter the appropriate descriptions for the dimensions (Step 3).

- For dimensions that consist of only a single InfoObject, you can activate the Line Item characteristic if necessary. To do this, activate the corresponding option of the dimension (Step 4).

Line Items

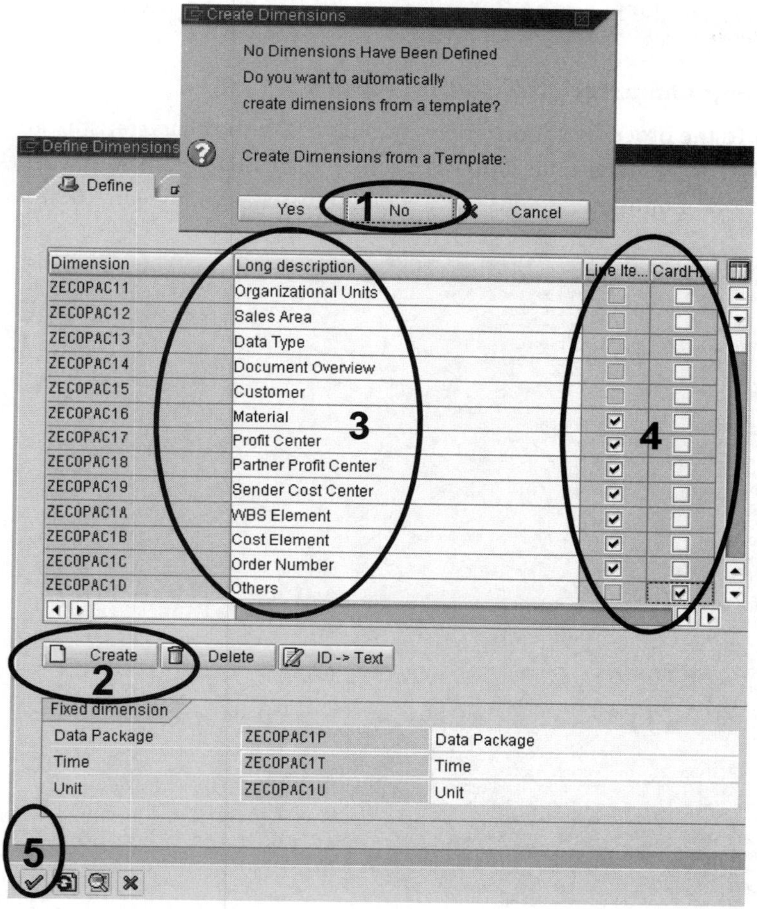

Figure 6.57 Defining Dimensions

- Similarly, you can set the **High Cardinality** option for dimensions that contain a large number of entries (see Figure 6.57, Step 4). If you set this characteristic, more appropriate index types will be selected for generating data structures for an InfoCube, which improves the read performance of these dimensions.

High Cardinality

- Confirm the settings by clicking on the **Next (Enter)** button (Step 5).

In the context help of the **Define Dimensions** popup, SAP recommends the following values for dimensions with a large number of entries: Size: Dimension reaches at least 20 % of the fact table size, measured in the number of sets.

Assigning Characteristics to Dimensions

Similar to the procedure described in Section 6.3.4, the characteristics are assigned to the dimensions (in particular, see the explanations for Figures 6.17 to 6.20) until the dimensions are defined as shown in Figure 6.58.

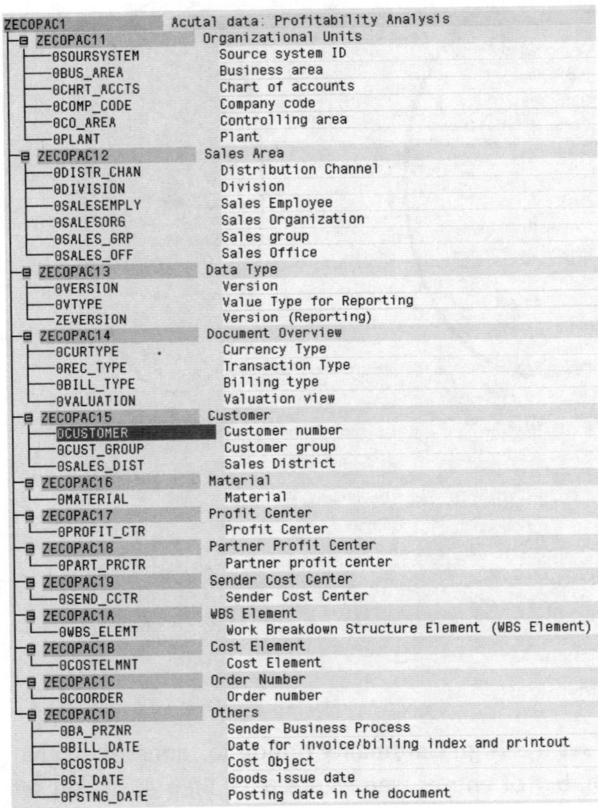

ZECOPAC1 Acutal data: Profitability Analysis
ZECOPAC11 Organizational Units
0SOURSYSTEM Source system ID
0BUS_AREA Business area
0CHRT_ACCTS Chart of accounts
0COMP_CODE Company code
0CO_AREA Controlling area
0PLANT Plant
ZECOPAC12 Sales Area
0DISTR_CHAN Distribution Channel
0DIVISION Division
0SALESEMPLY Sales Employee
0SALESORG Sales Organization
0SALES_GRP Sales group
0SALES_OFF Sales Office
ZECOPAC13 Data Type
0VERSION Version
0VTYPE Value Type for Reporting
ZEVERSION Version (Reporting)
ZECOPAC14 Document Overview
0CURTYPE Currency Type
0REC_TYPE Transaction Type
0BILL_TYPE Billing type
0VALUATION Valuation view
ZECOPAC15 Customer
0CUSTOMER Customer number
0CUST_GROUP Customer group
0SALES_DIST Sales District
ZECOPAC16 Material
0MATERIAL Material
ZECOPAC17 Profit Center
0PROFIT_CTR Profit Center
ZECOPAC18 Partner Profit Center
0PART_PRCTR Partner profit center
ZECOPAC19 Sender Cost Center
0SEND_CCTR Sender Cost Center
ZECOPAC1A WBS Element
0WBS_ELEMT Work Breakdown Structure Element (WBS Element)
ZECOPAC1B Cost Element
0COSTELMNT Cost Element
ZECOPAC1C Order Number
0COORDER Order number
ZECOPAC1D Others
0BA_PRZNR Sender Business Process
0BILL_DATE Date for invoice/billing index and printout
0COSTOBJ Cost Object
0GI_DATE Goods issue date
0PSTNG_DATE Posting date in the document

Figure 6.58 Dimensions of the Actual-Data InfoCube of the Profitability Analysis

Key figures and time characteristics

When you transferred the InfoObjects from the ODS object template, all time characteristics and key figures of the ODS object were transferred as well. Therefore, the required key figures and time characteristics are available in their entirety (see Appendix D, *InfoCube Actual Data: Profit and Loss Statement*).

After activation, the Actual-data InfoCube can be used for additional tasks.

Activation

6.4.5 Creating an InfoCube for Plan Data of the Profitability Analysis

Dedicated Plan-data InfoCube

The profitability analysis data that was generated in the course of a SAP BW-integrated planning must also be stored in an InfoCube. However, as described in Section 6.3.5, the SAP BW-BPS component has specific requirements for such a BasicCube. Apart from this, in profitability analysis the granularity of plan data is significantly lower than that of the actual data. Therefore a separate InfoCube must be created for the plan data of the profitability analysis.

Plan Profitability Analysis

The requirements for the plan profitability analysis correspond to those of the Actual-data cube. Therefore, we will use the latter as a template. Planning will be carried out with the granularity year, accounting sector, country and region of the customer, and product hierarchy for aggregate key figures up to profit margin II.

Differences to the Actual-data InfoCube

With regard to characteristics and time characteristics, the Actual-data InfoCube of the profitability analysis can be used as a template for the Plan-data InfoCube. The **Country** (0COUNTRY) and **Region** (0REGION) characteristics of the customer, as well as the **Product hierarchy** (0PROD_HIER) characteristic—all of which are relevant for planning—must be included in the InfoCube. For the key figures, you must select different InfoObjects. Lastly, you should optimize the dimensions.

Creating the Plan-Data InfoCube

- To create the InfoCube, start the **InfoProvider** view of the SAP BW Administrator Workbench.
- At the beginning, you should proceed as you did when you created the Plan-data InfoCube (see Section 6.3.5, Figure 6.24): Select the Actual-data InfoCube ZECOPAC1 as a template and the InfoCube type **transactional.**

Retransferring unused characteristics

- In the **Edit InfoCube: Characteristics** dialog screen, highlight the basic characteristics that are not relevant for planning (see Figure 6.59, Step 1), and click on the **Retransfer fields b**utton (Step 2).
- This will reduce the list of characteristics in the InfoCube structure.
- Repeat these steps for the region and the product hierarchy.

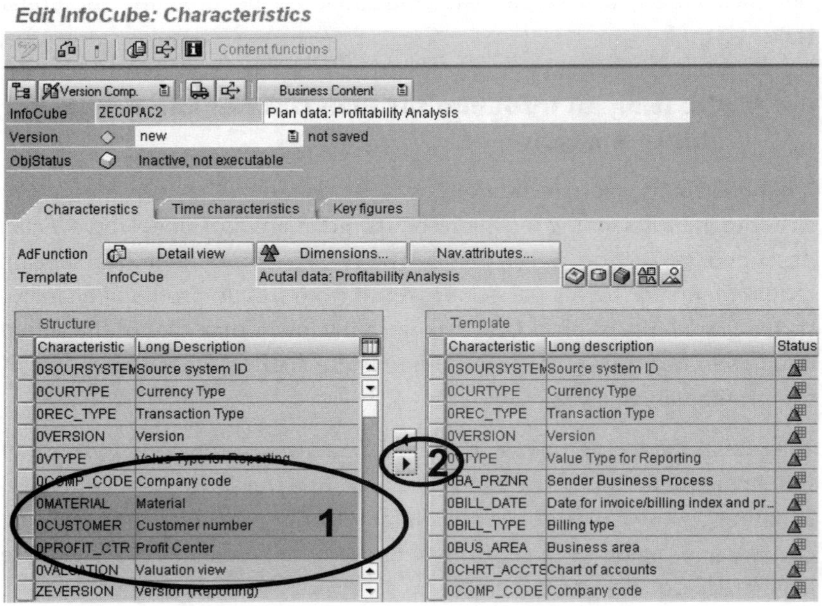

Figure 6.59 Retransferring Unused Characteristics

Transferring Characteristics

Characteristics relevant for planning that are not available in the template for the InfoCube must be transferred. To do this, you must search for them in the (default) template **All InfoObjects**.

- In the **Edit InfoCube: Characteristics** dialog screen, click on the **Find** button (see Figure 6.60, Step 1).
- Then the **Determine Search Criterion** popup will open. In this popup, enter the **Object name** (in this case 0COUNTRY) or the **Meaning** as search criterion (Step 2).
- Click on the **Next (Enter)** button (Step 3); if the search criterion is found, the cursor will be appended to the corresponding characteristic in the template.
- You can now highlight the characteristic (see Figure 6.61, Step 1) and transfer it into the InfoCube structure by clicking on the **Transfer fields** button (Step 2).
- Repeat these steps for the region and the product hierarchy.

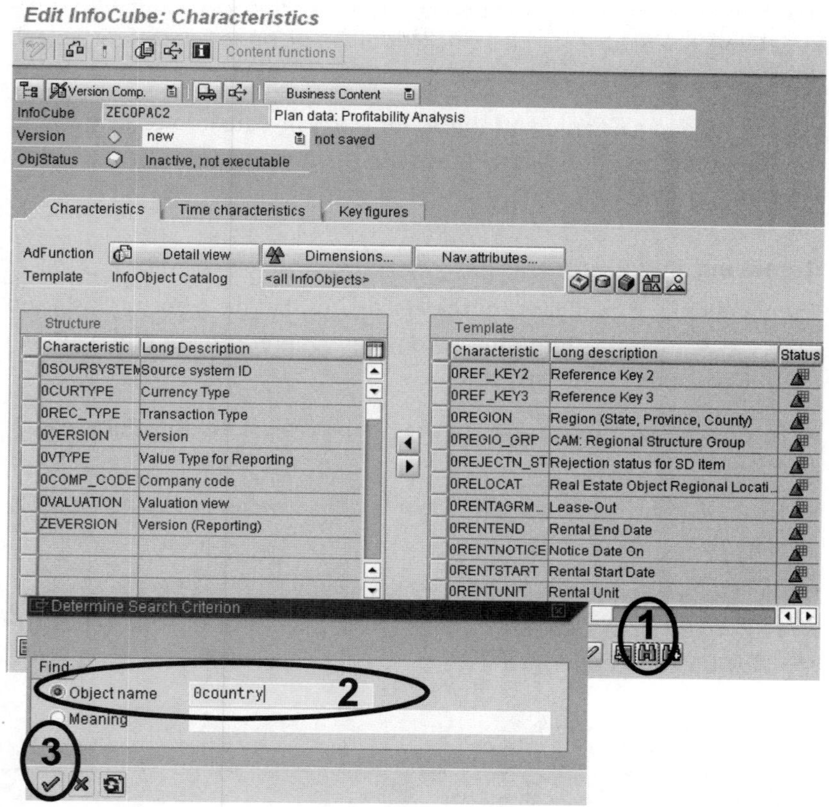

Figure 6.60 Selecting Additional Characteristics

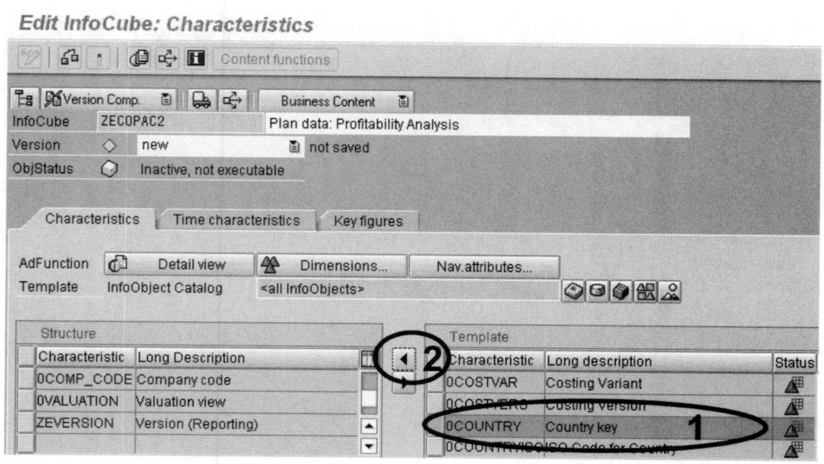

Figure 6.61 Transferring Individual InfoObjects

Modeling

To model the dimensions, the procedure is the same as the one described in Section 6.4.4. Due to the small number of basic characteristics, all dimensions can be created as line item dimensions.

Navigation attributes and time characteristics

You don't need navigation attributes for the Plan-data InfoCube. Because the Plan-data InfoCube was created with the template of the Actual-data InfoCube, the time characteristics are always available.

Removing Key Figures

For planning, the granularity of the key figures that have been transferred from the Actual-data InfoCube is too high. Therefore, we must remove the key figures from the structure.

- To do this, go to the **Key figures** tab in the **Edit InfoCube** dialog screen.
- Then click on the **Select all** button in the structure (see Figure 6.62, Step 1).
- All key figures in the structure are now highlighted (Step 2).
- To remove all key figures from the structure, click on the **Retransfer fields button** (Step 3).

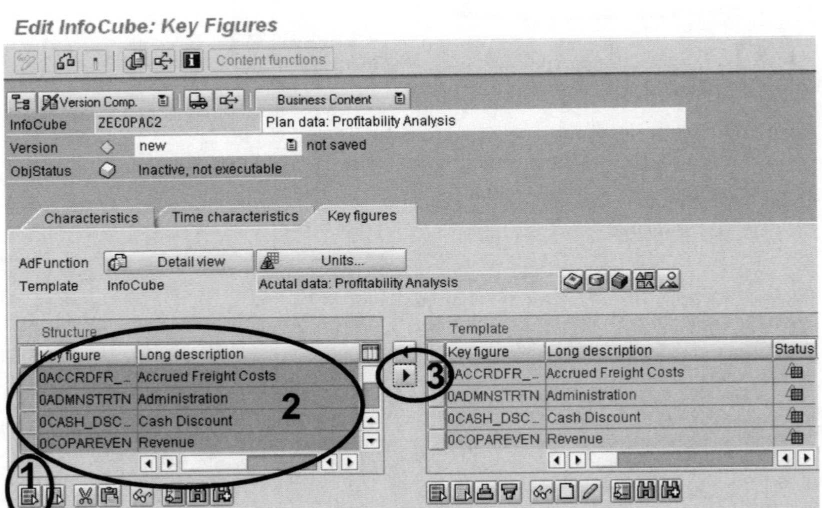

Figure 6.62 Removing Key Figures

Choosing Key Figures

To select key figures for planning, in the **All InfoObjects** template, highlight the first key figure that you want to transfer. Similar to the procedure described in Figure 6.60, we now select the key figure **Gross Sales** (ZEBRUMS) (see Figure 6.63, Steps 1 to 3).

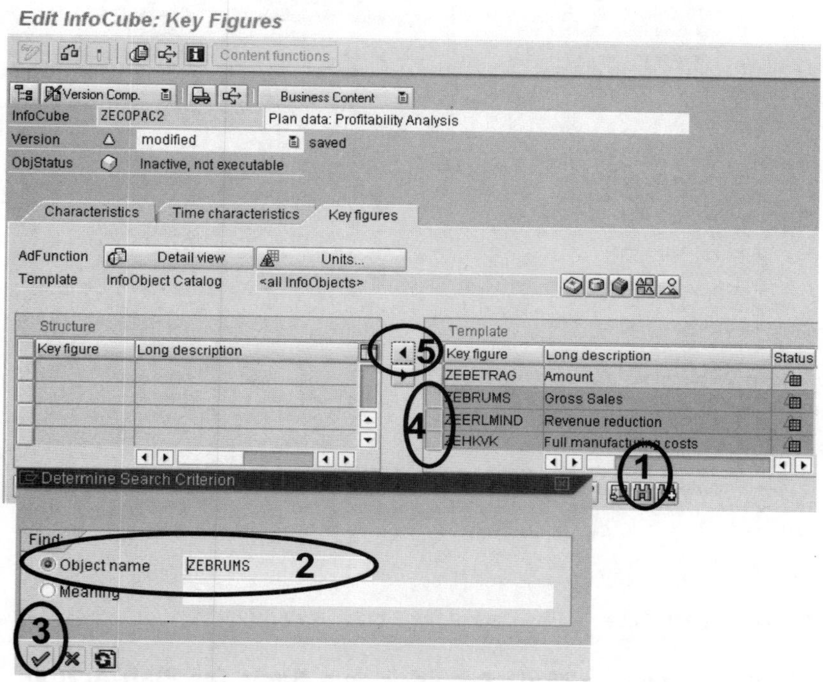

Figure 6.63 Transferring Key Figures

- Now highlight the three key figures relevant for planning by clicking on them (Step 4).
- Finally, transfer them into the InfoCube structure by using the **Transfer fields** button (Step 5).
- Then you must activate the InfoCube.

Activation

The InfoCube structure is now available for planning, as shown in Figure 6.64.

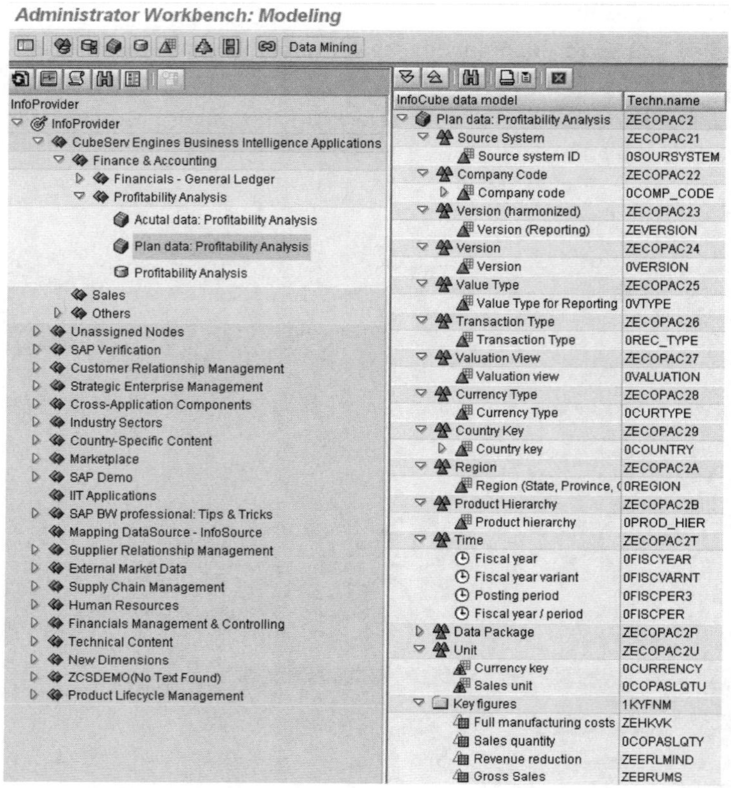

Figure 6.64 InfoCube for Plan Data of the Profitability Analysis

6.4.6 Creating a MultiProvider as a Basis for Plan-Actual Comparisons

As mentioned in Section 6.3.5, due to the separate storage of actual data and plan data in the InfoCubes **Actual-data: Profitability analysis** (ZECOPAC1) and **Plan-data: Profitability analysis** (ZECOPAC2), plan-actual comparisons are not yet possible, which is why the InfoCubes of the profitability analysis are combined in a MultiProvider. To do this, proceed as described in Section 6.3.5 and choose ZECOPAM1 as the name of the MultiProvider and ZECOPAC1 as well as ZECOPAC2 as InfoCubes involved.

Defining Dimensions with Templates

- In the **Edit MultiProvider: Characteristics** dialog screen, use the **Select all** and **Transfer fields** buttons to select all characteristics of the InfoCubes involved.

▶ When asked whether you want to create the dimensions from a template, click on **Yes** in the **Create Dimensions** popup (see Figure 6.65, Step 1).

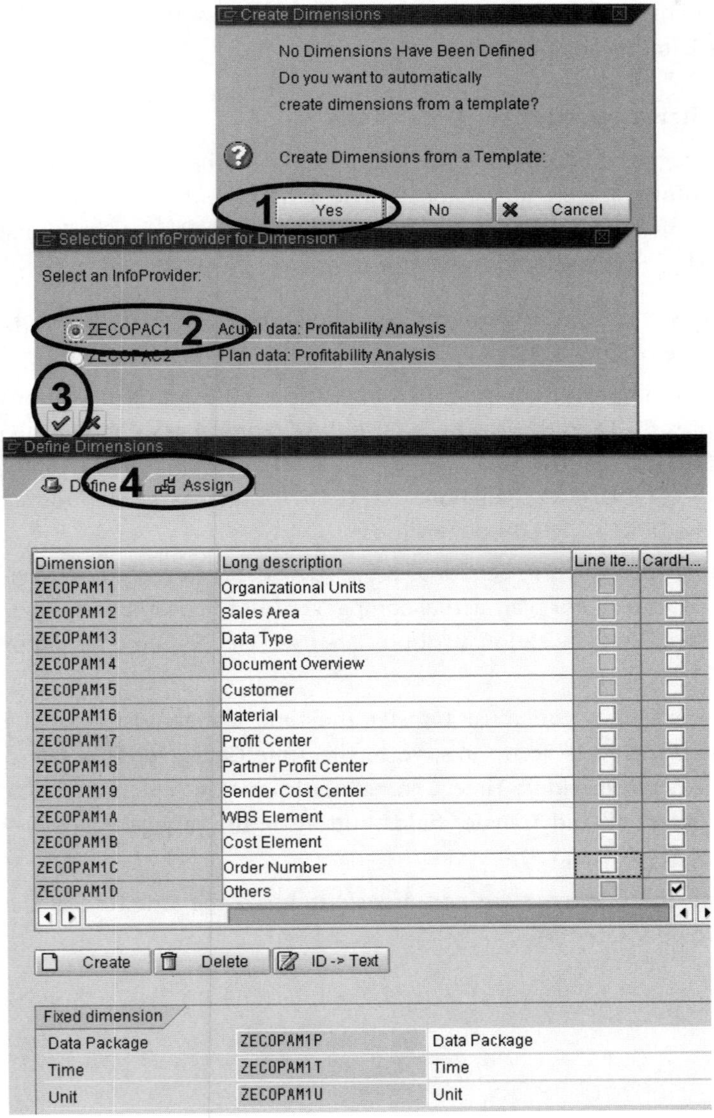

Figure 6.65 Transferring a Dimension from a Template

- In the following popup **Selection of InfoProvider for Dimension,** select the Actual-data InfoCube ZECOPAC1 (Step 2).
- Confirm your entries by clicking **Next (Enter)** (Step 3).
- The dimensions of the template InfoCube are now displayed in the **Define Dimensions** popup.

Adding Characteristics to Dimensions

When the suggested dimension was transferred, the characteristics of the template InfoCube were automatically assigned to the dimensions of the template. This means that you now have to assign only the additional characteristics from the Plan-data InfoCube.

- To do this, click on the **Assign** tab in the **Define Dimensions** popup (see Figure 6.65, Step 4).
- Similar to the procedure described in Section 6.3.3 (see explanations for Figures 6.18 and 6.19), you can use the **Graphical assignment** button to assign the still **unassigned characteristics to the Customer Country (0COUNTRY), Region** (0REGION), and **Material** (Product hierarchy (0PROD_HIER)) dimensions.

Navigation attributes

- Proceed as described in Section 6.3.5, Figure 6.32, to switch on navigation attributes. For plan-actual comparisons of the profitability analysis, all available navigation attributes are used (see Figure 6.66, Steps 1 and 2).

Time characteristics

- In the next step, you must transfer the time characteristics of the InfoCubes involved. To do this, go to the **Time Characteristics** tab in the **Edit MultiProvider: Time Characteristics** dialog screen and click on the **Select all** and **Transfer fields** buttons in the template (see Figure 6.67, Steps 1 and 2).
- The time characteristics are now transferred into the structure of the MultiProvider (Step 3).

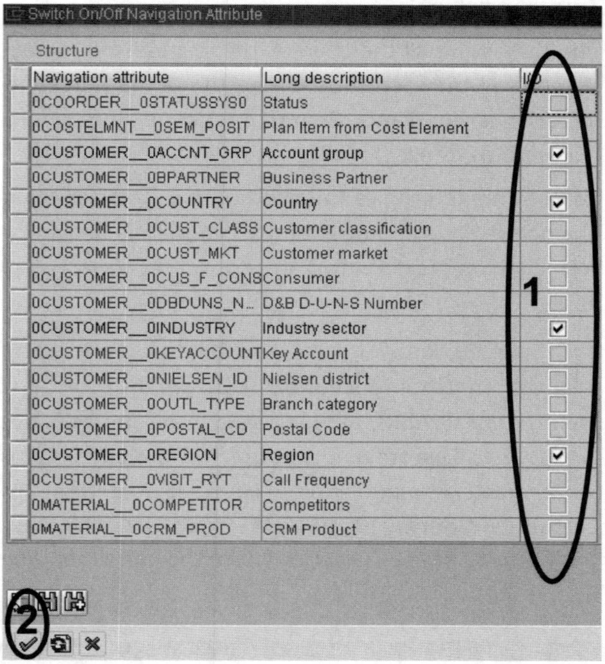

Figure 6.66 Navigation Attributes of the Profitability Analysis MultiProvider

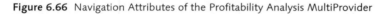

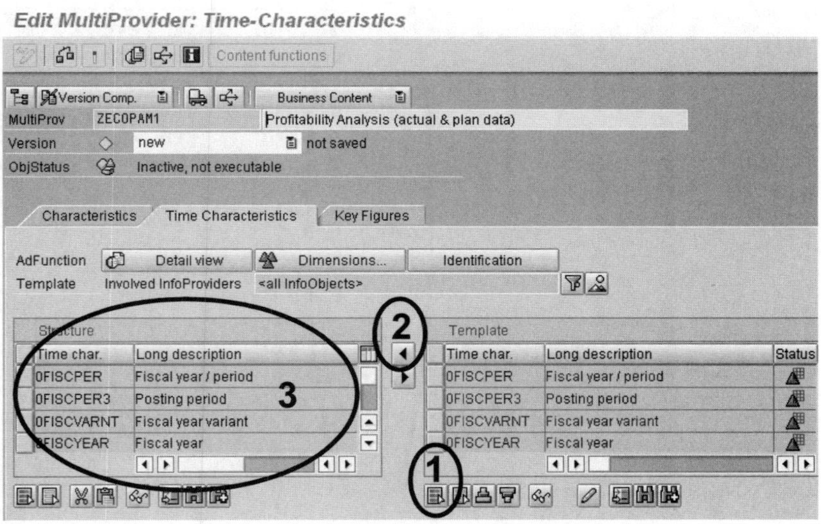

Figure 6.67 Transferring the Time Characteristics

Identifying the Characteristics

- You must determine the origins of the characteristics and time characteristics. To do this, click on the **Identification** button in the **Edit MultiProvider: Characteristics** or **Time Characteristics** dialog screen respectively (see Figure 6.67, Step 4).
- In the **Identification of Characteristics Involved** popup, you can specify the origin of characteristics and navigation attributes by activating the **Equal to** option; click on **Next (Enter)** to confirm this (see Figure 6.68, Steps 1 and 2).

Linking characteristics with navigation attributes

Whereas the country of the customer is provided for the reporting of actual data via the navigation attribute **Country** (0COUNTRY) for basic characteristic **Customer** (0CUSTOMER), the Plan-data InfoCube does not contain the basic characteristic **Customer**. The country of the customer is used directly as a basic characteristic in planning. Hence it is necessary to link the navigation attribute **Country** 0CUSTOMER__0COUNTRY with the basic characteristic **Country key** (0COUNTRY) (see the corresponding lines in Figure 6.68).

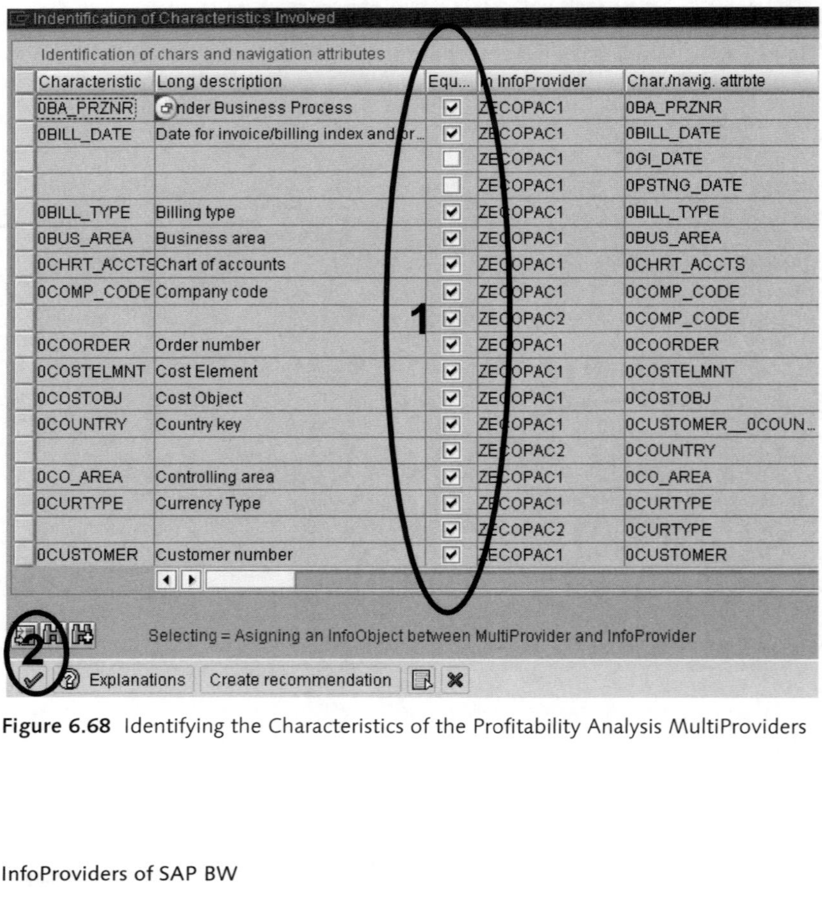

Indentification of Characteristics Involved
Identification of chars and navigation attributes
Characteristic
Long description
Equ...
InfoProvider
Char./navig. attrbte
0BA_PRZNR
nder Business Process
0BILL_DATE
Date for invoice/billing index and
0BILL_TYPE
Billing type
0BUS_AREA
Business area
0CHRT_ACCTS
Chart of accounts
0COMP_CODE
Company code
0COORDER
Order number
0COSTELMNT
Cost Element
0COSTOBJ
Cost Object
0COUNTRY
Country key
0CO_AREA
Controlling area
0CURTYPE
Currency Type
0CUSTOMER
Customer number
0GI_DATE
0PSTNG_DATE
0CUSTOMER__0COUN...
1
2
Selecting = Asigning an InfoObject between MultiProvider and InfoProvider
Explanations
Create recommendation

Figure 6.68 Identifying the Characteristics of the Profitability Analysis MultiProviders

Choosing Key Figures

- Go to the **Key Figures** tab in the **Edit MultiProvider** dialog screen to select the key figures of the InfoCubes to be used for the MultiProvider.
- Transfer all key figures into the structure of the MultiProvider by using the **Select all** and **Transfer fields** button, similar to the procedure when transferring characteristics (see Figure 6.69, Steps 1 to 3).

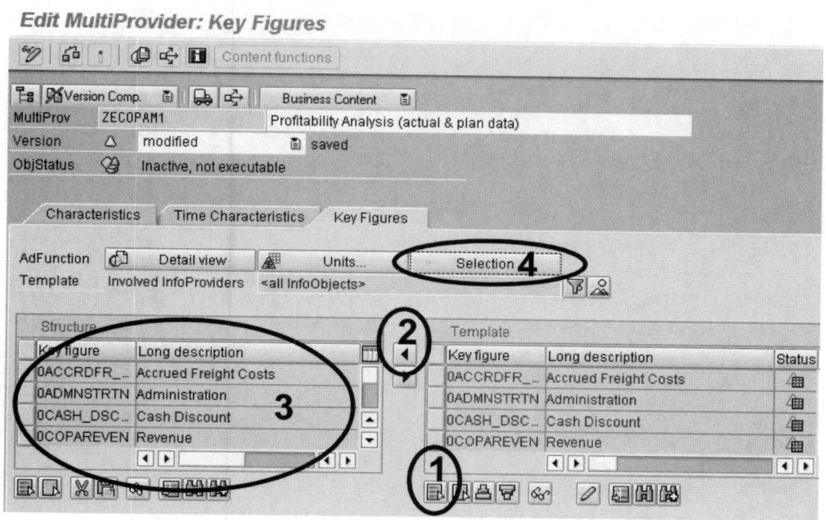

Figure 6.69 Transferring the Key Figures into the MultiProvider and Calling the Selection

Selecting the Key Figures

You can then determine the origin of the key figures by clicking on the **Selection** button (see Figure 6.69, Step 4).

- For those key figures that are contained in only one of the relevant InfoCubes—for example, for key figure **Revenue** (0COPAREVEN) from the Actual-data InfoCube (ZECOPAC1)—SAP BW automatically sets the selection flag (see Figure 6.70, Step 1).
- Only for those key figures that are contained in more than one of the involved InfoProviders is a manual selection required. Both the actual and the planned sales quantities are stored in the **Sales quantity** (0COPASLQTY) key figure. Therefore, you must select both InfoCubes (Step 2).
- Confirm the selection by clicking on **Next (Enter)** (Step 3).

Activation After activation, the MultiProvider can be used for additional work.

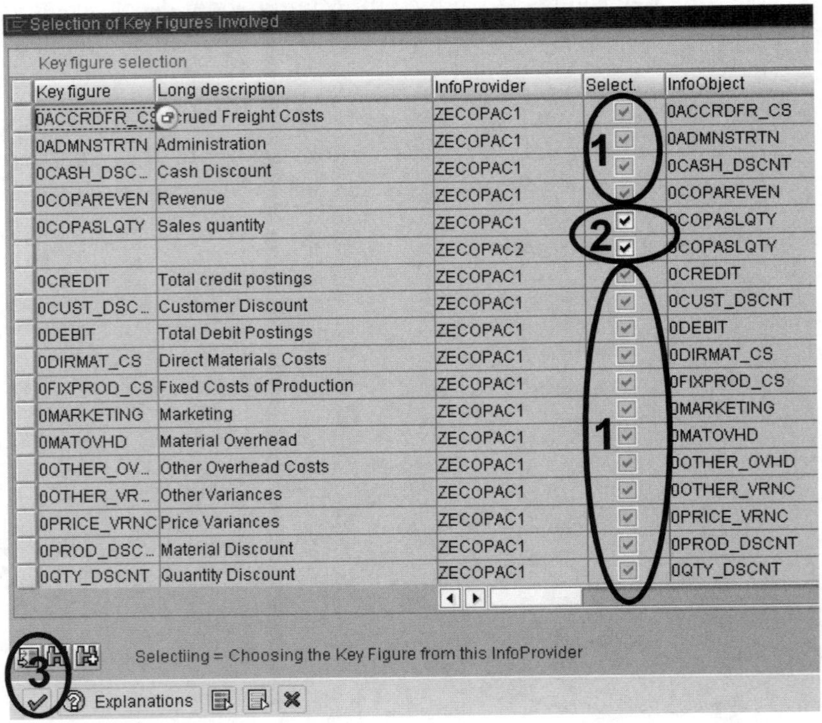

Figure 6.70 Selecting the Key Figures

6.5 Sales & Distribution

6.5.1 Requirements to Incoming-Order and Sales-Order-Stock Reporting

Due to the requirements of incoming-order reporting (see Chapter 4, *Sample Scenario*), various InfoProviders are needed. For document reporting, a highly granular InfoProvider (an ODS object or an InfoCube depending on the document volume) is necessary. With the same high granularity, an average growth in the number of documents in the sales order stocks area would result in a structure of considerable size. This, in turn, would cause performance problems and make high requirements to the hardware used. As sales order stocks are required at only the aggregate level, a dedicated aggregate stock InfoCube will be created and used for sales-order-stock reporting.

6.5.2 ODS Objects for Incoming-Order Reporting: Usability of SAP Business Content and the Need for Enhancements

SAP Business Content ODS Objects

For the incoming orders area, we will create ODS objects for the header, item, and allocation data and a detailed InfoCube. With Business Content, SAP provides a large set of ODS objects (0SD_O01 to 0SD_O03) with their corresponding ETL components. You can use these objects for our model company, CubeServ Engines; however, they must be enhanced in order to be used extensively in real companies.

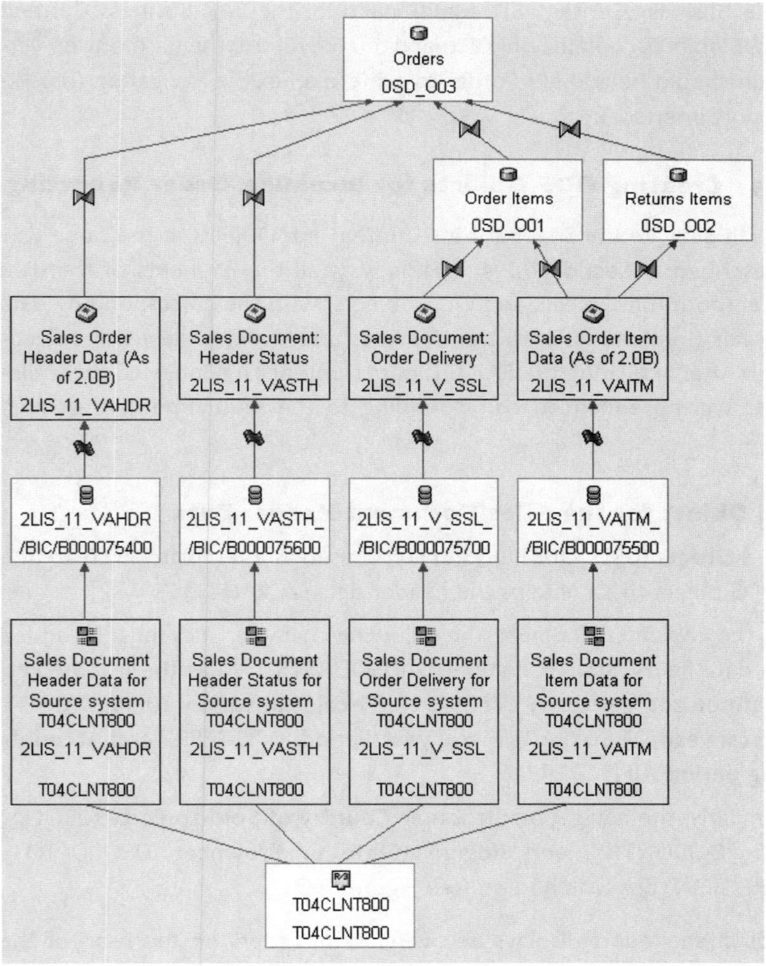

Figure 6.71 SAP Business Content ODS Objects as Templates for Header and Item Data of Sales Documents

Enhancements of SAP Business Content ODS objects

For the model company, the following enhancements are necessary:

- The SAP Business Content ODS objects do not contain the **Source System** InfoObject. However, because we must be able to identify data from various different source systems with regard to their origin, we must add the source system ID.
- The SAP Business Content ODS objects do not contain any time characteristics that would allow for an appropriate distinction of the document amount. Therefore, the required time characteristics must be added.
- The Business Content ETL functionality of the SAP Business Content ODS objects contains only actual data. Therefore, the harmonized version should be added in order to achieve a flexible navigation (report-report interface).

6.5.3 Creating ODS Objects for Incoming-Order Reporting

You can activate the SAP Business Content InfoObjects in the same way as described in Section 5.2.4. In this way, all the elements of the data model (both InfoObjects and ODS objects) with the corresponding data retrievals (InfoSources with transfer rules and update rules) will be activated. After activating the SAP Business Content ODS objects, these elements will be enhanced corresponding to the requirements described above.

ODS Object for the Sales Document Header Data

- The **Orders (0SD_O03)** ODS object is used as a template to create the ODS object that contains the header data (ZEVAHDO1).
- In the copied ODS object, the following characteristics must be added as data fields: **Source system ID** (0SOURSYSTEM) as the leading key, **Harmonized Version** (ZEVERSION), **Fiscal year variant** (0FISCVARNT), **Fiscal year** (0FISCYEAR), **Fiscal year/Period** (0FISCPER), and **Accounting period** (0FISCPER3).
- Similarly, the navigation attributes **Country of Sold-to Party** (0SOLD_TO__0COUNTRY) and **Region (State or Province)** (0SOLD_TO__0REGION) are switched on (see Figure 6.72).

A document report displays an overview of orders on the basis of the Sales Document (header data) ODS object (see Figure 6.73).

Key fields	
Source system ID	0SOURSYSTEM
Sales document	0DOC_NUMBER
Fiscal year variant	0FISCVARNT
Data Fields	
Delivery Status	0DLV_STS
Overall Delivery Status of All Items	0DLV_STSOI
Number of Document Items	0DOC_ITEMS
Cumulated Order Processing Time for All Document Items	0CUML_TME
Delivered early acc. req. delivery date	0DLVIEYCR
Value delivered early acc. req. delivery date	0DLVWEYCR
Delivered late acc. req. delivery date	0DLVILECR
Value of late deliveries acc. req. delivery date	0DLVWLECR
Delivered early/late according to req. delivery date	0DLVIELCR
Value delivered early/ late acc. req. delivery date	0DLVWELCR
More Delivered than Requested	0DLVIOVER
Value Delivered more Than Requested	0DLVWOVER
Less Delivered than Requested	0DLVIUNDR
Less then Requested Delivery Value	0DLVWUNDR
Returns	0DITM_RET
Value of Returns	0VAL_RET
Delivered early acc. schedule line date	0DLVIEYSC
Value of early deliveries acc. schedule line date	0DLVWEYSC
Delivered late acc. schedule line date	0DLVILESC
Value of late deliveries acc. schedule line date	0DLVWLESC
Delivered early/late according to schedule line date	0DLVIELSC
Value of early/late deliveries acc. schedule line date	0DLVWELSC
Confirmed as Requested	0ICOASREQ
Value Confirmed as Requested	0VCOASREQ
Delivery from Warehouse	0ISHP_STCK
Value with Delivery from Warehouse	0VSHP_STCK
Delivery Within 24 Hours	0DLV_24
Value with Delivery Within 24 Hours	0VAL_24
Date on which the record was created	0CREATEDON
Sold-to party	0SOLD_TO
Company code	0COMP_CODE
Customer group 1	0CUST_GRP1
Customer group 2	0CUST_GRP2
Customer group 3	0CUST_GRP3
Customer group 4	0CUST_GRP4
Customer group 5	0CUST_GRP5
Distribution Channel	0DISTR_CHAN
Sales Employee	0SALESEMPLY
Sales group	0SALES_GRP
Sales Office	0SALES_OFF
Sales Organization	0SALESORG
Division	0DIVISION
Document currency	0DOC_CURRCY
Requested Delivery Value	0REQU_VAL
Actual Delivered Value	0DLV_VAL
Net value of the order in document currency	0NET_VAL_HD
Header Deleted	0HEADER_DEL
Version	ZEVERSION
Fiscal year	0FISCYEAR
Fiscal year / period	0FISCPER
Posting period	0FISCPER3
NavAttribute	
Customer Account Group	0SOLD_TO__0ACCNT_GRP
Country of Sold-to Party	0SOLD_TO__0COUNTRY
Region (state, county)	0SOLD_TO__0REGION

Figure 6.72 Enhanced ODS Object ZEVAHDO1 (Order)

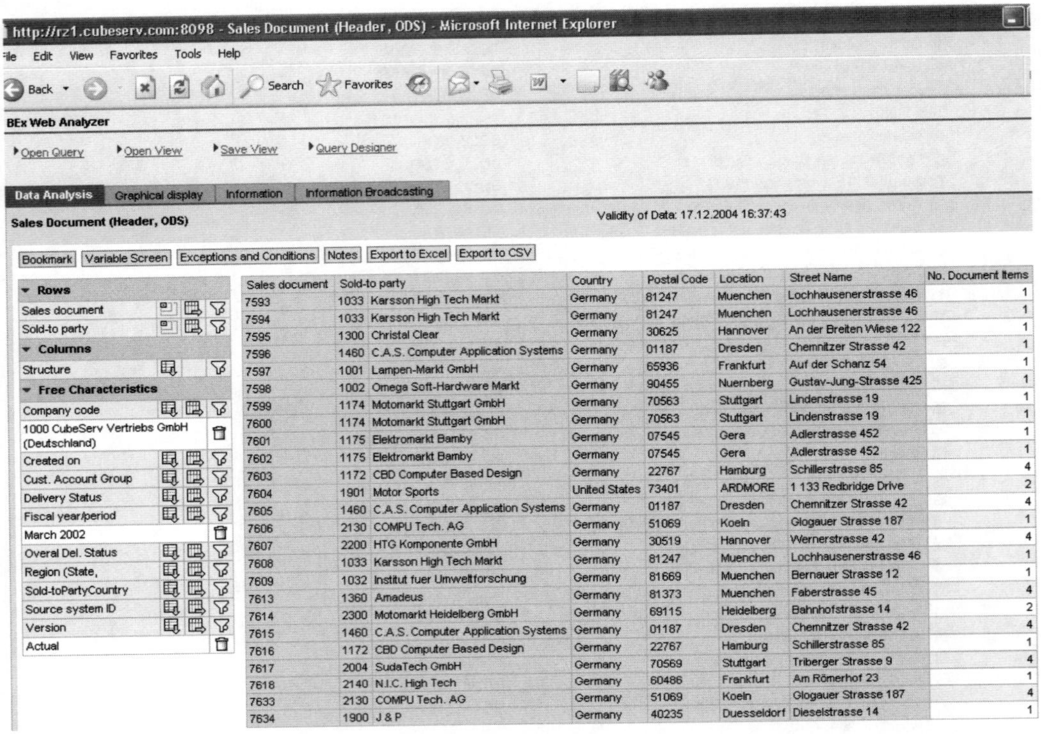

http://rz1.cubeserv.com:8098 - Sales Document (Header, ODS) - Microsoft Internet Explorer
File Edit View Favorites Tools Help
Back Search Favorites
BEx Web Analyzer
Open Query
Open View
Save View
Query Designer
Data Analysis
Graphical display
Information
Information Broadcasting
Sales Document (Header, ODS)
Validity of Data: 17.12.2004 16:37:43
Bookmark
Variable Screen
Exceptions and Conditions
Notes
Export to Excel
Export to CSV
Rows
Sales document
Sold-to party
Columns
Structure
Free Characteristics
Company code
1000 CubeServ Vertriebs GmbH (Deutschland)
Created on
Cust. Account Group
Delivery Status
Fiscal year/period
March 2002
Overal Del. Status
Region (State,
Sold-toPartyCountry
Source system ID
Version
Actual
Sales document | Sold-to party | Country | Postal Code | Location | Street Name | No. Document Items
7593 | 1033 Karsson High Tech Markt | Germany | 81247 | Muenchen | Lochhausenerstrasse 46 | 1
7594 | 1033 Karsson High Tech Markt | Germany | 81247 | Muenchen | Lochhausenerstrasse 46 | 1
7595 | 1300 Christal Clear | Germany | 30625 | Hannover | An der Breiten Wiese 122 | 1
7596 | 1460 C.A.S. Computer Application Systems | Germany | 01187 | Dresden | Chemnitzer Strasse 42 | 1
7597 | 1001 Lampen-Markt GmbH | Germany | 65936 | Frankfurt | Auf der Schanz 54 | 1
7598 | 1002 Omega Soft-Hardware Markt | Germany | 90455 | Nuernberg | Gustav-Jung-Strasse 425 | 1
7599 | 1174 Motomarkt Stuttgart GmbH | Germany | 70563 | Stuttgart | Lindenstrasse 19 | 1
7600 | 1174 Motomarkt Stuttgart GmbH | Germany | 70563 | Stuttgart | Lindenstrasse 19 | 1
7601 | 1175 Elektromarkt Bamby | Germany | 07545 | Gera | Adlerstrasse 452 | 1
7602 | 1175 Elektromarkt Bamby | Germany | 07545 | Gera | Adlerstrasse 452 | 1
7603 | 1172 CBD Computer Based Design | Germany | 22767 | Hamburg | Schillerstrasse 85 | 4
7604 | 1901 Motor Sports | United States | 73401 | ARDMORE | 1 133 Redbridge Drive | 2
7605 | 1460 C.A.S. Computer Application Systems | Germany | 01187 | Dresden | Chemnitzer Strasse 42 | 4
7606 | 2130 COMPU Tech. AG | Germany | 51069 | Koeln | Glogauer Strasse 187 | 1
7607 | 2200 HTG Komponente GmbH | Germany | 30519 | Hannover | Wernerstrasse 42 | 4
7608 | 1033 Karsson High Tech Markt | Germany | 81247 | Muenchen | Lochhausenerstrasse 46 | 1
7609 | 1032 Institut fuer Umweltforschung | Germany | 81669 | Muenchen | Bernauer Strasse 12 | 1
7613 | 1360 Amadeus | Germany | 81373 | Muenchen | Faberstrasse 45 | 4
7614 | 2300 Motomarkt Heidelberg GmbH | Germany | 69115 | Heidelberg | Bahnhofstrasse 14 | 2
7615 | 1460 C.A.S. Computer Application Systems | Germany | 01187 | Dresden | Chemnitzer Strasse 42 | 4
7616 | 1172 CBD Computer Based Design | Germany | 22767 | Hamburg | Schillerstrasse 85 | 1
7617 | 2004 SudaTech GmbH | Germany | 70569 | Stuttgart | Triberger Strasse 9 | 4
7618 | 2140 N.I.C. High Tech | Germany | 60486 | Frankfurt | Am Römerhof 23 | 1
7633 | 2130 COMPU Tech. AG | Germany | 51069 | Koeln | Glogauer Strasse 187 | 4
7634 | 1900 J & P | Germany | 40235 | Duesseldorf | Dieselstrasse 14 | 1

Figure 6.73 Overview of Orders on the Basis of the Sales Document (Header Data) ODS Object

ODS Object for the Sales Document Item Data (Order)

- The **Order Items** (0SD_O01) ODS object is used as a template to create the ODS object that contains the item data (ZEVAHDO1).
- Similar to the ODS object with header data, the copied ODS object will be enhanced in the key and data areas (see Figure 6.72).
- The same applies to the navigation attributes.
- Additionally, the navigation attributes **Product Hierarchy** (0MATERIAL__0PROD_HIER), **Country of Ship-To Party** (0SHIP_TO__0COUNTRY), and **Country of the payer** (0PAYER__0COUNTRY) are switched on, as shown in Figure 6.74.

On the basis of the order item ODS object, reporting at the document level is possible (see Figure 6.75)

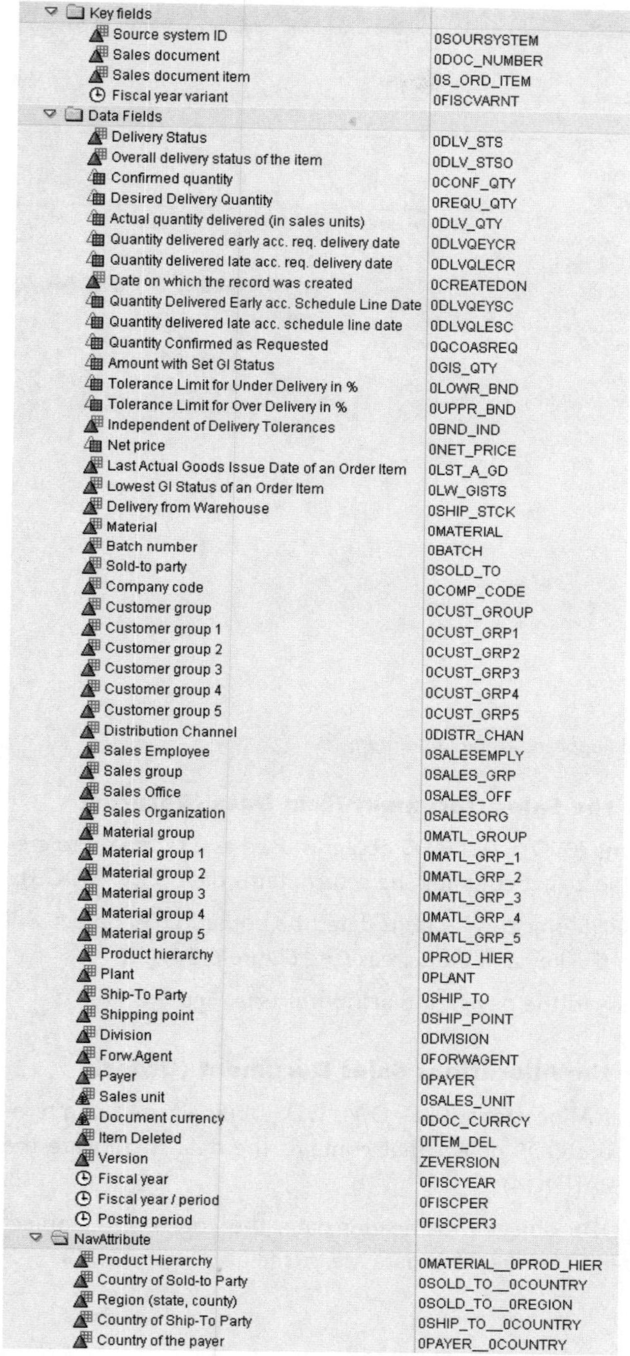

Key fields
Source system ID
0SOURSYSTEM
Sales document
0DOC_NUMBER
Sales document item
0S_ORD_ITEM
Fiscal year variant
0FISCVARNT
Data Fields
Delivery Status
0DLV_STS
Overall delivery status of the item
0DLV_STSO
Confirmed quantity
0CONF_QTY
Desired Delivery Quantity
0REQU_QTY
Actual quantity delivered (in sales units)
0DLV_QTY
Quantity delivered early acc. req. delivery date
0DLVQEYCR
Quantity delivered late acc. req. delivery date
0DLVQLECR
Date on which the record was created
0CREATEDON
Quantity Delivered Early acc. Schedule Line Date
0DLVQEYSC
Quantity delivered late acc. schedule line date
0DLVQLESC
Quantity Confirmed as Requested
0QCOASREQ
Amount with Set GI Status
0GIS_QTY
Tolerance Limit for Under Delivery in %
0LOWR_BND
Tolerance Limit for Over Delivery in %
0UPPR_BND
Independent of Delivery Tolerances
0BND_IND
Net price
0NET_PRICE
Last Actual Goods Issue Date of an Order Item
0LST_A_GD
Lowest GI Status of an Order Item
0LW_GISTS
Delivery from Warehouse
0SHIP_STCK
Material
0MATERIAL
Batch number
0BATCH
Sold-to party
0SOLD_TO
Company code
0COMP_CODE
Customer group
0CUST_GROUP
Customer group 1
0CUST_GRP1
Customer group 2
0CUST_GRP2
Customer group 3
0CUST_GRP3
Customer group 4
0CUST_GRP4
Customer group 5
0CUST_GRP5
Distribution Channel
0DISTR_CHAN
Sales Employee
0SALESEMPLY
Sales group
0SALES_GRP
Sales Office
0SALES_OFF
Sales Organization
0SALESORG
Material group
0MATL_GROUP
Material group 1
0MATL_GRP_1
Material group 2
0MATL_GRP_2
Material group 3
0MATL_GRP_3
Material group 4
0MATL_GRP_4
Material group 5
0MATL_GRP_5
Product hierarchy
0PROD_HIER
Plant
0PLANT
Ship-To Party
0SHIP_TO
Shipping point
0SHIP_POINT
Division
0DIVISION
Forw.Agent
0FORWAGENT
Payer
0PAYER
Sales unit
0SALES_UNIT
Document currency
0DOC_CURRCY
Item Deleted
0ITEM_DEL
Version
ZEVERSION
Fiscal year
0FISCYEAR
Fiscal year / period
0FISCPER
Posting period
0FISCPER3
NavAttribute
Product Hierarchy
0MATERIAL__0PROD_HIER
Country of Sold-to Party
0SOLD_TO__0COUNTRY
Region (state, county)
0SOLD_TO__0REGION
Country of Ship-To Party
0SHIP_TO__0COUNTRY
Country of the payer
0PAYER__0COUNTRY

Figure 6.74 Enhanced ODS Object ZEVAHDO2 (Order Item)

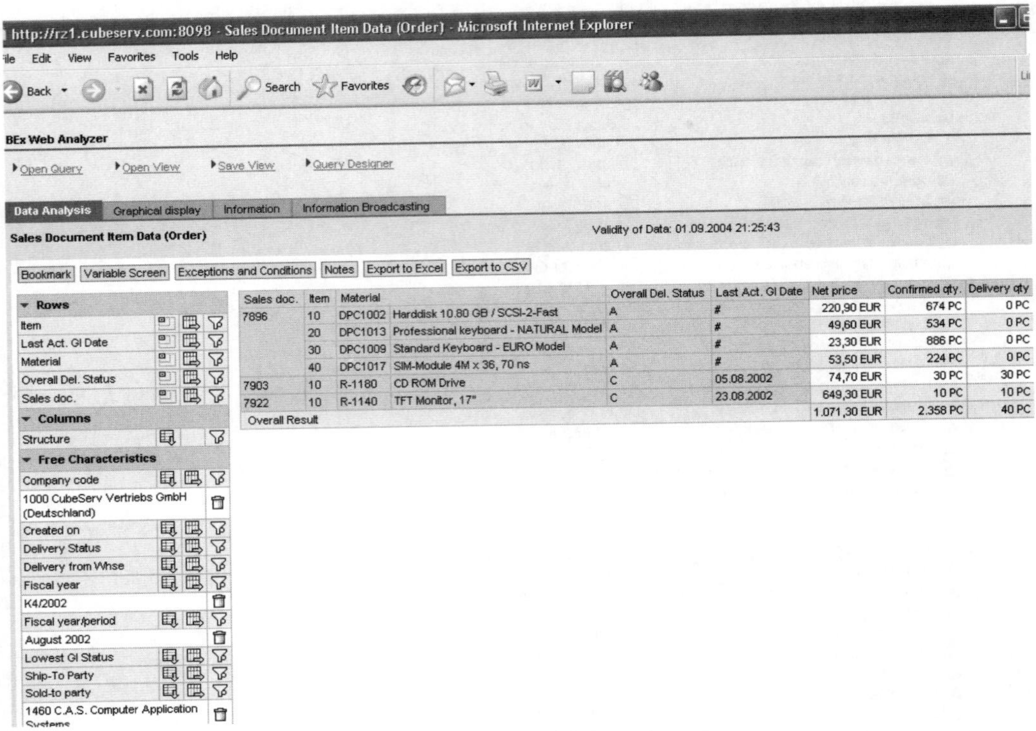

Figure 6.75 Detailed Reporting at the Order Item Level

ODS Object for the Sales Document Item Data (Returns)

- The **Return Items** (0SD_O02) ODS object is used as a template to create the ODS object that contains the return items data (ZEVAHDO3).
- Similar to the ODS object with item data, the copied ODS object will be enhanced in the key and data areas (see Figure 6.74).
- The same applies to the navigation attributes (see Figure 6.76).

ODS Object for the Allocations Sales Document (Order)

- The **Open Order Allocations** (0SD_O04) ODS object is used as a template to create the ODS object that contains the data to allocate the order items (ZEVAHDO4).
- Similar to the ODS object with header data, the copied ODS object will be enhanced in the key and data areas (see also Figure 6.72).

Key fields	
Source system ID	0SOURSYSTEM
Sales document item	0S_ORD_ITEM
Sales document	0DOC_NUMBER
Fiscal year variant	0FISCVARNT
Data Fields	
Cumulative order quantity in sales units	0CML_OR_QTY
Net price	0NET_PRICE
Date on which the record was created	0CREATEDON
Material	0MATERIAL
Batch number	0BATCH
Sold-to party	0SOLD_TO
Company code	0COMP_CODE
Customer group	0CUST_GROUP
Customer group 1	0CUST_GRP1
Customer group 2	0CUST_GRP2
Customer group 3	0CUST_GRP3
Customer group 4	0CUST_GRP4
Customer group 5	0CUST_GRP5
Distribution Channel	0DISTR_CHAN
Sales Employee	0SALESEMPLY
Sales group	0SALES_GRP
Sales Office	0SALES_OFF
Sales Organization	0SALESORG
Material group	0MATL_GROUP
Material group 1	0MATL_GRP_1
Material group 2	0MATL_GRP_2
Material group 3	0MATL_GRP_3
Material group 4	0MATL_GRP_4
Material group 5	0MATL_GRP_5
Product hierarchy	0PROD_HIER
Plant	0PLANT
Ship-To Party	0SHIP_TO
Shipping point	0SHIP_POINT
Division	0DIVISION
Forw.Agent	0FORWAGENT
Payer	0PAYER
Document currency	0DOC_CURRCY
Sales unit	0SALES_UNIT
Version	ZEVERSION
Fiscal year	0FISCYEAR
Fiscal year / period	0FISCPER
Posting period	0FISCPER3
NavAttribute	
Product Hierarchy	0MATERIAL__0PROD_HIER
Country of Sold-to Party	0SOLD_TO__0COUNTRY
Region (state, county)	0SOLD_TO__0REGION
Country of Ship-To Party	0SHIP_TO__0COUNTRY
Country of the payer	0PAYER__0COUNTRY

Figure 6.76 Enhanced ODS Object ZEVAHDO3 (Return Item)

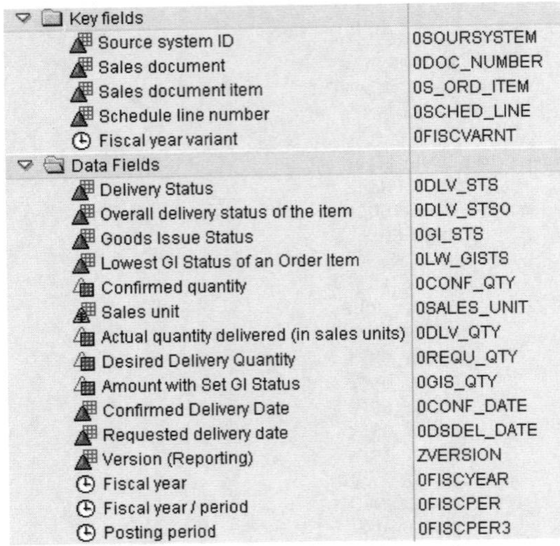

Key fields
Source system ID | 0SOURSYSTEM
Sales document | 0DOC_NUMBER
Sales document item | 0S_ORD_ITEM
Schedule line number | 0SCHED_LINE
Fiscal year variant | 0FISCVARNT
Data Fields
Delivery Status | 0DLV_STS
Overall delivery status of the item | 0DLV_STSO
Goods Issue Status | 0GI_STS
Lowest GI Status of an Order Item | 0LW_GISTS
Confirmed quantity | 0CONF_QTY
Sales unit | 0SALES_UNIT
Actual quantity delivered (in sales units) | 0DLV_QTY
Desired Delivery Quantity | 0REQU_QTY
Amount with Set GI Status | 0GIS_QTY
Confirmed Delivery Date | 0CONF_DATE
Requested delivery date | 0DSDEL_DATE
Version (Reporting) | ZVERSION
Fiscal year | 0FISCYEAR
Fiscal year / period | 0FISCPER
Posting period | 0FISCPER3

Figure 6.77 Enhanced ODS Object ZEVAHDO4 (Allocation)

6.5.4 Creating an InfoSet for Reporting with the Allocations of Sales Document Items

Missing characteristics for reporting

The ODS object **Allocations of sales document items** (ZEVAHDO4) does not contain important characteristics relevant to reporting. Some relevant characteristics for selection (for example, Accounting sector and Sold-to party of the sales document) are missing. Important list characteristics, such as the **Sold-to party of the sales document** or the **Material of the sales document item** are also missing. However, because ODS objects are objects of the data layer, for which only document reporting is permitted, we will not supplement the ODS object with the allocations of the sales document item.

InfoSets as the solution

Instead, we will work from the basis of the ODS objects **Allocation of sales order item** (ZEVAHDO4) and **Sales order items** (ZEVAHDO2) to define an *InfoSet* that links the required information.

Creating an InfoSet

- To create an InfoSet, start the Administrator Workbench of SAP BW.
- In the **InfoProvider** view, select all the InfoAreas to be assigned to the InfoSet (see Figure 6.78, Step 1).
- Right-click to open the context menu and select **Create InfoSet...** (step 2).

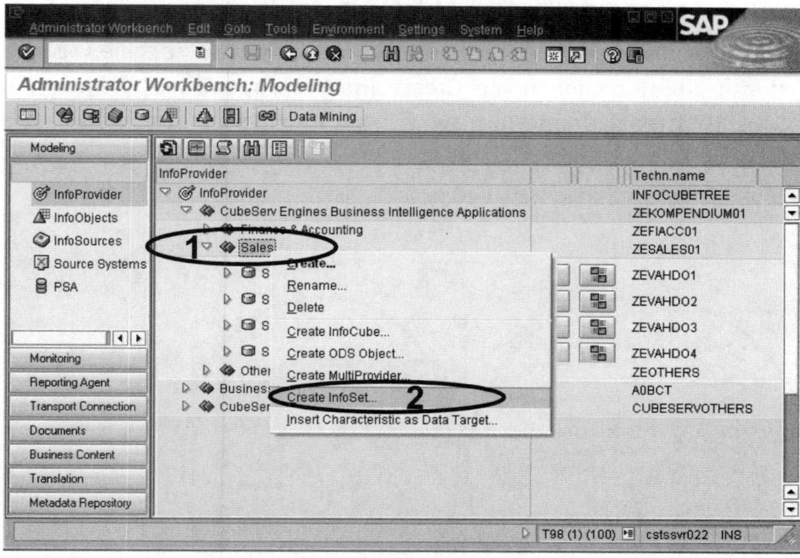

Figure 6.78 Starting the "Create InfoSet" Function

- Enter the technical name and the description in the **Create InfoSet** popup (see Figure 6.79, Step 1).
- Then define the InfoProvider (ODS object or InfoObject) with which the definition of the InfoSet should begin (Step 2). For our example, select the ODS object with allocations of the sales order item.
- Confirm your entries with the **Next (Enter)** button (Step 3).

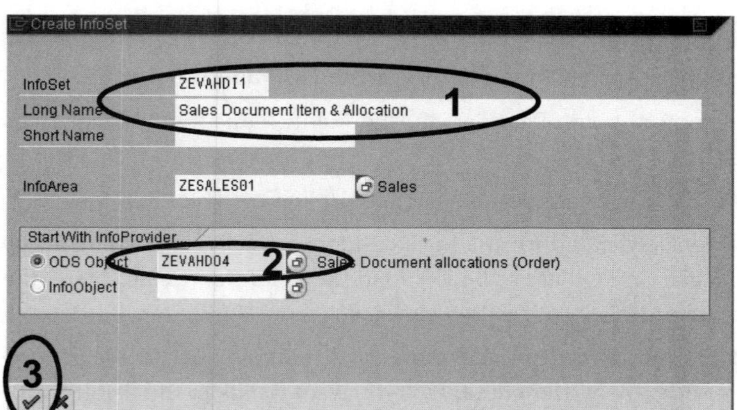

Figure 6.79 Setting the Name, Description, and the Starting InfoProviders of the InfoSet

▶ SAP BW then starts the **Change InfoSet...** dialog screen.

▶ The right frame displays the InfoProvider that you specified as the starting InfoProvider in the **Create InfoSet** popup (see Figure 6.80, Step 1). The left frame displays the InfoProviders that can be linked with the starting InfoProvider (Step 2).

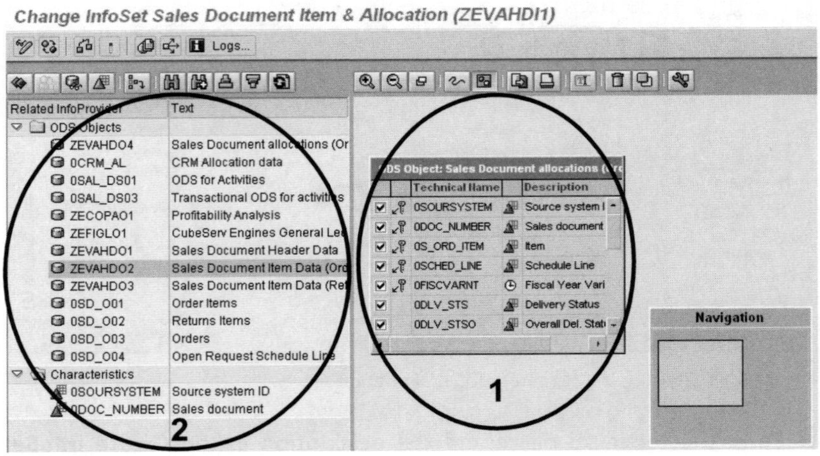

Figure 6.80 "Change InfoSet..." Dialog Screen

Join with another InfoProvider

A join to the ODS object with the item data (ZEVAHDO2) is required to link the allocation information with the information available at the item level.

▶ To create the join, select the desired InfoProvider in the left frame (see Figure 6.81, Step 1). In this case, it is the ODS object noted above.

▶ Then copy the InfoProvider to the right frame with Drag&Drop (Step 2).

▶ Both ODS objects are now available to define the link (Step 3).

▶ The links are defined for the InfoProviders recorded in the InfoSet by selecting an InfoObject to be linked in the first InfoProvider (here, the allocations ODS object) with a click (see Figure 6.82, Step 1).

▶ Hold the mouse button and move to the InfoObject in the second InfoProvider (here: **item data**) that you want to link to the first InfoObject (Step 2).

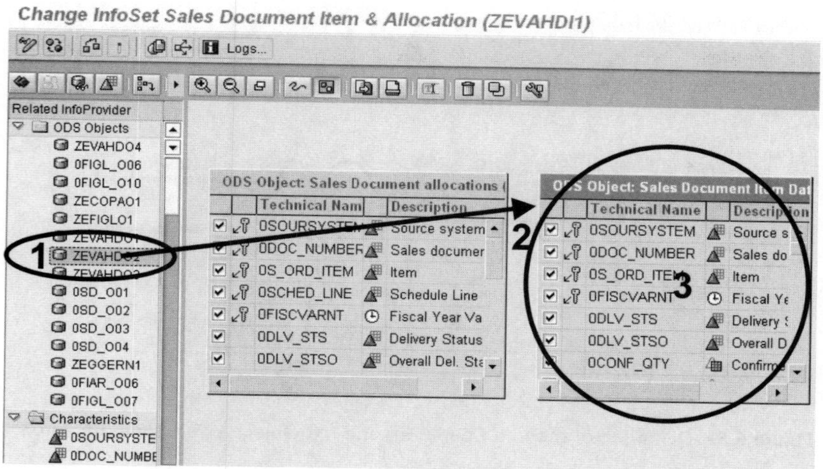

Figure 6.81 Adding InfoProviders to Define the Table Join

- After you release the mouse button, SAP BW displays the links with connecting lines for fields that can be linked. For the task at hand, you must define links between the ODS object **Allocation of sales order item** (ZEVAHDO4) and **Sales order items** (ZEVAHDO2) for the following InfoObjects:
  - **Source system** (0SOURSYSTEM)
  - **Sales document** (0DOC_NUMBER)
  - **Item** (0S_ORD_ITEM)
  - **Fiscal year variant** (0FISCVARNT)
- In the list of available InfoObjects, you must now select from the InfoProviders the InfoObjects to be made available for reporting (see Figure 6.82, Steps 4 and 5).

Selecting InfoObjects of ODS Objects for InfoSets

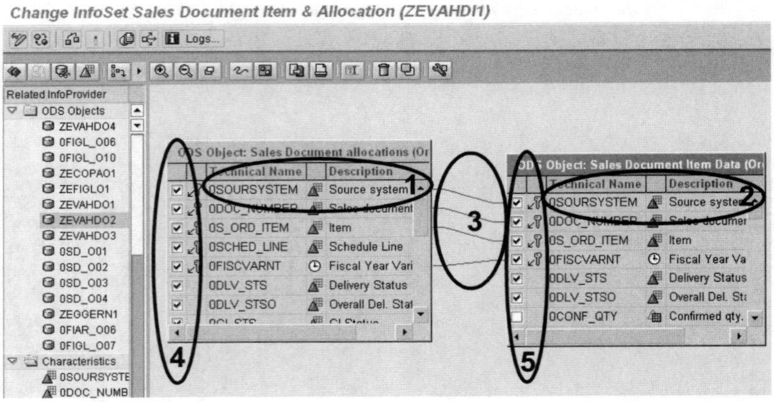

Figure 6.82 Definition of the Join Conditions and InfoObjects Available in the InfoSet

Reporting on InfoSets

- Based on the InfoSets selected in this manner by using join conditions, SAP BEx queries can be defined (see Figure 6.83).

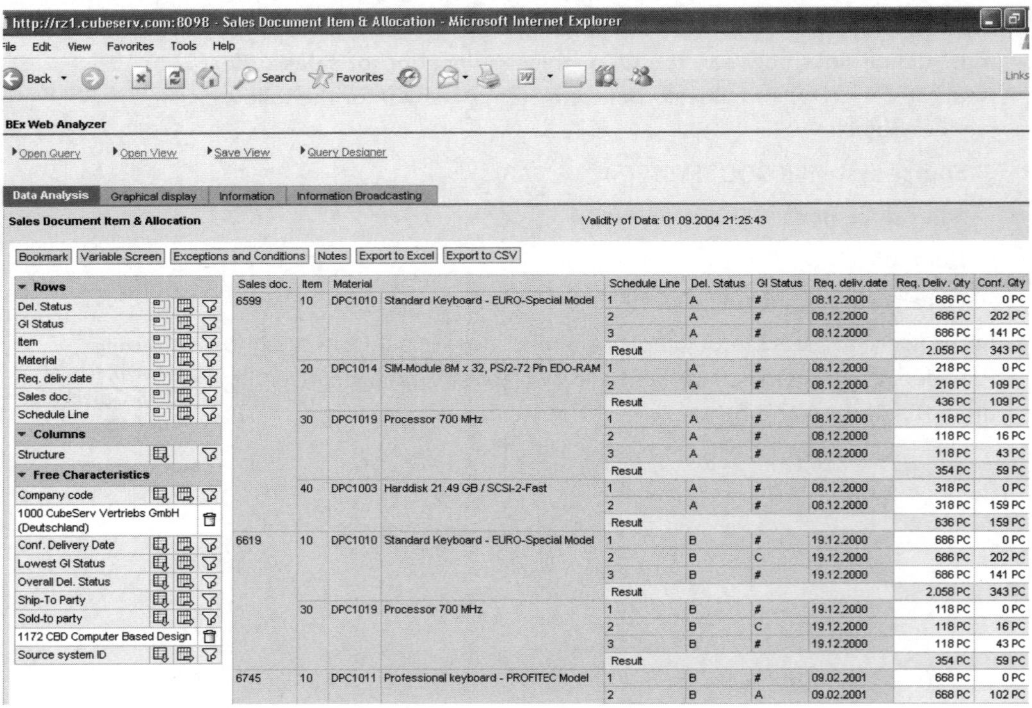

Figure 6.83 SAP BEx Query Based on an InfoSet

6.5.5 Creating InfoCubes for Incoming-Order Reporting

InfoCubes for Header, Item, and Allocation Data

InfoCubes for the various levels of the sales document are required for reporting on incoming orders. Separate InfoCubes are created for sales document header data, sales order items, and the allocation of sales order items.

InfoCube for Sales Orders

For the most part, the InfoCube for sales orders contains the same InfoObjects as the corresponding ODS object **Sales document header data** (ZEVAHDO1): see Section 6.5.3.

- The **Document number** InfoObject (0DOC_NUMBER) is not relevant for OLAP analyses and is therefore not included in the InfoCube.
- Nevertheless, reporting on incoming orders requires the number of sales orders to calculate the average value of sales orders. Therefore, the **Sales document header data** InfoCube is enhanced with the key figures of the **Sales document header data** ODS object (ZEVAHDO1) and the key figure of the **Number of orders** (0ORDERS).
- For flexible aggregation of the time dimension, all time characteristics are recorded in the InfoCube, unlike the case with the ODS object.

Navigation attributes of the header data InfoCube

- The following attributes of the sold-to party are used as navigation attributes:
  - **Customer Account Group** (0SOLD_TO__0ACCNT_GRP)
  - **Country of Sold-to Party** (0SOLD_TO__0COUNTRY)
  - **Region (State, county)** (0SOLD_TO__0REGION)
  - **Key account** (0SOLD_TO__0KEYACCOUNT)

Creating an InfoCube with a template ODS

- Creation of the **Sales document header data** InfoCube (ZEVAHDC1) is done with the procedure described in Section 6.4.3, based on the **Sales document header data** ODS object (ZEVAHDO1).
- Enhancing the InfoCube with the **Number of orders** key figure (0ORDERS) is analogous to the procedure described in Section 6.3.3, Figure 6.13 and Figure 6.14.

Line Items

- As much as possible, the dimensions are defined as line item dimensions (see Figure 6.84).

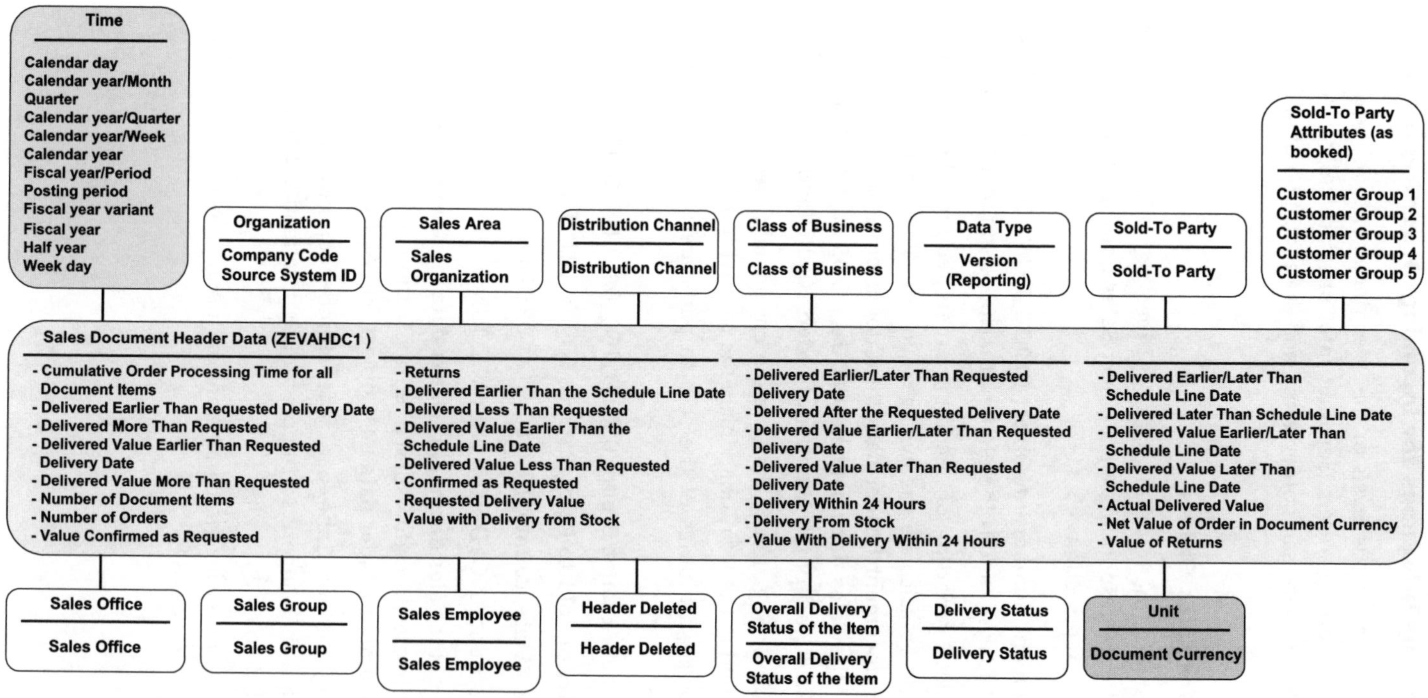

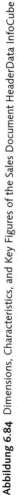

Abbildung 6.84 Dimensions, Characteristics, and Key Figures of the Sales Document HeaderData InfoCube

InfoCube for Sales Order Items

For the most part, the InfoCube for sales order items contains the same InfoObjects as the corresponding ODS object **Sales document item data (order)** (ZEVAHDO2): see Section 6.5.3.

- The **Sales document** (0DOC_NUMBER) and **Sales document item** (0S_ORD_ITEM) are not relevant for OLAP analyses.
- The **Batch number** (0BATCH) is also irrelevant here. Consequently, these InfoObjects are not included in the InfoCube.
- Nevertheless, reporting on incoming orders requires the **number of sales order items t**o calculate the average value of the sales order item. For that reason, the **Sales document item data (orders and returns)** InfoCube is enhanced with the key figures of the **Sales document item data (order)** ODS object (ZEVAHDO2) and the key figure of the **Number of document items** (0DOC_ITEMS).
- Because our model company, CubeServ Engines, considers returns as decreases in the number of orders, the InfoCube is enhanced with the **Cumulated order quantity in sales units** (0CML_OR_QTY) InfoCube of the **Sales document item data (returns)** (ZEVAHDO3) ODS object.
- For flexible aggregation of the time dimension, all time characteristics are included in the item data InfoCube, unlike the case with the ODS object.

Navigation attributes of the Item Data InfoCube

- The following attributes of the sold-to party, the ship-to party, the payer, and the material are used as navigation attributes:
  - **Customer Account Group** (0SOLD_TO__0ACCNT_GRP)
  - **Country of Sold-to Party** (0SOLD_TO__0COUNTRY)
  - **Region (State, county)** (0SOLD_TO__0REGION)
  - **Key account** (0SOLD_TO__0KEYACCOUNT)
  - **Country of Ship-to Party** (0SHIP_TO__0COUNTRY)
  - **Country of the payer** (0PAYER__0COUNTRY)
  - **Product Hierarchy** (0MATERIAL__0PROD_HIER)

Creating an InfoCube with a template ODS

- Creation of the **Sales document item data** InfoCube **(orders and returns)** (ZEVAHDC2) is done with the procedure described in Section 6.4.3, based on the **Sales document item data (order)** ODS object (ZEVAHDO2).
- Enhancing the InfoCube with the InfoObjects noted above is similar to the procedure described in Section 6.3.3, Figure 6.13 and Figure 6.14.

Line Items

- As much as possible, the dimensions are defined as line item dimensions (see Figure 6.85).

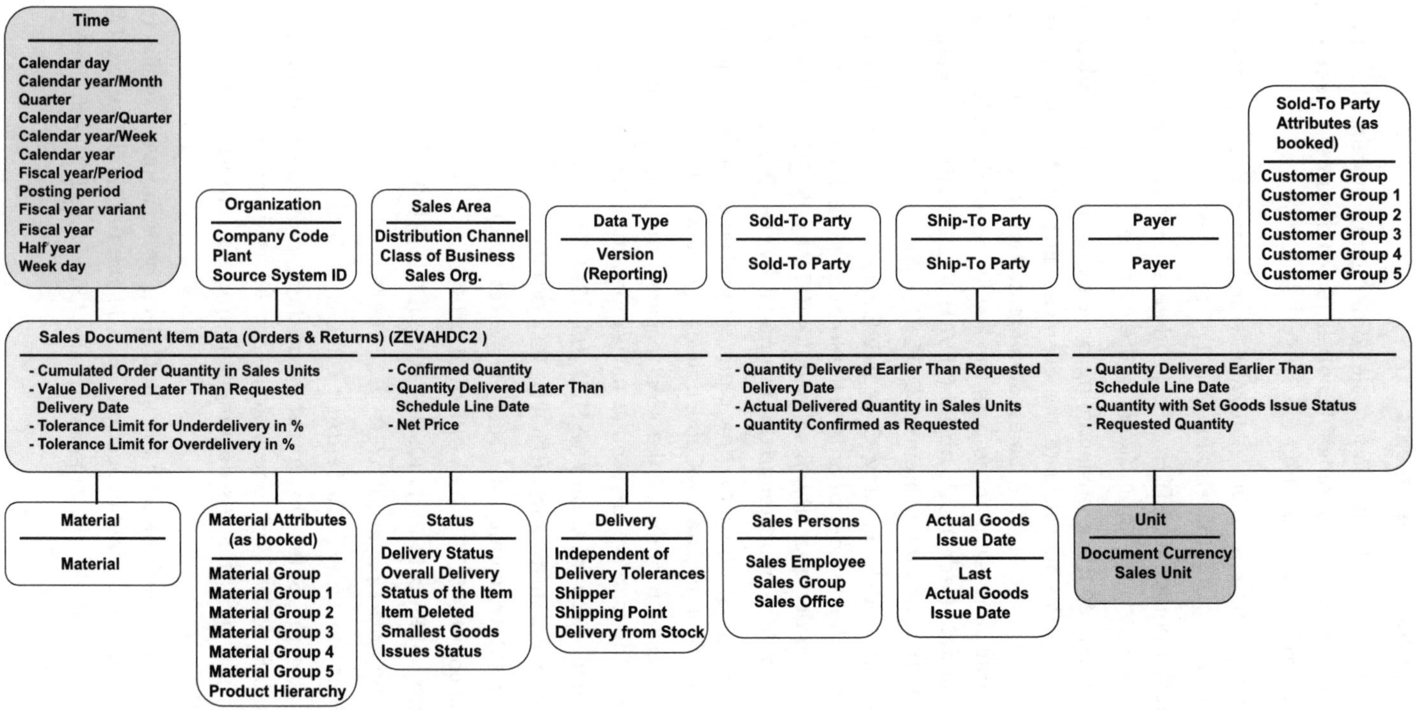
Time
Calendar day
Calendar year/Month
Quarter
Calendar year/Quarter
Calendar year/Week
Calendar year
Fiscal year/Period
Posting period
Fiscal year variant
Fiscal year
Half year
Week day
Organization
Company Code
Plant
Source System ID
Sales Area
Distribution Channel
Class of Business
Sales Org.
Data Type
Version (Reporting)
Sold-To Party
Sold-To Party
Ship-To Party
Ship-To Party
Payer
Payer
Sold-To Party Attributes (as booked)
Customer Group
Customer Group 1
Customer Group 2
Customer Group 3
Customer Group 4
Customer Group 5
Sales Document Item Data (Orders & Returns) (ZEVAHDC2)
- Cumulated Order Quantity in Sales Units
- Value Delivered Later Than Requested Delivery Date
- Tolerance Limit for Underdelivery in %
- Tolerance Limit for Overdelivery in %
- Confirmed Quantity
- Quantity Delivered Later Than Schedule Line Date
- Net Price
- Quantity Delivered Earlier Than Requested Delivery Date
- Actual Delivered Quantity in Sales Units
- Quantity Confirmed as Requested
- Quantity Delivered Earlier Than Schedule Line Date
- Quantity with Set Goods Issue Status
- Requested Quantity
Material
Material
Material Attributes (as booked)
Material Group
Material Group 1
Material Group 2
Material Group 3
Material Group 4
Material Group 5
Product Hierarchy
Status
Delivery Status
Overall Delivery
Status of the Item
Item Deleted
Smallest Goods
Issues Status
Delivery
Independent of
Delivery Tolerances
Shipper
Shipping Point
Delivery from Stock
Sales Persons
Sales Employee
Sales Group
Sales Office
Actual Goods Issue Date
Last
Actual Goods
Issue Date
Unit
Document Currency
Sales Unit

Abbildung 6.85 Dimensions, Characteristics, and Key Figures of the Sales Document Item Data InfoCube

InfoCube for Allocating the Sales Order Items

On the whole, the InfoCube for allocating the sales order items contains the same InfoObjects as the **Sales document item data (orders and returns)** InfoCube (ZEVAHDC2), enhanced with the InfoObjects of the **Sales document allocations (order)** ODS object (ZEVAHDO4): see Section 6.5.3.

- The **Sales document** (0DOC_NUMBER), **Sales document item** (0S_ORD_ITEM), and the **Schedule line** (0SCHED_LINE) are not relevant for OLAP analyses. Therefore, these InfoObjects are not included in the InfoCube.
- Nevertheless, reporting on incoming orders requires the number of allocations to calculate various delivery key figures. Consequently, the **Sales document allocations (orders)** InfoCube is enhanced with the key figures of the **Sales document allocations (order)** ODS object (ZEVAHDO4) and the **Number of scheduled allocations** (0NUM_SCHED) key figure.
- For flexible aggregation of the time dimension, all time characteristics are recorded in the **Sales document allocations (order)** InfoCube, unlike the case with the ODS object.

Navigation attributes

- The navigation attributes of the **Sales document item data (sales and returns)** (ZEVAHDC2) InfoCube are used as navigation attributes.

Creating an InfoCube with a template ODS

- Creation of the **Sales document allocations (order)** InfoCube (ZEVAHDC3) is done with the procedure described in Section 6.3.3, based on the **Sales document item data (sales and returns)** InfoCube (ZEVAHDC2).
- Enhancing the InfoCube with the InfoObjects noted above is similar to the procedure described in Section 6.3.3 and illustrated in Figure 6.13 and Figure 6.14.

Line Items

- As much as possible, the dimensions are defined as line item dimensions (see Figure 6.86).

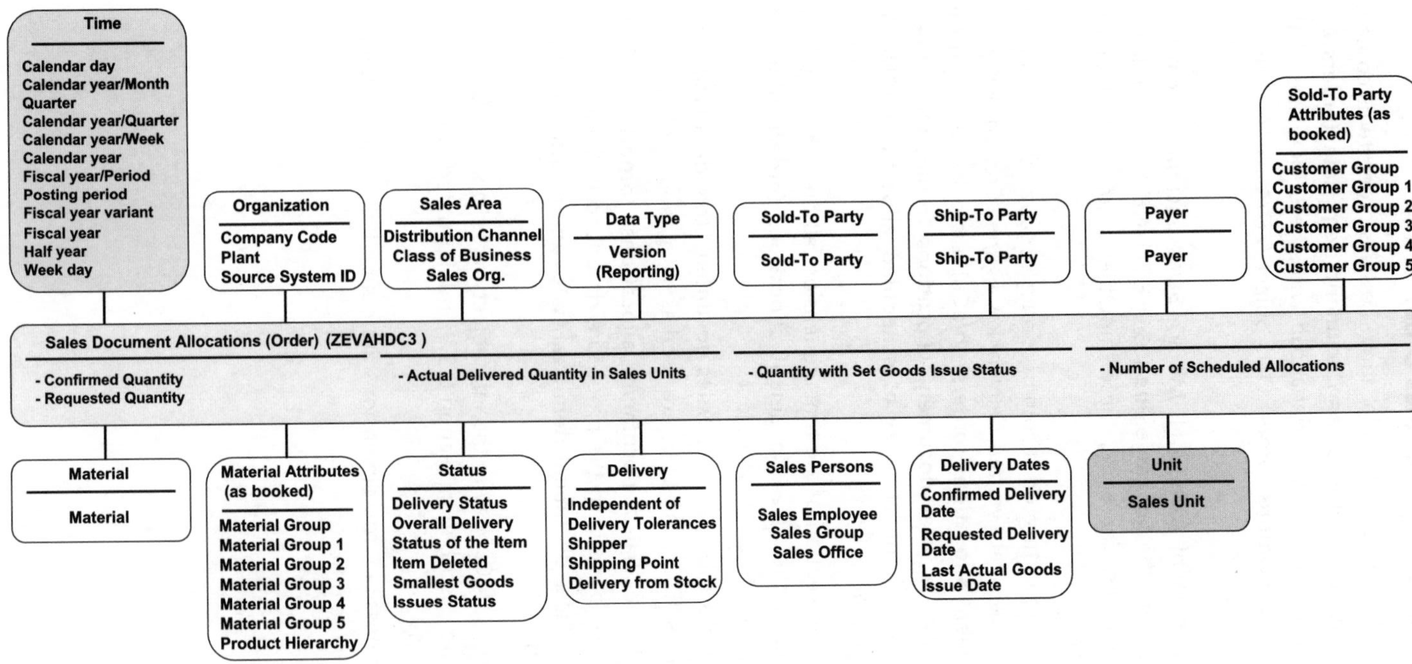

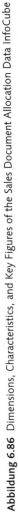

Abbildung 6.86 Dimensions, Characteristics, and Key Figures of the Sales Document Allocation Data InfoCube

6.5.6 Creating a MultiProvider for Incoming-Order Reporting

MultiProviders for OLAP Analyses

A MultiProvider combines the InfoCubes for reporting on incoming orders. The MultiProvider enables comprehensive and combined analyses of all components, such as the average value of allocations.

The following three incoming-order InfoCubes are combined for the required analyses:

- **Sales document header data** (ZEVAHDC1)
- **Sales document item data (order and returns)** (ZEVAHDC2)
- **Sales document schedule lines (order)** (ZEVAHDC3)

All available InfoObjects are used and linked.

Creating the Incoming-Order MultiProvider

The procedure to create the MultiProvider for reporting on incoming orders is similar to procedure described in Section 6.3.5 and is illustrated in Figure 6.87 and Figure 6.88. InfoObjects are grouped in the MultiProvider according to business criteria (see Appendix E, *MultiProviders*).

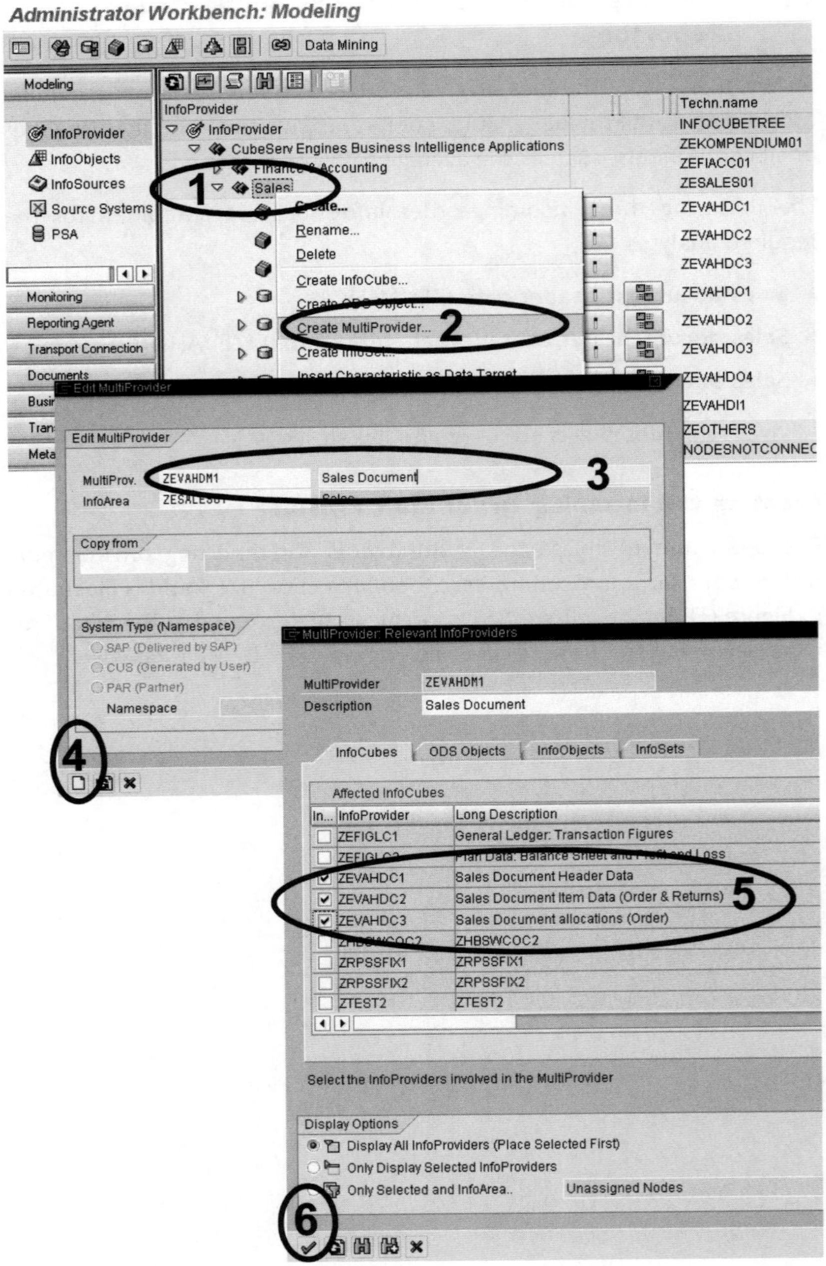

Figure 6.87 Creating the Sales Document MultiProvider, Part 1

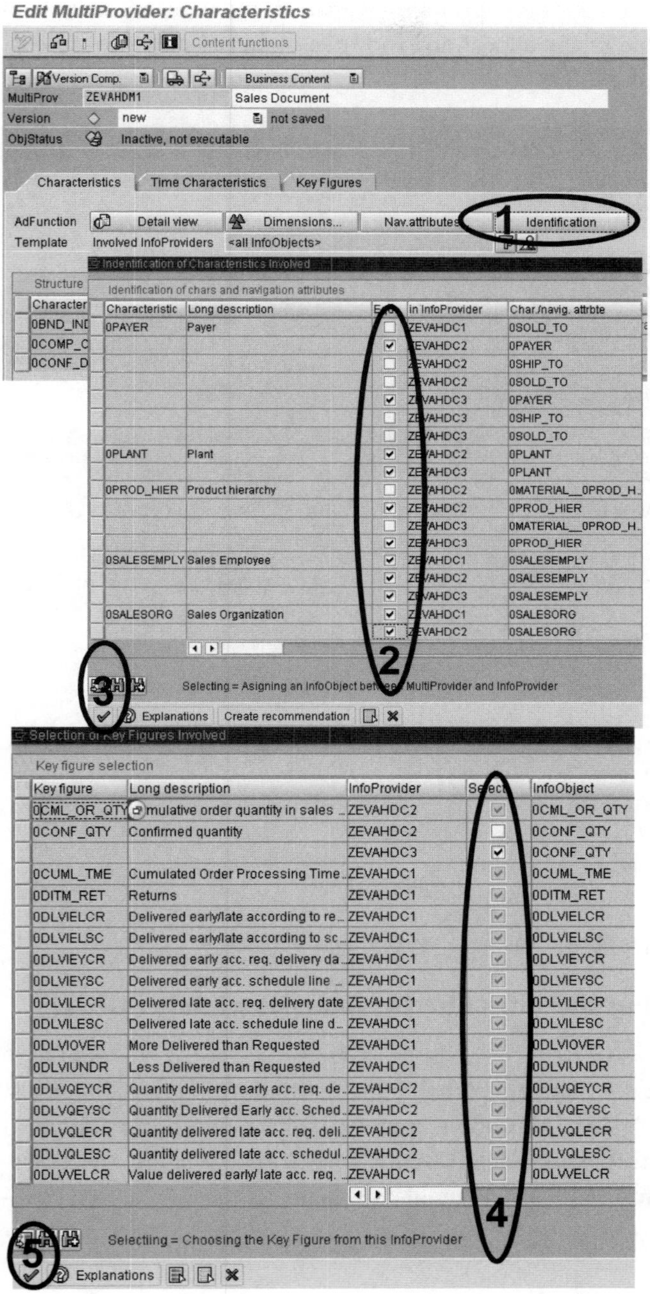

Edit MultiProvider: Characteristics

Content functions

Version Comp. | Business Content
MultiProv ZEVAHDM1 Sales Document
Version ◇ new | not saved
ObjStatus ⊗ Inactive, not executable

| Characteristics | Time Characteristics | Key Figures |

☑	ZEVAHDC2	0PAYER
		☐	ZEVAHDC2	0SHIP_TO
		☐	ZEVAHDC2	0SOLD_TO
		☑	ZEVAHDC3	0PAYER
		☐	ZEVAHDC3	0SHIP_TO
		☐	ZEVAHDC3	0SOLD_TO
0PLANT	Plant	☑	ZEVAHDC2	0PLANT
		☑	ZEVAHDC3	0PLANT
0PROD_HIER	Product hierarchy	☐	ZEVAHDC2	0MATERIAL__0PROD_H..
		☑	ZEVAHDC2	0PROD_HIER
		☐	ZEVAHDC3	0MATERIAL__0PROD_H..
		☑	ZEVAHDC3	0PROD_HIER
0SALESEMPLY	Sales Employee	☑	ZEVAHDC1	0SALESEMPLY
		☑	ZEVAHDC2	0SALESEMPLY
		☑	ZEVAHDC3	0SALESEMPLY
0SALESORG	Sales Organization	☑	ZEVAHDC1	0SALESORG
0CML_OR_QTY	Cumulative order quantity in sales ..	ZEVAHDC2	☑	0CML_OR_QTY
0CONF_QTY	Confirmed quantity	ZEVAHDC2	☐	0CONF_QTY
		ZEVAHDC3	☑	0CONF_QTY
0CUML_TME	Cumulated Order Processing Time	ZEVAHDC1	☑	0CUML_TME
0DITM_RET	Returns	ZEVAHDC1	☑	0DITM_RET
0DLVIELCR	Delivered early/late according to re..	ZEVAHDC1	☑	0DLVIELCR
0DLVIELSC	Delivered early/late according to sc..	ZEVAHDC1	☑	0DLVIELSC
0DLVIEYCR	Delivered early acc. req. delivery da..	ZEVAHDC1	☑	0DLVIEYCR
0DLVIEYSC	Delivered early acc. schedule line ..	ZEVAHDC1	☑	0DLVIEYSC
0DLVILECR	Delivered late acc. req. delivery date	ZEVAHDC1	☑	0DLVILECR
0DLVILESC	Delivered late acc. schedule line d..	ZEVAHDC1	☑	0DLVILESC
0DLVIOVER	More Delivered than Requested	ZEVAHDC1	☑	0DLVIOVER
0DLVIUNDR	Less Delivered than Requested	ZEVAHDC1	☑	0DLVIUNDR
0DLVQEYCR	Quantity delivered early acc. req. de..	ZEVAHDC2	☑	0DLVQEYCR
0DLVQEYSC	Quantity Delivered Early acc. Sched..	ZEVAHDC2	☑	0DLVQEYSC
0DLVQLECR	Quantity delivered late acc. req. deli..	ZEVAHDC2	☑	0DLVQLECR
0DLVQLESC	Quantity delivered late acc. schedul..	ZEVAHDC2	☑	0DLVQLESC
0DLVWELCR	Value delivered early/ late acc. req. ..	ZEVAHDC1	☑	0DLVWELCR

4

5

Selectiing = Choosing the Key Figure from this InfoProvider

✓ Explanations

Figure 6.88 Creating the Sales Document MultiProvider, Part 2

The data model enables comprehensive analyses, such as an analysis of the average value of the allocations and thus of partial deliveries to customers (see Figure 6.89).

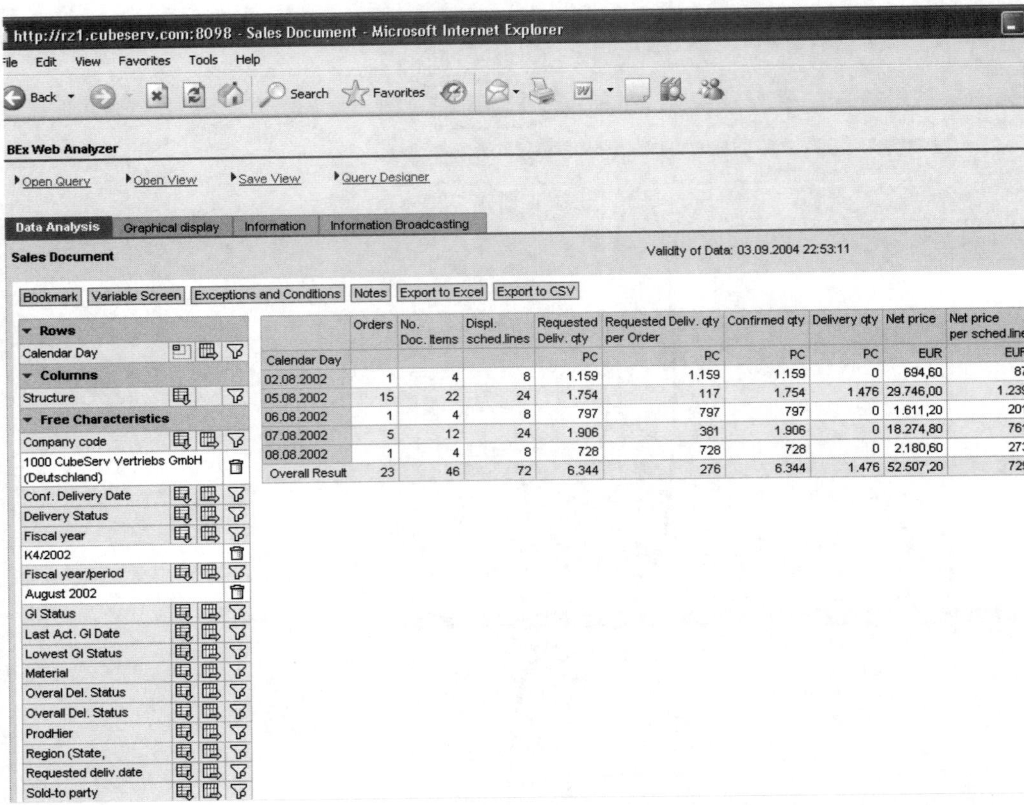

	Orders	No. Doc. Items	Displ. sched.lines	Requested Deliv. qty	Requested Deliv. qty per Order	Confirmed qty	Delivery qty	Net price	Net price per sched.line
Calendar Day				PC	PC	PC	PC	EUR	EUR
02.08.2002	1	4	8	1.159	1.159	1.159	0	694,60	87
05.08.2002	15	22	24	1.754	117	1.754	1.476	29.746,00	1.239
06.08.2002	1	4	8	797	797	797	0	1.611,20	201
07.08.2002	5	12	24	1.906	381	1.906	0	18.274,80	761
08.08.2002	1	4	8	728	728	728	0	2.180,60	273
Overall Result	23	46	72	6.344	276	6.344	1.476	52.507,20	729

Figure 6.89 Comprehensive Analyses Based on the MultiProvider

6.5.7 Creating the InfoCube for Analysis of Sales Order Stocks

Sales order stock InfoCube

Sales order stock is analyzed in an independent InfoCube (see Chapter 4, *Sample Scenario*). This InfoCube is modeled with a group orientation. It uses the **Inventory value** (ZEBESTAND) inventory key figure and therefore the **Amount** (ZEBETRAG) cumulative value.

InfoObjects of the InfoCube for Sales Order Stock

The following characteristics are used to analyze sales order stock:

- **Company code** (0COMP_CODE)
- **Plant** (0PLANT)
- **Source system ID** (0SOURSYSTEM)

- **Distribution channel** (0DISTR_CHAN)
- **Division** (0DIVISION)
- **Sales group** (0SALES_GRP)
- **Sales employee** (0SALESEMPLY)
- **Sales organization** (0SALESORG)
- **Sales office** (0SALES_OFF)
- **Customer group** (0CUST_GROUP)
- **Customer number** (0CUSTOMER)
- **Sales district** (0SALES_DIST)
- **Material** (0MATERIAL)
- **Fiscal year/period** (0FISCPER)
- **Posting period** (0FISCPER3)
- **Fiscal year** (0FISCYEAR)

The following characteristics are required to identify the data:

- **Fiscal year variant** (0FISCVARNT)
- **Version** (0VERSION)
- **Value Type for Reporting** (0VTYPE)
- **Version (reporting)** (ZEVERSION)
- **Invoice type** (0BILL_TYPE)
- **Valuation view** (0VALUATION)
- **Currency type** (0CURTYPE)

Contents of the Key Figures

Inventory increases (incoming orders) and inventory decreases (invoices) are stored in the cumulative value **Amount** (ZEBETRAG). The sales order stock is determined with the **Inventory value** (ZEBESTAND) key figure.

Template InfoCube

Principally, the **Sales order stock** InfoCube contains the same InfoObjects as the **Actual-data** InfoCube—**Profitability analysis** (ZECOPAC1) and can therefore be used as a template. The navigation attributes of the template InfoCube are used as navigation attributes. The creation of the InfoCube is analogous to the procedure described in Section 6.3.3.

Line Items

Typically, the dimensions are defined as line item dimensions.

Removing Unused Characteristics

- After you call the **Create InfoCube** function and enter the name, description, and the template InfoCube, the screen displays the **Edit InfoCube: Characteristics** dialog (the start view is the **Characteristics** tab).
- Highlight the InfoObjects that you do not need to analyze the sales order stock (see Figure 6.90, Step 1).
- Then remove these InfoObjects from the structure of the InfoCube with the **Retransfer fields** button (Step 2).

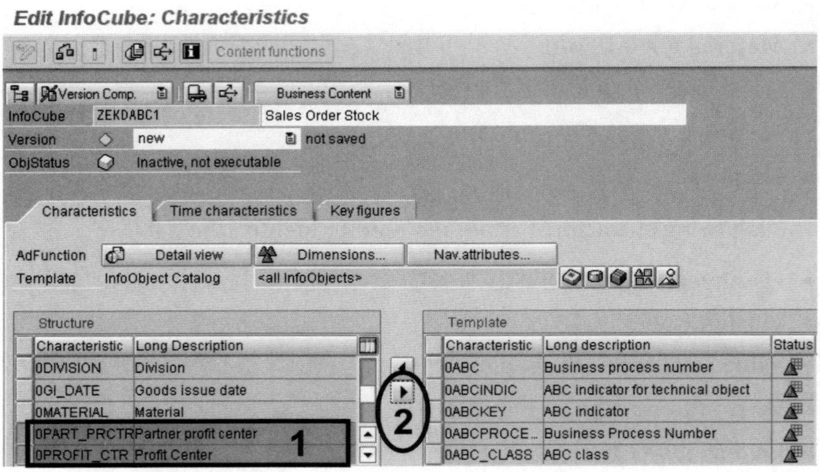

Figure 6.90 Removing the Characteristics That You Don't Need to Analyze the Sales Order Stock

Removing all Key Figures of the Template InfoCube

- Click on the **Key figures** tab to display the **Edit InfoCube: Key Figures** dialog screen (see Figure 6.91, Step 1).
- Then use the **Select all** button (Step 2) to mark all the key figures of the template InfoCube (Step 3).
- Remove these key figures from the structure of the InfoCube with the **Retransfer fields** button (Step 4).

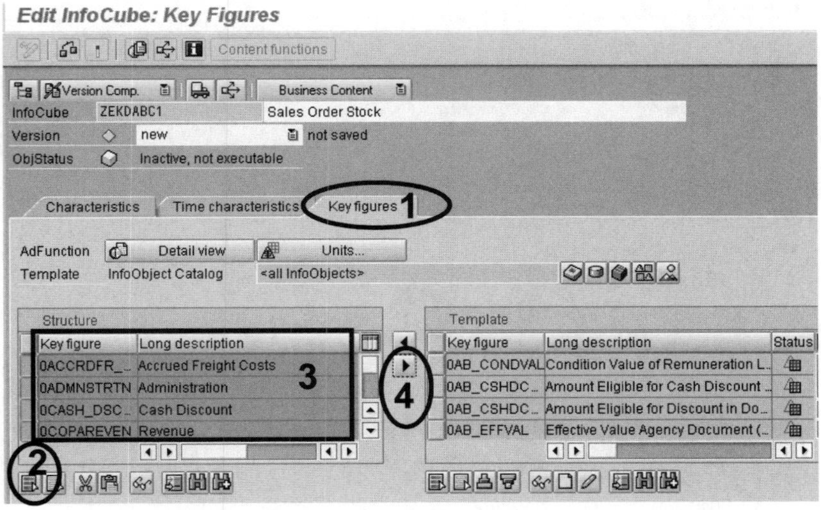

Figure 6.91 Removing All Key Figures of the Template InfoCube

Including Key Figures

- To include the key figure, click on the **Find** button in the template (see Figure 6.92, Step 1).
- Then enter the search criterion (here: ZEB* for technical names ZEBESTAND and ZEBETRAG, Step 2).
- Then start the search by clicking the **Next (Enter)** button (Step 3).
- The key figure template is then positioned as desired (Step 4).
- After you select the desired key figures, you can use the **Transfer fields** button (Step 5) to include the key figures in the structure of the InfoCube.
- The time characteristics are transferred from the template InfoCube and meet the requirements.

Time Characteristics

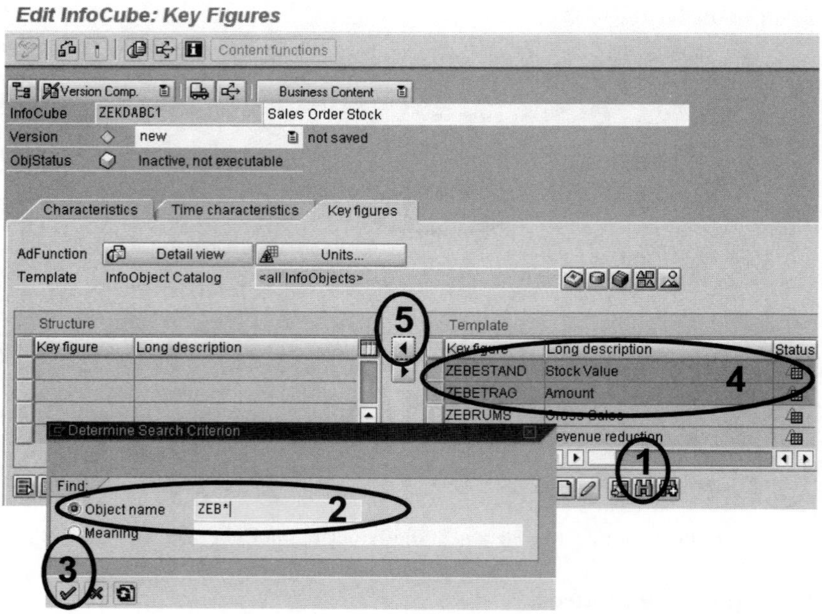

Figure 6.92 Recording the Key Figures in the Sales Order Stock InfoCube

Dimensions

- You then define the dimensions (see Figure 6.93, Step 1) much as you did with the procedure described in Section 6.4.3 (Figure 6.52 and Figure 6.53).
- You can use the **Tree Display** button to display the structure of the InfoCube while you configure it (Step 2).

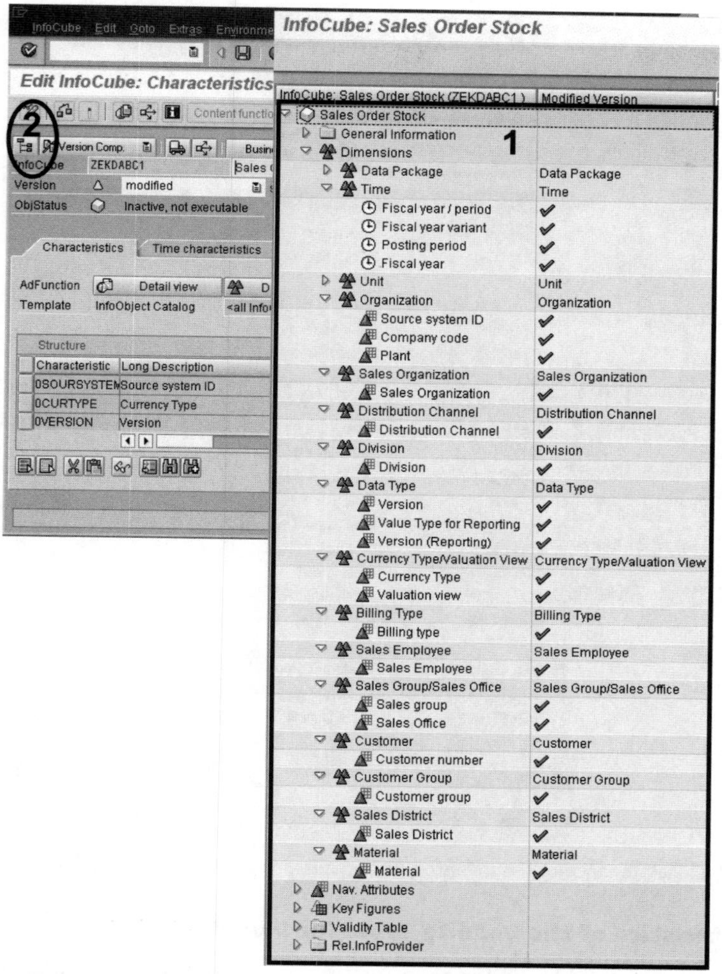

Figure 6.93 The Dimensions of the Sales Order Stock InfoCube

Inventory Parameters

Because the **Sales order stock** InfoCube uses an inventory key figure, you must maintain the inventory parameters.

- Select the **Extras** menu to call this function (see Figure 6.94, Step 1).
- Then select the **Maintain non-cumulative values** menu option (Step 2).
- The **Non-cumulative Value Parameters for the InfoCube** popup displays the correct reference characteristic for time-related aggregation of **Fiscal year/period** (0FISCPER).

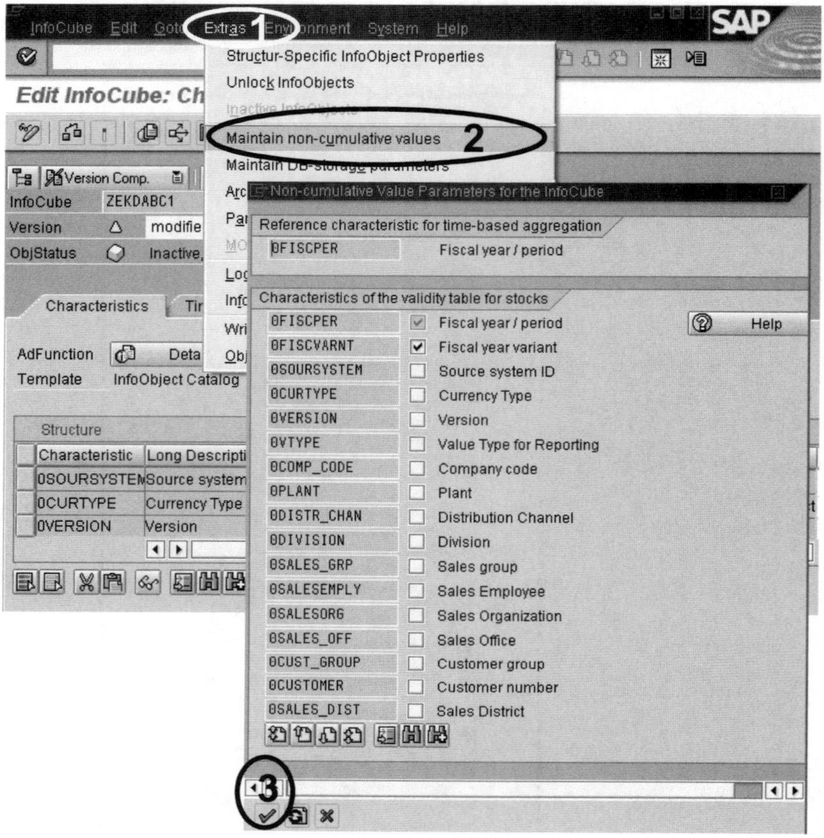

Figure 6.94 Maintenance of the Inventory Parameters

Characteristics of the Validity Table for Inventories

The reference characteristic for time-related aggregation is automatically included (it is also mandatory) in the list of **Characteristics of the validity table for stocks.** Because the **Fiscal year/period** (0FISCPER) involves a fiscal time characteristic compounded to the fiscal year variant, it is automatically transferred to the validity table.

SAP explains the following in the help entries for the validity table: The InfoCube contains inventory key figures. A validity table is created for these inventory key figures. The validity table stores the time interval for which the inventory values are valid.

The validity table automatically contains the most refined of the selected time characteristics. If none exist, the user must define it (record it in the InfoCube). In addition to the most refined time characteristics, other characteristics of the InfoCube can be included in the validity table. Examples of such characteristics include:

- A plan-actual ID if plan and actual values exist for various time intervals (actual values for the current fiscal year and plan values for the next fiscal year)
- The **Plant** characteristic if the inventory key figures are reported for each plant and if a value exists for a specific period for plant A but not for plant B

In principle, additional characteristics can be included in the validity table. However, this feature is not needed to meet the requirements of our model company, CubeServ Engines.

- Simply transfer the settings for the validity table by clicking the **Next (Enter)** button (see Figure 6.94, Step 3).
- You can then activate the InfoCube.
- Posting the incoming order and billing data generates values for the **Amount** cumulative value (see Figure 6.95).
- The inventory values are determined on the basis of the cumulative value and displayed in reporting (see Figure 6.96).

Data tgt. browser: "ZEKDABC1", List output

Company co...	0SOURSYSTE	Version	0CURTYPE	Material	0FISCP...	0FISCVARNT	Currency	ZEBETRAG
1000	R0	100	B0	1300-410	2003012	K4	USD	17.388,51-
1000	R0	100	B0		2003012	K4	USD	70.432,96
1000	R0	100	B0		2003012	K4	USD	53.044,45
1000	R0	100	B0		2004001	K4	USD	152.505,13-
1000	R0	100	B0		2004001	K4	USD	63.328,29
1000	R0	100	B0		2004001	K4	USD	89.176,84-
1000	R0	100	B0		2004002	K4	USD	156.294,64-
1000	R0	100	B0		2004002	K4	USD	56.415,91
1000	R0	100	B0		2004002	K4	USD	99.878,73-
1000	R0	100	B0		2004003	K4	USD	160.442,89-
1000	R0	100	B0		2004003	K4	USD	59.598,91
1000	R0	100	B0		2004003	K4	USD	100.843,98-
1000	R0	100	B0		2004004	K4	USD	148.744,97-
1000	R0	100	B0		2004004	K4	USD	61.345,34
1000	R0	100	B0		2004004	K4	USD	87.399,63-
1000	R0	100	B0		2004005	K4	USD	164.208,42-
1000	R0	100	B0		2004005	K4	USD	62.158,71
1000	R0	100	B0		2004005	K4	USD	102.049,71-
1000	R0	100	B0		2004006	K4	USD	148.601,91-
1000	R0	100	B0		2004006	K4	USD	60.689,00
1000	R0	100	B0		2004006	K4	USD	87.912,91-
1000	R0	100	B0	AM2-850-H	2003012	K4	USD	26.491,80-
1000	R0	100	B0		2003012	K4	USD	35.035,98
1000	R0	100	B0		2003012	K4	USD	8.544,18
1000	R0	100	B0		2004001	K4	USD	26.990,82-
1000	R0	100	B0		2004001	K4	USD	28.330,27
1000	R0	100	B0		2004001	K4	USD	1.339,45
1000	R0	100	B0		2004002	K4	USD	28.083,28-
1000	R0	100	B0		2004002	K4	USD	27.122,22
1000	R0	100	B0		2004002	K4	USD	961,06-
1000	R0	100	B0		2004003	K4	USD	29.190,67-
1000	R0	100	B0		2004003	K4	USD	24.687,80
1000	R0	100	B0		2004003	K4	USD	4.502,87-
1000	R0	100	B0		2004004	K4	USD	27.337,97-
1000	R0	100	B0		2004004	K4	USD	27.328,32
1000	R0	100	B0		2004004	K4	USD	9,65-
1000	R0	100	B0		2004005	K4	USD	27.616,82-
1000	R0	100	B0		2004005	K4	USD	27.227,00
1000	R0	100	B0		2004005	K4	USD	389,82-
1000	R0	100	B0		2004006	K4	USD	26.208,61-
1000	R0	100	B0		2004006	K4	USD	22.234,19
1000	R0	100	B0		2004006	K4	USD	3.974,42-

Figure 6.95 Physical Storage in the InfoCube: Only the Cumulative Value Amount Is Updated

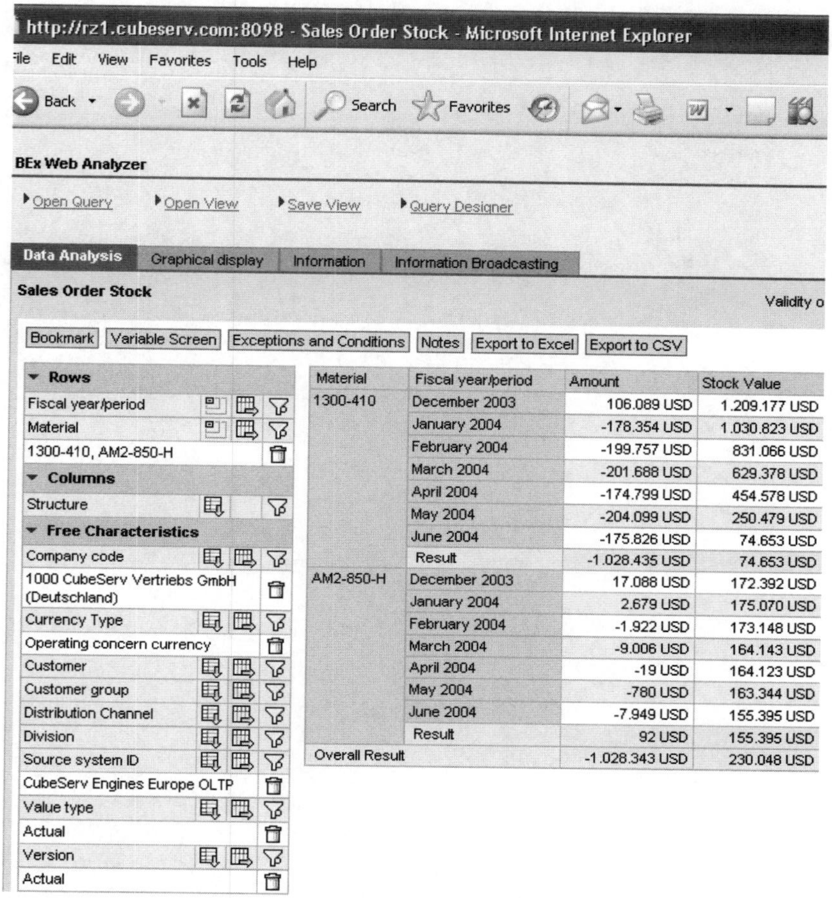

Figure 6.96 Display of Cumulative Value and Inventory Value in Reporting

7 SAP Business Content

This chapter describes SAP Business Content, the pre-configured solution that SAP delivers with SAP BW. In particular, this chapter presents the solution's strengths and weaknesses, and makes recommendations regarding how you can best use Business Content for your own purposes.

The SAP Business Content solution comprises a wide range of predefined analytical solutions that are part of the SAP BW package:

> *SAP Business Content consists of preconfigured, role-related, and task-related information model, based on consistent metadata in the SAP Business Information Warehouse. SAP Business Content provides selected roles within a company with the range of available information that employees need to complete their daily tasks.*[1]

Benefits of SAP Business Content

Because these predefined models contain all the necessary components—from extraction to the data model to reports—they greatly help to reduce the time and effort required to set up and implement SAP Business Information Warehouse (SAP BW). Therefore, as part of a new SAP BW installation, SAP Business Content means much shorter setup times, even if it is being used only as a template. This makes it possible to implement an application such as Profit Center Reporting relatively easily and quickly. Needless to say, for this to be possible, the systems in question must have been installed correctly.

We are not aware of any other data warehousing product that provides such comprehensive business content. This is particularly true in cases where a sufficient amount of data from SAP R/3 is made available in SAP BW for reporting purposes.

We should also note that the quality of the Business Content is improved with each new release of SAP BW (and an improvement in the quality of the existing data is preferable to an increase in the quantity of data).

Problems of SAP Business Content

As we will demonstrate in this section, you should not accept the standard preconfigured solution unquestioningly, even with all its benefits. This is because frequently the solution does not adequately fulfill the require-

1 SAP AG, SAP BW online documentation, *http://help.sap.com/saphelp_bw33/helpdata/de/37/5fb13cd0500255e10000000a114084/content.htm*

ments of the real-world company. You should always determine whether you can use the Business Content directly *as is*, or whether it would make more sense to use it as a template to create your own objects.

You should also note that the overall quality of the delivered data can vary widely. For example, as we will see, the Business Content in the Financial Accounting and Controlling areas corresponds to real-world requirements much better than does the data in Logistics or Human Resources.

In this chapter, we will focus exclusively on Business Content in the Data Modeling area. For the Extraction and Reporting areas, you should seek other volumes of the SAP BW Library.[2]

7.1 Elements of SAP Business Content

The following are the main object types for the Data Modeling area that are released with SAP BW 3.5:

Object types

- InfoObjects
  - Characteristics
  - Key figures
- DataProvider
  - Basic InfoCubes
  - ODS Objects
  - MultiProviders

The number of objects included in the delivery has become almost unmanageable: Approximately 14,000 InfoObjects and 691 Basic InfoCubes are delivered with Release 3.5.2 of Business Content. Section 5.2 of this book describes in detail how to activate SAP Business Content.

7.2 Fundamental Problems of SAP Business Content

The option of directly implementing the Business Content solution is restricted by the fact that the solution is unlikely to fulfill the technical requirements of every company that may use it. This deficit is due to the data model, which is not optimal from a technical point of view. However,

2 This book is the first volume of the new *SAP BW Library* series. See Appendix L of this book for an overview of the subsequent volumes in this series.

it is unlikely that all the weaknesses of the solution will be solved in the long term. This is because the weaknesses are partly due to the multitude of requirements that companies have, and also because it is simply not within the scope of a general solution to fulfill all the possible requirements.

> We recommend that you carefully consider whether you want to implement SAP Business Content as is; otherwise, you may end up creating applications that don't correspond to your company's requirements. Unfortunately, this is a common scenario, which leads to general dissatisfaction with SAP BW. Also, besides the project costs, the customer also incurs the considerable costs of operating the application in question without enjoying the corresponding benefits.

7.2.1 Technical Problems

Common requirements

Although technical requirements do vary from one company to another, there are nonetheless several requirements that apply to all projects, but that are not included in Business Content. Section 7.4 contains some examples of these requirements. It would be a welcome improvement if these requirements were included in future releases of Business Content.

7.2.2 Data Model

Common problems

The Business Content data model contains several less-than-optimal solutions and even errors. These solutions and errors can cause the following problems:

- Incorrect reporting data
- Complicated navigation in the reporting function
- Performance problems

Examples of these problems are provided in the following sections.

InfoObjects: Attributes

It is not always apparent how to assign attributes to InfoObjects. Also, the way in which attributes are assigned, while technically correct, can reduce the usability of the application. For example, the **Organizational Unit** characteristic (0ORGUNIT) can have attributes from the Purchasing and Sales Organization areas, which, in turn, have references to the Organizational Unit (see Figure 7.1). This means that Sales Organization attributes are also visible in a purchasing application, and vice versa.

We therefore recommend that you delete any attributes that are not required, or that you create your own InfoObjects rather than using the SAP Business Content InfoObjects.

Organizational Unit	0ORGUNIT	
InfoCube		
InfoObject Catalog		
InfoObject		
Business Partner	0BPARTNER	Has attribute : 0ORGUNIT [IOBJ]
Employee	0EMPLOYEE	Has attribute : 0ORGUNIT [IOBJ]
Position	0HRPOSITION	Has attribute : 0ORGUNIT [IOBJ]
User Name	0USERNAME	Has attribute : 0ORGUNIT [IOBJ]
Recipients	0WS_TAROBJ	Has attribute : 0ORGUNIT [IOBJ]
Purchasing Group	0BBP_PURGRP	Refers to characteristic : 0ORGUNIT [IOBJ]
Purchasing Organization	0BBP_PURORG	Refers to characteristic : 0ORGUNIT [IOBJ]
Responsible Organizational Unit in Purchasing	0CRMPU_OG_R	Refers to characteristic : 0ORGUNIT [IOBJ]
Responsible Organizational Unit in Sales	0CRMSA_OG_R	Refers to characteristic : 0ORGUNIT [IOBJ]
Responsible Organizational Unit (Service)	0CRMSE_OG_R	Refers to characteristic : 0ORGUNIT [IOBJ]
Executing CRM Service Organization	0CRMSRVTGRP	Refers to characteristic : 0ORGUNIT [IOBJ]
CRM Sales Group	0CRM_SALGRP	Refers to characteristic : 0ORGUNIT [IOBJ]
CRM Sales Office	0CRM_SALOFF	Refers to characteristic : 0ORGUNIT [IOBJ]
Sales Organization CRM	0CRM_SALORG	Refers to characteristic : 0ORGUNIT [IOBJ]
Service Organization CRM	0CRM_SRVORG	Refers to characteristic : 0ORGUNIT [IOBJ]

Figure 7.1 Attributes of the Organizational Unit (0ORGUNIT)

Attributes as navigation attributes

Time-dependent attributes are also frequently used with characteristics that are likely to have a high number of instances. Examples of this are **Material** (0MATERIAL) and **Employee** (0EMPLOYEE). If a situation occurs where these attributes have to be used as navigation attributes for technical reasons, you should expect performance problems. This situation arises because the time and effort required to define meaningful aggregates for the InfoCubes are simply not justifiable.

InfoObjects: Compounding

Characteristics should be compounded in a manner that preserves the uniqueness of the master data for this InfoObject. With Business Content, the characteristics are delivered in such a way that the compounding corresponds to the data model of an individual SAP R/3 system. For example, the G/L account is compounded with the Chart of Accounts and the plant material is compounded with the plant. However, in actuality, there is usually more than one source system.

Ensure that you evaluate the extent of this problem in detail and early in the project, even if data is initially extracted from only one source system. This is because extending the compounding later on in a live application is very time-consuming.

Characteristics without master data

Characteristics that don't contain any master data in SAP BW are generally not compounded. Therefore, the document item (for example, 0ID_ITMNUM) is not compounded with the document header (for example, 0ID_DOCNUM). This applies to all documents, such as accounting documents and sales documents, and leads to incorrect results in report navigation if the user positions the cursor in the document item on a list where document number and document item have been drilled down, and if the user selects the **Filters and drilldown** function. The incorrect results occur because the document number is ignored in the filter.

If you require this navigation in the queries, we recommend that you extend the compounding accordingly.

InfoCubes: Design of the Star Schema

The design of the star schema is a deciding factor in the performance of the reporting function. The SAP BW documentation states the following:

> *In one dimension, characteristics that logically belong together should be summarized (for example, District and Area both belong to the regional dimension). If this design criterion is adhered to, the dimensions can be kept largely independent and the data volume in the dimension tables is kept small, which has a positive effect on performance.*[3]

All characteristics in a dimension

However, Business Content contains a range of InfoCubes in which this is not the case. An example of an InfoCube where all characteristics, except the time characteristic, are stored in a single dimension is the **IC Interaction Statistics** (0CRM_CTI2) InfoCube from the CRM area (see Figure 7.2).

We strongly recommend that you optimize the star schema. In doing so, it is essential that you always keep in mind the requirements of the data that will be used in the real-life application.

3 SAP AG, SAP BW online documentation, *http://help.sap.com/saphelp_bw33/helpdata/de/4c/89dc37c7f2d67ae10000009b38f889/content.htm*

InfoCube data model	Techn.name
IC Interaction Statistics (with Reference to CRM Info.)	0CRM_CTI2
Dimension1	0CRM_CTI21
Executing Interaction Center	0CRM_EXC_CC
Indicator: Connection Canceled	0CRM_FLGABD
CRM Marketing Element (Campaign and Marketing Plan)	0CRM_MKTELM
Current Catalog: Reasons	0CRM_RCA
Current Code: Reasons	0CRM_RCO
Current Code Group: Reasons	0CRM_RG
Activity Reason (Code)	0CRM_RSN_CO
Activity Reason (Code Group)	0CRM_RSN_GR
Activity Reason (Catalog)	0CRM_RSN_TY
Contact Partner	0BP_ACTIVIT
Contact Persons	0BP_CONTPER
Responsible Employee	0BP_EMPLO
Category	0CRM_CAT
Communication Type	0CRM_COMTYP
Direction	0CRM_DIRECT
Communication Direction	0CRM_CDIR
Time	0CRM_CTI2T
Data Package	0CRM_CTI2P
Key figures	1KYFNM
Navigation attributes	1ATTRIBUTE

Figure 7.2 Data Model of InfoCube 0CRM_CTI2

InfoCubes: Time Characteristics

Time characteristic types

SAP BW has two different types of time characteristics: *calendar* characteristics (0CALDAY, 0CALMONTH2, 0CALMONTH, 0CALQUARTER, 0CALYEAR, among others) and *fiscal* characteristics (0FISCVARNT, 0FISCPER3, 0FISCPER, and 0FISCYEAR).

Summarizing different time characteristics

The Business Content InfoCubes don't use characteristics consistently. For example, some InfoCubes contain calendar characteristics, while others use fiscal characteristics. Other InfoCubes also contain a mixture of both types. This results in a situation whereby if you want to group together in a MultiProvider two InfoCubes in which time characteristics are used differently, the time characteristics cannot be used for the grouping. Figure 7.3 shows that InfoCube 0IC_C03 contains only calendar characteristics, and InfoCube 0COPC_C04 contains only fiscal characteristics.

It is therefore advisable that you include all the appropriate calendar and fiscal time characteristics, down to the smallest unit (such as day or month), in every InfoCube. This need not be a particularly time-consuming task.

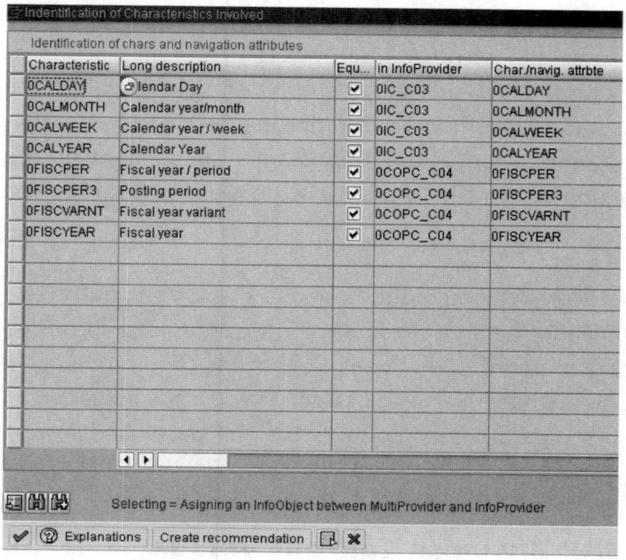
Indentification of Characteristics Involved

Identification of chars and navigation attributes

Characteristic	Long description	Equ...	in InfoProvider	Char./navig. attrbte
0CALDAY	Calendar Day	☑	0IC_C03	0CALDAY
0CALMONTH	Calendar year/month	☑	0IC_C03	0CALMONTH
0CALWEEK	Calendar year / week	☑	0IC_C03	0CALWEEK
0CALYEAR	Calendar Year	☑	0IC_C03	0CALYEAR
0FISCPER	Fiscal year / period	☑	0COPC_C04	0FISCPER
0FISCPER3	Posting period	☑	0COPC_C04	0FISCPER3
0FISCVARNT	Fiscal year variant	☑	0COPC_C04	0FISCVARNT
0FISCYEAR	Fiscal year	☑	0COPC_C04	0FISCYEAR

Selecting = Asigning an InfoObject between MultiProvider and InfoProvider

Explanations | Create recommendation

Figure 7.3 Assigning the Time Characteristics in MultiProvider

ODS as Data Warehouse Layer

The literature on this subject generally takes an architectural approach—constructing data marts for the analysis on top of an initial data warehousing layer. While the data stored in the data warehouse is in an uncompressed format, the data in the data mart is compressed and may be stored there in a format suitable for a specific reporting purpose. In SAP BW, the corresponding object types are ODS for the data warehouse, and InfoCubes for the data marts. In Business Content, however, this approach is used in only some cases.

> In those cases where this approach is employed, we recommend that it is used for all data and that you create corresponding ODS objects. However, this is not always the case in Business Content.

ODS: Reporting Directly to the ODS Object

In some cases (such as appraisals in Human Resources 0PAH_DS03), data is updated in only one ODS object. The reporting process is then carried out directly in this ODS, which causes significant performance problems.

> In such cases, we recommend that you update the data in an additional InfoCube. This InfoCube is then used for reporting purposes.

Using MultiProviders

Optimizing the data model

Business Content uses almost no MultiProviders to optimize the data model. This often causes a high number of empty cells, along with all the associated problems for data storage and reporting performance.[4] However, because the composition of the data is highly dependent on the customer's transaction systems, it is often not possible to optimize the Business Content.

Within the scope of an implementation project, this aspect should be examined in detail, and the data model should be optimized, because this usually is less time-consuming than taking steps to improve performance. It is also advisable in many cases that you store actual data and plan data in separate Basic InfoCubes, as the data has varying degrees of granularity.

7.3 Using SAP Business Content Versus Proprietary Objects

At the start of almost every project, a discussion occurs regarding whether the Business Content objects should be used *as is* or possibly changed as required, or whether a general approach of using proprietary objects should be adopted. While the most popular decision is often to use proprietary objects for the InfoProviders and to use the Business Content as a template only, the part of the discussion concerning the InfoObjects is far more controversial.

We recommend that you create your own objects rather than use Business Content objects, for the following reasons:

- Changed, active Business Content objects can be destroyed when Business Content is reactivated. This is not very likely, but still possible, and the resulting damage can be considerable.
- Therefore, if you want to activate Business Content for testing purposes—for example, in order to test new functionality after an upgrade—you should do so on a sandbox system only. However, this kind of system is often unavailable.

Partially transfer InfoObjects?

The following compromise is sometimes implemented in projects. InfoObjects that are not being changed are copied from Business Con-

4 See Egger, 2004, p. 192.

tent, and InfoObjects that are being changed—by taking on new attributes, for example—are created as new objects. This approach, however, soon causes the problem that objects may need to be changed again at a later stage, making it impossible to agree whether to use Business Content objects or proprietary objects when the object is created. It is quite time-consuming to change InfoObjects later on in a live application.

To ensure that we have covered this topic thoroughly, we would like to point out that SAP Business Content must be used for certain types of InfoObjects (such as time characteristics).

7.4 SAP Business Content in Selected Application Areas

The Business Content for the SAP BW 3.5 data model is divided into the following main areas:

- Customer Relationship Management (CRM)
- Supplier Relationship Management (SRM)
- Supply Chain Performance Management (SCPM)
- Product Lifecycle Management (PLM)
- Financials (FI)
- Human Resources (HR)
- Business Content for various Industry Solutions (IS)

Because a comprehensive, detailed analysis exceeds the scope of this book, we will concentrate here on selected sub-areas from the Financials, Supply Chain Performance Management, and Human Resources areas.

7.4.1 Business Content for Financials

Comprehensive implementation

The implementation of Business Content in the Financials area has been quite comprehensive since the early releases of SAP BW. While this instance was at first primarily intended for copying and storing totals records, it also evolved into a solution for copying line items (for General Ledger Accounting and Profit Center Accounting, for example). SAP BW 3.5 provides new components for Credit Management, Real Estate Management, and Budget Management.

Low level of adaptation required

Because the Financials area is highly standardized compared to other areas (for example, cost-center reporting is largely the same in all companies, regardless of the industry), Business Content can often be used with a relatively low level of adaptation required.

Weaknesses

Nonetheless, there are some weaknesses in Business Content, examples of which are given below:

- The document item characteristics are not compounded with the document (see Section 7.2.2).
- The important **Group G/L Account** attribute (BILKT field in SAP R/3 G/L account master record) is not available in the **G/L Account** (0GL_ACCOUNT) characteristic. This attribute is often required in this characteristic to combine data from companies with different Chart of Accounts in SAP BW.
- The InfoCube **CO-OM-CCA: Costs and Allocations** (0CCA_C11) is delivered in Business Content with 12 dimensions. The **Origin** dimension contains a range of characteristics that don't have a high degree of correlation (see Figure 7.4). We recommend that you use the maximum possible number of dimensions and distribute the characteristics of the **Origin** dimension across several dimensions.

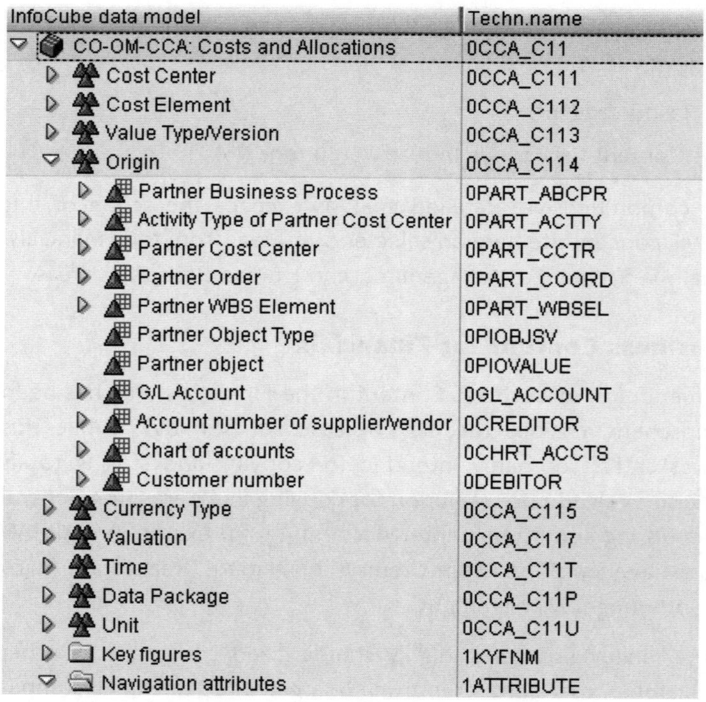

Figure 7.4 Data Model InfoCube 0CCA_C11

- Special characteristics are used for the **Account** characteristic (see Table 7.1) in the SAP R/3 modules Financial Accounting, Overhead Costs Controlling, and Profit Center Accounting.

Module	Characteristic
Financial Accounting	G/L account (0GL_ACCOUNT)
Overhead Costs Controlling	Cost element (0COSTELMNT)
Profit Center Accounting	Account (0ACCOUNT)

Table 7.1 InfoObjects for the Account Characteristic

Even if these characteristics are not completely identical, it is still preferable if each account is available as an attribute, so that the data in Multi-Providers can be interconnected.

7.4.2 Business Content for Supply Chain Performance Management

Industry details

Business Content for Supply Chain Performance Management (SCPM) is a wide area. There are also other specific solutions in the Business Content versions for the Industry Solutions. Because SCPM requirements vary so much from one industry to the other, and because many companies also have very specific reporting requirements, you should consider carefully whether you can use Business Content directly. Some problems with Business Content arising from the aforementioned facts are outlined below.

Characteristic: Material

Empty attributes

The 0MATERIAL characteristic in Business Content contains several attributes (see Figures 7.5 to 7.7.). In actuality, many of these attributes are empty, because no content was assigned to them in the application in question, either in the current system or the source system.

> Because there can often be many material master records (up to several hundred thousands), you should evaluate the attributes and determine whether some of them could be deleted. This reduces the amount of storage space required and increases the clarity of the process for defining queries. We recommend that you delete any attributes that are no longer required, and that you fill any empty attributes.

Object overview	Field	InfoObject
Material		
Characteristics		
AFS Elementary Field "Color"	AF_COLOR	0AF_COLOR
AFS Fabric Content Code	AF_FCOCO	0AF_FCOCO
AFS Grid	AF_GRID	0AF_GRID
AFS Intersection	AF_STYLE	0AF_STYLE
AFS Target Group	AF_GENDER	0AF_GENDER
ATC Code	HC_ATCCODE	0HC_ATCCODE
Active Ingredient 1 (Main Active Ingredient)	HC_AGENT1	0HC_AGENT1
Active Ingredient 2	HC_AGENT2	0HC_AGENT2
Active Ingredient 3	HC_AGENT3	0HC_AGENT3
Anesthetic Indicator	HC_ANESIND	0HC_ANESIND
Approval Type	HC_APPRTYP	0HC_APPRTYP
Basic material (basic constituent of a material)	BASIC_MATL	0BASIC_MATL
Brand	RF_BNDID	0RF_BNDID
Catalog 1 Indicator	HC_CATIND1	0HC_CATIND1
Catalog 2 Indicator	HC_CATIND2	0HC_CATIND2
Catalog 3 Indicator	HC_CATIND3	0HC_CATIND3
Certification Type	UCCERTIFTY	0UCCERTIFTY
Collection	RT_SEAROLL	0RT_SEAROLL
Color	RT_COLOR	0RT_COLOR
Competitors	COMPETITOR	0COMPETITOR
Construction Class	UCCONSTCLA	0UCCONSTCLA
Cross-Plant Configur. Material	RT_CONFMAT	0RT_CONFMAT
Date on which the record was created	CREATEDON	0CREATEDON
Division	DIVISION	0DIVISION
European Article Numbers/Universal Product Code	EANUPC	0EANUPC
External material group	EXTMATLGRP	0EXTMATLGRP
Fashion Grade	RT_FASHGRD	0RT_FASHGRD
Function Class	UCFUNCCLAS	0UCFUNCCLAS

Figure 7.5 Attributes for Characteristic 0MATERIAL, Part 1

Function Class	UCFUNCCLAS	0UCFUNCCLAS
General Analysis Characteristic	RF_FRECHAR	0RF_FRECHAR
Hazardous Substance Indicator	HC_HAZMIND	0HC_HAZMIND
Import Material Indicator	HC_IMPMIND	0HC_IMPMIND
Industry Standard Description (such as DIN)	STD_DESCR	0STD_DESCR
Industry sector	IND_SECTOR	0IND_SECTOR
Manufacturer	MANUFACTOR	0MANUFACTOR
Manufacturer Part Number	MANU_MATNR	0MANU_MATNR
Master Data Release Status	RT_MDRELST	0RT_MDRELST
Material	MATERIAL	0MATERIAL
Material Group Hierarchy Level 1	RPA_WGH1	0RPA_WGH1
Material Group Hierarchy Level 2	RPA_WGH2	0RPA_WGH2
Material Group Hierarchy Level 3	RPA_WGH3	0RPA_WGH3
Material Group Hierarchy Level 4	RPA_WGH4	0RPA_WGH4
Material category	MATL_CAT	0MATL_CAT
Material group	MATL_GROUP	0MATL_GROUP
Material type	MATL_TYPE	0MATL_TYPE
Price Band Category	RT_PRBAND	0RT_PRBAND
Procurement Rule	RT_PRRULE	0RT_PRRULE
Product	APO_PROD	0APO_PROD
Product	BBP_PROD	0BBP_PROD
Product	CRM_PROD	0CRM_PROD
Product hierarchy	PROD_HIER	0PROD_HIER
Season Category	RT_SEASON	0RT_SEASON
Season Year	RT_SEAYR	0RT_SEAYR
Season Year	RT_SEASYR	0RT_SEASYR

Figure 7.6 Attributes for Characteristic 0MATERIAL, Part 2

Size	RT_SIZE	0RT_SIZE
Size 2	RF_SIZE2	0RF_SIZE2
Size/dimension	SIZE_DIM	0SIZE_DIM
Source System	LOGSYS	0LOGSYS
Source of Supply	RT_SUPS	0RT_SUPS
Type of Med. Category for ATC Code	HC_ATCMTYP	0HC_ATCMTYP
Usage	MSA_USAGE	0MSA_USAGE
Vendor	VENDOR	0VENDOR
Key Figures		
Gross contents	GROSS_CONT	0GROSS_CONT
Gross weight	GROSS_WT	0GROSS_WT
Height	HEIGHT	0HEIGHT
Length	LENGHT	0LENGHT
Net contents	NET_CONT	0NET_CONT
Net weight of item	NET_WEIGHT	0NET_WEIGHT
Planned Purchase Price	RTPLCST	0RTPLCST
Volume	VOLUME	0VOLUME
Width	WIDTH	0WIDTH
Units		
Base Unit of Measure	BASE_UOM	0BASE_UOM
Content unit	CONT_UNIT	0CONT_UNIT
Local currency	LOC_CURRCY	0LOC_CURRCY
Order unit	PO_UNIT	0PO_UNIT
Unit of dimension for length/width/height	UNIT_DIM	0UNIT_DIM
Volume unit	VOLUMEUNIT	0VOLUMEUNIT
Weight unit	UNIT_OF_WT	0UNIT_OF_WT

Figure 7.7 Attributes for Characteristic 0MATERIAL, Part 3

InfoCube: Purchasing Data

Missing time characteristics

The 0PUR_C01 InfoCube (see Figure 7.8) contains purchasing data that is used to carry out analyses of material groups, vendors, and material. It should be noted, however, that the time characteristics are incomplete; in other words, this InfoCube does not contain all the possible calendar and fiscal characteristics. For reasons that are not clear, 0FISCYEAR, 0FISCPER3, and 0CALMONTH2 are missing.

We recommend that you fill the empty time characteristics.

Avoiding empty cells

The InfoCube is updated from the **Purchasing Data** InfoSource **(document schedule line level) from 2.0B** (2LIS_02_SCL) and the **Purchasing Data** InfoSource **(document item level) from 2.0B** (2LIS_02_ITM). This creates several empty cells, and the associated storage and performance problems. A better approach would be to create a Basic Provider for each InfoSource. All the Basic Providers would then be combined using a MultiProvider.

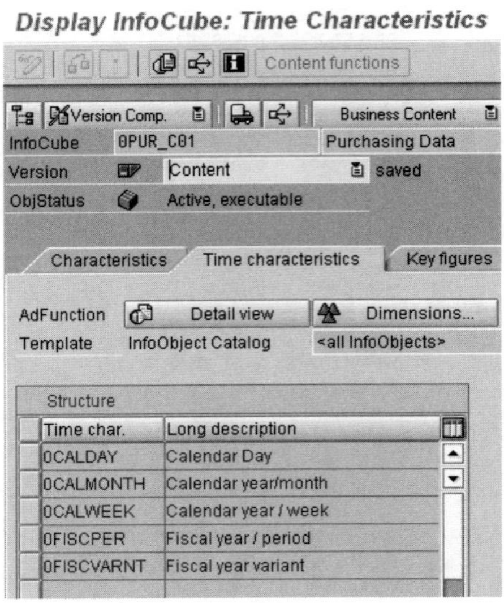

Figure 7.8 InfoCube 0PUR_C01, Time Characteristics

InfoCube: Goods Movement

Performance problems

InfoCube 0IC_C03 contains data on goods movements and stocks. Because this InfoCube uses stock key figures, you need to specify a reference characteristic for the time-based aggregation. In Business Content, this characteristic is the calendar day (0CALDAY). For large data volumes, however, performance problems will probably occur here.

> We therefore recommend that you determine whether the calendar day is required as the time reference characteristic or, whether it could be compressed to the month instead. This would improve performance greatly.

Version and value type

Also, the InfoCube does not contain any characteristics for version and value type, because only actual data is transferred to it from the R/3 system.

> However, even if you initially want to transfer only the actual data, we recommend that you also include the **version** and **value type** characteristics in order to give yourself the option of adding plan data to the application at a later stage (using a flat file upload, for example) without incurring any problems.

InfoCube: Sales Overview

Administration problems

The 0SD_C03 InfoCube (see Figure 7.9) contains data from the SAP R/3 SD (Sales & Distribution) module. This InfoCube is updated from several different InfoSources. (You should note, however, that InfoSources 2LIS_01_S260 to 2LIS_01_S263 should no longer be used.) This yields a high number of empty cells, thereby making it harder to administer the InfoCube in normal operations.

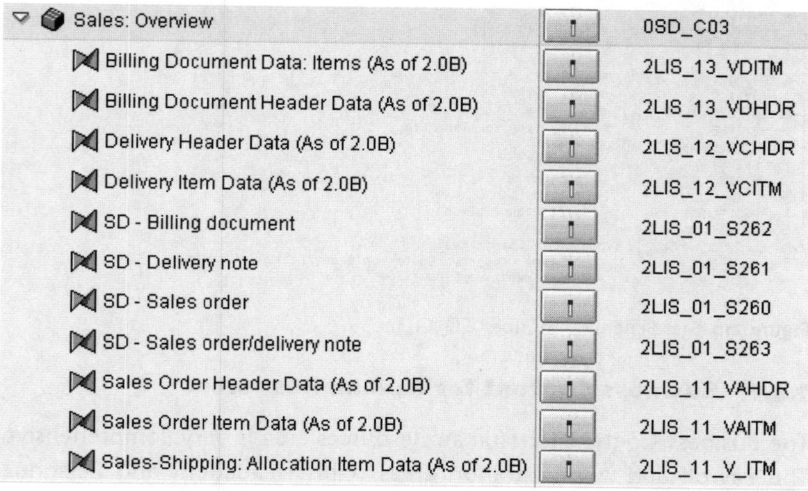

Figure 7.9 Updating InfoCube 0SD_C03

Assigning characteristics

In many projects, the volume of sales data is very large. Therefore, we recommend that you pay particular attention to assigning characteristics to dimensions in the star schema. Only eight of the possible 13 dimensions are used in Business Content (see Figure 7.10).

The data model should be optimized to include all 13 dimensions. To do this, a close analysis needs to be carried out on the data involved in the real-life application. Either the **Organization** dimension or the **Customer** dimension would be a good place to start. The **Customer** dimension will need to be revised only if there are several cases where there is not a one-to-one relationship between Sold-to party, Payer, Goods Recipient, and Bill-to party.

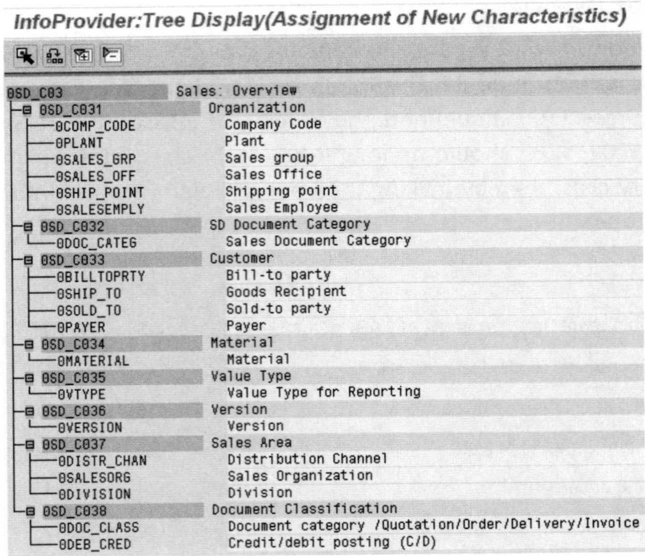

Figure 7.10 Star Schema InfoCube 0SD_C03

7.4.3 Business Content for Human Resources

The Business Content for Human Resources area is very comprehensive. The Payroll and Administration areas (with Headcount and Personnel Action) are the most important areas for everyday use.

Necessary corrections

Based on our experience, several corrections need to be made to Business Content in order to make it correspond to real-world requirements. We have provided you with some examples of these corrections below.

Employee Attributes

Only one entry date

Although the **Employee** characteristic (0EMPLOYEE) does have several attributes in Business Content, some common everyday requirements are not covered. For example, it has only one **entry date** (0ENTRYDATE), although several entry dates are often required, such as the following:

- Date of entry to the company
- Date of entry to the group
- Accountable date of entry for calculating seniority

Time-dependent employee attributes

Furthermore, the employee attributes are time-dependent. With the usual real-world employee numbers (often several tens of thousands), you should expect performance problems when using navigation attributes simultaneously.

Employee and Person Characteristics

Separate master data

The master data for Person and the master data for Employee are stored separately in the OPERSON and OEMPLOYEE InfoObjects. The attributes assigned to the **Person** characteristic include **date of birth** and **nationality**, while the **Employee** characteristic has attributes relating to employment, such as **entry date** and **personnel area**.

At first glance, this model is perfectly correct, as the **Person** characteristic is used in other InfoCubes, and not every person is also an employee.

Problems

However, in a case where a list has been drilled down by **Employee** in the Reporting function, this results in the list also having to be drilled down by **Person** so that the **Nationality** attribute, for example, becomes visible (see Figure 7.11).

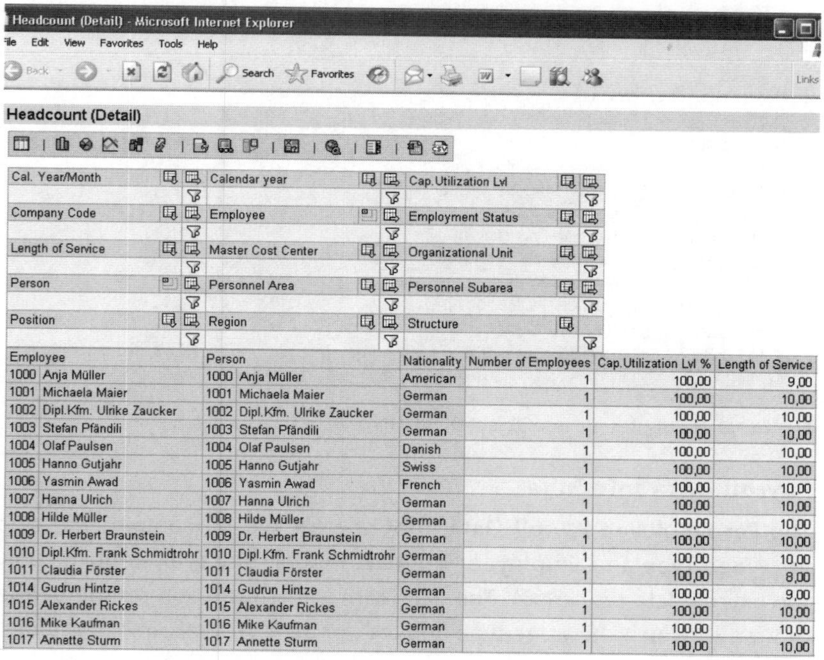

Employee		Person		Nationality	Number of Employees	Cap.Utilization Lvl %	Length of Service
1000	Anja Müller	1000	Anja Müller	American	1	100,00	9,00
1001	Michaela Maier	1001	Michaela Maier	German	1	100,00	10,00
1002	Dipl.Kfm. Ulrike Zaucker	1002	Dipl.Kfm. Ulrike Zaucker	German	1	100,00	10,00
1003	Stefan Pfändili	1003	Stefan Pfändili	German	1	100,00	10,00
1004	Olaf Paulsen	1004	Olaf Paulsen	Danish	1	100,00	10,00
1005	Hanno Gutjahr	1005	Hanno Gutjahr	Swiss	1	100,00	10,00
1006	Yasmin Awad	1006	Yasmin Awad	French	1	100,00	10,00
1007	Hanna Ulrich	1007	Hanna Ulrich	German	1	100,00	10,00
1008	Hilde Müller	1008	Hilde Müller	German	1	100,00	10,00
1009	Dr. Herbert Braunstein	1009	Dr. Herbert Braunstein	German	1	100,00	10,00
1010	Dipl.Kfm. Frank Schmidtrohr	1010	Dipl.Kfm. Frank Schmidtrohr	German	1	100,00	10,00
1011	Claudia Förster	1011	Claudia Förster	German	1	100,00	8,00
1014	Gudrun Hintze	1014	Gudrun Hintze	German	1	100,00	9,00
1015	Alexander Rickes	1015	Alexander Rickes	German	1	100,00	10,00
1016	Mike Kaufman	1016	Mike Kaufman	German	1	100,00	10,00
1017	Annette Sturm	1017	Annette Sturm	German	1	100,00	10,00

Figure 7.11 Query with Person Attribute

> We therefore recommend that you include the **Person** attributes in the employee details, in order to make the Reporting function more user-friendly.

Organizational Unit Attributes

Missing Human Resources attributes

The **Organizational Unit** attribute (0ORGUNIT) contains several Purchasing and CRM attributes (see Figure 7.12). Human Resources attributes, however, are missing and therefore may have to be added as part of the implementation project.

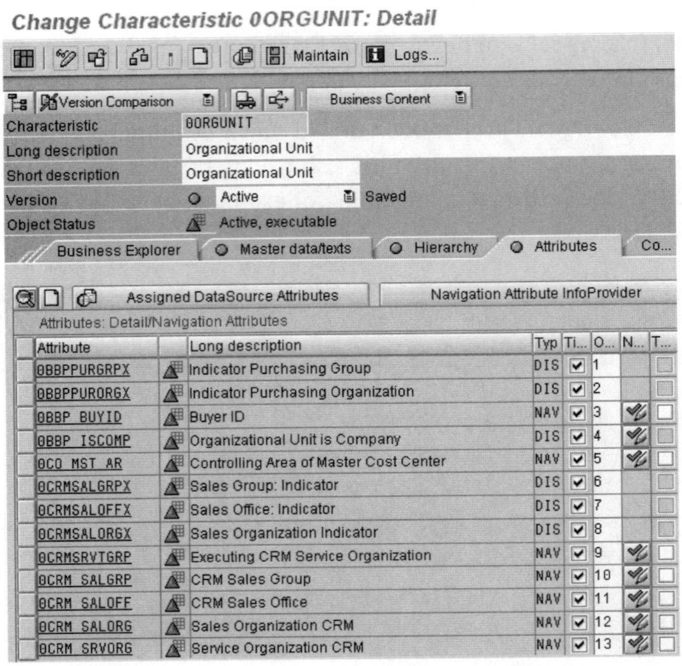

Figure 7.12 Attributes for InfoObject 0ORGUNIT

Payroll Data InfoCube

In-period and for-period

The **Per-Employee Payroll Data** InfoCube (0PY_C02) contains the data for **Wage Type** and **Employee**. The data model, however, contains only the payroll date (*in-period*). The date with the information on the period of time to which the wage type applies (*for-period*) is missing. Therefore, reporting information is available regarding when a payroll was run for overtime work, for example, but no information is available on when that work was actually done.

While plug-in 2004.1 can be used to select and extract the period in question, it is still not possible to select both pieces of time information,[5] although based on our experience, both pieces of information are used

5 See OSS Note 697225.

regularly. However, the extra work required to adapt the InfoCube applies mainly to the extraction process from SAP R/3.

Headcount and Personnel Actions InfoCube

Empty cells

The following two structurally different data records are updated in the **Headcount and Personnel Actions** InfoCube (0PA_C01):

- Employees (contains headcount), InfoSource 0HR_PA_0
- Personnel actions, InfoSource 0HR_PA_1

This causes several empty cells to occur in this InfoCube, which has a negative effect on performance and storage requirements.[6]

> It is preferable to create one Basic InfoCube for headcount and one for personnel actions. Then, these InfoCubes can be easily combined again using a MultiProvider. Using this data model makes it easier to administrate the InfoCubes in day-to-day operations.

7.5 Conclusion

Our examples have shown that when using Business Content for the Data Modeling area, you should consider it from several different perspectives. You should always determine whether you can use the Business Content directly *as is*, or whether it would be preferable to use it as a template for creating your own objects. You should also note that the overall quality of the delivered data can vary widely. For example, the Business Content in the Financial Accounting and Controlling areas applies to real-world requirements far more accurately than does the data in Logistics or Human Resources.

For this reason, before you activate SAP Business Content, check whether it can be used for your company's individual requirements without any adjustments. Sometimes the best thing to do may be to make changes to Business Content before using it; other times, it may be better to circumvent it altogether.

Because of the current scope of SAP Business Content, it would be impossible for us to make individual recommendations for your company here. However, the following general advice, which you can use to support your work, can be drawn from the examples provided in this chapter:

6 See Egger, 2004.

- Do not implement SAP Business Content without examining it closely first. Otherwise, it may not be suitable for your company's real-life requirements, resulting in additional project costs and general dissatisfaction with SAP BW.
- Consider whether optimizing the star schema may be necessary for your individual requirements. The design of the star schema is a deciding factor in the performance of the reporting function.
- Consider whether your data model could be optimized by using MultiProviders. This can often help to avoid empty cells and achieve significant improvements in performance.
- Note that there are considerable advantages to creating your own objects as opposed to using Business Content objects.

Whatever your situation, it will always prove worthwhile for you to invest time in familiarizing yourself with SAP Business Content. Despite all the difficulties at the detail level, Business Content is and will continue to be an excellent tool for greatly reducing the implementation time for SAP BW and will therefore make your implementation project considerably easier.

A Abbreviations

ABAP	Advanced Business Application Programming
ADK	Archiving Development Kit
ALE	Application Link Enabling
API	Application Programming Interface
ASCII	American Standard Code for Information Interchange
AWB	Administrator Workbench
BAPI	Business Application Programming Interface
BCT	Business Content
RRI	Report-to-Report Interface
BEx	Business Explorer
BW	Business Information Warehouse
CSV	Comma Separated Values (or Variables)
DDIC	Data Dictionary
DIM ID	Dimension Identification
DWH	Data Warehouse
ETL	Extraction, Transformation, and Loading
IDoc	Intermediate Document
LUW	Logical Unit of Work
ODBO	OLE DB (Object Linking and Embedding Database) for OLAP
ODS	Operational Data Store
OLAP	Online Analytical Processing
OLTP	Online Transaction Processing
RFC	Remote Function Call
SAPI	Service API
SID	Surrogate Identification
SOAP	Simple Object Access Protocol
SQL	Structured Query Language
TCT	Technical Content
TRFC	Transactional RFC
WAD	Web Application Designer
WAS	Web Application Server
XML	Extensible Markup Language

B InfoObjectCatalogs

CubeServ BW Documentation Tool

The *CubeServ BW Documentation Tool* created all the screenshots displayed at the site. The CubeServ BW Documentation Tool is the first professional documentation tool for SAP Business Information Warehouse (SAP BW). You can use it to create documentation from SAP BW at the touch of a button. You can employ various navigation options to use the documentation on line or as a printout.[1]

B.1 InfoObjectCatalog ZECOPA01CHA01

InfoArea:	ZECOPA01
InfoObjectCatalog:	ZECOPA0101

Profitability Analysis Characteristics

Type:	Characteristic

0BA_PRZNR	Sender Business Process
0BA_STO_BNR	
0BA_STO_PNR	
0BILL_DATE	Date for Billing/Invoice Index and Printing
0BILL_TYPE	Invoice Type
0BUS_AREA	Business Area
0CHRT_ACCTS	Chart of Accounts
0COMP_CODE	Company Code
0COORDER	Order Number
0COSTELMNT	Cost Element
0COSTOBJ	Cost Object
0CO_AREA	Controlling Area
0CURTYPE	Currency Type
0CUSTOMER	Customer Number
0CUST_GROUP	Customer Group
0DISTR_N	Distribution
0DIVISION	Division
0DOC_NUMBER	
0GI_DATE	Goods Issue Date
0ID_DOCNUM	
0ID_ITMNUM	
0INDUSTRY	
0MAINMATGRP	
0MATERIAL	Material
0MATL_GROUP	Material Group
0ME_REFDOC	
0ME_REFITEM	
0PART_PRCTR	Partner Profit Center

1 For more information on the *CubeServ BW Documentation Tool*, please visit *www.cubeserv.com*.

0PLANT	Plant
0PROFIT_CTR	Profit Center
0PSTNG_DATE	Posting Date on the Document
0REC_TYPE	Record Type
0SALESEMPLY	Sales Employee
0SALESORG	Sales Organization
0SALES_DIST	Sales District
0SALES_GRP	Sales Group
0SALES_OFF	Sales Office
0SEND_CCTR	Sending Cost Center
0SOURSYSTEM	Source System ID
0S_ORD_ITEM	
0VALUATION	Valuation View
0VERSION	Version
0VTYPE	Value Type for Reporting
0WBS_ELEMT	Work Breakdown Structure Element (WBS Element)
ZEVERSION	Version (Reporting)

B.2 InfoObjectCatalog ZECOPA01KYF01

InfoArea: ZECOPA01

InfoObjectCatalog: ZECOPA0101

Profit and Loss Statement Key Figures

Type: Key Figure

0ACCRDFR_CS	Accrued Freight Costs
0ADMNSTRTN	Administration
0CASH_DSCNT	Cash Discount
0COPAREVEN	Revenue
0COPASLQTY	Sales Quantity
0CUST_DSCNT	Customer Discount
0DIRMAT_CS	Direct Material Costs
0FIXPROD_CS	Fixed Production Costs
0MARKETING	Marketing
0MATOVHD	Material Overhead Costs
0OTHER_OVHD	Other Overhead Costs
0OTHER_VRNC	Other Variances
0PRICE_VRNC	Price Variances
0PROD_DSCNT	Material Discount
0QTY_DSCNT	Quantity Discount
0QUANT_VRNC	Quantity Variances
0RSRCH_DEV	Research and Development
0SALES_CMSN	Sales Commission
0SALES_CS	Sales Costs
0SPCDSLS_CS	Special Direct Costs of Sales
0VARPROD_CS	Variable Production Costs
0VOL_REBATE	Volume-Based Rebate
ZEBRUMS	Gross Sales

ZEERLMIND	Sales Revenue Reductions
ZEHKVK	Full Costs of Manufacturing

B.3 InfoObjectCatalog ZEFIGL01CHA01

InfoArea: ZEFIGL01

InfoObjectCatalog: ZEFIGL0101

Financials—General Ledger Characteristics

Type: Characteristic

0CHRT_ACCTS	Chart of Accounts
0COMP_CODE	Company Code
0COSTCENTER	Cost Object
0CO_AREA	Controlling Area
0CURTYPE	Currency Type
0FUNC_AREA	Functional Area
0GL_ACCOUNT	General Ledger Account
0PROFIT_CTR	Profit Center
0SEGMENT	Segment for Segment Reporting
0VALUATION	Valuation View
0VERSION	Version
0VTYPE	Value Type for Reporting
ZECHRTACC	
ZEKONZKTO	
ZEVERSION	Version (Reporting)

B.4 InfoObjectCatalog ZEFIGL01KYF01

InfoArea: ZEFIGL01

InfoObjectCatalog: ZEFIGL0101

Financials—General Ledger Characteristics

Type: Key Figure

0BALANCE	Cumulative Balance
0CREDIT	Total of Credit Postings
0DEBIT	Total of Debit Postings
0SALES	Sales per Period

B.5 InfoObjectCatalog ZESALES01VAHDRCHA01

InfoArea: ZESALES01

InfoObjectCatalog: ZESALES01VAHDR01

Sales Document Header Characteristics

Type: Characteristic

0COMP_CODE	Company Code
0CREATEDON	

0CUST_GRP1	Customer Group 1
0CUST_GRP2	Customer Group 2
0CUST_GRP3	Customer Group 3
0CUST_GRP4	Customer Group 4
0CUST_GRP5	Customer Group 5
0DISTR_N	Distribution Channel
0DIVISION	Division
0DLV_STS	Delivery Status
0DLV_STSOI	Overall Delivery Status of all Items
0DOC_NUMBER	
0HEADER_DEL	Header Deleted
0SALESEMPLY	Sales Employee
0SALESORG	Sales Organization
0SALES_GRP	Sales Group
0SALES_OFF	Sales Office
0SOLD_TO	Sold-To Party
0SOURSYSTEM	Source System ID
ZEVERSION	Version (Reporting)

B.6 InfoObjectCatalog ZESALES01VAHDRKYF01

InfoArea: ZESALES01

InfoObjectCatalog: ZESALES01VAHDR01

Sales Document Header Key Figures

Type: Key Figure

0CUML_TME	Cumulative Order Processing Time for all Document Items
0DITM_RET	Returns
0DLVIELCR	Delivered Earlier/Later than Requested Delivery Date
0DLVIELSC	Delivered Earlier/Later than Schedule Line Date
0DLVIEYCR	Delivered Earlier/Later than Requested Delivery Date
0DLVIEYSC	Delivered Earlier/Later than Schedule Line Date
0DLVILECR	Delivered after the Requested Delivery Date
0DLVILESC	Delivered after the Schedule Line Date
0DLVIOVER	Delivered More than Requested
0DLVIUNDR	Delivered Less then Requested
0DLVVELCR	Delivered Value Earlier/Later than the Requested Delivery Date
0DLVVELSC	Delivered Value Earlier/Later than the Schedule Line Date
0DLVVEYCR	Delivered Value Earlier/Later than the Requested Delivery Date
0DLVVEYSC	Delivered Value Earlier/Later than the Schedule Line Date
0DLVVLECR	Delivered Value Earlier/Later than the Requested Delivery Date
0DLVVLESC	Delivered Value Later than Schedule Line Date
0DLVVOVER	Delivered Value More than Requested
0DLVVUNDR	Value Less the Requested
0DLV_24	Delivery within 24 Hours
0DLV_VAL	Actual Delivered Value
0DOC_ITEMS	Number of Document Items
0ICOASREQ	Confirmed as Requested
0ISHP_STCK	Delivery from Stock

0NET_VAL_HD	Net Value of Order in Document Currency
0ORDERS	Number of Orders
0REQU_VAL	Requested Delivery Value
0VAL_24	Value with Delivery within 24 Hours
0VAL_RET	Value of Returns
0VCOASREQ	Value Confirmed as Requested
0VSHP_STCK	Value with Delivery from Stock

B.7 InfoObjectCatalog ZESALES01VAITMCHA01

InfoArea: ZESALES01

InfoObjectCatalog: ZESALES01VAITM01

Sales Document Item Characteristics

Type: Characteristic

0BATCH	
0BND_IND	Independent of Delivery Tolerance
0COMP_CODE	Company Codes
0CREATEDON	
0CUST_GROUP	Customer Group
0CUST_GRP1	Customer Group 1
0CUST_GRP2	Customer Group 2
0CUST_GRP3	Customer Group 3
0CUST_GRP4	Customer Group 4
0CUST_GRP5	Customer Group 5
0DISTR_N	Distribution Channel
0DIVISION	Division
0DLV_STS	Delivery Status
0DLV_STSO	Overall Delivery Status of the Item
0DOC_NUMBER	
0FORWAGENT	Shipper
0ITEM_DEL	Item Deleted
0LST_A_GD	Last Actual Goods Issue Date of an Order Item
0LW_GISTS	Smallest Goods Issue Status of an Order Item
0MATERIAL	Material
0MATL_GROUP	Material Group
0MATL_GRP_1	Material Group 1
0MATL_GRP_2	Material Group 2
0MATL_GRP_3	Material Group 3
0MATL_GRP_4	Material Group 4
0MATL_GRP_5	Material Group 5
0PAYER Payer	
0PLANT Plant	
0PROD_HIER	Product Hierarchy
0SALESEMPLY	Sales Employee
0SALESORG	Sales Organization
0SALES_GRP	Sales Group
0SALES_OFF	Sales Office
0SHIP_POINT	Shipping Point

0SHIP_STCK	Delivery from Stock
0SHIP_TO	Ship-To Party
0SOLD_TO	Sold-To Party
0SOURSYSTEM	Source System ID
0S_ORD_ITEM	
ZEVERSION	Version (Reporting)

B.8 InfoObjectCatalog ZESALES01VAITMKYF01

InfoArea: ZESALES01

InfoObjectCatalog: ZESALES01VAITM01

Sales Document Item Key Figures

Type: Key Figure

0CML_OR_QTY	Cumulated Order Quantity in Sales Units
0CONF_QTY	Confirmed Quantity
0DLVQEYCR	Value Delivered Earlier than Requested Delivery Date
0DLVQEYSC	Value Delivered Earlier than Schedule Line Date
0DLVQLECR	Value Delivered Later than Requested Delivery Date
0DLVQLESC	Value Deliver Later than Schedule Line Date
0DLV_QTY	Actual Delivered Quantity in Sales Units
0GIS_QTY	Quantity with Set Goods Issue Status
0LOWR_BND	Tolerance Limit for Underdelivery in %
0NET_PRICE	Net Price
0QCOASREQ	Quantity Confirmed as Requested
0REQU_QTY	Requested Delivery Quantity
0UPPR_BND	Tolerance Limit for Overdelivery in %

B.9 InfoObjectCatalog ZESALES01VASCLCHA01

InfoArea: ZESALES01

InfoObjectCatalog: ZESALES01VASCL01

Sales Document Requirement Item Characteristics

Type: Characteristic

0BATCH	
0BND_IND	Independent of Delivery Tolerance
0COMP_CODE	Company Code
0CONF_DATE	Confirmed Delivery Date
0CREATEDON	
0CUST_GROUP	Customer Group
0CUST_GRP1	Customer Group 1
0CUST_GRP2	Customer Group 2
0CUST_GRP3	Customer Group 3
0CUST_GRP4	Customer Group 4
0CUST_GRP5	Customer Group 5
0DISTR_N	Distribution Channel
0DIVISION	Division

0DLV_STS	Delivery Status
0DLV_STSO	Overall Delivery Status of the Items
0DOC_NUMBER	
0DSDEL_DATE	Requested Delivery Date
0FORWAGENT	Shipper
0GI_STS	Goods Issue Status
0ITEM_DEL	Item Deleted
0LST_A_GD	Last Actual Goods Issue Date of an Order Item
0LW_GISTS	Smallest Goods Issue Status of an Order Item
0MATERIAL	Material
0MATL_GROUP	Material Group
0MATL_GRP_1	Material Group 1
0MATL_GRP_2	Material Group 2
0MATL_GRP_3	Material Group 3
0MATL_GRP_4	Material Group 4
0MATL_GRP_5	Material Group 5
0PAYER Payer	
0PLANT Plant	
0PROD_HIER	Product Hierarchy
0SALESEMPLY	Sales Employee
0SALESORG	Sales Organization
0SALES_GRP	Sales Group
0SALES_OFF	Sales Office
0SHIP_POINT	Shipping Point
0SHIP_STCK	Delivery from Stock
0SHIP_TO	Ship-To Party
0SOLD_TO	Sold-To Party
0SOURSYSTEM	Source System ID
0S_ORD_ITEM	
ZEVERSION	Version (Reporting)

B.10 InfoObjectCatalog ZESALES01VASCLKYF01

InfoArea: ZESALES01

InfoObjectCatalog: ZESALES01VASCL01

Sales Document Requirement Item Key Figures

Type: Key Figure

0CONF_QTY	Confirmed Quantity
0DLV_QTY	Actual Delivered Quantity in Sales Units
0GIS_QTY	Quantity with Set Goods Issue Status
0NUM_SCHED	Number of Requirement Items
0REQU_QTY	Requested Delivery Quantity

C ODS Objects

All the screenshots displayed at the site were created with the *CubeServ BW Documentation Tool*, which is the first professional documentation tool for SAP Business Information Warehouse (BW).[1]

C.1 ODS Object ZECOPAO1

InfoArea:	ZECOPA01
InfoProvider:	ZECOPAO1
ODS:	ZECOPAO1
Description:	Profit and Loss Statement
Last Changed by:	EGGERN
Last Change:	30.08.2004/06:19:58
BEx Reporting:	no
Type of ODS object:	Standard
Unique Data Records:	no
Check Table for InfoObject:	
Set Quality Status to OK Automatically:	yes
Activate Data of the ODS Object Automatically:	yes
Update Data Targets from ODS Object Automatically:	yes

C.1.1 Key Fields

Text	InfoObject	Data Type	Length
Source System ID	0SOURSYSTEM	CHAR	2
Currency Type	0CURTYPE	CHAR	2
Record Type	0REC_TYPE	CHAR	1
Version	0VERSION	CHAR	3
Value Type for Reporting	0VTYPE	NUMC	3
Fiscal Year Variant	0FISCVARNT	CHAR	2
Fiscal Year/Period	0FISCPER	NUMC	7

1 You can use the *CubeServ BW Documentation Tool* to create documentation from SAP BW at the touch of a button. You can employ various navigation options to use the documentation on line or as a printout. For more information on the *CubeServ BW Documentation Tool*, please visit *www.cubeserv.com*.

Text	InfoObject	Data Type	Length
Document Number	0ID_DOCNUM	NUMC	10
Document Item Number	0ID_ITMNUM	NUMC	6

C.1.2 Characteristics

Text	InfoObject	Data Type	Length
Company Code	0COMP_CODE	CHAR	4
Plant	0PLANT	CHAR	4
Sales Organization	0SALESORG	CHAR	4
Material	0MATERIAL	CHAR	18
Customer Number	0CUSTOMER	CHAR	10
Profit Center	0PROFIT_CTR	CHAR	10
Partner Profit Center	0PART_PRCTR	CHAR	10
Sending Cost Center	0SEND_CCTR	CHAR	10
Work Breakdown Structure Element (WBS Element)	0WBS_ELEMT	CHAR	24
Cost Element	0COSTELMNT	CHAR	10
Sender Business Process	0BA_PRZNR	CHAR	12
Cancelled Document	0BA_STO_BNR	CHAR	10
Cancelled Document Item	0BA_STO_PNR	CHAR	6
Date for Billing/Invoice Index and Printing	0BILL_DATE	DATS	8
Billing Type	0BILL_TYPE	CHAR	4
Business Area	0BUS_AREA	CHAR	4
Chart of Accounts	0CHRT_ACCTS	CHAR	4
Order Number	0COORDER	CHAR	12
Cost Object	0COSTOBJ	CHAR	12
Controlling Area	0CO_AREA	CHAR	4
Customer Group	0CUST_GROUP	CHAR	2
Distribution Channel	0DISTR_CHAN	CHAR	2
Division	0DIVISION	CHAR	2
Sales Document	0DOC_NUMBER	CHAR	10

Text	InfoObject	Data Type	Length
Sales Document Item	0S_ORD_ITEM	NUMC	6
Goods Issue Date	0GI_DATE	DATS	8
Industry Key	0INDUSTRY	CHAR	4
Main Material Group	0MAINMATGRP	NUMC	2
Material Group	0MATL_GROUP	CHAR	9
Reference Document Number of the Individual Item on the Profit and Loss Statement	0ME_REFDOC	CHAR	10
Item Number of the Reference Document (Profit and Loss Statement)	0ME_REFITEM	CHAR	6
Posting Date on the Document	0PSTNG_DATE	DATS	8
Sales Employee	0SALESEMPLY	NUMC	8
Sales District	0SALES_DIST	CHAR	6
Sales Group	0SALES_GRP	CHAR	3
Sales Office	0SALES_OFF	CHAR	4
Valuation View	0VALUATION	NUMC	1
Version (Reporting)	ZEVERSION	CHAR	10
Fiscal Year	0FISCYEAR	NUMC	4
Posting Period	0FISCPER3	NUMC	3
Currency Key	0CURRENCY	CUKY	5
Sales Unit	0COPASLQTU	UNIT	3

C.1.3 Key Figures

Text	InfoObject	Data Type	Length
Accrued Freight Costs	0ACCRDFR_CS	CURR	9
Administration	0ADMNSTRTN	CURR	9
Cash Discount	0CASH_DSCNT	CURR	9
Revenue	0COPAREVEN	CURR	9
Sales Quantity	0COPASLQTY	QUAN	9
Customer Discount	0CUST_DSCNT	CURR	9
Direct Material Costs	0DIRMAT_CS	CURR	9

Text	InfoObject	Data Type	Length
Fixed Production Costs	0FIXPROD_CS	CURR	9
Marketing	0MARKETING	CURR	9
Material Overhead Costs	0MATOVHD	CURR	9
Other Overhead Costs	0OTHER_OVHD	CURR	9
Other Variances	0OTHER_VRNC	CURR	9
Price Variances	0PRICE_VRNC	CURR	9
Material Discount	0PROD_DSCNT	CURR	9
Quantity Discount	0QTY_DSCNT	CURR	9
Quantity Variances	0QUANT_VRNC	CURR	9
Research and Development	0RSRCH_DEV	CURR	9
Sales Commission	0SALES_CMSN	CURR	9
Cost of Sales	0SALES_CS	CURR	9
Special Costs of Sales	0SPCDSLS_CS	CURR	9
Variable Production Costs	0VARPROD_CS	CURR	9
Volume Rebate	0VOL_REBATE	CURR	9

C.2 ODS Object ZEFIGLO1

InfoArea:	ZEFIGL01
InfoProvider:	ZEFIGLO1
ODS:	ZEFIGLO1
Description:	CubeServ
Engines General Ledger:	Transaction Figures
Last Changed by:	EGGERN
Last Change:	25.08.2004/19:32:46
BEx Reporting:	yes
Type of ODS object:	Standard
Unique Data Records:	no
Check Table for InfoObject:	
Set Quality Status to OK Automatically:	yes
Activate Data of the ODS Object Automatically:	yes
Update Data Targets from the ODS Object Automatically:	yes

C.2.1 Key Fields

Text	InfoObject	Data Type	Length
Version	0VERSION	CHAR	3
Company Code	0COMP_CODE	CHAR	4
Fiscal Year/Period	0FISCPER	NUMC	7
General Ledger Account	0GL_ACCOUNT	CHAR	10
Functional Area	0FUNC_AREA	CHAR	16
Cost Center	0COSTCENTER	CHAR	10
Value Type for Reporting	0VTYPE	NUMC	3
Profit Center	0PROFIT_CTR	CHAR	10
Segment for Segment Reporting	0SEGMENT	CHAR	10
Fiscal Year Variant	0FISCVARNT	CHAR	2
Currency Type	0CURTYPE	CHAR	2
Valuation View	0VALUATION	NUMC	1
Currency Key for Transaction Currency	0CURKEY_TC	CUKY	5
Quantity Unit	0UNIT	UNIT	3
Source System ID	0SOURSYSTEM	CHAR	2

C.2.2 Characteristics

Text	InfoObject	Data Type	Length
Controlling Area	0CO_AREA	CHAR	4
Chart of Accounts	0CHRT_ACCTS	CHAR	4
Currency Key	0CURRENCY	CUKY	5
Version (Reporting)	ZEVERSION	CHAR	10

C.2.3 Key Figures

Text	InfoObject	Data Type	Length
Total of all Debit Postings	0DEBIT	CURR	9
Cumulated Balance	0BALANCE	CURR	9
Total of all Credit Postings	0CREDIT	CURR	9

C.3 ODS Object ZEVAHDO1

InfoArea:	ZESALES01
InfoProvider:	ZEVAHDO1
ODS:	ZEVAHDO1
Description:	Sales Document Header Data
Last Changed by:	EGGERN
Last Change:	30.08.2004/19:54:08
BEx Reporting:	yes
Type of ODS object	Standard
Unique Data Records:	no
Check Table for InfoObject:	
Set Quality Status to OK Automatically:	yes
Activate Data of the ODS Object Automatically:	yes
Update Data Targets from the ODS Object Automatically:	yes

C.3.1 Key Fields

Text	InfoObject	Data Type	Length
Source System ID	0SOURSYSTEM	CHAR	2
Sales Document	0DOC_NUMBER	CHAR	10
Fiscal Year Variant	0FISCVARNT	CHAR	2

C.3.2 Characteristics

Text	InfoObject	Data Type	Length
Delivery Status	0DLV_STS	CHAR	1
Overall Delivery Status of all Items	0DLV_STSOI	CHAR	1
Date of Creation of Record	0CREATEDON	DATS	8
Sold-To Party	0SOLD_TO	CHAR	10
Company Code	0COMP_CODE	CHAR	4
Customer Group 1	0CUST_GRP1	CHAR	3
Customer Group 2	0CUST_GRP2	CHAR	3
Customer Group 3	0CUST_GRP3	CHAR	3
Customer Group 4	0CUST_GRP4	CHAR	3

Text	InfoObject	Data Type	Length
Customer Group 5	0CUST_GRP5	CHAR	3
Distribution Channel	0DISTR_CHAN	CHAR	2
Sales Employee	0SALESEMPLY	NUMC	8
Sales Group	0SALES_GRP	CHAR	3
Sales Office	0SALES_OFF	CHAR	4
Sales Organization	0SALESORG	CHAR	4
Division	0DIVISION	CHAR	2
Document Currency	0DOC_CURRCY	CUKY	5
Header Deleted	0HEADER_DEL	CHAR	1
Version (Reporting)	ZEVERSION	CHAR	10
Fiscal Year	0FISCYEAR	NUMC	4
Fiscal Year/Period	0FISCPER	NUMC	7
Posting Period	0FISCPER3	NUMC	3

C.3.3 Key Figures

Text	InfoObject	Data Type	Length
Number of Document Items	0DOC_ITEMS	DEC	9
Cumulative Order Processing Time for all Document Items	0CUML_TME	INT4	4
Delivered Earlier than the Requested Date	0DLVIEYCR	INT4	4
Delivered Value Earlier than the Requested Delivery Date	0DLVVEYCR	CURR	9
Delivered Later than the Requested Date	0DLVILECR	INT4	4
Delivered Value Later than the Requested Delivery Date	0DLVVLECR	CURR	9
Delivered Earlier/Later than the Requested Delivery Date	0DLVIELCR	INT4	4
Delivered Value Earlier/Later than the Requested Delivery Date	0DLVVELCR	CURR	9
Delivered More than Requested	0DLVIOVER	INT4	4
Delivered Value More than Requested	0DLVVOVER	CURR	9
Delivered Less than Requested	0DLVIUNDR	INT4	4

Text	InfoObject	Data Type	Length
Delivered Value Less than Requested	0DLVVUNDR	CURR	9
Returns	0DITM_RET	INT4	4
Value of Returns	0VAL_RET	CURR	9
Delivered Earlier than the Schedule Line Date	0DLVIEYSC	INT4	4
Delivered Value Earlier than the Schedule Line Date	0DLVVEYSC	CURR	9
Delivered Later than the Schedule Line Date	0DLVILESC	INT4	4
Delivered Value Later than the Schedule Line Date	0DLVVLESC	CURR	9
Delivered Earlier/Later than the Schedule Line Date	0DLVIELSC	INT4	4
Delivered Value Earlier/Later than the Schedule Line Date	0DLVVELSC	CURR	9
Confirmed as Requested	0ICOASREQ	INT4	4
Value Confirmed as Requested	0VCOASREQ	CURR	9
Delivery from Stock	0ISHP_STCK	INT4	4
Value with Delivery from Stock	0VSHP_STCK	CURR	9
Delivery within 24 Hours	0DLV_24	INT4	4
Value with Delivery within 24 Hours	0VAL_24	CURR	9
Requested Delivery Value	0REQU_VAL	CURR	9
Actual Delivered Value	0DLV_VAL	CURR	9
Net Value of Order in Document Currency	0NET_VAL_HD	CURR	9

C.3.4 Navigation Attributes

Text	InfoObject	Data Type	Length
Sold-To Account Group	0SOLD_TO__0ACCNT_GRP	CHAR	4
Country Key	0SOLD_TO__0COUNTRY	CHAR	3
Region (State or Province)	0SOLD_TO__0REGION	CHAR	3

C.4 ODS Object ZEVAHDO2

InfoArea:	ZESALES01
InfoProvider:	ZEVAHDO2
ODS:	ZEVAHDO2
Description: (Order)	Sales Document Item Data
Last Changed by:	EGGERN
Last Change:	30.08.2004/20:37:05
BEx Reporting:	yes
Type of ODS object:	Standard
Unique Data Records:	no
Check Table for InfoObject:	
Set Quality Status to OK Automatically:	yes
Activate Data of the ODS Object Automatically:	yes
Update Data Targets from the ODS Object Automatically:	yes

C.4.1 Key Fields

Text	InfoObject	Data Type	Length
Source System ID	0SOURSYSTEM	CHAR	2
Sales Document	0DOC_NUMBER	CHAR	10
Sales Document Item	0S_ORD_ITEM	NUMC	6
Fiscal Year Variant	0FISCVARNT	CHAR	2

C.4.2 Characteristics

Text	InfoObject	Data Type	Length
Delivery Status	0DLV_STS	CHAR	1
Overall Delivery Status of Item	0DLV_STSO	CHAR	1
Date of Creation of Record	0CREATEDON	DATS	8
Independent of Delivery Tolerances	0BND_IND	CHAR	1
Last Actual Goods Issue Date of an Order Item	0LST_A_GD	DATS	8
Smallest Goods Issues Status of an Order Item	0LW_GISTS	CHAR	1

Text	InfoObject	Data Type	Length
Delivery from Stock	0SHIP_STCK	CHAR	1
Material	0MATERIAL	CHAR	18
Batch Number	0BATCH	CHAR	10
Sold-To Party	0SOLD_TO	CHAR	10
Company Code	0COMP_CODE	CHAR	4
Customer Group	0CUST_GROUP	CHAR	2
Customer Group 1	0CUST_GRP1	CHAR	3
Customer Group 2	0CUST_GRP2	CHAR	3
Customer Group 3	0CUST_GRP3	CHAR	3
Customer Group 4	0CUST_GRP4	CHAR	3
Customer Group 5	0CUST_GRP5	CHAR	3
Distribution Channel	0DISTR_CHAN	CHAR	2
Sales Employee	0SALESEMPLY	NUMC	8
Sales Group	0SALES_GRP	CHAR	3
Sales Office	0SALES_OFF	CHAR	4
Sales Organization	0SALESORG	CHAR	4
Material Group	0MATL_GROUP	CHAR	9
Material Group 1	0MATL_GRP_1	CHAR	3
Material Group 2	0MATL_GRP_2	CHAR	3
Material Group 3	0MATL_GRP_3	CHAR	3
Material Group 4	0MATL_GRP_4	CHAR	3
Material Group 5	0MATL_GRP_5	CHAR	3
Product Hierarchy	0PROD_HIER	CHAR	18
Plant	0PLANT	CHAR	4
Ship-To Party	0SHIP_TO	CHAR	10
Shipping Point	0SHIP_POINT	CHAR	4
Division	0DIVISION	CHAR	2
Forwarding Agent	0FORWAGENT	CHAR	10
Payer	0PAYER	CHAR	10
Sales Unit	0SALES_UNIT	UNIT	3

Text	InfoObject	Data Type	Length
Document Currency	0DOC_CURRCY	CUKY	5
Item Deleted	0ITEM_DEL	CHAR	1
Version (Reporting)	ZEVERSION	CHAR	10
Fiscal Year	0FISCYEAR	NUMC	4
Fiscal Year/Period	0FISCPER	NUMC	7
Posting Period	0FISCPER3	NUMC	3

C.4.3 Key Figures

Text	InfoObject	Data Type	Length
Confirmed Quantity	0CONF_QTY	QUAN	9
Requested Quantity	0REQU_QTY	QUAN	9
Actual Delivered Quantity in Sales Units	0DLV_QTY	QUAN	9
Quantity Delivered Earlier than the Requested Delivery Date	0DLVQEYCR	QUAN	9
Quantity Delivered Later than the Requested Delivery Date	0DLVQLECR	QUAN	9
Quantity Delivered Earlier than the Schedule Line Date	0DLVQEYSC	QUAN	9
Quantity Delivered Later than the Schedule Line Date	0DLVQLESC	QUAN	9
Quantity Confirmed as Requested	0QCOASREQ	QUAN	9
Quantity with Set Goods Issue Status	0GIS_QTY	QUAN	9
Tolerance Limit for Underdelivery in %	0LOWR_BND	DEC	9
Tolerance Limit for Overdelivery in %	0UPPR_BND	DEC	9
Net Price	0NET_PRICE	CURR	9

C.4.4 Navigation Attributes

Text	InfoObject	Data Type	Length
Product Hierarchy	0MATERIAL__0PROD_HIER	CHAR	18
Sold-To Country	0SOLD_TO__0COUNTRY	CHAR	3

Text	InfoObject	Data Type	Length
Region (State or Province)	0SOLD_TO__ 0REGION	CHAR	3
Ship-To Country	0SHIP_TO__ 0COUNTRY	CHAR	3
Payer Country	0PAYER__ 0COUNTRY	CHAR	3

C.5 ODS Object ZEVAHDO3

InfoArea:	ZESALES01
InfoProvider:	ZEVAHDO3
ODS:	ZEVAHDO3
Description: (Returns)	Sales Document Item Data
Last Changed by:	EGGERN
Last Change:	30.08.2004/21:01:34
BEx Reporting:	yes
Type of ODS object:	Standard
Unique Data Records:	no
Check Table for InfoObject:	
Set Quality Status to OK Automatically:	yes
Activate Data of the ODS Object Automatically:	yes
Update Data Targets from the ODS Object Automatically:	yes

C.5.1 Key Fields

Text	InfoObject	Data Type	Length
Source System ID	0SOURSYSTEM	CHAR	2
Sales Document Item	0S_ORD_ITEM	NUMC	6
Sales Document	0DOC_NUMBER	CHAR	10
Fiscal Year Variant	0FISCVARNT	CHAR	2

C.5.2 Characteristics

Text	InfoObject	Data Type	Length
Date of Creation of Record	0CREATEDON	DATS	8
Material	0MATERIAL	CHAR	18
Batch Number	0BATCH	CHAR	10
Sold-To Party	0SOLD_TO	CHAR	10
Company Code	0COMP_CODE	CHAR	4
Customer Group	0CUST_GROUP	CHAR	2
Customer Group 1	0CUST_GRP1	CHAR	3
Customer Group 2	0CUST_GRP2	CHAR	3
Customer Group 3	0CUST_GRP3	CHAR	3
Customer Group 4	0CUST_GRP4	CHAR	3
Customer Group 5	0CUST_GRP5	CHAR	3
Distribution Channel	0DISTR_CHAN	CHAR	2
Sales Employee	0SALESEMPLY	NUMC	8
Sales Group	0SALES_GRP	CHAR	3
Sales Office	0SALES_OFF	CHAR	4
Sales Organization	0SALESORG	CHAR	4
Material Group	0MATL_GROUP	CHAR	9
Material Group 1	0MATL_GRP_1	CHAR	3
Material Group 2	0MATL_GRP_2	CHAR	3
Material Group 3	0MATL_GRP_3	CHAR	3
Material Group 4	0MATL_GRP_4	CHAR	3
Material Group 5	0MATL_GRP_5	CHAR	3
Product Hierarchy	0PROD_HIER	CHAR	18
Plant	0PLANT	CHAR	4
Ship-To Party	0SHIP_TO	CHAR	10
Shipping Point	0SHIP_POINT	CHAR	4
Division	0DIVISION	CHAR	2
Forwarding Agent	0FORWAGENT	CHAR	10
Payer	0PAYER	CHAR	10

Text	InfoObject	Data Type	Length
Document Currency	0DOC_CURRCY	CUKY	5
Sales Unit	0SALES_UNIT	UNIT	3
Version (Reporting)	ZEVERSION	CHAR	10
Fiscal Year	0FISCYEAR	NUMC	4
Fiscal Year/Period	0FISCPER	NUMC	7
Posting Period	0FISCPER3	NUMC	3

C.5.3 Key Figures

Text	InfoObject	Data Type	Length
Cumulated Order Quantity in Sales Units	0CML_OR_QTY	QUAN	9
Net Price	0NET_PRICE	CURR	9

C.5.4 Navigation Attributes

Text	InfoObject	Data Type	Length
Product Hierarchy	0MATERIAL__0PROD_HIER	CHAR	18
Sold-To Country	0SOLD_TO__0COUNTRY	CHAR	03
Region (State or Province)	0SOLD_TO__0REGION	CHAR	03
Ship-To Country	0SHIP_TO__0COUNTRY	CHAR	03
Payer Country	0PAYER__0COUNTRY	CHAR	03

C.6 ODS Object ZEVAHDO4

InfoArea:	ZESALES01
InfoProvider:	ZEVAHDO4
ODS:	ZEVAHDO4
Description:	Sales Document Schedule Lines (Order)
Last Changed by:	EGGERN
Last Change:	01.09.2004/19:24:23
BEx Reporting:	yes
Type of ODS object:	Standard
Unique Data Records:	no

Check Table for InfoObject:

Set Quality Status to OK Automatically: yes

Activate Data of the ODS Object Automatically: yes

Update Data Targets from the ODS Object Automatically: yes

C.6.1 Key Fields

Text	InfoObject	Data Type	Length
Source System ID	0SOURSYSTEM	CHAR	2
Sales Document	0DOC_NUMBER	CHAR	10
Sales Document Item	0S_ORD_ITEM	NUMC	6
Schedule Line Number	0SCHED_LINE	NUMC	4
Fiscal Year Variant	0FISCVARNT	CHAR	2

C.6.2 Characteristics

Text	InfoObject	Data Type	Length
Delivery Status	0DLV_STS	CHAR	1
Overall Delivery Status of Item	0DLV_STSO	CHAR	1
Goods Issue Status	0GI_STS	CHAR	1
Smallest Goods Issue Status of an Order Item	0LW_GISTS	CHAR	1
Sales Unit	0SALES_UNIT	UNIT	3
Confirmed Delivery Date	0CONF_DATE	DATS	8
Requested Delivery Date	0DSDEL_DATE	DATS	8
Version (Reporting)	ZEVERSION	CHAR	10
Fiscal Year	0FISCYEAR	NUMC	4
Fiscal Year/Period	0FISCPER	NUMC	7
Posting Period	0FISCPER3	NUMC	3

C.6.3 Key Figures

Text	InfoObject	Data Type	Length
Confirmed Quantity	0CONF_QTY	QUAN	9
Actual Delivered Quantity in Sales Units	0DLV_QTY	QUAN	9

Text	InfoObject	Data Type	Length
Requested Quantity	0REQU_QTY	QUAN	9
Quantity with Set Goods Issue Status	0GIS_QTY	QUAN	9

D InfoCube »Actual Data: Profit and Loss Statement«

The *CubeServ BW Documentation Tool* created all the screenshots displayed at the site. The CubeServ BW Documentation Tool is the first professional documentation tool for SAP Business Information Warehouse (SAP BW).[1]

D.1 InfoAreas with InfoCubes

D.1.1 InfoArea ZECOPA01 Profit and Loss Statement

InfoCube		Cube Type
ZECOPAC1	Actual data: Profit and Loss Statement	BasicCube
ZECOPAC2	Plan data: Profit and Loss Statement	BasicCube

D.1.2 InfoArea ZEFIGL01 Financials—General Ledger

InfoCube		Cube Type
ZEFIGLC1	General Ledger Transaction Figures	BasicCube
ZEFIGLC2	Plan data: Balance sheet/profit and loss	BasicCube

D.1.3 InfoArea ZESALES01 Sales

InfoCube		Cube Type
ZEKDABC1	Sales Order Stock	BasicCube
ZEVAHDC1	Sales Document Header Data	BasicCube
ZEVAHDC2	Sales Document Item Data (Order and Returns)	BasicCube
ZEVAHDC3	Sales Document Schedule Lines (Order)	BasicCube

1 You can use the *CubeServ BW Documentation Tool* to create documentation from SAP BW at the touch of a button. You can employ various navigation options to use the documentation on line or as a printout. For more information on the *CubeServ BW Documentation Tool*, please visit *www.cubeserv.com*.

D.2 InfoCube ZECOPAC1

InfoArea:	ZECOPA01
InfoCube	ZECOPAC1
Actual data: Profit and Loss Statement	
Cube Type	BasicCube

Key Figures

0ACCRDFR_CS	Accrued Freight Costs
0ADMNSTRTN	Administration
0CASH_DSCNT	Cash Discount
0COPAREVEN	Revenue
0COPASLQTY	Sales Quantity
0CUST_DSCNT	Customer Discount
0DIRMAT_CS	Direct Material Costs
0FIXPROD_CS	Fixed Production Costs
0MARKETING	Marketing
0MATOVHD	Material Overhead Costs
0OTHER_OVHD	Other Overhead Costs
0OTHER_VRNC	Other Variances
0PRICE_VRNC	Price Variances
0PROD_DSCNT	Material Discount
0QTY_DSCNT	Quantity Discount
0QUANT_VRNC	Quantity Variances
0RSRCH_DEV	Research and Development
0SALES_CMSN	Sales Commission
0SALES_CS	Sales Costs
0SPCDSLS_CS	Special Direct Costs of Sales
0VARPROD_CS	Variable Production Costs
0VOL_REBATE Rebate	Dimension ZEFIGLM11 Organizational Units
0COMP_CODE	Company Code
0COSTCENTER	Cost Object
0CO_AREA	Controlling Area
0FUNC_AREA	Functional Area
0PROFIT_CTR	Profit Center
0SEGMENT	Segment for Segment Reporting
0SOURSYSTEM	Source System ID

Dimension ZECOPAC11 Organization

0BUS_AREA	Business Area
0CHRT_ACCTS	Chart of Accounts
0COMP_CODE	Company Code
0CO_AREA	Controlling Area
0PLANT	Plant
0SOURSYSTEM	Source System ID

Dimension ZECOPAC12 Sales Area

0DISTR_CHAN	Distribution Channel
0DIVISION	Division
0SALESEMPLY	Sales Employee
0SALESORG	Sales Organization
0SALES_GRP	Sales Group
0SALES_OFF	Sales Office

Dimension ZECOPAC13 Data Type

0VERSION	Version
0VTYPE	Value Type for Reporting
ZEVERSION	Version (Reporting)

Dimension ZECOPAC14 Document Information

0BILL_TYPE	Billing Type
0CURTYPE	Currency Type
0REC_TYPE	Record Type
0VALUATION	Valuation View

Dimension ZECOPAC15 Customer

0CUSTOMER	Customer Number
0CUSTOMER	Customer Number 0ACCNT_GRP Account Group Customer
0CUSTOMER	Customer Number 0COUNTRY Country Key
0CUSTOMER	Customer Number 0INDUSTRY Industry Key
0CUSTOMER	Customer Number 0REGION Region
0CUST_GROUP	Customer Group
0SALES_DIST	Sales District

Dimension ZECOPAC16 Material

Line Item: yes

0MATERIAL	Material
0MATERIAL	Material 0MATL_GROUP Material Group
0MATERIAL	Material 0PROD_HIER Product Hierarchy

Dimension ZECOPAC17 Profit

Line Item: yes

0PROFIT_CTR	Profit Center

Dimension ZECOPAC18 Partner Profit Center

Line Item: yes

0PART_PRCTR	Partner Profit Center

Dimension ZECOPAC19 Sending Cost Center

Line Item: yes

0SEND_CCTR	Sending Cost Center

Dimension ZECOPAC1A Work Breakdown Structure Element

Line Item: yes

0WBS_ELEMT	Work Breakdown Structure Element (WBS Element)

Dimension ZECOPAC1B Cost Element

Line Item: yes

0COSTELMNT	Cost Element

Dimension ZECOPAC1C Order Number

0COORDER	Order Number

Dimension ZECOPAC1D Other

0BA_PRZNR	Sender Business Process
0BILL_DATE	Date for Billing/Invoice Index and Printing
0COSTOBJ	Cost Object
0GI_DATE	Goods Issue Date
0PSTNG_DATE	Posting Date on the Document

Dimension ZECOPAC1P Data Package

0CHNGID	Change Run ID
0RECORDTP	Record Type
0REQUID	Request ID

Dimension ZECOPAC1T Time

0FISCPER	Fiscal Year/Period
0FISCPER3	Posting Period
0FISCVARNT	Fiscal Year Variant
0FISCYEAR	Fiscal Year

Dimension ZECOPAC1U Unit

0COPASLQTU	Sales Quantity Unit
0CURRENCY	Currency Key

D.3 InfoCube ZECOPAC2

InfoArea:	ZECOPA01
InfoCube	ZECOPAC2

Plan data: Profit and Loss Statement

Cube Type	BasicCube

Key Figures

0COPASLQTY	Sales Quantity
ZEBRUMS	Gross Sales
ZEERLMIND	Revenue Reductions
ZEHKVK	Full Manufacturing Costs

Dimension ZECOPAC21 Source System

Line Item: yes

0SOURSYSTEM	Source System ID

Dimension ZECOPAC22 Company Code

Line Item: yes

0COMP_CODE	Company Code

Dimension ZECOPAC23 Version (harmonized)

Line Item: yes

ZEVERSION	Version (Reporting)

Dimension ZECOPAC24 Version

Line Item: yes

0VERSION	Version

Dimension ZECOPAC25 Value Type

Line Item: yes

0VTYPE	Value Type for Reporting

Dimension ZECOPAC26 Record Type

Line Item: yes

0REC_TYPE	Record Type

Dimension ZECOPAC27 Valuation View

Line Item: yes

0VALUATION	Valuation View

Dimension ZECOPAC28 Currency Type

Line Item: yes

0CURTYPE	Currency Type

Dimension ZECOPAC29 Country Key

Line Item: yes

0COUNTRY	Country Key

Dimension ZECOPAC2A Region

Line Item: yes

0REGION	Region (State, Province, or County)

Dimension ZECOPAC2B Product Hierarchy

Line Item: yes

0PROD_HIER	Product Hierarchy

Dimension ZECOPAC2P Data Package

0CHNGID	Change Run ID
0RECORDTP	Record Type
0REQUID	Request ID

Dimension ZECOPAC2T Time

0FISCPER	Fiscal Year/Period
0FISCPER3	Posting Period
0FISCVARNT	Fiscal Year Variant
0FISCYEAR	Fiscal Year

Dimension ZECOPAC2U Unit

0COPASLQTU	Sales Quantity Unit
0CURRENCY	Currency Key

D.4 InfoCube ZEFIGLC1

InfoArea:	ZEFIGL01
InfoCube	ZEFIGLC1
General Ledger Transaction Figures	
Cube Type	BasicCube

Key Figures

0BALANCE	Cumulative Balance
0CREDIT	Total of Credit Postings
0DEBIT	Total of Debit Postings
0SALES	Sales per Period

Dimension ZEFIGLC11 Company Code

Line Item: yes

0COMP_CODE	Company Code	
0COMP_CODE	Company Code	0COMPANY Company

Dimension ZEFIGLC12 Controlling Area

Line Item: yes

0CO_AREA	Controlling Area

Dimension ZEFIGLC13 Source System ID

Line Item: yes

0SOURSYSTEM	Source System ID

Dimension ZEFIGLC14 Functional Area

Line Item: yes

0FUNC_AREA	Functional Area

Dimension ZEFIGLC15 Segment

Line Item: yes

0SEGMENT	Segment for Segment Reporting

Dimension ZEFIGLC16 Chart of Accounts

Line Item: yes

0CHRT_ACCTS	Chart of Accounts

Dimension ZEFIGLC17 General Ledger Account

Line Item: yes

0GL_ACCOUNT	General Ledger Account		
0GL_ACCOUNT	General Ledger Account	0BAL_FLAG	Flag: Stock Account
0GL_ACCOUNT	General Ledger Account	0INCST_FLAG	Flag: Erf.Rechn.Konto
0GL_ACCOUNT	General Ledger Account	0SEM_POSIT	Planning Item
0GL_ACCOUNT	General Ledger Account	ZECHRTACC	Chart of Accounts (Group Account)
0GL_ACCOUNT	General Ledger Account	ZEKONZKTO	Group Account Number

Dimension ZEFIGLC18 Data Type

Line Item: yes

0VERSION	Version
0VTYPE	Value Type for Reporting
ZEVERSION	Version (Reporting)

Dimension ZEFIGLC19 Currency Type

Line Item: yes

0CURTYPE	Currency Type

Dimension ZEFIGLC1A Valuation View

Line Item: yes

0VALUATION	Valuation View

Dimension ZEFIGLC1B Cost Center

Line Item: yes

0COSTCENTER	Cost Center

Dimension ZEFIGLC1C Profit Center

Line Item: yes

0PROFIT_CTR	Profit Center

Dimension ZEFIGLC1P Data Package

0CHNGID	Change Run ID
0RECORDTP	Record Type
0REQUID	Request ID

ZEFIGLC1T Time

0FISCPER	Fiscal Year/Period
0FISCPER3	Posting Period

0FISCVARNT	Fiscal Year Variant
0FISCYEAR	Fiscal Year

Dimension ZEFIGLC1U Unit

0CURRENCY	Currency Key

D.5 InfoCube ZEFIGLC2

InfoArea:	ZEFIGL01
InfoCube	ZEFIGLC2

Plan data: Balance sheet/profit and loss

Cube Type	BasicCube

Key Figures

0BALANCE	Cumulative Balance
0CREDIT	Total of Credit Postings
0DEBIT	Total of Debit Postings
0SALES	Sales per Period

Dimension ZEFIGLC21 Company Code

Line Item: yes

0COMP_CODE	Company Code	
0COMP_CODE	Company Code	0COMPANY Company

Dimension ZEFIGLC27 Planning Item

Line Item: yes

0SEM_POSIT	Planning Item	
0SEM_POSIT	Planning Item 0SEM_POSCAT	Item Type

Dimension ZEFIGLC28 Data Type

0VERSION	Version
0VTYPE Value	Type for Reporting
ZEVERSION	Version (Reporting)

Dimension ZEFIGLC29 Currency Type

Line Item: yes

0CURTYPE	Currency Type

Dimension ZEFIGLC2A Valuation View

Line Item: yes

0VALUATION	Valuation View

Dimension ZEFIGLC2P Data Package

0CHNGID	Change Run ID
0RECORDTP	Record Type
0REQUID	Request ID

Dimension ZEFIGLC2T Time

0FISCPER	Fiscal Year/Period
0FISCPER3	Posting Period
0FISCVARNT	Fiscal Year Variant
0FISCYEAR	Fiscal Year

Dimension ZEFIGLC2U Unit

0CURRENCY	Currency Key

D.6 InfoCube ZEKDABC1

InfoArea:	ZESALES01
InfoCube	ZEKDABC1
Sales Order Stock	
Cube Type	BasicCube

Key Figures

ZEBESTAND	Stock Value
ZEBETRAG	Amount

Dimension ZEKDABC11 Organization

0COMP_CODE	Company Code
0PLANT	Plant
0SOURSYSTEM	Source System ID

Dimension ZEKDABC12 Sales Organization

Line Item: yes

0SALESORG	Sales Organization

Dimension ZEKDABC13 Distribution Channel

Line Item: yes

0DISTR_CHAN	Distribution Channel

Dimension ZEKDABC14 Division

Line Item: yes

0DIVISION	Division

Dimension ZEKDABC15 Data Type

0VERSION	Version
0VTYPE	Value Type for Reporting
ZEVERSION	Version (Reporting)

Dimension ZEKDABC16 Currency Type/Valuation View

0CURTYPE	Currency Type
0VALUATION	Valuation View

Dimension ZEKDABC17 Billing Type

Line Item: yes

0BILL_TYPE	Billing Type

Dimension ZEKDABC18 Sales Employee

Line Item: yes

0SALESEMPLY	Sales Employee

Dimension ZEKDABC19 Sales Group/Sales Office

0SALES_GRP	Sales Group
0SALES_OFF	Sales Office

Dimension ZEKDABC1A Customer

Line Item: yes

0CUSTOMER	Customer Number		
0CUSTOMER	Customer Number	0ACCNT_GRP	Customer Account Group
0CUSTOMER	Customer Number	0COUNTRY	Country Key
0CUSTOMER	Customer Number	0INDUSTRY	Industry Key
0CUSTOMER	Customer Number	0REGION	Region

Dimension ZEKDABC1B Customer Group

Line Item: yes

0CUST_GROUP	Customer Group

Dimension ZEKDABC1C Sales District

Line Item: yes

0SALES_DIST	Sales District

Dimension ZEKDABC1D Material

Line Item: yes

0MATERIAL	Material		
0MATERIAL	Material	0MATL_GROUP	Material Group
0MATERIAL	Material	0PROD_HIER	Product Hierarchy

Dimension ZEKDABC1P Data Package

0CHNGID	Change Run ID
0RECORDTP	Record Type
0REQUID	Request ID

Dimension ZEKDABC1T Time

0FISCPER	Fiscal Year/Period	Posting Period
0FISCVARNT	Fiscal Year Variant	
0FISCYEAR	Fiscal Year	

Dimension ZEKDABC1U Unit

0CURRENCY	Currency Key

D.7 InfoCube ZEVAHDC1

InfoArea:	ZESALES01
InfoCube	ZEVAHDC1

Sales Document Header Data

Cube Type	BasicCube

Key Figures

0CUML_TME	Cumulative Order Processing Time for all Document Items
0DITM_RET	Returns
0DLVIELCR	Delivered Earlier/Later than the Requested Delivery Date
0DLVIELSC	Delivered Earlier/Later than the Schedule Line Date
0DLVIEYCR	Delivered Earlier than the Requested Date
0DLVIEYSC	Delivered Earlier than the Schedule Line Date
0DLVILECR	Delivered after the Requested Delivery Date
0DLVILESC	Delivered after the Schedule Line Date
0DLVIOVER	Delivered More than Requested
0DLVIUNDR	Delivered less than Requested
0DLVVELCR	Delivered Value Earlier/Later than the Requested Delivery Date
0DLVVELSC	Delivered Value Earlier/Later than the Schedule Line Date
0DLVVEYCR	Delivered Value Earlier than the Requested Delivery Date
0DLVVEYSC	Delivered Value Earlier than the Schedule Line Date
0DLVVLECR	Delivered Value Later than Requested Delivery Date
0DLVVLESC	Delivered Later than the Schedule Line Date

0DLVVOVER	Delivered Value More than RequestedDelivered Value Less than Requested
0DLV_24	Delivery within 24 Hours
0DLV_VAL	Actual Delivered Value
0DOC_ITEMS	Number of Document Items
0ICOASREQ	Confirmed as Requested
0ISHP_STCK	Delivery from Stock
0NET_VAL_HD	Net Value of Order in Document Currency
0ORDERS	Number of Orders
0REQU_VAL	Requested Delivery Value
0VAL_24	Value with Delivery within 24 Hours
0VAL_RET	Value of Returns
0VCOASREQ	Value Confirmed as Requested
0VSHP_STCK	Value with Delivery from Stock

Dimension ZEVAHDC11 Organization

0COMP_CODE	Company Code
0SOURSYSTEM	Source System ID

Dimension ZEVAHDC12 Sales Area

Line Item: yes

0SALESORG	Sales Organization

D.8 Dimension ZEKDABC13 Distribution Channel

Line Item: yes

0DISTR_CHAN	Distribution Channel

Dimension ZEVAHDC14 Division

Line Item: yes

0DIVISION	Division

Dimension ZEVAHDC15 Data Type

Line Item: yes

ZEVERSION	Version (Reporting)

Dimension ZEVAHDC16 Sold-To Party

Line Item: yes

0SOLD_TO	Sold-To Party		
0SOLD_TO	Sold-To Party	0ACCNT_GRP	Customer Account Group
0SOLD_TO	Sold-To Party	0COUNTRY	Country Key
0SOLD_TO	Sold-To Party	0KEYACCOUNT	Key Account
0SOLD_TO	Sold-To Party	0REGION	Region

Dimension ZEVAHDC17 Sold-To Party Attribute (as posted)

0CUST_GRP1	Customer Group 1
0CUST_GRP2	Customer Group 2
0CUST_GRP3	Customer Group 3
0CUST_GRP4	Customer Group 4
0CUST_GRP5	Customer Group 5

Dimension ZEVAHDC18 Sales Office

Line Item: yes

0SALES_OFF	Sales Office

Dimension ZEVAHDC19 Sales Group

Line Item: yes

0SALES_GRP	Sales Group

Dimension ZEVAHDC1A Sales Employee

Line Item: yes

0SALESEMPLY	Sales Employee

Dimension ZEVAHDC1B Header Deleted

Line Item: yes

0HEADER_DEL	Header Deleted

Dimension ZEVAHDC1C Overall Delivery Status of All Items

Line Item: yes

0DLV_STSOI	Overall Delivery Status of all Items

Dimension ZEVAHDC1D Delivery Status

Line Item: yes

0DLV_STS	Delivery Status

Dimension ZEVAHDC1P Data Package

0CHNGID	Change Run ID
0RECORDTP	Record Type
0REQUID	Request ID

Dimension ZEVAHDC1T Time

0CALDAY	Calendar Day
0CALMONTH	Calendar Year/Month
0CALMONTH2	Calendar Month

0CALQUART1	Quarter
0CALQUARTER	Calendar Year/Quarter
0CALWEEK	Calendar Year/Week
0CALYEAR	Calendar Year
0FISCPER	Fiscal Year/Period
0FISCPER3	Posting Period
0FISCVARNT	Fiscal Year Variant
0FISCYEAR	Fiscal Year
0HALFYEAR1	Half Year
0WEEKDAY1	Weekday

Dimension ZEVAHDC1U Unit

0DOC_CURRCY	Document Currency

D.9 InfoCube ZEVAHDC2

InfoArea: ZESALES01

InfoCube ZEVAHDC2

Sales Document Item Data (Order and Returns)

Cube Type BasicCube

Key Figures

0CML_OR_QTY	Cumulated Order Quantity in Sales Units
0CONF_QTY	Confirmed Quantity
0DLVQEYCR	Quantity Delivered Earlier than Requested Delivery Date
0DLVQEYSC	Quantity Delivered Earlier than Schedule Line Date
0DLVQLECR	Delivered Quantity Later than Requested Delivery Date
0DLVVLESC	Delivered Quantity Later than the Schedule Line Date
0DLV_QTYR	Actual Delivered Quantity in Sales Units
0GIS_QTY	Quantity with Set Goods Issue Status
0LOWR_BND	Tolerance Limit for Underdelivery in %
0NET_PRICE	Net Price
0QCOASREQ	Quantity Confirmed as Requested
0REQU_QTY	Requested Delivery Quantity
0UPPR_BND	Tolerance Limit for Overdelivery in %

Dimension ZEVAHDC21 Organization

0COMP_CODE	Company Code
0PLANT	Plant
0SOURSYSTEM	Source System ID

Dimension ZEVAHDC22 Sales Area

0DISTR_CHAN	Distribution Channel
0DIVISION	Division
0SALESORG	Sales Organization

D.10 Dimension ZEVAHDC23 Data Type

Line Item: yes

ZEVERSION	Version (Reporting)

Dimension ZEVAHDC24 Sold-To Party

Line Item: yes

0SOLD_TO	Sold-To Party	
0SOLD_TO	Sold-To Party	0ACCNT_GRP Customer Account Group
0SOLD_TO	Sold-To Party	0COUNTRY Country Key
0SOLD_TO	Sold-To Party	0KEYACCOUNT Key Account
0SOLD_TO	Sold-To Party	0REGION Region

Dimension ZEVAHDC25 Ship-To Party

Line Item: yes

0SHIP_TO	Ship-To Party
0SHIP_TO	Ship-To Party0COUNTRYCountry Key

Dimension ZEVAHDC26 Payer

Line Item: yes

0PAYER	Payer
0PAYER	Payer0COUNTRY Country Key

Dimension ZEVAHDC27 Sold-To Party Attribute (as posted)

0CUST_GROUP	Customer Group
0CUST_GRP1	Customer Group 1
0CUST_GRP2	Customer Group 2
0CUST_GRP3	Customer Group 3
0CUST_GRP4	Customer Group 4
0CUST_GRP5	Customer Group 5

Dimension ZEVAHDC28 Material

Line Item: yes

0MATERIAL	Material	
0MATERIAL	Material	0PROD_HIER Product Hierarchy

Dimension ZEVAHDC29 Material Attribute (as posted)

0MATL_GROUP	Material Group
0MATL_GRP_1	Material Group 1
0MATL_GRP_2	Material Group 2
0MATL_GRP_3	Material Group 3
0MATL_GRP_4	Material Group 4

0MATL_GRP_5	Material Group 5
0PROD_HIER	Product Hierarchy

Dimension ZEVAHDC2A Status

0DLV_STS	Delivery Status
0DLV_STSO	Overall Delivery Status of Item
0ITEM_DEL	Item Deleted
0LW_GISTS	Lowest Goods Issue Status of an Order Item

Dimension ZEVAHDC2B Delivery

0BND_IND	Independent of Delivery Tolerances
0FORWAGENT	Forwarding Agent
0SHIP_POINT	Shipping Point
0SHIP_STCK	Delivery from Stock

Dimension ZEVAHDC2C Sales Person

0SALESEMPLY	Sales Employee
0SALES_GRP	Sales Group
0SALES_OFF	Sales Office

Dimension ZEVAHDC2D Actual Goods-Issue Date

Line Item: yes

0LST_A_GD	Last Actual Goods Issue Date of an Order Item

Dimension ZEVAHDC2P Data Package

0CHNGID	Change Run ID
0RECORDTP	Record Type
0REQUID	Request ID

Dimension ZEVAHDC2T Time

0CALDAY	Calendar Day
0CALMONTH	Calendar Year/Month
0CALMONTH2	Calendar Month
0CALQUART1	Quarter
0CALQUARTER	Calendar Year/Quarter
0CALWEEK	Calendar Year/Week
0CALYEAR	Calendar Year
0FISCPER	Fiscal Year/Period
0FISCPER3	Posting Period
0FISCVARNT	Fiscal Year Variant
0FISCYEAR	Fiscal Year
0HALFYEAR1	Half Year
0WEEKDAY1	Weekday

Dimension ZEVAHDC2U Unit

0DOC_CURRCY	Document Currency
0SALES_UNIT	Sales Unit

D.11 InfoCube ZEVAHDC3

InfoArea:	ZESALES01
InfoCube	ZEVAHDC3

Sales Document Schedule Lines (Order)

Cube Type	BasicCube

Key Figures

0CONF_QTY	Confirmed Quantity
0DLV_QTY	Actual Delivered Quantity in Sales Units
0GIS_QTY	Quantity with Set Goods Issue Status
0NUM_SCHED	Number of Schedule Line Items
0REQU_QTY	Requested Quantity

Dimension ZEVAHDC31 Organization

0COMP_CODE	Company Code
0PLANT	Plant
0SOURSYSTEM	Source System ID

Dimension ZEVAHDC32 Sales Area

0DISTR_CHAN	Distribution Channel
0DIVISION	Division
0SALESORG	Sales Organization

D.12 Dimension ZEVAHDC33 Data Type

Line Item: yes

ZEVERSION	Version (Reporting)

Dimension ZEVAHDC34 Sold-To Party

Line Item: yes

0SOLD_TO	Sold-To Party		
0SOLD_TO	Sold-To Party	0ACCNT_GRP	Customer Account Group
0SOLD_TO	Sold-To Party	0COUNTRY	Country Key
0SOLD_TO	Sold-To Party	0KEYACCOUNT	Key Account
0SOLD_TO	Sold-To Party	0REGION	Region

Dimension ZEVAHDC35 Ship-To Party

Line Item: yes

0SHIP_TO	Ship-To Party	
0SHIP_TO	Ship-To Party	0COUNTRY Country Key

Dimension ZEVAHDC36 Payer

Line Item: yes

0PAYER	Payer	
0PAYER	Payer	0COUNTRY Country Key

Dimension ZEVAHDC37 Sold-To Party Attribute (as posted)

0CUST_GROUP	Customer Group
0CUST_GRP1	Customer Group 1
0CUST_GRP2	Customer Group 2
0CUST_GRP3	Customer Group 3
0CUST_GRP4	Customer Group 4
0CUST_GRP5	Customer Group 5

Dimension ZEVAHDC38 Material

Line Item: yes

0MATERIAL	Material	
0MATERIAL	Material	0PROD_HIER Product Hierarchy

Dimension ZEVAHDC39 Material Attribute (as posted)

0MATL_GROUP	Material Group
0MATL_GRP_1	Material Group 1
0MATL_GRP_2	Material Group 2
0MATL_GRP_3	Material Group 3
0MATL_GRP_4	Material Group 4
0MATL_GRP_5	Material Group 5
0PROD_HIER	Product Hierarchy

Dimension ZEVAHDC3A Status

0DLV_STS	Delivery Status
0DLV_STSO	Overall Delivery Status of Item
0GI_STS	Goods Issue Status
0ITEM_DEL	Item Deleted
0LW_GISTS	Lowest Goods Issue Status of an Order Item

Dimension ZEVAHDC3B Delivery

0BND_IND	Independent of Delivery Tolerances
0FORWAGENT	Forwarding Agent

0SHIP_POINT	Shipping Point
0SHIP_STCK	Delivery from Stock

Dimension ZEVAHDC3C Sales Person

0SALESEMPLY	Sales Employee
0SALES_GRP	Sales Group
0SALES_OFF	Sales Office

Dimension ZEVAHDC3D Delivery Date

0CONF_DATE	Confirmed Delivery Date
0DSDEL_DATE	Requested Delivery Date
0LST_A_GD	Last Actual Goods Issue Date of an Order Item

Dimension ZEVAHDC3P Data Package

0CHNGID	Change Run ID
0RECORDTP	Record Type
0REQUID	Request ID

Dimension ZEVAHDC3T Time

0CALDAY	Calendar Day
0CALMONTH	Calendar Year/Month
0CALMONTH2	Calendar Month
0CALQUART1	Quarter
0CALQUARTER	Calendar Year/Quarter
0CALWEEK	Calendar Year/Week
0CALYEAR	Calendar Year
0FISCPER	Fiscal Year/Period
0FISCPER3	Posting Period
0FISCVARNT	Fiscal Year Variant
0FISCYEAR	Fiscal Year
0HALFYEAR1	Half Year
0WEEKDAY1	Weekday

Dimension ZEVAHDC3U Unit

0SALES_UNIT	Sales Unit

E MultiProviders

The *CubeServ BW Documentation Tool* created all the screenshots displayed at the site. The CubeServ BW Documentation Tool is the first professional documentation tool for SAP Business Information Warehouse (SAP BW).[1]

E.1 MultiProvider ZECOPAM1

InfoArea:	ZECOPA01
InfoCube	ZECOPAM1

Profit and Loss Statement (Actual and Plan Data)

Cube Type	MultiProviders

Key Figures

0ACCRDFR_CS	Accrued Freight Costs
0ADMNSTRTN	Administration
0CASH_DSCNT	Cash Discount
0COPAREVEN	Revenue
0COPASLQTY	Sales Quantity
0CUST_DSCNT	Customer Discount
0DIRMAT_CS	Direct Material Costs
0FIXPROD_CS	Fixed Production Costs
0MARKETING	Marketing
0MATOVHD	Material Overhead Costs
0OTHER_OVHD	Other Overhead Costs
0OTHER_VRNC	Other Variances
0PRICE_VRNC	Price Variances
0PROD_DSCNT	Material Discount
0QTY_DSCNT	Quantity Discount
0QUANT_VRNC	Quantity Variances
0RSRCH_DEV	Research and Development
0SALES_CMSN	Sales Commission
0SALES_CS	Sales Costs
0SPCDSLS_CS	Special Direct Costs of Sales
0VARPROD_CS	Variable Production Costs
0VOL_REBATE	Volume-Based Rebate
ZEBRUMS	Gross Sales
ZEERLMIND	Sales Revenue Reductions
ZEHKVK	Full Costs of Manufacturing

1 You can use the *CubeServ BW Documentation Tool* to create documentation from SAP BW at the touch of a button. You can employ various navigation options to use the documentation on line or as a printout. For more information on the *CubeServ BW Documentation Tool*, please visit *www.cubeserv.com*.

Dimension ZECOPAM11 Organization

0BUS_AREA	Business Area
0CHRT_ACCTS	Chart of Accounts
0COMP_CODE	Company Code
0CO_AREA	Controlling Area
0PLANT	Plant
0SOURSYSTEM	Source System ID

Dimension ZECOPAM12 Sales Area

0DISTR_CHAN	Distribution Channel
0DIVISION	Division
0SALESEMPLY	Sales Employee
0SALESORG	Sales Organization
0SALES_GRP	Sales Group
0SALES_OFF	Sales Office

Dimension ZECOPAM13 Data Type

0VERSION	Version
0VTYPE	Value Type for Reporting
ZEVERSION	Version (Reporting)

Dimension ZECOPAM14 Document Information

0BILL_TYPE	Billing Type
0CURTYPE	Currency Type
0REC_TYPE	Record Type
0VALUATION	Valuation View

Dimension ZECOPAM15 Customer

0COUNTRY	Currency Key
0CUSTOMER	Customer Number
0CUST_GROUP	Customer Group
0REGION	Region (State, Province, or County)
0SALES_DIST	Sales District

Dimension ZECOPAM16 Material

0MATERIAL	Material
0PROD_HIER	Product Hierarchy

Dimension ZECOPAM17 Profit Center

0PROFIT_CTR	Profit Center

Dimension ZECOPAM18 Partner Profit Center

0PART_PRCTR	Partner Profit

Dimension ZECOPAM19 Sending Cost Center

0SEND_CCTR	Sending Cost Center

Dimension ZECOPAM1A Work Breakdown Structure Element

0WBS_ELEMT	Work Breakdown Structure Element (WBS Element)

Dimension ZECOPAM1B Cost Element

0COSTELMNT	Cost Element

Dimension ZECOPAM1C Order Number

0COORDER	Order Number

Dimension ZECOPAM1D Other

0BA_PRZNR	Sender Business Process
0BILL_DATE	Date for Billing/Invoice Index and Printing
0COSTOBJ	Cost Object
0GI_DATE	Goods Issue Date
0PSTNG_DATE	Posting Date on the Document

Dimension ZECOPAM1P Data Package

0CHNGID	Change Run ID
0RECORDTP	Record Type
0REQUID	Request ID

Dimension ZECOPAM1T Time

0FISCPER	Fiscal Year/Period
0FISCPER3	Posting Period
0FISCVARNT	Fiscal Year Variant
0FISCYEAR	Fiscal Year

Dimension ZECOPAM1U Unit

0COPASLQTU	Sales Quantity Unit
0CURRENCY	Currency Key

InfoCubes Involved

ZECOPAC1	Actual data: Profit and Loss Statement
ZECOPAC2	Plan Data: Profit and Loss Statement

E.2 MultiProvider ZEFIGLM1

InfoArea:	ZEFIGL01
InfoCube:	ZEFIGLM1

Financials—General Ledger (Actual and Plan Data)

Cube Type:	MultiProvider

Key Figures

0BALANCE	Cumulative Balance
0CREDIT	Total of Credit Postings
0DEBIT	Total of Debit Postings
0SALES	Sales per Period

Dimension ZEFIGLM11 Organizational Unit

0COMP_CODE	Company Code
0COSTCENTER	Cost Center
0CO_AREA	Controlling Area
0FUNC_AREA	Functional Area
0PROFIT_CTR	Profit Center
0SEGMENT	Segment for Segment Reporting
0SOURSYSTEM	Source System ID

Dimension ZEFIGLM12 Accounts

0CHRT_ACCTS	Chart of Accounts
0GL_ACCOUNT	General Ledger Account
0SEM_POSIT	Plan Item

Dimension ZEFIGLM13 Data Type

0VERSION	Version
0VTYPE Value	Type for Reporting
ZEVERSION	Version (Reporting)

Dimension ZEFIGLM14 Currency Type

0CURTYPE	Currency Type

Dimension ZEFIGLM15 Valuation View

0VALUATION	Valuation View

Dimension ZEFIGLM1P Data Package

0CHNGID	Change Run ID
0RECORDTP	Record Type
0REQUID	Request ID

Dimension ZEFIGLM1T Time

0FISCPER	Fiscal Year Period
0FISCPER3	Posting Period
0FISCVARNT	Fiscal Year Variant
0FISCYEAR	Fiscal Year

Dimension ZEFIGLM1U Unit

0CURRENCY	Currency Key

Dimension InfoCubes Involved

ZEFIGLC1	General Ledger Transaction Figures
ZEFIGLC2	Plan Data: Balance sheet/profit and loss

E.3 MultiProvider ZEVAHDM1

InfoArea:	ZESALES01InfoCube:	ZEVAHDM1
Sales Document		
Cube Type:	MultiProvider	

Key Figures

0CML_OR_QTY	Cumulated Order Quantity in Sales Units
0CONF_QTY	Confirmed Quantity
0CUML_TME	Cumulative Order Processing Time for all Document Items
0DITM_RET	Returns
0DLVIELCR	Delivered Earlier/Later than Requested Delivery Date
0DLVIELSC	Delivered Earlier/Later than the Schedule Line Date
0DLVIEYCR	Delivered Earlier than the Requested Date
0DLVIEYSC	Delivered Earlier than the Schedule Line Data
0DLVIEYSC	Delivered Later than Requested Delivery Date
0DLVILECR	Delivered Later than the Schedule Line Date
0DLVIOVER	Delivered More than Requested
0DLVIUNDR	Delivered Less then Requested
0DLVQEYCR	Quantity Delivered Earlier than Requested Delivery Date
0DLVQEYSC	Quantity Delivered Earlier than Schedule Line Date
0DLVQLECR	Quantity Delivered Later than Requested Delivery Date
0DLVQLESC	Quantity Delivered Later than Schedule Line Date
0DLVVELCR	Delivered Value Earlier/Later than the Requested Delivery Date
0DLVVELSC	Delivered Value Earlier/Later than the Schedule Line Date
0DLVVEYCR	Delivered Value Earlier than the Requested Delivery Date
0DLVVEYSC	Delivered Value Earlier than the Schedule Line Date
0DLVVLECR	Delivered Value Later than the Requested Delivery Date
0DLVVLESC	Delivered Value Later than Schedule Line Date
0DLVVOVER	Delivered Value More than RequestedDelivered Value Less than Requested
0DLV_24	Delivery within 24 Hours

0DLV_QTY	Actual Delivered Quantity in Sales Units
0DLV_VAL	Actual Delivered Value
0DOC_ITEMS	Number of Document Items
0GIS_QTY	Quantity with Set Goods Issue Status
0ICOASREQ	Confirmed as Requested
0ISHP_STCK	Delivery from Stock
0LOWR_BND	Tolerance Limit for Underdelivery in %
0NET_PRICE	Net Price
0NET_VAL_HD	Net Value of the Order in Document Currency
0NUM_SCHED	Number of Schedule Lines
0ORDERS	Number of Orders
0QCOASREQ	Quantity Confirmed as Requested
0REQU_QTY	Requested Delivery Date
0REQU_VAL	Requested Delivery Value
0UPPR_BND	Tolerance Limit for Overdelivery in %
0VAL_24	Value with Delivery within 24 Hours
0VAL_RET	Value of Returns
0VCOASREQ	Value Confirmed as Requested
0VSHP_STCK	Value with Shipment from Stock

Dimension ZEVAHDM11 Organization

0COMP_CODE	Company Code
0PLANT	Plant
0SOURSYSTEM	Source System ID

Dimension ZEVAHDM12 Sales Area

0DISTR_CHAN	Distribution Channel
0DIVISION	Division
0SALESORG	Sales Organization

Dimension ZEVAHDM13 Data Type

ZEVERSION	Version (Reporting)

Dimension ZEVAHDM14 Sold-To Party

0CUST_GROUP	Customer Group
0CUST_GRP1	Customer Group 1
0CUST_GRP2	Customer Group 2
0CUST_GRP3	Customer Group 3
0CUST_GRP4	Customer Group 4
0CUST_GRP5	Customer Group 5
0SOLD_TO	Sold-To Party

Dimension ZEVAHDM15 Ship-To Party

0SHIP_TO	Ship-To Party

Dimension ZEVAHDM16 Payer

0PAYER	Payer

Dimension ZEVAHDM17 Shipping Point

0SHIP_POINT	Shipping Point

Dimension ZEVAHDM18 Material

0MATERIAL	Material
0MATL_GROUP	Material Group
0MATL_GRP_1	Material Group 1
0MATL_GRP_2	Material Group 2
0MATL_GRP_3	Material Group 3
0MATL_GRP_4	Material Group 4
0MATL_GRP_5	Material Group 5
0PROD_HIER	Product Hierarchy

Dimension ZEVAHDM19 Deletion Flag

0HEADER_DEL	Header Deleted
0ITEM_DEL	Item Deleted

Dimension ZEVAHDM1A Status

0DLV_STS	Delivery Status
0DLV_STSO	Overall Delivery Status of the Item
0DLV_STSOI	Overall Delivery Status of All Items
0GI_STS	Goods Issue Status
0LW_GISTS	Lowest Goods Issue Status of an Order Item

Dimension ZEVAHDM1B Delivery

0BND_IND	Independent of Delivery Tolerances
0FORWAGENT	Forwarding Agent
0SHIP_STCK	Delivery from Stock

Dimension ZEVAHDM1C Sales Person

0SALESEMPLY	Sales Employee
0SALES_GRP	Sales Group
0SALES_OFF	Sales Office

Dimension ZEVAHDM1D Delivery Date

0CONF_DATE	Confirmed Delivery Date
0DSDEL_DATE	Requested Delivery Date
0LST_A_GD	Last Actual Goods Issue Date of an Order Item

Dimension ZEVAHDM1P Data Package

0CHNGID	Change Run ID
0RECORDTP	Record Type
0REQUID	Request ID

Dimension ZEVAHDM1T Time

0CALDAY	Calendar Date
0CALMONTH	Calendar Year/Month
0CALMONTH2	Calendar Month
0CALQUART1	Quarter
0CALQUARTER	Calendar Year/Quarter
0CALWEEK	Calendar Year/Week
0CALYEAR	Calendar Year
0FISCPER	Fiscal Year/Period
0FISCPER3	Posting Period
0FISCVARNT	Fiscal Year Variant
0FISCYEAR	Business Year
0HALFYEAR1	Half Year
0WEEKDAY1	Weekday

Dimension ZEVAHDM1U Unit

0DOC_CURRCY	Document Currency
0SALES_UNIT	Sales Unit

InfoCubes Involved

ZEVAHDC1	Sales Document Header Data
ZEVAHDC2	Sales Document Item Data (Order and Returns)
ZEVAHDC3	Sales Document Schedule Lines (Order)

F InfoSets

The *CubeServ BW Documentation Tool* created all the screenshots displayed at the site. The CubeServ BW Documentation Tool is the first professional documentation tool for SAP Business Information Warehouse (SAP BW).[1]

F.1 InfoSet ZECOPAI1

ZECOPAI1 Profit and Loss Statement: Document Overview

F.1.1 ODS ZECOPAO1 Profit and Loss Statement

Field	InfoObject	Data Type	Length
Source System ID	0SOURSYSTEM	CHAR	2
Currency Type	0CURTYPE	CHAR	2
Record Type	0REC_TYPE	CHAR	1
Version	0VERSION	CHAR	3
Value Type	0VTYPE	NUMC	3
Fiscal Year Variant	0FISCVARNT	CHAR	2
Fiscal Year/Period	0FISCPER	NUMC	7
Document Number	0ID_DOCNUM	NUMC	10
Document Item Number	0ID_ITMNUM	NUMC	6
Company Code	0COMP_CODE	CHAR	4
Plant	0PLANT	CHAR	4
Sales Organization	0SALESORG	CHAR	4
Material	0MATERIAL	CHAR	18
Customer	0CUSTOMER	CHAR	10
Profit Center	0PROFIT_CTR	CHAR	10
Partner Profit Center	0PART_PRCTR	CHAR	10
Sender Cost Center	0SEND_CCTR	CHAR	10

1 You can use the *CubeServ BW Documentation Tool* to create documentation from SAP BW at the touch of a button. You can employ various navigation options to use the documentation on line or as a printout. For more information on the *CubeServ BW Documentation Tool*, please visit *www.cubeserv.com*.

Field	InfoObject	Data Type	Length
WBS Element	0WBS_ELEMT	CHAR	24
Cost Element	0COSTELMNT	CHAR	10
Sender Business Process	0BA_PRZNR	CHAR	12
Cancelled Document	0BA_STO_BNR	CHAR	10
Cancelled Document Item	0BA_STO_PNR	CHAR	6
Billing Date	0BILL_DATE	DATS	8
Billing Type	0BILL_TYPE	CHAR	4
Business Area	0BUS_AREA	CHAR	4
Chart of Accounts	0CHRT_ACCTS	CHAR	4
Order	0COORDER	CHAR	12
Cost Object	0COSTOBJ	CHAR	12
Controlling Area	0CO_AREA	CHAR	4
Customer Group	0CUST_GROUP	CHAR	2
Distribution Channel	0DISTR_CHAN	CHAR	2
Division	0DIVISION	CHAR	2
Sales Document	0DOC_NUMBER	CHAR	10
Item	0S_ORD_ITEM	NUMC	6
Goods Issue	0GI_DATE	DATS	8
Industry	0INDUSTRY	CHAR	4
Main Material Group	0MAINMATGRP	NUMC	2
Material Group	0MATL_GROUP	CHAR	9
CO-PA Reference Document Number	0ME_REFDOC	CHAR	10
CO-PA Reference Item	0ME_REFITEM	CHAR	6
Posting Date	0PSTNG_DATE	DATS	8
Sales Employee	0SALESEMPLY	NUMC	8
Sales District	0SALES_DIST	CHAR	6
Sales Group	0SALES_GRP	CHAR	3
Sales Office	0SALES_OFF	CHAR	4
Valuation View	0VALUATION	NUMC	1
Version	ZEVERSION	CHAR	10

Field	InfoObject	Data Type	Length
Fiscal Year	0FISCYEAR	NUMC	4
Posting Period	0FISCPER3	NUMC	3
Accrued Freight	0ACCRDFR_CS	CURR	9
Administration	0ADMNSTRTN	CURR	9
Cash Discount	0CASH_DSCNT	CURR	9
Revenue	0COPAREVEN	CURR	9
Sales Quantity	0COPASLQTY	QUAN	9
Customer Discount	0CUST_DSCNT	CURR	9
Direct Material Costs	0DIRMAT_CS	CURR	9
Fixed Production Costs	0FIXPROD_CS	CURR	9
Marketing	0MARKETING	CURR	9
Material Overhead Costs	0MATOVHD	CURR	9
Other Overhead	0OTHER_OVHD	CURR	9
Other Variances	0OTHER_VRNC	CURR	9
Price Variances	0PRICE_VRNC	CURR	9
Product Discount	0PROD_DSCNT	CURR	9
Quantity Discount	0QTY_DSCNT	CURR	9
Quantity Variance	0QUANT_VRNC	CURR	9
Research and Development	0RSRCH_DEV	CURR	9
Sales Commission	0SALES_CMSN	CURR	9
Cost of Sales	0SALES_CS	CURR	9
Other Direct Sales Costs	0SPCDSLS_CS	CURR	9
Variable Production Costs	0VARPROD_CS	CURR	9
Volume Rebate	0VOL_REBATE	CURR	9
Currency	0CURRENCY	CUKY	5
Sales Quantity Unit	0COPASLQTU	UNIT	3

F.2 InfoSet ZEVAHDI1

ZEVAHDI1 Sales Document Item and Schedule Line

F.2.1 ODS ZEVAHDO4 Sales Document Schedule Lines (Order)

Field	InfoObject	Data Type	Length
Source System ID	0SOURSYSTEM	CHAR	2
Sales Document	0DOC_NUMBER	CHAR	10
Item	0S_ORD_ITEM	NUMC	6
Schedule Line	0SCHED_LINE	NUMC	4
Fiscal Year Variant	0FISCVARNT	CHAR	2
Delivery Status	0DLV_STS	CHAR	1
Delivery Status of Item	0DLV_STSO	CHAR	1
Goods Issue Status	0GI_STS	CHAR	1
Lowest Goods Issue Status	0LW_GISTS	CHAR	1
Confirmed Quantity	0CONF_QTY	QUAN	9
Sales Unit	0SALES_UNIT	UNIT	3
Delivery Quantity	0DLV_QTY	QUAN	9
Quantity with Goods Issue Status	0GIS_QTY	QUAN	9
Confirmed Delivery Date	0CONF_DATE	DATS	8
Requested Delivery Date	0DSDEL_DATE	DATS	8
Version	ZEVERSION	CHAR	10
Fiscal Year	0FISCYEAR	NUMC	4
Fiscal Year/Period	0FISCPER	NUMC	7
Posting Period	0FISCPER3	NUMC	3

F.2.2 ODS ZEVAHDO2 Sales Document Item Data (Order)

Field	InfoObject	Data Type	Length
Source System ID	0SOURSYSTEM	CHAR	2
Sales Document	0DOC_NUMBER	CHAR	10
Item	0S_ORD_ITEM	NUMC	6
Fiscal Year Variant	0FISCVARNT	CHAR	2
Delivery Status	0DLV_STS	CHAR	1

Field	InfoObject	Data Type	Length
Delivery Status of Item	0DLV_STSO	CHAR	1
Requested Quantity	0REQU_QTY	QUAN	9
Quantity Delivered Earlier than Requested Delivery Date	0DLVQEYCR	QUAN	9
Quantity Delivered Later than Requested Delivery Date	0DLVQLECR	QUAN	9
Created on	0CREATEDON	DATS	8
Quantity Delivered Earlier than the Schedule Line Date	0DLVQEYSC	QUAN	9
Quantity Delivered Later than the Schedule Line Date	0DLVQLESC	QUAN	9
Quantity Confirmed as Requested	0QCOASREQ	QUAN	9
Tolerance Limit for Underdelivery in %	0LOWR_BND	DEC	9
Tolerance Limit for Overdelivery in %	0UPPR_BND	DEC	9
Independent of Delivery Tolerance	0BND_IND	CHAR	1
Net Price	0NET_PRICE	CURR	9
Last Actual Goods Issue Date	0LST_A_GD	DATS	8
Lowest Goods Issue Status	0LW_GISTS	CHAR	1
Delivery from Stock	0SHIP_STCK	CHAR	1
Material	0MATERIAL	CHAR	18
Batch	0BATCH	CHAR	10
Sold-To Party	0SOLD_TO	CHAR	10
Company Code	0COMP_CODE	CHAR	4
Customer Group	0CUST_GROUP	CHAR	2
Customer Group 1	0CUST_GRP1	CHAR	3
Customer Group 2	0CUST_GRP2	CHAR	3
Customer Group 3	0CUST_GRP3	CHAR	3
Customer Group 4	0CUST_GRP4	CHAR	3
Customer Group 5	0CUST_GRP5	CHAR	3
Distribution Channel	0DISTR_CHAN	CHAR	2
Sales Employee	0SALESEMPLY	NUMC	8
Sales Group	0SALES_GRP	CHAR	3
Sales Office	0SALES_OFF	CHAR	4

Field	InfoObject	Data Type	Length
Sales Organization	0SALESORG	CHAR	4
Material Group	0MATL_GROUP	CHAR	9
Material Group 1	0MATL_GRP_1	CHAR	3
Material Group 2	0MATL_GRP_2	CHAR	3
Material Group 3	0MATL_GRP_3	CHAR	3
Material Group 4	0MATL_GRP_4	CHAR	3
Material Group 5	0MATL_GRP_5	CHAR	3
Product Hierarchy	0PROD_HIER	CHAR	18
Plant	0PLANT	CHAR	4
Ship-To Party	0SHIP_TO	CHAR	10
Shipping Point	0SHIP_POINT	CHAR	4
Division	0DIVISION	CHAR	2
Forwarding Agent	0FORWAGENT	CHAR	10
Payer	0PAYER	CHAR	10
Sales Unit	0SALES_UNIT	UNIT	3
Document Currency	0DOC_CURRCY	CUKY	5
Item Deleted	0ITEM_DEL	CHAR	1
Version	ZEVERSION	CHAR	10
Fiscal Year	0FISCYEAR	NUMC	4
Fiscal Year/Period	0FISCPER	NUMC	7
Fiscal Period	0FISCPER3	NUMC	3

F.2.3 Link

ZEVAHDO2 Sales Document Item Data (Order)		ZEVAHDO4 Sales Document Schedule Lines (Order)	
Field	**InfoObject**	**Field**	**InfoObject**
Source System ID	0SOURSYSTEM	Source System ID	0SOURSYSTEM
Sales Document	0DOC_NUMBER	Sales Document	0DOC_NUMBER
Item	0_ORD_ITEM	Item	0_ORD_ITEM
Fiscal Year Variant	0FISCVARNT	Fiscal Year Variant	0FISCVARNT

G Transaction Codes

G.1 Transactions in SAP BW

Transaction	Meaning
BAPI	BAPI Explorer
CMOD	Project Management of SAP Extensions
FILE	Maintenance of Logical File Paths
LISTCUBE	List Viewer for Data Targets (→ BasicCubes, ODS Objects, Characteristic InfoObjects)
LISTSCHEMA	Schema Viewer for BasicCubes (including Aggregates)
PFCG	Role Maintenance
RRC1, RRC2, and RRC3	Create, Modify, and Display Definitions for Currency Conversion
RRMX	Start BEx Analyzer
RS12	Display and Delete Locked Entries (of Tables)
RSA1	Administrator Workbench (→ Modeling)
RSA11	Administrator Workbench (→ InfoProvider)
RSA12	Administrator Workbench (→ InfoSources)
RSA13	Administrator Workbench (→ Source Systems)
RSA14	Administrator Workbench (→ InfoObjects)
RSA3	Extractor Checker SAPI 3.0
RSA5	Transfer DataSources from Business Content
RSA6	Perform Follow-Up Work on DataSources and Application Component Hierarchy
RSA7	Maintenance of Delta Queue
RSA9	Transfer Application Components from Business Content
RSBBS	Maintain Blocked Lines for the Report-to-Report Interface (RRI)
RSCUSTV1	Change Settings for Flat Files (→ Thousands, Decimal, and Field Separators; Field Delimiters)
RSCUSTV6	Change Threshold Values for Data Loading (→ Package Size, Size of a PSA Partition, and IDOC Frequency Status)
RSCUSTV8	Change Settings for Aggregate Change Run (→ Threshold Value for Restructuring and Block Size)

Transaction	Meaning
RSD1, RSD2, and RSD3	Maintenance of InfoObjects: Characteristic/Flag/Unit Types
RSD4 and RSD5	Editing of Technical Characteristics and Time Characteristics
RSDBC	DB Connect: Select Tables and Views
RSDDV	Maintenance of Aggregates
RSDIOBC	Editing InfoObjectCatalogs
RSDMD	Maintenance of Master Data (for one Characteristic)
RSDMPROM	Editing MultiProviders
RSDODS	Editing ODS Objects
RSDV	Maintenance of the Validity Slice (→ BasicCubes with Flag Type of Non-Cumulative Value)
RSFH	Test Tool for Extraction of Transaction Data
RSIMG	SAP BW Customizing Implementation Guide
RSISET	Maintenance of InfoSets
RSKC	Maintenance of Permitted Additional Characters in SAP BW
RSMD	Test Tool for Extraction of Master Data
RSMO	Monitor
RSMON	Administrator Workbench (→ Monitoring)
RSMONCOLOR	Valuation of Requests
RSO2	Maintenance of Generic DataSources
RSO3	Setup of Delta Extraction for Attributes and Texts
RSOR	Administrator Workbench (→ Metadata Repository)
RSORBCT	Administrator Workbench (→ Business Content)
RSPC	Maintenance of Process Chains
RSRT	Query Monitor
RSRTRACE	Query Trace
RSRV	Analysis and Repair of SAP BW Objects
RSSM	Maintenance of Reporting Authorization Objects
RSU1/RSU2/RSU3	Create, Modify, and Display Update Rules (→ BasicCubes and ODS Objects)
SARA	Archive Administration

Transaction	Meaning
SBIW	Display of Implementation Guide (→ Customizing for Extractors)
SE03	Transport Organizer Tools
SE09	Transport Organizer
SE11	ABAP Dictionary
SE16	ABAP Data Browser
SE37	Function Builder (→ Maintenance of Function Modules)
SE38	ABAP Editor (→ Maintenance of ABAP Programs)
SE80	Object Navigator
SICF	Maintenance of System Internet Communication Framework
SM04	User List
SM12	Selection of Blocked Entries
SM21	Online Analysis of System Log
SM37	Job Overview
SM38	Queue (Job)—Definition
SM50	Process Overview
SM59	Maintenance of RFC Connections
SM62	Maintenance of Events
SM66	Global Work Process Overview
SMX	System → Own Jobs
SPRO	Customizing Guidelines
SQ02	Maintenance of SAP Query/InfoSets
SQ10	Assignment of Query/InfoSets to User and Role
ST03	SAP BW Statistics
ST05	Performance Analysis (→ SQL-Trace)
ST22	ABAP Dump Analysis
SU01	Maintenance of Users
SU24	Maintenance of Role Templates
SU53	Resolve Error Codes (at the Authorization Level)
TRSA	Test Tool for Service API

G.2 SAP R/3 Transactions Relevant to SAP BW

Transaction	Meaning
LBWE	Customizing Cockpit for Logistics Extract Structures
KEB0	Create, Display, and Delete CO-PA DataSource
RSA3	Extractor Checker SAPI 3.0
RSA5	Transfer DataSources from Business Content
RSA6	Perform Follow-Up Work on DataSources and Application Component Hierarchy
RSA7	Maintenance of Delta Queue
RSA9	Transfer Application Components from Business Content
RSO2	Maintenance of Generic DataSources
RSO3	Setup of Delta Extraction for Attributes and Texts
SBIW	Display of Implementation Guide (→ Customizing for Extractors)
SMQ1	qRFC Monitor (Output Queue)
TRSA	Test Tool for Service API

H Metadata Tables

H.1 InfoObject

Table	Meaning
RSDIOBJ	Directory of all InfoObjects
RSDIOBJT	Texts of InfoObjects
RSDATRNAV	Navigation Attributes
RSDATRNAVT	Navigation Attributes
RSDBCHATR	Master Data Attributes
RSDCHABAS	Basic Characteristics (for Characteristics, Time Characteristics, and Units)
RSDCHA	Characteristics Catalog
RSDDPA	Data Package Characteristic
RSDIOBJCMP	Dependencies of InfoObjects
RSKYF	Key Figures
RSDTIM	Time Characteristics
RSDUNI	Units

H.2 InfoCube

Table	Meaning
RSDCUBE	Directory of InfoCubes
RSDCUBET	Texts on InfoCubes
RSDCUBEIOBJ	Navigation Attributes
RSDDIME	Directory of Dimensions
RSDDIMET	Texts on Dimensions
RSDDIMEIOBJ	InfoObjects for each Dimension (Where-Used List)
RSDCUBEMULTI	InfoCubes Involved in a MultiCube
RSDICMULTIIOBJ	MultiProvider: Selection/Identification of InfoObjects
RSDICHAPRO	Characteristic Properties Specific to an InfoCube
RSDIKYFPRO	Flag Properties Specific to an InfoCube
RSDICVALIOBJ	InfoObjects of the Stock Validity Table for the InfoCube

H.3 Aggregate

Table	Meaning
RSDDAGGRDIR	Directory of Aggregates
RSDDAGGRCOMP	Description of Aggregates
RSDDAGGRT	Texts on Aggregates

H.4 ODS Object

Table	Meaning
RSDODSO	Directory of all ODS Objects
RSDODSOT	Texts of ODS Objects
RSDODSOIOBJ	InfoObjects of ODS Objects
RSDODSOATRNAV	Navigation Attribute for ODS Object
RSDODSOTABL	Directory of all ODS Object Tables

H.5 PSA

Table	Meaning
RSTSODS	Directory of all PSA Tables

H.6 DataSource (= OLTP Source)

Table	Meaning
ROOSOURCE	Header Table for SAP BW DataSources (SAP Source System/ BW System
RODELTAM	BW Delta Procedure (SAP Source System)
RSOLTPSOURCE	Replication Table for DataSources in BW

H.7 InfoSource

Table	Meaning
RSIS	Directory of InfoSources with Flexible Update
RSIST	Texts on InfoSources with Flexible Update
RSISFIELD	InfoObjects of an InfoSource

H.8 Communications Structure

Table	Meaning
RSKS	▶ Communications Structure for InfoSources with Flexible Update ▶ Communications Structure (View) for Attributes for an InfoSource with Direct Update
RSKSFIELD	Texts on InfoSources with Flexible Update
RSISFIELD	InfoObjects of an InfoSource with Flexible Update

H.9 Transfer Structure

Table	Meaning
RSTS	Transfer Structure in SAP BW
ROOSGEN	Generated Objects for a DataSource (Transfer Structure, for example) in SAP Source System

H.10 Mapping

Table	Meaning
RSISOSMAP	Mapping Between InfoSources and DataSources (= OLTP Sources)
RSOSFIELDMAP	Mapping Between DataSource Fields and InfoObjects

H.11 SAP BW Statistics

Table	Meaning
RSDDSTAT	Basic Table for InfoCubes/Queries
RSDDSTATAGGR	Detail Table for Aggregate Setup
RSDDSTATAGGRDEF	Detail Table of Navigation for each InfoCube/Query

I Glossary

Ad-hoc Query Designer
Web item that enables you to create and change ad-hoc queries in a Web application. You can use the Ad-hoc Query Designer in the Web Application Designer to design Web applications in which you can create or change queries.

ADK
see: Archiving Development Kit

Administrator Workbench (AWB)
Central tool for controlling, monitoring, and maintaining all processes involved in data retrieval and processing in SAP BW. The tasks are executed in the following functional areas:

- **Modeling** (Transaction RSA1)
  This functional area handles the creation and maintenance of (meta) objects in SAP BW relevant to the process of retrieving or loading data.
- **Monitoring** (Transaction RSMON)
  Monitoring enables you to observe and control the data loading process and other data processing activities in SAP BW.
- **Reporting Agent** (Transaction RSA1 • Pushbutton **Reporting Agent**)
  Tool for scheduling and executing reporting functions in the background (batch). The functions include evaluating exceptions and printing queries.
- **Transport connection** (Transaction RSA1 • Pushbutton **Transport connection**)
  With the transport connection, you can collect newly created and modified BW objects and use the Change and Transport Organizer (CTO) to transport them into other BW systems.
- **Documents** (Transaction RSA1 • Pushbutton **Documents**)
  This functional area enables you to link and search one or more documents in various formats, versions, and languages.
- **Business Content** (Transaction RSORBCT)
  Business Content offers preconfigured roles and task-related information models based on consistent metadata (*see*: Business Content).
- **Translation** (Transaction RSA1 • Pushbutton **Translation**)
  You can translate short and long texts of BW objects in this functional area.
- **Metadata Repository** (Transaction RSOR)
  The HTML-based BW Metadata Repository centrally administers all BW metaobjects and their links to each other, which enables a consistent and homogenous data model across all source systems (*see:* Metadata Repository).

Aggregate
Stores the dataset of a BasicCube redundantly and persistently in a summarized form in the database. Because aggregates use the same form of storage (fact and dimension tables) as BasicCubes, they are often called aggregate cubes. Aggrega-

tes enable you to access BasicCubes quickly for reporting. Thus, aggregates help to improve performance. Because a BasicCube can possess several aggregates, the Optimizer of the OLAP processor automatically accesses the most appropriate aggregate during execution of a query. In other words, the decision to use a BasicCube or an aggregate for reporting is not transparent to the end user. Information on aggregates, such as technical, content, and status properties, are stored in table RSDDAGGRDIR. Maintenance of aggregates in SAP BW:

- Transaction RSDDV
- Initial access: **AWB** · **Modeling** · **InfoProvider** · Select **InfoArea** · Select **maintain aggregate** in the context menu of the selected BasicCube.

When building an aggregate from the characteristics and navigation attributes of a BasicCube, you can group the data according to different aggregation levels:

- **All characteristic values (*)**
  Data is grouped according to all values of the combined characteristics or navigation attributes that define the aggregate.
- **Hierarchy level (H)**
  The data is grouped according to the nodes of a hierarchy level.
- **Fixed value (F)**
  The data is filtered and grouped according to an individual value of a characteristic or navigation attribute.

Logical data packages are used to load new data (requests) into an aggregate. When loading data, note the distinction between filling and rolling up. Aggregates enable you to access InfoCube data quickly for reporting. Thus, aggregates help to improve performance.

- **Activate and fill**
  This function builds the aggregate and fills it for the first time. An active and filled aggregate is used for reporting and can be populated with additional data by rolling up data packages.
- **Roll-Up**
  Loads data packages (requests) that are not yet contained in the aggregates of a BasicCube into all aggregates of the BasicCube. A roll-up is required as soon as the data of the BasicCube has changed to guarantee ensure the consistency of data between the aggregate and the BasicCube. After the roll-up, the new data is used in queries.
- **Roll-Up Hierarchy (aggregate hierarchy)**
  The roll-up hierarchy displays the dependency of aggregates to a BasicCube and among aggregates in terms of the roll-up. In other words, it displays whether an aggregate is filled by a superior aggregate or directly by the BasicCube during a roll-up. You can use the roll-up hierarchy to identify similar aggregates and this that information as the basis for manual and targeted optimization of the aggregates.

Additional functionalities:

- **On/Off Switch**
  If an aggregate is temporarily switched off, it is not used in the execution of a query. When the aggregate is switched back on, it does not have to be reactivated and refilled. This feature allows you to compare the runtime of the query with and without the aggregate to determine whether using the aggregate is judicious.
- **Deactivate**
  Deactivation of an aggregate means that all the data of the aggregate is deleted, although the structure of the aggregate remains in place.
- **Delete**
  Deletion deactivates the aggregate and its structure.
- **Compress**
  Compression of aggregates corresponds to the compression of BasicCubes. In other words, compressed requests can no longer be deleted from the aggregate. However, you can switch compression off after the roll-up so that the aggregate request remains in place.
- **Hierarchy/Attribute Change Run**
  If the hierarchy and navigation attributes of characteristics used in aggregates change, structural modifications are required in the aggregates to adjust the data accordingly. A structure modification changes the aggregates of all BasicCubes affected by modifications of hierarchies and navigation attributes:

  Initial access: **AWB · Tools · Execute Hierarchy/Attribute Modifications for Reporting**

  You can use the ABAP program "RSDDS_CHANGE" "RUN_MONITOR" to determine the attributes, hierarchies, and aggregates to be adjusted during the change run. Modifications of master data become effective only if a change run is executed for the master data. At a certain size of the change run, modification of the aggregates involves more work than rebuilding it. You can set this threshold value yourself:

  - Transaction RSCUSTV8
  - Initial access: **BW Customizing Guidelines · Business Information Warehouse · General BW Settings · Parameters for Aggregates**

Aggregation Level
Choice of characteristics and navigation attributes of an InfoCube from which aggregates are constructed. You have the following aggregation options:

- **All characteristic values (*)**: Data is grouped by all values of the characteristic or the navigation attribute.
- **Hierarchy level (H)**:
  The data is grouped according to the nodes of a hierarchy level.
- **Fixed value (F)**: Data is filtered according to a single value.

ALE
see: Application Link Enabling

Alert Monitor
A monitoring tool for displaying exceptions whose threshold values have been exceeded or have not been reached. The exceptions that occur are found in background processing with the help of the reporting agent. They are then displayed in the alert monitor as a follow-up action. Exceptions are displayed in the BEx Analyzer as well as in the reporting agent scheduler of the Administrator Workbench. Exceptions can be displayed as an alert monitor in a Web application.

And Process
Collective process of process chain maintenance. The use of an And process in process chain maintenance starts the application process only after successful triggers of all events of the preceding processes, including the last of the events for which it waited.

Application Process
A process that is automated in process chain maintenance. Example: a data loading process or an attribute change run.

Archiving
Data archiving enables you to archive data from BasicCubes and ODS objects (tables with active data). Therefore, you can store the data as a flat structure in a file system and delete it from the BasicCube or ODS object. You archive data for the following purposes:

- To lessen the volume or data and thus save storage space
- To improve performance because of the smaller volume of data during analyses, updates, roll-ups, and change runs, for example
- To meet legal requirements for the storage of data

See also: Archiving Development Kit, archiving process, and archiving objects

Archiving Process
The archiving process in SAP BW consists of the following subprocesses:

- **Writing data to the archive (Transaction SARA)**
- **Deleting the archived data from the BasicCube/ODS Object (Transaction SARA)**
  If you delete archived data from a BasicCube, it is also deleted from the aggregate that belongs to the BasicCube. If you delete data from an ODS object, archiving does not affect the data targets populated with data from the ODS object.
- **Restoring archived Data in the BW system**
  You can restore archived data with the export DataSource of the BasicCube or ODS object from which the data was archived. The ADK provides functions for

reading archived data. Later updates occur with the familiar data loading processes in the BW system.

Archiving Objects

All archiving requires archiving objects that describe related business data with a data structure and that are used to define and execute reading, writing, and deleting in the context of the archiving process. They are the link between the ADK and SAP BW objects. Creating an archiving object:

Initial access: **AWB** • **Modeling** • **InfoProvider** • Select **InfoArea** • In the context menu of the selected BasicCube or ODS object, select **Modify** • **Extras**• **Archiving.**

Archiving Development Kit (ADK)

The ADK of mySAP Technology-Basis is used for archiving. The ADK provides the runtime environment for archiving. It primarily helps read and write data to and from archive files. The ADK guarantees platform and release independence for archived data.

Application Link Enabling (ALE)

ALE supports the configuration and operation of distributed application systems—between SAP systems themselves and between SAP systems and external systems. For communication (data exchange) among distributed application systems, ALE provides tolls and services, such as consistency checks, monitoring of data transfer, error handling, and synchronous and asynchronous connections. It thus guarantees controlled data exchange among the distributed application systems and consistent data storage.

Attribute

Attributes are InfoObjects (characteristics or key figures) used to describe characteristics in more detail. Example: For the "cost center" characteristic, you can assign the following attributes:

- "Cost center manger" (characteristic as attribute)
- "Size of the cost center in square meters" (key figure as attribute)

When you maintain an InfoObject for a characteristic, you can also assign attributes with attribute properties to the characteristic:

- **Display**
  Attributes with this property can be used in reporting only as supplemental information in combination with the characteristic. That means that you cannot navigate in queries. Note the special case that occurs when you define InfoObjects. You can define InfoObjects (characteristics or key figures) as exclusive attributes. You cannot use these attributes as navigation attributes; you can use them only as display attributes.
- **Navigation Attribute**
  You can define attributes of InfoObject type "characteristic" as navigation attributes. These types of attributes can be used for navigation much like (dimension) characteristics in queries: All navigation functions of (dimension) charac-

teristics in queries also apply to navigation attributes. Unlike (dimension) characteristics, navigation attributes enable current and key-date data views at the query layer (→ Tracking History). To make these attributes available in reporting as navigation attributes, you must also switch them on at the data-target layer. A characteristic used as a navigation attribute can also have its own navigation attributes, which are called transitive attributes (= two-level navigation attribute). You can also switch on the transitive attributes and make them available for navigation in queries.

- **Time Dependency**
  You can flag both display and navigation attributes as time-dependent attributes if a validity area is required for each attribute value.

AWB
see: Administrator Workbench

Balanced Scorecard (BSC)
Robert S. Kaplan, professor or management at Harvard Business School, and Dr. David Norton introduced this management instrument in 1992, which began a profound and lasting change in performance management at leading companies. The *Harvard Business Review* calls the concept the most important management idea in the last 75 years.

The core of the theory is that the economic success of a company rests on influencing factors behind the target financial values that causatively determine the ability to reach the financial objective. The BSC usually considers meeting objects from the perspective of finances, processes, customers, and innovation. The evidence of historical key figures is supplemented by the knowledge of future developments.

BAPI (Business Application Programming Interface)
BAPIs are open, standard interfaces defined at the application layer (Transaction: BAPI). These interfaces provided by SAP enable communication between SAP systems and applications developed by third parties. Technically, calling a BAPI calls a function module with RFC or tRFC (*see also:* Staging BAPI).

BasicCube

- Creating BasicCubes:

  Initial access: **AWB** • **Modeling** • **InfoProvider** • Select **InfoArea** • In the context menu of the selected InfoArea, select **Create InfoCube** and select the type of **BasicCube.**

- Maintenance of BasicCubes: Transaction RSDCUBE

A BasicCube is a data container; reports and analyses in SAP BW are based on BasicCubes. An InfoCube is a closed, topically related dataset on which queries can be defined. A BasicCube contains two types of data: key figures and characteristics. It is supplied with transaction data relevant to analysis by one or more InfoSources with update rules. A BasicCube is the InfoCube that is relevant for multidimensional modeling because only objects that contain data are considered for the BW data model.

From a technical viewpoint, a BasicCube is a set of relational tables placed together according to the star schema: a large fact table in the center, surrounded by several dimension tables. The fact table is used to store all key figures at the lowest level of detail. The dimension tables help to store the characteristics required in reporting and during analysis of the key figures. Dimension tables are considered independently of each other. Only the fact table links the dimensions to the key figures. All data is thus stored multidimensionally in the BasicCubes:

- **Fact Tables**
  A BasicCube consists of two fact tables, each of which stores the key figures.
  - F table: Normal fact table (→ partitioned with respect to the request ID)
  - E table: Compressed fact table (→ F table without request ID)

  A maximum of 233 key figures can be stored. Use of the E table is optional (*see also:* Compression).
- **Dimension Tables**
  A BasicCube consists of a maximum of 16 dimension tables. Of these, the system automatically generates the time dimension and data package dimension tables. The system generates a unit dimension table only when at least one key figure is of the "amount" or "quantity" type. In this case, you must also supply a fixed or variable currency/unit along with the key figure (*see also*: Key Figures).
- **SID Tables/Master Data Tables**
  The relationship between the master data tables for a characteristic InfoObject and the dimension tables is created by system-generated INT4 keys, or SIDs (surrogate identifications) of each characteristic InfoObject. Dimension tables store only SIDs of each characteristic InfoObject; they never store characteristic values. A dimension table can contain a maximum of 248 SIDs of each characteristic InfoObject. The relationship between a fact table and the related dimension tables is created with artificially generated INT4 keys, or DIM IDs (dimension identifications).

Administering BasicCubes:

- **Selective Deletion (Content tab)**
  With this function and a previous selection, you can delete targeted data records that correspond to the selection criteria from a BasicCube. If you use selective deletion to delete erroneous data records from the BasicCube, you can replace the records with correct(ed) data records by using a repair request in the scheduler (**Scheduler** • Maintain **InfoPackage**).
- **Check, Delete, or Repair Indices (Performance tab)**
  An index of BasicCubes is created on the fact table for each DIM ID. The indices are required to ensure the optimal finding and selection of data. However, the database system must adjust the indices during write access, which can lead to considerable degradations of performance. The **Delete Indices** function enables you to accelerate write access during the updating of the BasicCubes. After the update ends, you must rebuild the indices with the **Repair Indices** function. You

can use the **Check Indices** function to determine whether indices are deleted (red light), rebuilt (yellow light), or active (green light).

- **Delete Requests (Requests tab)**
  You can use this function to deleted selected requests loaded into the Basic Cubes (if they have not been rolled up into aggregates).
- **Rebuild Requests (Rebuild tab)**
  You can use this function to recreate deleted requests for a BasicCube. You can also use these requests for other BasicCubes. This function works only if the PSA tables store the requests.
- **Roll-Up Requests (Roll-Up tab)**
  see: **Aggregate · Roll-Up**
- **Compress (Compress tab)**
  Every BasicCube has a data package dimension table (set by the system) that stores the SID for the 0REQUID (request ID) technical characteristic. Every load process fills this dimension table. Consequently, the fact table stores data with a higher level of detail than is required from a business viewpoint. Depending on the modeling of the BasicCube, the frequency of load processes, and the composition of loaded data, the level of detail can significantly affect the volume of data in the BasicCubes. After the disappearance of the request ID, the data volume can be reduced considerably without having to accept any disadvantages from the perspective of the business. To enable this reduction, each BasicCube consists of two fact tables:
  - F table: Normal fact table
  - E table: Compressed fact table (= F table without request ID)

  The **Compress** function fills the E table with data from the F table. The entire F table can be compressed, or only an older portion of the requests can be compressed. New requests are written to the F table and can then be compressed. The compression of aggregates behaves similarly. The disadvantage of the **Compression** function is that it cannot be reversed.

BCT
see: Business Content

BEx
see: Business Explorer

BI Cockpit
see: Business Intelligence Cockpit

BIS
see: Business Intelligence Systems

BSC
see: Balanced Scorecard

Business Application Programming Interface
see: BAPI

Business Content (BCT)
An important advantage of SAP BW over and above other data warehouse solutions is the Business Content (BCT) that SAP delivers with SAP BW. SAP continues the ongoing development of BCT, which requires a comprehensive, predefined information model for the analysis of business processes. It contains the entire definition of all required SAP BW objects, including the following: InfoAreas, InfoObjectCatalogs, roles, workbooks, query elements, InfoCubes, InfoObjects, ODS objects, update rules, InfoSources, transfer rules, currency conversion types, extractors, and DataSources. Two areas of BCT are distinguished:

- BCT for SAP source systems (component hierarchy and DataSources, for example)
- BCT for the BW system

BCT for SAP source systems (SAP R/3 systems: = Release 3.1 I) is imported with plug-ins. If SAP BW systems are connected to other Business Warehouse systems as a source system, the importing of plug-ins is not required. Before you can use elements of BCT, you must adopt or activate them explicitly. You do so with Transaction SBIW in the source system and Transaction RSORBCT in the BW system.

- **Object Versions**
  All SAP BW objects are first delivered in the D(elivered) version with BCT. The adoption of these objects from BCT creates an A(ctive) version; the D version remains in place. If the activated objects are modified, a new, M(odified) version is created. You can activate the M version and thus overwrite the older active version. Modifications of BW objects adopted from the BCT are not overwritten by adoption of a newer content version.

Business Explorer (BEx)
The BEx is the analysis and reporting tool of SAP Business Information Warehouse. You can use it to evaluate centrally stored data that comes from various sources. The BEx makes use of the following areas:

- **Query Design and Application Design**
  BEx Query Designer and BEx Web Application Designer
- **Analysis and Reporting**
  BEx Analyzer, BEx Web Applications, and Mobile Intelligence
- **Formatted Reporting**
  Crystal Reports integration
- **Organization**
  BEx Browser

Business Explorer Analyzer (BEx Analyzer)
- Transaction RRMX

The BEx Analyzer is the analysis and reporting tool of Business Explorer. It is embedded in Microsoft Excel and can therefore access all Excel functionality. In the Business Explorer Analyzer, you can use navigation to analyze selected InfoProvider Data in queries created in the BEx Query Designer and generate various views of the data, namely, query views. BEx Analyzer is used for the following:

- To create and modify reports
- To analyze reports and navigate within reports
- To call and to save reports in roles or as personal favorites
- To publish reports for Web reporting

Business Explorer Browser (BEx Browser)
The BEx Browser is a tool used to organize and manage workbooks and documents. You can use it to access all documents in SAP BW that have been assigned to your role and that you have stored in your list of favorites. You can work with the following types of documents in the BEx Browser:

- SAP BW workbooks
- Documents stored in the Business Document Service (BDS)
- Links (references to the file system and shortcuts)
- Links to Internet sites (URLs)
- SAP transaction calls
- Web applications and Web templates
- Crystal Reports

Business Explorer Map (BEx Map)
The BEx Map is a Geographical Information System (GIS) of Business Explorer that enables you to display and evaluate data with geographical references (characteristics such as customer, sales region, and country, for example) along with key figures relevant to the business on a map.

Business Explorer Mobile Intelligence (BEx Mobile Intelligence)
BEx Mobile Intelligence is a tool that enables you to use Web applications for mobile devices with an online connection to SAP BW.

Business Explorer Query Designer (BEx Query Designer)
BEx Query Designer is a tool used to define queries based on selected characteristics and key figures (InfoObjects) or reusable structures of an InfoProvider. In BEx Query Designer, you can parameterize queries by defining variables for characteristic values, hierarchies, hierarchy nodes, texts, or formulas. You can limit and refine the selection of InfoObjects by doing the following:

- Limiting characteristics and key figures to characteristic values, characteristic value intervals, and hierarchy nodes
- Defining calculated and limited key figures for reuse
- Defining structures for reuse

- Defining exceptions
- Defining conditions
- Defining exception cells

All queries defined in BEx Query Designer can also be used for OLAP reporting and for flat reporting.

Business Explorer Web Application (BEx Web Application)
Web-based application in Business Explorer for data analysis, reporting, and analytical applications on the Web. You can format and display your data in various ways in BEx Web Application Designer with a series of Web items (tables, filters, charts, maps, documents, and so on). In this manner, you can create Web applications (such as BI cockpits) individually and access them over the Internet or via an enterprise portal.

Business Explorer Web Application Designer (BEx Web Application Designer)
Desktop application for creating Web sites with SAP BW content. With the BEx Web Application Designer, you can place queries and HTML documents on an intranet, or on the Internet. The BEx Web Application Designer allows you to create an HTML page that contains BW-specific content such as tables, charts, and maps. Such HTML pages serve as the basis for Web applications with complex interaction, such as BI cockpits. You can save Web applications as a URL and then access them over an intranet or from mobile end devices. You can also save Web applications as an iView and integrate them into an enterprise portal.

Business Explorer Web Application Wizard (BEx Web Application Wizard)
An assistant that supports you in the creation of Web pages with SAP BW-specific content. This wizard enables you to use a simplified design procedure with an automated, step-by-step sequence. The BEx Web Application Wizard is integrated into the Web Application Designer.

Business Intelligence Cockpit (BI cockpit)
Synonyms: Web cockpit and information cockpit

Web-based switchboard with business intelligence content. Similar to a cockpit in an airplane, the BI cockpit displays an overview of all relevant business data to a company's management. With the Business Explorer Web Application Designer, you can create individual BI cockpits that display the relevant data in tables, charts, or maps. You can recognize critical data that has exceeded a threshold at a glance with the alert monitor, which is integrated into the BI cockpit. You can also insert additional data, such as documents, sketches, or hyperlinks, into the business data. BI cockpits offer the following options:

- Data can be collected from various data sources and displayed in various ways (tables, charts, maps, and so on).
- Structured (BI content) and unstructured (documents and so on) information supplement each other

- Personalized access: Parameters are automatically filled with user-specific values (references to the cost center, region, and so on)
- Role-specific variations: various BI cockpits for various roles

You can get a quick overview of various business news much like you would when reading the front page of a newspaper. You can then perform a detailed query with easy-to-use navigation elements such as hyperlinks, drop-down boxes, buttons, and so on.

Business Intelligence Systems (BIS)
Business Intelligence Systems are a family of IT systems tailored to meet the requirements of a specific user group: knowledge workers. Both observers of the IT industry and analysts differentiate between operating systems and business intelligence systems:

Operating systems

- Operative system help automates routines and makes tasks predictable.
- They are characterized by a multitude of small transactions whose effects are normally limited and that convert data into a format that can be processed by a computer.
- Business Intelligence systems
- Business intelligence systems help research, analyze, and present information.
- They typically involve a relatively small number of queries that are often comprehensive, or that have can have significant ramifications.
- The type of queries that might arise in the future cannot be predicted. Such systems always involve mining information from the system.

Characteristic
- Creating a characteristic InfoObject in the InfoObject tree:

  Initial access: **AWB** · **Modeling** · **InfoObjects** · Select **InfoArea** · Select **InfoObjectCatalog** of type characteristic. Select **Create InfoObject** in the context menu of the InfoObjectCatalog
- Maintenance of characteristics: Transactions RSD1 through RSD5

Type of InfoObject. Organization term, like company code, product, customer group, fiscal year, period, or region. Characteristic InfoObjects (such as customer or item) are reference objects. They are used to describe, select, and evaluate key figures. In addition, characteristic can carry master data (attributes, texts, and hierarchies) as master data tables:

- Attributes
- Texts
- Hierarchies

Characteristics indicate the classification options of a data set. In general, an InfoCube contains only a subset of the characteristic values from the master data table. The master data comprises the permitted values of a characteristic, the characteristic values. Characteristic values are discrete descriptions. For example, the "region" characteristic has the following properties:

- North
- Central
- South

Characteristics that carry master data can also be used as an InfoSource with direct update for loading master data. (Exception: Reference characteristics, unit InfoObjects, and characteristic 0SOURSYSTEM). Note the following special characteristics:

- Units (0CURRENCY (currency key) and 0UNIT (quantity unit), for example)
- Time characteristics (0CALYEAR (calendar year), for example)
- Technical characteristics (0REQUID (request ID), for example)

see also: Reference characteristic

Chart
Web item that refers to the data of a query view to create a diagram for a Web application. You can select from a variety of display options for the diagram. You can also navigate in interactive charts and analyze the data displayed in them.

Cleansing
Cleaning data before posting, checking data for plausibility before posting, or suppressing records with errors.

You can use transfer rules and update rules to homogenize and harmonize data from the source systems in terms of data structure and semantics before posting it to the data targets. You can filter out, cleanse, or correct erroneous information.

Collective Process
In process chain maintenance, a collective process enables you to combine several process strands into one, which makes multiple scheduling of the actual application process unnecessary. Process chain maintenance makes the following collective processes available:

- **And process (last):** The application process starts only after successful triggers of all events of the preceding processes, including the last of the events for which it waited.
- **Or Process (every):** The application process starts every time an event of the preceding process is triggered successfully.
- **Exor Process (first):** The application process starts only when the first event of the preceding process has been triggered successfully.

Common Warehouse Metamodel (CWM)
CWM is a standard recognized by the Object Management Group (OMG): it describes the exchange of metadata in the following areas:

- Data warehousing
- Business intelligence
- Knowledge management
- Portal technologies

CWM uses:

- UML to model metadata
- MOF to access metadata
- XMI to exchange metadata

You can find the specifications for CWM Version 1.0 at *www.omg.org*.

Communications Structure
The communications structure is independent of the source system and depicts the structure of an InfoSource. It contains all the InfoObjects that belong to an InfoSource. Data is updated into InfoCubes from this structure. The system always accesses the active, saved version of the communications structure.

An InfoSource with direct update always contains one communications structure for attributes and one for texts. Both are automatically generated by the system as an InfoSource during the creation of a characteristic. A communications structure for hierarchies is generated only if you select "PSA" as the transfer method.

The technical properties (length and type, for example) of the fields in the communications structure correspond to the InfoObjects of SAP Business Information Warehouse.

Component Hierarchy

- **In the SAP source system:** The component hierarchy is an element of the SAP source system Business Content that is imported with the plug-in. You can also maintain the hierarchy manually. The hierarchy helps organize DataSources. Modify component hierarchy:
  - Transaction RSA8
  - Initial access: **Transaction SBIW • Postprocessing of DataSources • Modify Component Hierarchy**
- **In the SAP BW system:** The component hierarchy is also an element of SAP BW – Business Content; you can maintain it manually here. It is advantageous to organize the InfoSource tree and PSA tables in the PSA tree.

Compounding
You will frequently need to compound characteristic values to enable the unambiguous assignment of characteristic values. Compounding is implemented in the maintenance of characteristic InfoObjects. You can use multiple characteristics as compounded characteristics. In general, you should use as few compounded characteristics as possible to avoid a negative affect on performance (→ compounded characteristics are elements of the primary key of the corresponding SID and mas-

ter data tables). Example: Cost center 100 in controlling area 1000 is purchasing and is sales in controlling area 2000: unambiguous evaluation is impossible. Compounding the cost center to the controlling area guarantees no ambiguity.

Condenser
A program that compresses the contents of an InfoCube fact table.

Control Query
An auxiliary query executed in the Web template before the queries whose results are used to parameterize the Web template.

CO-PA Updating
Transfer of account assignment data from Contract Accounts Receivable and Payable (FI-CA) into Profitability Analysis (CO-PA).

Crystal Enterprise
Server component for executing reports, scheduling reports, caching reports, and outputting reports to the Web. Content and user administration occur over the SAP BW server in the context of integration.

Crystal Report
BW object type. A report definition created with Crystal Reports Designer and stored in SAP BW. Several queries can be embedded in a Crystal Report (similar to an Excel workbook). A Crystal Report does not contain any current data.

Crystal Reports Designer
Design component to create a Crystal Report; it contains the layout (report definition).

CWM
see: Common Warehouse Metamodel

Data Dictionary (DDIC)
▶ Transaction SE11

The (ABAP) Data Dictionary enables central description and management of all the data definitions used in the system. The DDIC is completely integrated into the ABAP Workbench. The DDIC supports the definition of user-defined types (data elements, structures, and table types). You can also define the structure of database objects (tables, indices, and views) in the DDIC. You can use this definition for automatic creation of the objects in the database.

Data Manager
Part of the OLAP processor: it executes the database accesses that result from the definition of a query. Part of warehouse management: it writes data to the database.

Data Mart Interface
The data mart interface enables the updating of data from one data target into an additional data target. It allows you to update within an SAP BW system (Myself Data Mart/Myself System) and among multiple BW systems. If you use several BW systems, the system that delivers the data is called the source BW; the receiving system is called the target BW. Individual BWs in such a landscape are called data marts.

A transfer of data from one data target into another requires an export DataSource derived from the structure of the source data target. If the source data target is an ODS object, the export DataSource is automatically generated when you activate a newly created ODS object (which differs from the case with a BasicCube).

Data Marts
see: Data Mart Interface

Data Provider
An object that delivers data for one or more Web items. A data provider reflects the navigational status of a query at a specific point in time. The star view of a data provider corresponds to a query view. Navigation through the data or parameterization of the call can modify the state of a data provider.

Data Quality
Quality of data in terms of its usefulness for reporting and analysis. *See also:* Cleansing

Data Staging
Formatting process for retrieving data in SAP BW.

Data Warehouse (DWH)
A DWH is a system that stores data that is relevant to decisions made by a company. The functions of a data warehouse are to combine data from sources within a firm and outside of it, to cleanse the data, to consolidate the data, and to make it available consistently with analysis, reporting, and evaluation tools. The knowledge gained in this manner creates the foundation for decision-making that applies to the control of a company. A data warehouse is therefore a system primarily used to support enterprise control.

The integration of OLAP tools in a DWH system is not mandatory. Nevertheless, manufacturers currently offer increasingly more DWH systems with integrated OLAP tools. Such DWH systems are often called OLAP systems or DWH solutions. Accordingly, SAP BW is a DWH solution.

Database Shared Library
see: DB Connect

DataSource
Comprises a quantity of fields in SAP Business Information Warehouse offered in a flat structure, the extract structure, to transfer data. It also describes the properties of the corresponding extractor in terms of transferring data into SAP Business Information Warehouse.

A DataSource describes a business unit of master data (material master data, for example) and transaction data (sales data, for example). From the viewpoint of the source system, metainformation (fields and field descriptions of the master and transaction data and programs) belongs to each DataSource; the metainformation describes how the extraction is executed. This information is specific to each source system: a DataSource is dependent on the source system. In SAP source systems, the DataSource information is stored in tables ROOSOURCE and RODELTAM; in SAP BW systems, it is stored in table RSOLTPSOURCE. From a technical point of view, a DataSource distinguishes two types of field structures:

- Extract structure
- Transfer structure

Note the following types of DataSources:

- DataSources for transaction data
- DataSources for master data attributes
- DataSources for master data hierarchies

The definition of generic DataSources enables you to extract data from any DDIC tables and view, SAP queries and InfoSets, or function modules from SAP source systems. You can therefore extract data from SAP source systems that is not extracted by BCT DataSources (Transaction RSO2). You cannot extract data for external hierarchies with generic DataSources.

Data Granularity
Data granularity describes the level of detail of data. Very detailed data has a low granularity; increasing aggregation produces a higher granularity. Granularity affects disk space, the quantity of information, and read performance. In SAP BW, detailed data for reporting is stored in ODS objects; aggregated data is stored in BasicCubes or aggregates.

Data Requirement
Describes the requirement set on the source system by the scheduler, the quantity of data and information generated in SAP BW and the source system because of the requirement, and the loading procedure.

Data Quality
see: Data Quality

Data Target
A data target is a BW object into which data can be loaded: it is a physical object. These objects include BasicCubes, ODS objects, and InfoObjects (characteristics

with attributes, texts, or hierarchies). Note the distinction between pure data targets for which queries cannot be created or executed, and data targets for which queries can be defined. The latter are also called InfoProviders. A data target is a physical object that is relevant during the modeling of the BW data model and when loading the data. Data targets can be the following:

- BasicCubes
- ODS objects
- Characteristic InfoObjects

DB Connect
Enables the connection to various (external) relational database systems and the transfer of data from tables or views from the database system into the SAP Business Information Warehouse.

SAP DB MultiConnect is used to create a connection to the database management system (DBMS) of the external database. Reading metadata and the original data makes it easy to generate the required structures in SAP BW and to load the data. The precondition is that SAP supports the DBMS involved. You can then use DataSources to make the data known to SAP BW and to extract it. SAP supports the following DBMS:

- SAP DB
- Informix
- Microsoft SQL Server
- Oracle
- IBM DB2 390//400/UDB

In addition, you must also install the SAP-specific part of the Database Shared Library (DBSL) interface on the SAP BW application server for each source DBMS.

DBSL (Database Shared Library)
see: DB Connect

DDIC
see: Data Dictionary

Decision-Support System (DSS)
Development of decision-support systems began in the 1970s: Managers wanted query and analysis instruments that were based on flexible database systems and allowed them to perform what-if scenarios and ad-hoc analyses. Three main reasons contributed to the failure of this DSS design:

1. The DSS offered at the time used complex languages and inflexible model structures; they required a great deal of effort to learn and had prohibitively high start-up costs.
2. To justify the enormous investments in the DSS infrastructure and the high cost of IT specialists, increasingly more lists and reports were created.

3. The sheer quantity and unmanageability of the reports and lists made it impossible to make any reasonable management decisions.
4. It became apparent that endless lists of numbers for the controller did not determine the success of an enterprise. Success depended on the consistent implementation of strategic goals, coupled with quick decisions.

Delta Process
Extractor feature. It specifies how the data is to be transferred. As a DataSource attribute, it specifies how the DataSource data is to be transmitted to the data target. The user can determine, for example, with which data targets a DataSource is compatible, how the data is to be updated, and how serialization is to take place.

Delta Queue
Data storage in the source system of a BW system. Data records are automatically written to the delta queue in the source system with a posting procedure, or are written after a data request from BW via extraction with a function module. The data is transferred to SAP BW during a delta requirement of the BW scheduler.

Delta Update
A delta update requests that data has been created since the last update. It fills the corresponding data targets with the (new) data. Before you can request a delta update, you must initialize the data process. A delta update is independent of the DataSource. In SAP source systems, the DataSource properties are stored in tables ROOSOURCE and RODELTAM; in SAP BW systems, the DataSource properties are stored in the table RSOLTPSOURCE.

DIM ID
see: Dimension Identification

Dimension
A dimension is the grouping of logically related characteristics into one generic term. A total of 248 characteristics can be combined within one dimension. Technically, a dimension consists of a BasicCube from a dimension table (if it is not a line item dimension, SID tables, and master data tables). During the definition of an InfoCube, characteristics are grouped into dimensions in order to store them in a table of the star schema (dimension table). *See also*: Line Item Dimension

Dimension Identification (DIM ID)
The relationship between a fact table and its dimension tables to a BasicCube is created with a system-generated INT4 key, or DIM ID. During the loading of transaction data into the BasicCube, DIM ID values are assigned unambiguously: each DIM ID value is explicitly assigned to a combination of SID values of the various characteristics.

Dimension Table
see: BasicCube

Drilldown
Hierarchies can be defined for every dimension. The hierarchies can contain multiple levels. The higher the hierarchy level is, the higher the aggregation level of the displayed data. The deeper a user drills down into the hierarchy, the more detailed the information becomes. Drilldown can occur within a dimension (by moving in the product hierarchy from main product groups to product groups, and then to individual products), or by inserting characteristics from other dimensions (*see also*: Hierarchy).

DSS
see: Decision Support System

DWH
see: Data Warehouse

DWH Systems
see: Data Warehouse

EIS
see: Executive Information System

Elementary Test
Component of a test that cannot be split up into subtests. An elementary test checks the consistency of logical objects that belong together.

Error Handling
You can use the **Error Handling** function on the **Update Parameters** tab in the InfoPackage of the scheduler when loading data with the PSA table in order to control the behavior of SAP BW when data records with errors appear. You then have the following options:

- No posting and no reporting (default)
- Posting of valid records and no reporting (request is red)
- Posting of valid records and reporting is possible (request is green)

You can also determine after how many error records the loading process aborts. If you do not make any entries here, the loading process aborts when the first error occurs.

The request is considered an error when the number of received records does not agree with the number of posted records (key figure: "Aggregation not allowed").

E Table:
see: BasicCube

ETL Process
An ETL process consists of the following subprocesses:

- Extraction of data from a source system
- Transformation of the data (including cleansing and data quality assurance)
- Loading the data into the BW system

Event
A signal to background control that a specific state in the SAP system has been reached. Background control then starts all the processes waiting for the event.

Event Collector
An event collector is a set of several, independent, and successfully completed events to which background processing is to react. The event collector corresponds to the "And" process of process chain maintenance. If an application process is scheduled with a event collector, it starts when all the events of the preceding processes have been triggered successfully.

Executive Information System (EIS)
After the era of controllers and the decision-support systems of the 1970s, the evolution of planning systems took an entirely new path in the 1980s. Instead of automatic decision generators or decision-support systems operated by expensive specialists, developers decided to focus on what they could actually accomplish.

1. Upper management would be supported by Executive Information Systems (EIS).
2. If a decision-maker needed information, it was to be available at the push of a button.
3. Development did not want to be limited to a company's own data, but, to integrate external data instead.

However, the EIS approach failed technologically. It was too expensive and did not offer optimal performance. The continuing weaknesses of EIS tools, especially regarding the integration of external data) and a lack of acceptance among upper management also contributed to the failure of this approach. Instead, divisional solutions came into being, such as marketing, sales, and financial, and product information systems.

Export DataSource
see: Data Mart Interface

eXtensible Markup Language
see: XML

External Hierarchies
In SAP BW, the term "external hierarchy" is understood as presentation hierarchies that store the properties of a characteristic for structuring in hierarchy tables. In other words, they are triggered by the attributes and texts of a characteristic Info-

Object and can thus be maintained independently of the attributes and texts of the characteristic InfoObject. When the **With Hierarchy** flag is set, you can also create hierarchies for a characteristic (not reference characteristics) within SAP BW and load them from the SAP source system or with flat files into SAP BW.

Maintenance of hierarchies for a characteristic:

- Transaction RSH1
- Initial access: **AWB** • **Modeling** • **InfoObjects** • Select **InfoArea** • Select **Create Hierarchy** in the context menu of the selected characteristic InfoObject

  Existing hierarchies for a characteristic are displayed in the InfoObject tree beneath this characteristic and can be edited from the corresponding context menu.

Properties of external hierarchies:

- **Version-independence**
  External hierarchies can be used in various versions. Version-dependent hierarchies can be used for planning and other reporting tasks similar to simulation. In other words, hierarchy versions can be compared with each other in a query.
- **Time-dependence**
  Note the following distinctions related to time-dependence:
  - **Time-dependent whole hierarchy:** The time-dependence relates to the hierarchy root and is thus transferred to all nodes of the hierarchy. Depending on the key data chosen in the query, you can use various hierarchies.
  - **Time-dependent hierarchy structure:** The time-dependency refers to the nodes of the hierarchy. Here you can determine the time period of the nodes for which the hierarchy should stand at the indicated location.
- **Hierarchy interval**
  You can append characteristic properties as intervals beneath a hierarchy node. For example, instead of appending the cost element properties to material costs individually in a cost element hierarchy, you can specify cost element properties as cost elements 100 through 1000.
- **Plus/minus sign reversal for nodes**
  You can use this function to reverse the plus or minus sign of values assigned in a hierarchy node.

External System
An external, non-SAP data source for a BW system used to transfer data and metadata with staging BAPIs. External systems are non-SAP systems (including SAP R/3 system and SAP R/3 systems with a release level lower than 3.1I) that make data available to SAP BW and thus serve it as a source system. The extraction, transformation, and load of this data can occur with staging BAPIs and third-party tools.

Extractor
A program that fills the extract structure of a DataSource with data from the data stored in the SAP source system. Extractors are imported into the SAP source sys-

tem with the DataSources as a plug-in. An extractor is a program that is used for the following purposes:

- To make metadata from an SAP source system available with the extract structure of a DataSource
- To process data requests
- To perform the extraction

Extract Structure

- Transaction in the source system: SBIW

In the extract structure, the data of a DataSource is made available in the source system. The extract structure contains all the fields of the SAP source system that the extractors make available in the source system for the data-loading process. You can define, edit, and extend the extract structures of DataSources in the source system. The extract structure contains the number of fields that are offered by the extractor in the source system for the data-loading process in SAP BW.

F Table:
see: BasicCube

Fact Table
A table in the middle of the star schema of an InfoCube. It contains the key fields of the dimension table and the key figures of the InfoCube. The key is built with reference to the entries of the dimensions of the InfoCube. Together with the dimension tables assigned to it, the fact table builds the InfoCube for transaction data (*see also*: BasicCube and InfoCube).

Filter (QD)
A Web item that displays the filter values for a query view generated by navigation in a Web application and enables the selection of individual values.

The data container includes a column for a filter flag. You can use this flag to have the data container use several graphic proxies, but access different data sets. This feature makes the creation of a specific data container for every graphic proxy superfluous.

Flat File
Data can be imported into SAP BW with a file interface. Two data formats are supported as source files for SAP BW:

- **ASCII (American Standard Code for Information Interchange)**
  Files with fixed field lengths
- **CSV (Comma Separated Variables)**
  Files with variable length: users can define the separator (Transaction RSCUSTV1)

You can use flat files to reduce the number of problems involved with interfaces; however, you must then maintain the metadata (the transfer structure, for example) manually in SAP BW.

Formatted Reporting

Design for reports with master data, ODS objects, and multidimensional InfoProviders. You can use formatted reporting to make data available for interactive analyses and in formatted print layouts. Formatted reporting is based on the queries defined in the BEx Analyzer. Formatted reporting uses Crystal Reports from Crystal Decision, which is integrated into SAP BW.

Formatted reporting contains all the elements of formatting reports: fonts, font sizes, colors, graphics, and styles. It enables pixel-exact assignment of reporting elements without being limited to a tabular display. It focuses on form-based reports and print output. No analytical functionality: Options for interaction are considered when the report is designed.

Full Update

A full update requests all the data that corresponds to the selection criteria set in **Scheduler • InfoPackage**. Unlike a delta update, every DataSource here supports a full update.

Generation Template

A template from which a program is generated. A generation template is used when the desired program cannot be written generically and therefore must be generated anew and tailored for each new situation.

Granularity

The fineness or level of detail of data.

Hierarchy

A hierarchy usually means an array of objects related to each other. In this sense, SAP BW has hierarchies in the dimension, attribute, and hierarchy tables. In DWH terminology, the term hierarchy is closely related to the term drilldown (→ predefined drilldown path) (*see also:* External Hierarchies).

Hierarchy Attribute

Attribute that mirrors the properties of the entire hierarchy. The level table type is an example: it indicates the form of the level table.

Homogenization

see: Cleansing

IDoc (Intermediate Document)

A (data) IDoc is a data contained for the exchange of data among SAP systems, non-SAP systems, and external systems. It uses ALE technology. An IDoc consists of the following components:

- **Header record**
  The header contains information on the sender, recipient, and the type of message and IDoc.
- **Connected data segments**
  Every data segment contains a standard header that consists of a sequential segment number and a description of the segment type, and a 1000 byte field list that describes the data of the segment.
- **Status records**
  Status records describe the previous processing steps of the IDoc.

These IDocs are used to load data into the SAP BW system if transfer method PSA was selected during the maintenance of the transfer method.

InfoArea

InfoAreas help to organize metaobjects in SAP BW. They are the highest organization criterion of InfoProviders and InfoObjects in SAP BW. You can use InfoObjectCatalogs to assign InfoObjects a data target property; you can also sign them to various InfoAreas.

Every data target is assigned to an InfoArea. The Administrator Workbench (AWB) then displays this hierarchy. The hierarchy organized the objects in appropriate trees:

- InfoProvider tree
- InfoObject tree

Every InfoProvider must be assigned to exactly one InfoArea in the InfoProvider. You can assign InfoObjects to various InfoAreas in the InfoObject tree with InfoObjectCatalogs. As with other SAP BW objects, you define InfoAreas with a technical name and a description, and create them within the InfoProvider tree or InfoObject tree.

InfoCube

- Creating an InfoCube in an InfoProvider tree:
  Initial access: **AWB** • **Modeling** • **InfoProvider** • Select **InfoArea** • Select **Create InfoCube** in the context menu of the InfoArea.
- Editing InfoCubes: Transaction RSDCUBE

InfoCubes are the central objects in SAP BW; multidimensional analyses and reports are based on InfoCubes. From a reporting viewpoint (the viewpoint of the end user of reporting), an InfoCube describes a closed data set of a business report. Queries are defined and executed on an InfoCube. The data set can be evaluated with BEx Query. InfoCubes can function as data targets and InfoProviders.

An InfoCube is a set of relational tables placed together according to the star schema: a large fact table in the center, surrounded by several dimension tables. SAP BW distinguishes among the following types of InfoCubes:

- BasicCube
- General RemoteCube
- SAP RemoteCube
- Virtual InfoCube with services

InfoObject

- Creating an InfoObject in the InfoObject tree:

  Initial access: **AWB** · **Modeling** · **InfoObjects** · Select **InfoArea** · Select **InfoObjectCatalog** · Select **Create InfoObject** in the context menu of the InfoObjectcatalog.
- Maintenance of InfoObjects: Transactions RSD1 through RSD5

In SAP BW, business evaluation objects (customers, revenue, and so on) are called InfoObjects. They are therefore the smallest information module (field) that can be identified unambiguously with their technical name. InfoObjects are divided into characteristics, key figures, units, time characteristics, and technical characteristics (such as a request number, for example).

As a component of the Metadata Repository, InfoObjects carry the technical and user information of the master and transaction data in SAP BW. They are used throughout the system to build tables and structures, which allows SAP BW to map the information in a structured form. InfoObjects are subdivided into the following classes, according to their function and task:

- **Key figure (revenue and quantity, for example)**
  Key figure InfoObjects supply the values that are to be evaluated with characteristics and characteristic combinations.
- **Characteristic (material, customer, and source system ID, for example)**
  Characteristic InfoObjects are business reference objects used to evaluate the key figures.
- **Time characteristic (calendar day or month, for example)**
  Time characteristics build the reference framework for many data analyses and evaluations. These characteristics are delivered with BCT; you can also define you own time characteristics.
  - **Unit (currency key or quantity unit, for example)**
    InfoObjects can be entered with the key figures to enable linkage between the values of the key figures and the related units in the evaluations.
  - **Technical characteristic**
    These characteristics have an organizational meaning in SAP BW. For example, technical characteristic "0REQUID" supplies the numbers assigned by the system during the loading of requests. Technical characteristic "0CHNGID" supplies the numbers assigned during aggregate change runs.

InfoObjectCatalog

- Creating an InfoObjectCatalog in the InfoObject tree:

  Initial access: **AWB · Modeling · InfoObject** · Select **InfoArea** · Select **Create InfoObjectCatalog** in the context menu of the InfoArea.

- Editing InfoObjectCatalogs:Transaction RSDIOBC

An InfoObjectCatalog is a grouping of InfoObjects according to application-specific viewpoints. It is used solely for organizational purposes and not for any kind of assessment.

An InfoObjectCatalog is assigned to an InfoArea in the InfoObject tree. The type of InfoObjectCatalog is either "characteristic" or "key figure" and therefore contains a characteristic or key figure, depending on its type.

InfoPackage

An InfoPackage describes which data is to be requested from a source system with a DataSource. The data can be selected with selection parameters, such as only from controlling area 001 in period 10.1997. An InfoPackage can request the following types of data:

- Transaction data
- Attributes of master data
- Hierarchies of master data
- Master data texts

You can define several InfoPackages for a DataSource. You can define several InfoPackages for a DataSource.

- Creating an InfoPackage in the InfoObject tree:

  Initial access: **AWB · Modeling · InfoSources** · Select **InfoSource** · Select **Source System** · Select **Create InfoPackage** (and schedule in the scheduler) in the context menu of the source system)

  Existing InfoPackages are displayed in the InfoSource tree beneath the source system and can be edited using the context menu.

InfoPackage Group

Combines logically related InfoPackages.

InfoProvider

An InfoProvider is an SAP BW object you can use to create and execute queries. InfoProviders include objects that physically contain data, for example, data targets like InfoCubes, ODS objects, and InfoObjects (characteristics with attributes, texts, or hierarchies). They also include objects that do not represent physical data storage: RemoteCubes, SAP RemoteCubes, and MultiProviders. InfoProviders are objects or views relevant to reporting. InfoProviders can include the following:

- InfoCubes (BasicCubes and virtual cubes)
- ODS objects

- Characteristic InfoObjects (with attributes or texts)
- InfoSets
- MultiProviders

Information Cockpit
see: Business Intelligence Cockpit

InfoSet

- Creating an InfoSet in an InfoProvider tree:

  Initial access: **AWB** • **Modeling** • **InfoProvider** • Select **InfoArea** • Select **Create InfoSet** in the context menu of the InfoArea.
- Maintenance of InfoSets: Transaction RSISET

An InfoSet is an InfoProvider that does not contain any data. It consists of a query definition that can usually be read in the BW system with joins of ODS objects or characteristic InfoObjects (with attributes or texts) at the runtime of data analysis. Unlike a traditional InfoSet, this view of the data is specific to SAP BW.

Reporting on master data is a possible use of InfoSets. InfoSets are created and modified in the InfoSet Builder. Based on InfoSets, you can define reports with the Query Designer.

InfoSet Builder
A tool to create and modify InfoSets with SAP BW repository objects (InfoObjects with master data and ODS objects).

InfoSet Query (ISQ)
Corresponds to the InfoSet query (BC-SRV-QUE) familiar in SAP R/3 Basis. The ISQ is a tool used to create lists. The data to be evaluated is combined in InfoSets. SAP List Viewer is the output medium for InfoSet Query.

InfoSource

- Creating an InfoSource in the InfoSources tree:

  Initial access: **AWB** • **Modeling** • **InfoSources** • Select **Create InfoSource** in the context menu of an application component • Select **InfoSource type**

A set of all the data available on a business event or a type of business events (such as cost center accounting, for example). An InfoSource is a set of logically related InfoObjects that contain all the information available on a business process (such as cost center accounting, for example). InfoSources can include transaction data and master data (attributes, texts, and hierarchies).

The structure that stores InfoSources is called the communications structure. Unlike the transfer structure, the communications structure is independent of the source system. You can assign several DataSources to an InfoSource. However, you can assign a DataSource to only one InfoSource within a source system. Note the following two types of InfoSources:

- **InfoSource with direct update**
  With this type of InfoSource, the master data (attributes and texts) of a characteristic InfoObject is updated directly (one to one with a communications structure) to the corresponding master data tables (exception: a transfer routine is created for a characteristic used as an InfoSource with direct update). The following applies to hierarchies: If you select transfer method "PSA," the system generates a communications structure used to load the data into the corresponding hierarchy tables. If you select transfer method "IDoc," the system does not generate a communications structure: the data is updated directly with the transfer structure. In this case, you also cannot define any (local) transfer rules. (With hierarchies, transfer method "PSA" is independent of DataSources: see table ROOSOURCE.) InfoSources with direct update cannot be used for transaction data.
- **InfoSource with flexible update**
  With this type of InfoSource, you can use update rules to load attribute, text, and transaction data into data targets (BasicCubes, ODS objects, and characteristic InfoObject) with a communications structure. You cannot update hierarchies flexibly.

InfoSpoke
Object for data export within Open Hub Services. The following are defined in the InfoSpoke:

- The open hub data source from which the data is extracted
- The extraction mode in which the data is delivered
- The open hub destination into which the data is delivered

Intermediate Document
see: IDoc

Key Figure
- Creating a key figure InfoObject in the InfoObject tree:
  Initial access: **AWB** · **Modeling** · **InfoObjects** · Select **InfoArea** · Select **InfoObjectCatalog of key figure type** · Select **Create InfoObject** in the context menu of the InfoObjectcatalog.
- Maintenance of key figures: Transactions RSD1 through RSD5

Values or quantities. In addition to the key figures stored in the database, you can also define calculated (derived) key figures during query definition in Business Explorer. You can calculate such key figures with a formula from the key figures of the InfoCube.

Examples for key figures:

- Revenue
- Fixed costs
- Sales quantity
- Number of employees

Examples for derived key figures:

- Revenue per employee
- Deviation in percent
- Contribution margin

Key figure InfoObjects like revenue and quantity deliver the values to be evaluated with characteristics or combinations of characteristics. SAP BW differentiates among the following types of key figures:

- Amount
- Quantity
- Number
- Integer
- Date
- Time

If you select the amount of quantity type of key figure, you must also enter corresponding units: the key figured is linked to a unit InfoObject or to a fixed value for a unit.

- Key figure as cumulative value (= value that refers to a period of time)
  Values for this key figure must be posted in every time unit for which values are to be calculated for this key figure (revenue, for example).
- Key figure as non-cumulative value (= value that refers to a specific point in time)
  For non-cumulative values, values must be stored for only selected points in time. The values of the other points in time are calculated from the value in a specific point in time and the intermediary balance sheet changes (such as warehouse inventory). You have two options for defining non-cumulative values:
  - **Non-cumulative with balance sheet changes:** Definition of the non-cumulative values also requires a cumulative value as a key figure InfoObject, a balance sheet change, which agrees with the non-cumulative value to be defined in the definition of the type.
  - **Non-cumulative with acquisitions and retirements:** Definition of the non-cumulative value requires two cumulative values, "acquisition" and "retirement," which agree with the non-cumulative value to be defined in the definition of the type.
- Aggregation of Key Figures
  - **Standard Aggregation (SUM/Max/Min):** With standard aggregation, you set how the key is aggregated in the BasicCube in key figure maintenance. This setting plays a role with an ODS object only when you select "addition" (you do not choose "overwrite") as the update type in maintenance of the update rules.
  - **Exception aggregation (last value, first value, maximum, minimum, and so on):** With exception aggregation, which you set in key figure maintenance, you can perform more complex aggregations of key figures. Example: The "number of employees" key figure is total with the "cost center" character-

istic (→ Standard-Aggregation). In this case, you could also enter a time characteristic as a reference characteristic for exception aggregation "last value."

- **Reference key figure**
  You can create a key figure with a reference to another key figure (= reference key figure). You usually need a reference key figure for the elimination of inter-company sales.

Line Item
see: Line Item Dimension
see: Dimension

Line Item Dimension
Characteristics can be defined as line items, which means that no additional characteristics can be assigned to a dimension along with this characteristic. Such a dimension is called a line item dimension (= degenerate dimension). Unlike a typical dimension, a line item dimension does not receive a dimension table. The SID table of the line item is linked directly with the fact table here over a foreign–primary key relationship. This option is used if a characteristic, such as an order number, has a large quantity of values. Using this option can improve the performance of queries (*see also*: Dimension).

List of Conditions
Web item that lists the existing conditions with their states (active/not active/not applicable/not used) for a query view in a Web application.

List of Exceptions
Web item that lists the existing conditions with their states (active/not active) for a query view in a Web application.

Master Data ID (SID)
Internal key (type INT4) used for characteristics carrying master data to master data, especially for hierarchy nodes and for characteristic names.

Master data IDs and characteristic values are stored in a master data table (SID table). Information on time-independent and time-dependent master data stored in a P or Q table is stored once again in an X or Y table by using SIDs in place of the characteristic values.

MDX
Multidimensional expressions. Query language for queries on data stored in multidimensional cubes.

Metadata Repository
The Metadata Repository contains the various classes of metadata. This type of data storage and presentation results in a consistent and homogenous data model across all source system. The Metadata Repository comprises all metaobjects

(InfoCubes, InfoObjects, queries, and so on) in SAP BW and their relationships to each other.

- Transaction RSOR
- Initial access: **AWB • Metadata Repository**

Metadata

Metadata is data or information about data. Metadata describes the origin, history, and other aspects of the data. Metadata enables the effective use of the information stored in SAP BW for reporting and analysis. Note the following types of metadata:

- **Technical metadata**
  For example: the storage structure of the data, like the number format of a key figure
- **Business metadata and effective metadata**
  For example: the person responsible for data and the origin of the data

Mobile Application

A Web application on a mobile device with an online connection to the SAP BW system. Superordinate term of: PDA application and WAP application

MOLAP (Multidimensional OLAP)

Multidimensional online analytical processing. Multidimensional data storage in special data structures based on arrays or cubes. MOLAP is primarily used in comparison with or as an alternative to ROLAP (*see also*: OLAP).

MOLAP Aggregate

Aggregate of a MOLAP cube. Like the MOLAP cube itself, the aggregate in stored in MOLAP storage.

MOLAP Cube

A BasicCube whose data is physically stored in MOLAP storage. Superordinate term: MOLAP Storage

MOLAP Storage

see: MOLAP

Monitor

Monitoring tool of the Administrator Workbench. You can use the monitor to keep an eye on data requests and processing in SAP BW.

You can use the monitor to observe data requests and processing within the AWB.

- Transactions RSMON (monitoring) and RSMO (monitor)
- Initial access: **AWB • Monitoring**

Multidimensional Expressions
see: MDX

Multidimensional OLAP
see: MOLAP

Multidimensional Online Analytical Processing
see: MOLAP

MultiProviders
Initial access: **AWB** · **Modeling** · **InfoProvider** · Select **InfoArea** · In the context menu of the selected InfoArea, select **Create MultiProvider** and select the **InfoProvider**.

A MultiProvider is a special InfoProvider that merges data from several InfoProviders and makes the data available for reporting. The MultiProvider does not contain any data; its data comes exclusively from the InfoProviders upon which it is based. Like InfoProviders, MultiProviders are objects or views relevant to reporting. A MultiProvider can merge various combinations of InfoProviders:

- InfoCube
- ODS object
- Characteristic InfoObject (with attributes or texts)
- InfoSet

Myself Data Mart
see: Myself System

Myself System
A system connected to itself for data extraction over the data mart interface. Such a connection means that data from data targets can be updated to additional data targets (*see also*: Data Mart Interface).

Navigation
Analysis of InfoProvider data by displaying various views of a query's data or of a Web application. You can use various navigation functions (such as Set Filter Value, Insert Outline After) to generate various views of the data (query views) that are then presented in the results area of the query or in a Web application. Changing views is referred to as navigation.

Navigation Attribute
Attribute in which the query can be selected.

Node Attribute
An attribute at the node level. Every node of the hierarchy has this attribute, for example, date fields DATETO and DATEFROM, if the hierarchy structure is time-dependent.

Nodes
Objects that build a hierarchy. A node can have subnodes. Note the distinction between the following two types of nodes:

- Nodes that can be posted to
- Nodes that cannot be posted to

ODS Object
An operational data store (ODS) object stores consolidated and cleansed data (transaction or master data) at the document level. An ODS object contains key fields (characteristics) and data fields that can also be key figures and characteristics, which differs from a BasicCube.

An ODS object describes a consolidated data set from one or more InfoSources. You can evaluate the data set with a BEx query. An ODS object contains a key (such as a document number or item) and data fields that can also contain character fields (such as customer) as key figures. The data of an ODS object can be updated with a delta update into InfoCubes or additional ODS objects in the same system or across systems. Unlike multidimensional data storage with InfoCubes, the data of ODS objects is stored in flat database tables. Contrary to BasicCubes, ODS objects consist of three (flat)tables:

- **Activation queue (= initial table of ODS objects)**
  New data is stored in this table before it is activated. Its structure is similar to that of a PSA table: the key is built from the request, data package, and data record number. After all the requests in the activation queue have been successfully activated, they are deleted from the activation queue.
- **Table with the active data**
  This table stores the current state of the data. This table has a semantic key (such as order number or item) that the modeler can define. Reporting draws upon this table. If the connected data targets are supplied in the full update method of updating, the data targets are updated with the active data from this table.
- **Change log (= output table for connect data targets)**
  During an activation run, the modifications are stored in the change log, which contains all the complete (activation) history of the modifications because the contents of the change log are not automatically deleted. If the connected data targets are supplied from the ODS object in a delta process, the data targets are updated from the change log. The change log is a PSA table and can be maintained in the PSA tree of the AWB. The change log has a technical key derived from the request, data package, and data record number.

The new state of the data is written in parallel into the change log and into the table with the active data. Note the following types of ODS objects:

- **Standard ODS object**
  - Creating a standard ODS object:

  Initial access: **AWB** · **Modeling** · **InfoProvider** · Select **InfoArea** · Select **Create ODS Object** in the context menu of the selected InfoArea.

- Editing standard ODS objects: Transaction RSDODS
- Managing a standard ODS object:

Initial access: **AWB** • **Modeling** • **InfoProvider** • Select **InfoArea** • Select **Manage** in the context menu of the selected ODS object.

This object involves the ODS object (→ three tables) described above. As with BasicCubes, ODS objects are supplied with data from one or more InfoSources with update rules.

The update rules include rules that apply to BasicCubes and an additional option to overwrite data fields.

- **Selective deletion** (**Contents** tab): Similar to the situation with a BasicCube, you can make a selection to delete targeted data records that correspond to the selection criteria from the ODS object. Selective deletion affects only the table with the active data. In other words, only entries in this table are deleted.

If you use selective deletion to delete erroneous data records from the ODS object, you can replace the records with correct(ed) data records by using a repair request in the scheduler (→ **Scheduler** • **Maintain InfoPackage**).

- **Delete requests** (**Requests** tab): You can use this function to delete targeted requests that have been loaded into the ODS object if they have not yet been updated into the connected data targets. Note the following two initial situations:
- **Non-activated requests**: In this case, the requests are deleted only from the activation queue.
- **Activated requests**: In this case, the requests are deleted from the table with the active data and from the change log.
- **Rebuild requests** (**Rebuild** tab): You can use this function to recover previously deleted requests for an ODS object. The recovered requests are then stored once again in the activation queue. This function works only if the PSA table stored the requests.
- **Delete change log**: You can use this function to delete requests from the change log, requests that are no longer needed for updates or to rebuild the connected data targets. We recommend that you delete the change log requests if you do not need the change log at all.

Management: **Environment** • **Delete Change Log Data**

- **Transactional ODS Object**
  - Creating a transactional ODS object:

Initial access: **AWB** • **Modeling** • **InfoProvider** • Select **InfoArea** • Select **Create ODS Object** in the context menu of the selected InfoArea. Select ODS object under the **Type** settings • Select **Modify Type** in the context menu.

- Editing standard ODS objects: Transaction RSDODS

This type of ODS object has only the table with active data. Therefore, this ODS object cannot be linked to the staging process because neither the activation queue nor the change log are used. These ODS object types can be filled by

APIs and read with a BAPI. They help store data for external applications, such as SAP Strategic Enterprise Management (SAP SEM). Transactional ODS objects are not automatically available for reporting. You must first define an InfoSet with these ODS objects; you can then use the InfoSet to define and execute queries.

OLAP (Online Analytical Processing)
The core of this software technology is multidimensional retrieval of data. Multidimensionality allows the creation of very flexible query and analysis tools that then enable rapid, interactive, and flexible access to the relevant information.

- **ROLAP (Relational OLAP)**
  The task of the ROLAP engine is to format relational data (with the star schema) in a multidimensional structure to enable efficient access. SAP BW is an example of a ROLAP system.
- **MOLAP (Multidimensional OLAP)**
  Data is physically stored here in multidimensional structures (cell and array structures), so that further formatting of the analysis tools is no longer necessary. This approach requires rapid response times for queries and calculations. So far, MOLAP systems are less appropriate than ROLAP systems for large sets of data.

OLAP Reporting
Reporting based upon multidimensional data sources. OLAP reporting enables simultaneous analysis of multiple dimensions (such as time, location, product, and so on). The goal of OLAP reporting is the analysis of key figures, such as a revenue analysis of a specific product over a specific period. The business question is formulated in a query that contains key figures and characteristics; the query is required for analysis and a response to the question. The data displayed in the form of a table serves as the starting point for detailed analysis that can address many questions.

Several interaction options such as sorting, filtering, exchanging characteristics, and recalculating values enable the flexible navigation in the data at runtime. In SAP BW, the data in the Business Explorer can be analyzed in the following areas:

- In BEx analyzer in the form of queries
- In BEx Web Applications

Unlike table-based reporting, the number of columns is dynamic here. Data analysis is the primary concern. The layout, formatting, and printing of the reports is secondary.

Synonyms: analytical reporting and multidimensional reporting

OLAP (Online Transaction Processing)
The core of this software technology is the relational retrieval of data for processing and the documentation of business processes (billing and inventory management, for example). However, the required standardization (→ as a rule, the third standard form → ensures data consistency and referential integrity) makes the

queries increasingly more complex, because many tables must be read. (The traditional SAP R/3 system is an example of an OLTP system.)

OLAP Systems
see: Data Warehouse

OLAP Tools
see: Data Warehouse

Online Analytical Processing
see: OLAP

Online Transaction Processing
see: OLTP

Open Hub Service
A service that enables the sharing of data from an SAP BW system with non-SAP data marts, analytical applications, and other applications. The open hub service ensures the controlled distribution and consistency of data across several systems.

Operational Data Store Object
see: ODS Object

Original Source System
Source system from which newly created or modified objects are transported into another system, the target source system. In the context of a system landscape consisting of OLTP and BW systems, an original source system is an OLTP development system. The target source system is the OLTP system linked to the BW target system. To be able to transport objects specific to a source system (such as transfer structure), you must enter the logical system name for the source system into a mapping table in the BW target system before and after the transport.

Or Process
Collective process of process chain maintenance. When you use or process in process chain maintenance, the application process starts each time that an event of the preceding process was triggered successfully.

PDA Application
Web application on a PDA device with Pocket IE.

P Table
Master data table for time-independent master data. This table includes the following fields:

- The characteristic that carries master data itself
- The characteristics associated with this characteristic ("superordinate characteristics")
- All time-independent attributes

CHANGED (D: record to delete; I: insert record; space: no modification; modifications are evaluated only with activation)

OBJEVERS (A: active version; M: modified and therefore not the active version)

These fields build the key.

Persistent Staging Area (PSA)
The persistent staging area (PSA) represents the initial view into SAP BW architecture. The PSA consists of transparent database tables (PSA tables) that can be used for (temporary) storage of unmodified data from the source system. One PSA is created for each DataSource and source system. The basic structure of PSA tables corresponds to the transfer structure. To be precise, it consists of the following: key fields of the PSA + fields of the transfer structure. The key consists of the request, data package, and data record number. The system generates PSA tables (technical name: /BIC/B000*) for each DataSource at activation of the transfer rules only if you selected "PSA" as the transfer method in maintenance of the transfer rules.

You can select from the following posting types in the scheduler when loading data into data targets (characteristic InfoObject, BasicCube, and ODS object):

- **PSA followed by data target (by package)**
  This type of posting first extracts a data package of a request from the source system and writes it to the PSA table. Posting of the data to the data targets begins as soon as the data package has been completely transferred into the PSA table. Extraction of the next data package begins at the same time as the posting, so that extraction and posting are executed concurrently.
- **PSA followed by data targets in parallel (by package)**
  Parallel posting to the data targets begins at the same time as writing the data packages to the PSA table.
- **Only PSA followed by updating to the data targets**
  This type of posting first posts all the data packages of a request to the PSA table and then posts them to the data targets. Posting and extraction do not occur in parallel here.
- **Only PSA**
  This posting type enables you to store all the extracted data packages of a request in a PSA table without updating them to the data targets. You can trigger follow-up posting at a later time.
- **Only data target**
  The data packages of a request are posted directly to the data targets. The data packages are not stored temporarily in a PSA table.

Process
A procedure within or external to an SAP system. A process has a defined beginning and end.

Process Chain

▶ Maintenance of Process Chains: Transaction RSPC

A process chain is a series of processes that are scheduled in the background (= batch) and are waiting for an event. Some of the processes trigger their own event, which can then start other processes. You can use process chains for the following:

▶ To automate complex flows (like the loading process) in SAP BW with event-driven processing

▶ To display flows with the use of network graphics

▶ To control and monitor the running of the processes centrally

Process Instance

A property of a process. The process instance contains the most important information that the process might want to communicate to subsequent processes. During a loading process, for example, this information would be the name of the request. The instance is determined by the process itself at runtime. The logs for the process are stored beneath the process instance.

Process Type

The type of process, such as the load process. The process type determines the tasks that a process has and what properties it has in maintenance.

Process Variant

Name of the process. A process can have various variants. For example, with the loading process, the name of the InfoPackage represents the variant of the process. Users define a variant at scheduling.

PSA

see: Persistent Staging Area

PSA Table

see: Persistent Staging Area

Q Table

Master data table for time-dependent master data. In terms of its fields, the Q table corresponds to the P table.

Query

A combination of characteristics and key figures (InfoObjects) to analyze the data of an InfoProvider. You can use a query to combine characteristics and key figure InfoObjects in the query designer to analyze the data of an InfoProvider. A query always refers to one InfoProvider, but any number of queries can be defined for an InfoProvider.

A query is defined in BEx query designed by selecting InfoObjects or reusable structures of an InfoProvider and setting a view of the data (query view) by distributing filters, rows, columns, and free characteristics. You can save the defined starting view of the query in the query designer among your favorites or roles. You use the saved query view as the basis for data analysis and reporting in BEx analyzer, BEx Web applications, BEx mobile intelligence, or formatted reporting.

Query Designer
see: Business Explorer Query Designer

Query View
Saved navigational view of a query.

Record
In a relational database table: a set of related values. A record is stored in the relational database management system (DBMS) as a line.

Reference Characteristic
You can use reference characteristics to reuse defined characteristic InfoObjects. Reference characteristics deliver technical properties to another characteristic. You can maintain these properties only with a reference characteristic. Technical properties include master data tables (attributes, texts, and hierarchies), data type, length, number and type of compounded characteristics, lower case letters, and conversion routines (*see also*: Characteristic).

Referential Integrity
A check of referential integrity can occur only for transaction and master data updated flexibly (→ InfoSource with flexible update). The check determines the valid values of the InfoObject. The check occurs after filling the communications structure, but before application of the update rules. The check occurs against the SID table of a characteristic or against an ODS object highlighted in maintenance of a characteristic InfoObject. To be able to use the check for referential integrity, you must always select the option to post data, even if no master data for the data exists, in the Update table of the scheduler (Maintain InfoPackage). You must also flag the characteristic InfoObjects that are to be checked against SID tables and ODS objects in the Referential Integrity column in InfoSource maintenance.

Relational OLAP
see: ROLAP

Relational Online Analytical Processing
see: ROLAP

RemoteCube
An InfoCube whose transaction data is managed externally rather than in SAP Business Information Warehouse. Only the structure of the RemoteCube is defined in SAP BW. The data is read with a BAPI from another system for reporting.

Remote Function Call (RFC)
You can use RFC to transfer data reliably between SAP systems and programs that you have developed. RFC can be used to call a function module in another SAP system, BW system, a program you have developed, or within an SAP system. The data is transmitted with TCP/IP or X.400 as a byte stream. If the call is asynchronous, it is referred to as transactional RFC (tRFC).

Reporting Agent
A tool that you can use to schedule reporting functions in the background. You can execute the following functions:

- Evaluation of exceptions
- Printing of queries
- Precalculation of Web templates

Results Area
In Business Explorer Analyzer, the result area is the portion of the worksheet that shows the results of a query. The results area corresponds to the Web item table in Web applications.

Reusable Structure
A component of a query stored for reuse in an InfoCube. You define a query template when you want to use parts of a query definition in other queries. For example, you can save structures as query templates. Structures are freely defined evaluations that consist of combinations of characteristics and basic key figures (as calculated or limited key figures, for example) of the InfoCube. For instance, a structure can be a plan-actual comparison or a contribution margin scheme.

RFC
see: Remote Function Call

ROLAP
Relational Online Analytical Processing. The storage of multidimensional data in a relational database: in tables organized in a star schema. Opposite model: MOLAP (*see also:* OLAP).

SAP Exit
A type of processing for variables delivered with SAP BW Business Content. The variables are processed by automatic substitution in a default substitution path (SAP Exit).

SAP RemoteCube
Access to transaction data in other SAP systems, based on an InfoSource with flexible update. The objects in SAP BW that do not store data include: InfoSets, RemoteCubes, SAP RemoteCubes, virtual InfoCubes with services, and MultiProviders (*see also:* InfoProviders).

SAPI (Service API)
The (BW) SAPI is the interface imported with the plug-in. SAPI is used for communication and data exchange among SAP systems (SAP SEM, SAP CRM, SAP APO, and SAP R/3) and the SAP BW system, between XML files and the SAP BW system, and between SAP BW systems. The SAPI is based exclusively on SAP technology and is available for SAP system as of Basis Release 3.1I. SAP BW service API technology is used in various places within the architecture of SAP BW:

- To transfer data and metadata from SAP systems
- To transfer data between SAP BW data targets within an SAP BW system
- (data mart Myself interface) or into another SAP BW system (data mart interface)
- To transfer data from XML files

Scheduler
You use the scheduler to determine which data (transaction data, master data, texts, or hierarchies) is requested and updated from which InfoSource, DataSource, and source system at which point in time.

Scheduling Package
Logical combination of multiple reporting agent settings for background processing.

see: SAPI

SID
see: Surrogate Identification

SID Table
see: Master Data Tables

Source SAP Business Information Warehouse
see: Source SAP BW

Source SAP BW (Source SAP Business Information Warehouse
SAP Business Information Warehouse that serves as the source system for additional BW servers. Data Mart Interface

Source System
System available to SAP Business Information Warehouse for data extraction. Source systems are instances that deliver data to SAP BW.

- External Systems (Non-SAP Systems, SAP R/2 Systems, and SAP R/3 Systems <3,1I)
- SAP systems
- BW systems (data marts)
- Databases (DB connect)
- Flat files (CSV and ASCII files)

- Flat files for external market data (from Dun & Bradstreet (D&B), for example)
- XML file

Staging
The process of retrieving data in a data warehouse.

Staging BAPI
You can use staging BAPIs to transfer data (metadata, master data, and transaction data) from external systems in SAP BW (*see also*: BAPI).

Star Schema
The classic star schema is intended for relational database systems at the physical design level. A drawing of the start schema looks like a star in which multidimensional data structures are mapped in two types of tables (*see also* BasicCube):

1. **In a single fact table:** The table contains the key figures and a combined key with an element for each dimension.
2. **In dimension tables (one per dimension):** These tables are completely non-normalized and contain a composed primary key from all the attributes required for non-ambiguity, the hierarchical structure of the related dimension, and a level attribute that displays all the individual entries on affiliation for a hierarchy level.

Start Process
Defines the start of a process chain.

Surrogate Identification (SID)
SIDs are system-generated INT4 keys. An SID key is generated for each characteristic. This assignment is implemented in an SID table for each characteristic: the characteristic is the primary key of the SID table. The SID table is linked to the related master data tables (if present) with the characteristic key. If a characteristic is assigned to a BasicCube when it is created, the SID table of the characteristic is linked to the corresponding dimension table after activations of the BasicCube. SID values are generated during loading of master data or transaction data and written to the appropriate SID tables. For transaction data, the values are also written to the dimension tables to set up the DIM ID. Use of INT4 keys (SID and DIM ID keys) enables faster access to the data than long alphanumeric keys do. The SID technique in the SAP BW star schema also enables use of master data across BasicCubes.

Surrogate Index
A special SAP BW index of all key figures of a fact table. The surrogate index is created on a fact table in place of the primary index. Unlike the primary index, the surrogate index does not have a UNIQUE limitation.

Reporting is based on one-dimensional tables: analysis is limited to one dimension with its attributes. Contrary to OLAP reporting, you can assign columns however you want during the design of a query in tabular editing mode of BEx query designer. For example, you can place a characteristics column between two key figure columns. The column presentation is fixed and is set at the time of design.

Target BW

A BW system connected to another BW system as a source system and into which data can be loaded with export DataSources (*see also*: Data Mart Interface).

TCT

see: Technical Content

Technical Content (TCT)

TCT makes the required SAP BW objects and tools available for the use of SAP BW Statistics. SAP BW Statistics is a tool for the analysis and optimization of processes, such as access time to data with queries and loading times. The data of SAP BW Statistics is stored in SAP BW and is based on a MultiProvider that is founded on several SAP BW BasicCubes. TCT is transferred in the same manner as BCT.

To use SAP BW Statistics, you must activate it ahead of time for selected InfoProviders. (Initial access: **AWB · Tools · BW Statistics for InfoProviders**).

Temporal Join

A join that contains at least one time-dependent characteristic. The time dependencies are evaluated to determine the set of results. Each record of the set of results is assigned a time interval that is valid for that record (valid time interval).

Test

A check for the consistency of internal information with SAP BW objects. A repair is offered in some circumstances. A test consists of a series of elementary tests. To avoid performing unnecessary checks, you can select elementary tests individually. *Synonym:* Analysis

Test Package

A sequence of elementary tests as the result of a selection of specific tests or elementary tests. You can save a test package and schedule it for a later run.

Text

Texts (such as the description of a cost center) belong to master data in SAP BW, as do attributes and hierarchies. In maintenance of a characteristic Info Object (→ Master Data/Texts tab), you can determine whether the characteristic should have texts. If so, you must select at least one text: short, medium, and long text (20, 40, and 60 characters). You can also determine whether the texts are time- or language-dependent. Texts are stored in a master data table for texts related to the characteristic.

T-Logo Object

Logical transport object. A T-logo object consists of the total of several table entries that are transported together. Example: The T-logo object "InfoObject" consists of table entries of the InfoObject table, the characteristics table, the text table, and the basic characteristics table.

Traditional InfoSet
Corresponds to the InfoSet familiar in SAP R/3 Basis: Element of an SAP query. An InfoSet determines the tables or table fields to which a query refers. InfoSets are primarily created with table joins or logical databases.

Transaction BasicCube
Transaction BasicCubes are typically used with SAP Strategic Enterprise Management (SAP SEM). Data of such a BasicCube is accessed in a transactional manner: Data is written to the BasicCube (sometimes by several users simultaneously) and might be read immediately. Standard BasicCubes are not appropriate for such use. You should use standard BasicCubes for read-only access.

Transaction Data
The transaction data of a system has a dynamic character.

Transfer Routine
In maintenance of a characteristic InfoObject, you can create a (global) transfer routine (ABAP routine/no formula editor). Contrary to a local transfer rule, you can use a global transfer routine across all source systems. The transfer routine is employed only if the characteristic is used as an InfoSource with direct update. If both a local and a global transfer routine are used, the local transfer routine runs first, followed by the global transfer routine.

Transfer Rule

- Editing transfer rules:

  Initial access: **AWB** • **Modeling** • **InfoSources** • Select **Application Component** • Select **InfoSource** • Select **Source System** • Select **Modify/Delete Transfer Rules**

The transfer rules determine how source data is transferred to the communications structure over the SAP BW transfer structure. In other words, transfer rules apply only to the data from one source system. Therefore, one usually speaks of local transfer rules. Note the differentiation of the following transfer rules:

- Data is updated 1:1.
- Supply with a constant: During the load process, the fields of the communication structure can be supplied with fixed values: the fields are not supplied via the transfer structure.
- You can use ABAP routines and the formula editor to design transfer rules.

see also: Cleansing

Transfer Structure
The structure in which data from the source system is transferred into SAP Business Information Warehouse. The transfer structure helps BW retrieve all the

metadata of an SAP source system on a business process or a business unit. The structure represents the selection of the fields of an extract structure of the SAP source system. In the maintenance of the transfer structure in SAP BW, you assign the DataSource and InfoSource to determine which fields should be used for the load process. When you activate the transfer rules, the transfer structure is generated in the SAP BW system and in the SAP source system. The transfer structure in the SAP BW system is stored in table RSTS; in the SAP source system, it is stored in table ROOSGEN. The data is copied 1:1 from the transfer structure of the SAP source system into the transfer structure of SAP BW and then transmitted to the communications structure of SAP with the transfer rules. If the source system is a file system, the metadata is maintained in SAP BW, so that the transfer structure must also be defined manually in SAP BW. The structure of the transfer structure must describe the structure of the file (*see also*: InfoSource).

UML

Unified Modeling Language (UML) is the standard recognized by the Object Management Group (OMG) for semantic analysis of objects and for the design of object-oriented models with graphic tools. The UML standard is integrated in XMI. You can find the specifications for UML at *www.omg.org*.

Unified Modeling Language

see: UML

Update Rules

Via the communications structure of an InfoSource with flexible updating, the master data and transaction data are transferred into the data targets (BasicCubes, ODS objects, and characteristic InfoObjects with attributes or texts) based on the logic defined in the update rules.

Update rules are not specific to a source system, but to a data target, which is how they differ from transfer rules. However, you can copy the update rules of one data target for use with another data target. These rules help you supply the data targets of one or more InfoSources. They help post data in the data targets and with modifications and enhancements of the data.

- Definition of update rules:

  Initial access: **AWB** • **Modeling** • **InfoProvider** • Select **InfoArea** • Select **Create Update Rules** in the context menu of the selected data target.

Examples of update rules include the following:

- Reading master data attributes
- Filling fields in the data target with constants
- Using a routing (ABAP coding) or a formula (transformation library) to supply the fields of a data target
- Currency conversion

With an update, you must select one of the following update types:

- **Addition/Maximum/Minimum**
  The standard aggregation behavior of a key figure is set in the maintenance of key figures and offered in the update rules for this key figure as addition, maximum, or minimum. In particular, addition is an option for data fields of ODS objects, as long as the ODS objects have a numeric data type. This update type is invalid for characteristic InfoObjects as a data target.
- **Overwrite**
  This type of update is not available for BasicCubes; it is available only for ODS objects and characteristic InfoObjects.
- **No update**
  If you select this type of update, no value is calculated for the affected key figure. In addition, no calculation is performed for the corresponding characteristics and key fields.

see also: Cleansing

Update Types
see: Update Rules

Variables
Parameters of a query created in BEx query designer. The parameters are filled with values only when the query is inserted into a workbook. Variables function as placeholders for characteristic values, hierarchies, hierarchy nodes, texts, and formula elements. They can be processed in various ways. Variables in SAP Business Information Warehouse are global variables: They are defined unambiguously and are available for the definition of all queries.

Virtual Cube
Virtual cubes are special InfoCubes in SAP BW. A virtual cube represents a logical view. Unlike BasicCubes, however, virtual cubes do not physically store any data. The data is retrieved from the source systems during the execution of queries. In terms of data collection, note the following types of virtual cubes:

- **SAP RemoteCube**
  An SAP RemoteCube allows the definition of queries with direct access to the transaction data in other SAP systems. Requirements for the use of SAP Remote Cubes:
  - The functionality of BW SAPI is installed (contained in the plug-in of the SAP source system).
  - The release level of the source system is at least 4.0B.
  - DataSources from the source system are assigned to the InfoSource of the RemoteCube. The DataSources are released for direct access and no transfer rules are active for this combination. To determine whether a DataSource supports direct access, view table ROOSOURCE: Direct access is supported if field VITCUBE is populated with a 1 or a 2.

- **General RemoteCube**
  A general RemoteCube enables reporting on data from non-SAP systems. The external system uses BAPIs to transfer the requested data to the OLAP processor. The data must be delivered in the source system because it is required for analysis. You cannot define any transfer rules in the SAP BW system.
- **Virtual InfoCube with services**
  This type of virtual cube enables you to analyze the data with a self-developed function module. It is used for complex calculations that queries with formulas and exception aggregations cannot perform, such as those involved in Strategic Enterprise Management (SEM).

Web Application
see: Business Explorer Web Application

Web Application Designer
see: Business Explorer Web Application Designer

Web Application Wizard
see: Business Explorer Web Application Wizard

Web Cockpit
see: Business Intelligence Cockpit

Web Item
An object that refers to the data of a Data Provider and makes it available in HTML in a Web application. Examples include generic navigation blocks, tables, filters, text elements, alert monitors, maps, and charts.

Web Item Paging
A mechanism to distribute the Web items of a Web template across several pages that are linked to an overview page that is generated automatically.

Web Template
An HTML document that helps to set the structure of a Web application. It contains placeholders for Web items, Data Providers, and SAP BW URLs. Web template is a superordinate term of Master Web template, standard Web template, and device-specific Web template.

Wireless Application Protocol
A transmission protocol optimized for compression transfer of the Wireless Markup Language (WML) content in mobile networks.

Wireless Markup Language
see: WML

WML
Wireless Markup Language. An Internet language standard used to describe pages for mobile WAP devices.

Workbook
A file with several worksheets (an expression from Microsoft Excel terminology). You insert one or more queries in the workbook in order to display them in the Business Explorer Analyzer. You can save the workbook in your Favorites or in your rolls.XMI (XML Metadata Interchange).

A standard, XML-based format to exchange metadata between UML-based modeling tools and MOF-based metadata repositories in distributed, heterogeneous development environments. The exchange occurs with data flows or files.

In addition to UML and MOF, SMI forms the core of the Metadata Repository architecture of the Object Management Group (OMG). You can find the specifications for XMI at *www.omg.org*.

XML (eXtensible Markup Language)
A descriptive markup language that can be enhanced. XML is a subset of the Standard Generalized Markup Language (SGML) developed for users on the World Wide Web. XML documents consist of entities that contain parsed or unparsed data. A parsed entity contains text: a sequence of characters. Note the following types of characters:

- Character data
- Markup (smart tags, end tags, tags for empty elements, entity references, character references, comments, limits for CDATA sections, document-type declarations, and processing instructions)

The XML 1.0 specification was designed by the Word Wide Web Consortium (W3C) and accepted by the W3C as a recommendation in 1998. You can view the specification at *www.w3.org*.

Several standards (XLink, Xpointer, XSL, XSLT, and DOM, for example) have been developed based on XML. More standards are still being developed.

XML for Analysis
A protocol specified by Microsoft to exchange analytical data between client applications and servers via HTTP and SOAP as a service on the Web. XML for Analysis is not limited to a specific platform, application, or development language.

You can view the specification for XML for Analysis at *www.msdn.microsoft.com/library*: **Web Development · XML and Web Services · XML (General) · XML for Analysis Spec**. The use of XML for Analysis in SAP Business Information Warehouse enables direct communication between a third-party reporting tool connect to SAP BW and the online analytical processing (OLAP) processor.

XML Integration
Data exchange with XML is based on standards defined by the Object Management Group (OMG), which aims to develop industry standards for data exchange among various systems. In SAP BW, such transfer methods for the integration of data are implemented with XML. Transfer of XML data into SAP BW occurs with the Simple Object Access Protocol (SOAP) and the use of the Hypertext Transfer Protocol (HTTP). The data is described in XML format. The data is first written to the delta queue and then updated over a DataSource for the Myself source system into the desired data targets. Do not use this transfer method for mass data; use the flat file interface for large data sets.

XML Metadata Interchange
see: XMI

X Table
Attribute SID table for time-independent master data. This table includes the following fields:

- The SID of the characteristic
- OBJEVERS (object version); both fields build the key
- The values of the superordinate characteristics
- The value of the characteristic itself carries master data
- CHANGED
- SIDs of the time-independent attributes

For more information on OBJEVERS and CHANGED,
see: P Table

Y Table
Attribute SID table for time-dependent master data. In terms of its fields, the Y table corresponds to the X table.

J Literature

Balanced Scorecard Institute: *http://www.balancedscorecard.org.*

Codd, Edgar Frank: A Relational Model of Data For Large Shared Data Banks, Communications of the ACM 26, No. 1, January 1983.

Codd, Edgar Frank et al.: Providing OLAP (Online Analytical Processing) to User-Analysts: An IT Mandate, 1993. See also: *http://www.fpm.com/refer/codd.html.*

Egger, Norbert: SAP BW Professional, SAP PRESS, 2004.

Fischer, Roland: Business Planning with SAP SEM, SAP PRESS, 2004.

Imhoff, Claudia; Galemmo, Nicholas; Geiger, Jonathan G.: Mastering Data Warehouse Design: Relational and Dimensional Techniques, John Wiley, 2003.

Inmon, William H.: Building the Data Warehouse, John Wiley, 3. Edition 2002.

Inmon, William H.; Imhoff, Claudia, Sousa, Ryan: Corporate Information Factory, John Wiley, 2. Edition 2000.

Kaiser, Bernd-Ulrich: Corporate Information with SAP-EIS: Building a Data Warehouse and a MIS-Application with Insight. Academic Press, 1998.

Kaplan, Robert S.; Norton, David P.: The Balanced Scorecard. Translating Strategy Into Action, 1996.

Kimball, Ralph; Merz, Richard: The Data Warehouse Toolkit: Building the Web-Enabled Data Warehouse, John Wiley, 2000.

Kimball, Ralph; Reeves, Laura; Ross, Margy; Thornthwaite, W.: The Data Warehouse Lifecycle Toolkit: Expert Methods for Designing, Developing, and Deploying Data Warehouses, John Wiley, 1998.

Kimball, Ralph; Ross, Margy: The Data Warehouse Toolkit: The Complete Guide to Dimensional Modeling, John Wiley, 2. Edition 2002.

Pendse, Nigel: The OLAP Report. What is OLAP? An analysis of what the increasingly misused OLAP term is supposed to mean, *http://www.olapreport.com.*

Rafanelli, Maurizio: Multidimensional Databases: Problems and Solutions, Idea Group Publishing, 2003.

Thomsen, Erik: OLAP Solutions: Building Multidimensional Information Systems, John Wiley, 2. Edition 2002.

Totok, Andreas: Modellierung von OLAP- und Data-Warehouse-Systemen, Deutscher Universitäts-Verlag, 2000.

J.1 The SAP BW Library

With this special edition, SAP PRESS offers you valuable, expert knowledge on every aspect of SAP BW. All volumes share the same, practical approach. Step by step and with easily understood sample cases, you'll learn how to master all the important topical areas in SAP Business Information Warehouse (SAP BW). All authors are SAP BW specialists of the CubeServ Group. This ensures profound, expert knowledge and a uniform, application-oriented conception of all the books.

Egger, Fiechter, Salzmann, Sawicki, Thielen

SAP BW Data Retrieval

The ETL process with master data, transaction data, and SAP Business Content in SAP BW 3.5.

The correct approach to data retrieval from the very beginning. This book offers fundamental advice on how to set up, execute, and optimize data retrieval in SAP BW. It takes you through all important areas of data retrieval step by step and introduces you to working with master data, transaction data, and SAP Business Content. You'll learn how to master a successful extraction, transformation, and loading (ETL) process with perfect interaction among these three factors. This book is based on the current release: SAP BW 3.5.

ISBN 1–59229–044–2

Egger, Fiechter, Rohlf, Rose, Schrüffer

SAP BW Reporting and Analysis

Reporting with SAP BW 3.5

Quick and targeted access to the information you want. This book offers a fundamental guide to setting up, executing, and optimizing (Web) reporting, Web applications, and the resulting analysis options in SAP BW for your specific needs. The book first familiarizes you with the basic concepts of BEx Query Designer, BEx Web Application Designer, BEx Web Applications, BEx Analyzer, and SAP Business Content. It then takes you through the creation of individual reports and analyses step by step. You'll learn how to create your own SAP BW Web Cockpit successfully. This book is based on the current release: SAP BW 3.5.

ISBN 1–59229–045–0

Egger, Fiechter, Rohlf, Rose, Weber

SAP BW Business Planning and Simulation

The planning environment, planning functions, and manual planning in SAP BW 3.5

Active enterprise control with SAP BW-BPS: This is the only book available that introduces you to this current and supplemental topic in SAP BW. A walk-through introduces you step by step to the new functions in SAP BW 3.5. Whatever your interest—planning environment, manual planning, or Web interface builder—this book offers you the basic knowledge you need to execute successful planning with SAP BW. Learn about recent innovations and take advantage of all the SAP BW functionality. This book shows you how.

ISBN 1–59229–046–9

Authors

The authors are all acknowledged SAP Business Information Warehouse (SAP BW) specialists of the CubeServ Group (*www.cubeserv.com*). The CubeServ Group (CubeServ AG, CubeServ GmbH, and CubeServ Technologies AG) specializes in Business Intelligence (BI) solutions and has practical experience with SAP BW dating back to 1998. It has already worked on hundreds of projects with SAP BW and SAP Strategic Enterprise Management (SAP SEM).

Meet the Experts! Would you like to speak with the authors of this book and submit additional questions? An Internet forum is available for this purpose. Stop by for a visit to exchange ideas with the business intelligence community:
www.bw-forum.com

Norbert Egger is the Managing Director of the CubeServ Group, which specializes in BI solutions. In 1996, he established the world's first data warehouse based on SAP. Since then, he has implemented hundreds of projects with SAP BW and SAP SEM. He has many years of experience in the operation of SAP-based BI solutions.

Norbert Egger wrote Chapter 4, *Sample Scenario*; Chapter 5, *InfoObjects of SAP BW*; and Chapter 6, *InfoProviders of SAP BW*.

If you want to discuss the topics of this book in more detail with him, we invite you to contact Norbert Egger directly at:
n.egger@cubeserv.com

Jean-Marie R. Fiechter has worked as a data warehousing consultant at CubeServ AG (Jona, Switzerland) since 2003 and is a certified SAP NetWeaver '04 Business Intelligence consultant. Before joining CubeServ, he worked in the area of data warehousing for 15 years at Teradata, IBM, and SAS. He has international, practical experience in the areas of data warehousing, business intelligence, parallel processing, and management information systems

(MIS). For several years, he has taught data warehousing at various universities and colleges. He also conducts seminars.

Jean-Marie R. Fiechter wrote Chapter 1, *Data Warehousing Concepts*; Chapter 2, *SAP Business Information Warehouse—Overview of Components*; and Chapter 3, *Introduction to Data Modeling*.

If you want to discuss the topics of this book in more detail with him, we invite you to contact Jean-Marie R. Fiechter directly at:
j-m.fiechter@cubeserv.com

Jens Rohlf is the Managing Director of CubeServ GmbH, which specializes in business intelligence solutions and is headquartered in Flörsheim am Main, Germany. After studying business administration, he first worked in production controlling at Linotype-Hell AG in Kiel, Germany and then established the SAP Business Intelligence area of autinform in Wiesbaden, Germany. He also served as the area's Director. He has many years of experience with SAP R/3, SAP BW, and SAP SEM (with a focus on planning and the balanced scorecard) and has directed numerous projects in various industries.

Jens Rohlf wrote Chapter 7, *SAP Business Content*.

If you want to discuss the topics of this book in more detail with him, we invite you to contact Jens Rohlf directly at:
j.rohlf@cubeserv.com

Wiebke Hübner joined the CubeServ Group in 2004 as Project Manager for SAP publications. She has many years of experience in the preparation and communication of specialized topics. After studying Liberal Arts, she worked in project management for a cross-regional museum. In 2001, she became Managing Editor at Galileo Press (Bonn, Germany) for business-oriented SAP literature.

Index

A

ABAP/4 coding 77, 79, 84
Account-oriented data model 119
Activating Drag&Drop 137
Activating indices 232
Activation of InfoObject 187
Activation of SAP Business Content 151
Actual data 129, 173, 195, 199, 224, 235, 240, 241, 246, 298
Actual-data InfoCube 129, 211, 220, 240, 241
Addition 79
Ad-hoc analysis 49, 90
Ad-hoc reports 85
Administration 50
Administrative metadata 50
Administrator Workbench 67, 135, 137, 143, 260
Aggregated key figures 126
Aggregates 42
Aggregation 56, 185, 223
Aggregation hierarchies 43
Aggregation layer 43
Aggregation level 57
Aggregation tables 42
ALE 68
Alert monitor 85, 87
Allocation data 265, 270, 271
Allocation InfoCube 269
ALPHA 176, 177
ALPHA conversion 176, 177
Analysis of sales order stocks 274, 276
Analysis tools 47, 81
Analytical applications 124, 134
Application Link Enabling 68
Application-specific InfoObjects 130
Architecture of SAP BW 67
Assigning characteristics 204, 240
Assignment of a constant value 77
Associations 48
Attribute 237, 287, 300
Authorization check 180
Authorization relevant 180
Automatic consistency check 170

B

Backup 50
BAPI interface 82
Basic characteristics 237
Basic InfoCube 292
BasicCube 71, 199, 241
Best-practice OLAP 94
Best-practice solution 74, 99
BEx 81, 90, 178, 189
BEx Analyzer 85, 89, 90, 94, 95, 128
BEx Broadcaster 90, 91
BEx information broadcasting 90
BEx Portfolio 91
BEx query 82, 83, 89, 264
BEx Query Designer 91
BEx Reporting 225
BEx Web analyzer 90
BEx Web Application Designer 91
BEx Web applications 90, 128
Bitmap index 44
Boolean comparison 44
Boolean operators 44
Budget Management 293
Business blueprint phase 98
Business budgeting 49
Business Consolidation 127
Business Content *see* SAP Business Content 146
Business Explorer queries 89
Business Explorer *see* BEx 189
Business Explorer workbooks 89
Business Information Warehouse *see* SAP BW 285
Business intelligence applications 121
Business intelligence solutions 124
Business metadata 51
Business planning 49
Business planning and budgeting 49
BW *see* Business Information Warehouse 285
BW-BPS 241

C

Cardinality 239
Central data warehouse system 45

Central monitoring 96
CHAR 176
CHAR InfoObjects 176
Characteristic 139, 173, 174, 190, 202
Characteristic as data target 190
Characteristic hierarchies 124
Characteristic is document attribute 178
Characteristic properties 176
Characteristic without conversion routine 177
Characteristic-oriented data model 119
Characteristics 55, 63, 88, 97, 129, 218, 260, 266, 268, 270, 276, 286, 289, 294
Characteristics InfoObjectCatalog 229
Characteristics without conversion 176
Chart of accounts 220
Chart of accounts properties 158
Charts 87
Choosing key figures 251
Clustering 48
Codd, E.F. 24
Coded presentation 167
Cognos 124
Column selection 84
Column-oriented data model 119
Company code currency 183
Company codes 123
Company fixed costs 126
Compounded attributes 163
Compounding 182, 288
Comprehensive InfoObjects 130
Consistency check 170
Consolidation 124, 127
Consolidation paths 55
Content Version 153
Controlling 98, 286
Controlling—Profitability Analysis 127, 223
Conversion routine 176, 177
Cost center reporting 293
Create MultiProvider 216
Creating an InfoObject 174
Creating dimensions 221
Creating your own InfoObjects 172
Credit Management 293
CRM 293, 302
Crystal Reports 124
Cube 52, 55, 57, 59
Cumulative value 182, 183, 185, 282
Currency conversion 183
Customer exit 84
Customer orders 129
Customer Relationship Management *see* CRM 293
Customer-specific InfoObjects 183
Customer-specific ODS object 198

D

Data acquisition 38, 50, 75
Data acquisition layer 37
Data acquisition process 75
Data auditing tools 40
Data capture 49
Data cleansing 38, 40
Data copy 38, 41
Data cube 54
Data distribution 49
Data export 96
Data fields 231
Data mart systems 41
Data marts 46, 47, 96, 291
Data mining 49
Data mining tools 48
Data model 54, 223, 286, 287, 292, 294
Data modeling 74, 121, 128
Data presenation 96
Data presentation layer 37
Data providers 86
Data provision 47
Data retrieval 121
Data sources
  database systems 75
  non-SAP systems 75
  SAP Systems 75
  structured interface files 75
  XML data 75
Data storage 41, 96
Data storage layer 37
Data target 190
Data type 174
Data warehouse 37, 42, 57, 169, 291
Data warehouse architecture 34
Data warehouse design 30

Data warehouse environment 25, 37
Data warehouse layer 291
Data warehouse solution 94
Data warehouse system 42, 45
Data warehousing 28
Data warehousing product 285
Database tables 96
Databases 24
Dataflow 223
DataProvider 286
DataSource 76, 173, 181, 224
DataSources
  Business Content 76
DB for OLAP interface 82
Dedicated inventory key figures 183
Default InfoObjectCatalog 133
Define Dimensions 213
Deleting Dimensions 213
Deliveries 125
Delta load 38
Delta upload 79
Delta-extract mode 96
Design criterium 289
Developed star schema 62, 65
Dicing 58, 59
Dimension hierarchy 55, 61
Dimension tables 61, 289, 415
Dimensions 55, 56, 57, 61, 63, 199, 239, 240, 246, 268, 270, 278, 289, 415
Direct transfer 77, 79
Display attributes 64
Display of decimal places 167
Distributed data warehouse system 45
Document attribute 178
Document characteristics 236, 237
Document level 256
Document ODS object 227
Document tables 183
Drag&drop 136, 230
Drag&Relate 170
Drill across 60
Drill down 60
Drill through 60
Dropdown boxes 87
DSS 27
DWH 24, 41
DWH environment 35

E

Edit MultiProvider 218
EIS 28, 48
EIS tools 48
End applications 37
Enterprise Controlling—Consolidation 127
Enterprise data warehouse 96
ERP software 24
ETL 38, 127, 169, 253
ETL components 253
ETL process 39, 67, 76, 80, 169, 196, 226
ETL processes 50
Excel 89
Excel workbooks 89
Exception analysis 92
Exception reporting 92
Exceptions 81, 92
Excursus 142
Executive information systems 48
Export DataSource 181
Extraction 39, 46, 223, 286, 303
Extraction methods 127
Extraction mode 96

F

Fact table 55, 61, 415
FI 293
Filter selection 180
Filtering 38
Finance & Accounting 98, 134
Financial Accounting 286, 295
Financial Accounting—General Ledger Accounting 127
Financial reporting 124, 126, 129, 192, 223
Financial Reporting MultiProvider 223
Financials 134, 293
Fiscal dimension 123
Fiscal posting periods 124
Fiscal year variant 123, 263
Flat file 96, 298
Flat file upload 298
Flow logic 84
Forecasting 49
Formula variables 84
Formulas 77, 79

For-period 302
Front-end tool 82
Frontends 94
Full costs of manufacturing 126
Full load 38
Full upload 79
Full-extract mode 96
Fuzzy logic 48

G

General ledger 124
General Ledger Accounting 127
Goods movements 298
Granularity 56, 57, 126, 129, 241, 244, 252, 292
Group currency 183

H

Header data 258, 265, 266, 271
Header data InfoCube 265
Hierarchy 84, 124, 181, 237
Hierarchy node variables 84
Hierarchy table 64
Hierarchy variables 84
High cardinality 239
High granularity 244
HOLAP 51
HR 293
HR reporting 131
HTML 92
  standard functionality 85
HTML browser 95
HTML technology 85
Hub 96
Human Resources 286, 293, 300
Hybrid OLAP 51, 53
HyperCube 54
Hyperion 124

I

Identification 219
Implementation project 302
Implementation steps 131
Impressible summation 167
In dataflow afterwards 143
In dataflow before 143, 150, 151
In dataflow before and afterwards 144
Incoming-Order InfoCubes 271
Incoming-Order MultiProvider 271
Incoming-Order Reporting 252, 254, 265
Incremental load 38
Indexing scheme 44
Indices 232
Industry Solutions 293, 295
InfoArea 133, 135, 224
InfoArea creation 135
InfoArea hierarchy 138
InfoCube 63, 71, 96, 97, 127, 128, 151, 154, 189, 199, 209, 219, 223, 241, 252, 267, 286, 289, 297, 413
  aggregate 74
InfoCube structure 213, 245
InfoObject 78, 96, 127, 128, 129, 133, 135, 142, 158, 175, 183, 189, 197, 225, 235, 274, 286, 287, 292
  general ledger account 157
InfoObject creation 178
InfoObject selection 226, 236
InfoObject types 293
InfoObjectCatalogs 130, 133, 139, 148, 153, 197, 224, 228
InfoObjects of SAP Business Content 142, 145
InfoPackages 79
InfoProvider 78, 83, 128, 135, 173, 189, 252, 260, 292
  RemoteCube 74
  SAP RemoteCube 73
  virtual InfoCube 74
InfoProvider types 189
Information broadcasting 90
InfoSets 71, 128, 189, 260, 413
InfoSource 77, 299
InfoSpoke 96
Initial load 39
In-period 302
Integration 31
Integrity constraints 41
Interval variables 84
Inventory changes 186
Inventory key figure 186, 187
Inventory parameters 279, 280
Inventory values 182, 281
Invoice item 183
Invoices 125

IT systems 124
Item 263
Item data 262, 265, 268, 271
Item data InfoCube 267
Item type 214
ITS 88
iView 92

J
Java Script 85
Join 262
Join conditions 264
Join index 44
Join operations 62

K
Key fields 227, 228
Key figure hierarchies 124
Key figure structures 88
Key figure-oriented data model 119
Key figures 61, 88, 97, 127, 129, 141, 166, 182, 221, 223, 230, 240, 251, 268, 270, 275, 276, 286, 415
Key value 169

L
Layers 43
Line Items 209, 239, 269, 275
Line-Item characteristic 239
Line-Item Setting 209
Line-Item table 228
Load 38, 41
Log files 39
Logical architecture 35
Logistic extract structure customizing cockpit 128
Logistics 131, 286
Logs 39
Lowercase letters 174

M
Machine learning 48
Main Material Group 237
Management information systems 48
Management reporting 125, 126
Maps 87
Master data 63, 289
Master data maintenance 180
Master data query 191
Master data reporting 189
Material 295
Materialized aggregates 65
Materialized views 41, 42
Matrix 58
Measures 54
Metadata 50, 152, 285
Metadata management 38
Metadata repository 37, 50, 51
Microsoft Excel 89, 95, 124
MIS 26, 48
MIS tools 48
Model 301
Modeling 190, 208
MOLAP 51
Monitor 79
Monitor programs 39
Monitoring 50, 67, 80, 96
Multidimensional analysis tools 47
Multidimensional data model 54
Multidimensional data sets 58
Multidimensional OLAP 51
MultiProvider 71, 128, 173, 189, 216, 221, 223, 246, 271, 286, 290, 295, 413

N
Navigation 58, 287
Navigation attributes 64, 164, 199, 218, 230, 237, 244, 248, 258, 265, 267
Navigation components 85
Navigational attribute 269
Navigational states 86
Net revenue 125
Non-SAP source system connections 68
Non-volatile 33
Non-volatility 33
NUMC 176
NUMC InfoObjects 176

O
Object type 98
ODS 41, 154, 223, 224, 286, 291
ODS object 79, 154, 189, 195, 223, 224, 228, 232, 252, 291
ODS object template 240
ODS objects 96, 97, 129, 286

ODS tables 41
ODS-Layer 128
OLAP 23, 41, 47
OLAP Analyses 271
OLAP design 48, 51
OLAP functionality 89
OLAP implementations 58
OLAP reporting 85, 94
OLAP technologies 41
OLE DB for OLAP interface 82
OLTP 60, 158, 169
OLTP system 24, 158, 169
Online analytical processing 47
Open Hub 67
Open Hub Service 96
Open-hub data sources 96
Open-hub destination 96
Operating profit 126
Operational data stores 41
Operational environment 25
Operational systems 37
Operative metadata 50
Optimization 42
Optional default values 84
Order item ODS object 256
Order items 260
Organization 55
Organizational forms 44
Organizational unit 287, 302
Overhead Costs Controlling 295
Overview of components 67
Overview of orders 256

P

Parameter variables 84
Payroll data 302
Performance improvement 292
Performance problems 287, 298
Persistent staging area (PSA) 80
Physical storage 282
Plan cost rates 126
Plan data 126, 129, 173, 210, 241, 246, 298
Plan prices 126
Plan Profitability Analysis 241
Plan-actual comparison 216, 246
Plan-actual differentiation 173
Plan-data InfoCube 129, 210, 241
Planning and simulation 121
Planning functions 126
Planning horizon 126
Planning interface 128
Planning item 213, 215
Plug-in 302
Portals 49
Preaggregations 42
Preparation 47
Presenation 48
Presentation objects 85
Presentation tools 37
Primary key 61
Product 55
Product Lifecycle Management 293
Profit Center 285, 293
Profit Center Accounting 293, 295
Profit Center Reporting 285
Profit margin 125
Profitability analysis 124, 127, 129, 134, 223, 224, 228, 229, 232, 240, 241, 246
Profitability analysis MultiProvider 249, 250
Project costs 287
Publish and subscribe process 49
Purchasing data 297

Q

Qualitative data 54
Quality assurance 49
Quantitative data 54
Queries 86, 90, 91, 295
Queries in workbooks 89
Query 47, 190, 223, 301
Query creation 190
Query Designer 83, 85
Query elements 84
Query execution 183
Query optimization 41
Query structures 53
Query tools 47
Query views 86

R

Ranging 58, 59
Real Estate Management 293
Realtime data 42
Recode 173

Recovery 39
Referenced InfoObject 159
Regressions 48
Relational OLAP 51, 52
Relational, detailed data layer 43
Reloading 38, 39
Remote access 74
Remote function call 68
RemoteCubes 71, 189, 413
Removing key figures 244, 245
Report tools 47
Reporting 49, 91, 183, 237, 256, 260, 264, 281, 286, 287, 291, 301
Reporting agent 81, 85
Reporting and analysis 121
Reporting and analysis tools 81
Reporting at the document level 256
Reporting Functionality 91, 94
Reporting objects 91
Reporting on InfoSets 264
Reporting tools 128
Reporting version 181
Reporting-relevant settings 179
Reports 285
Report-to-report interface 170
Repository 37, 50, 51
Repository models 51
Retransferring characteristics 241
Retransferring document characteristics 236
Revenue reductions 125, 126
RFC 68
ROLAP 51
ROLAP data structures 53
Role menu 87, 89
Rollup 43, 60
Rotation 58
Routines 77, 79
RRI 170
Runtime environment 88

S

Sales 134, 299
Sales & Distribution 124, 125, 127, 252, 299
Sales document 263, 266, 268, 270, 273
Sales document (header data) ODS object 254
Sales document allocation data 270
Sales document header data 266
Sales document item 267
Sales document item data 256, 268
Sales order items 267, 269
Sales order stock 183, 274, 278
Sales orders 265
Sales-Order-Stock Reporting 252
Sample Scenario 121
SAP BEx Analyzer *see* BEx Analyzer 88
SAP Business Content 97, 98, 127, 133, 142, 146, 172, 192, 253, 285, 288, 293, 300
SAP Business Content activation 143
SAP Business Content BasicCube 199
SAP Business Content Components 192
SAP Business Content InfoObjects 153, 254, 288
SAP Business Content Objects 292
SAP Business Content ODS Objects 195, 253, 254
SAP Business Explorer 81
  Ad-hoc queries 88
  Analyzer 81, 88
  bookmarks 92
  calculated key figures 83
  conditions 85
  exception 85
  formulas 83
  Information broadcasting 81, 90
  iView 92
  master data reporting 83
  mobile reporting 81, 92
  personalization 91
  query designer 83
  reporting agent 92
  restricted key figures 83
  structures 83
  tabular reporting 83
  URLs specific to SAP BW 87
  variables 84
  Web application designer 81, 85
  Web applications 81, 88
  Web templates 85
SAP Business Explorer Analyzer *see* BEx Analyzer 94

SAP Business Explorer query *see* BEx query 82
SAP Business Information Warehouse *see* SAP BW 99, 121, 183, 285
SAP BW 86, 99, 121, 128, 172, 183, 260, 285, 289
SAP BW 2.0 94
SAP BW 3.0 94
SAP BW add-on 88
SAP BW components 81, 97
SAP BW Library 121, 131
SAP BW objects 86, 96
SAP BW reporting functions 91
SAP BW role 91
SAP BW standard functionality 82
SAP BW system 163
SAP components 127
SAP Enterprise Portal 81, 82, 90, 91, 124
SAP exit 84
SAP Internet Transaction Server 88
SAP ITS 88
SAP NetWeaver 124
SAP R/3 24, 39, 99, 127, 158, 223, 228, 288, 303
  core functions 97
SAP R/3 Basis technology 97
SAP R/3 document tables 183
SAP R/3 reporting components 99
SAP R/3 source system 228
SAP R/3 upstream system 127, 223
SAP RemoteCubes 71, 189, 413
SAP source systems
  connections 68
SAP Web Application Server 88
SAP Web reporting 88
Scheduling 38, 67, 79
SCM 293
SD 299
Select option variables 84
Selection 179, 221, 251, 252
Selection objects 85
Selection of key figures 251
SEM 127
SEM-BCS 127
SID 64
SID table 64
Siebel 24
Simulation 49
Single sign-on 92
Slicing 58
Snowflake schema 62
Source system 39, 76, 169, 263, 295
Source system compounding 169, 170
Source system groups 169
Source system ID 254
SRM 293
Standard reporting 49
Standard Web template 85
Star index 44
Star schema 61, 62, 289, 300
Start views 91
Starting InfoProvider 261
Stock InfoCube 252
Strategic Enterprise Management *see* SEM 127
Strategic Enterprise Management—Business Consolidation *see* SEM-BCS 127
Style sheets 85
Substitution paths 84
Summation 167
Supplier Relationship Management *see* SRM 293
Supply Chain Performance Management 293, 295
Surrogate ID 64
Surrogate key 63
System stress 26

T

Tab 86, 181
Table JOIN 263
Technical metadata 50
Template InfoCube 275, 276
Template ODS 235, 265, 267, 269
Text elements 87
Text table 64
Text variables 84
Third-party front-end tools
  dynaSight 95
  inSight 95
Third-party frontend tools 95
  Business Objects 95
  Cognos 95
Third-party reporting tools 82

Third-party tools 79, 81, 82, 95
Time 55
Time characteristics 229, 240, 248, 277, 290, 293, 298
Time dimension 57
Time variant 32, 33
Transactional InfoCube 128, 212
Transfer rules 77
Transfer structure 76
Transformation 38
Type/Unit 185

U

Unbalanced hierarchies 63
Uniformity 32
Update rules 78
Upflow 43
Upstream systems 127, 173

V

Validity table 280
Validity table for inventories 280
Value type 298
Views 41, 42
Virtual data warehouse 45
Virtual InfoCubes 71, 189, 413

W

Web Application Designer 85, 86
Web applications 88, 90, 91
Web browser 85
Web design API 87
Web items 86
Web reporting 88
Web templates 85, 86, 91
Webserver 49
WML 92
Workbooks 89
Workflow management 49

X

XMLA interface 82

Make the most of BEx Query Designer, Web and SAP BW Information Broadcasting

SAP BW Reporting and Analysis

SAP BW – Reporting and Analysis

[illegible]

> BW with a comprehensive [illegible]

[illegible] you need to know [illegible] planning, the planning [illegible] documents and the Web Interface Builder

SAP BW Business Planning and Simulation

[illegible]

SAP BW
Business Planning and Simulation

Planning and [illegible] with SAP BW can be a complex [illegible], you can take advantage of [illegible] this book [illegible] gives you a [illegible] introduction and help you [illegible] common challenges.

A detailed, step-by-step examination of the new [illegible] SAP BW [illegible] help you, whether you intend to use the planning [illegible] planning, or the Web Interface Builder. You'll discover everything that's essential to success [illegible] planning [illegible] of the wide range of [illegible] SAP BW, and much more.

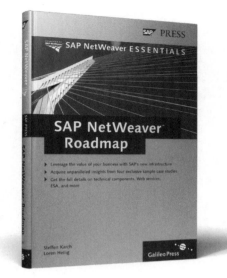

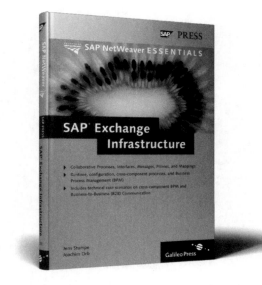

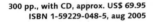